DAVID JASON

Sir David Jason was born in 1940 in North London. His acting career has been long and varied: from his theatre work in the West End to providing voices for Mr Toad from *The Wind in the Willows*, *Danger Mouse* and *The BFG*; and from *Open All Hours* and *The Darling Buds of May* to his starring roles as Detective Inspector Frost in *A Touch of Frost* and, of course, Derek 'Del Boy' Trotter in *Only Fools and Horses*.

He lives with his wife, Gill, and their daughter, Sophie, in Buckinghamshire.

Praise for David Jason: My Life

'As good as it gets ... so much on every page ... a great, great book.'
Chris Evans

'It's a romp of a chronicle, a life according to Del Boy, the ultimate cheeky chappy.' *Daily Telegraph*

'Jason's account of his 'busy and fulfilling life' is as genuinely genial as the man himself ... his hugely likeable memoirs reveal he's had the last laugh.' *Daily Mail - Book of the Week*

'The book is terrific.' *Richard Bacon*

'How the son of a market porter gave up a career as an electrician to become one of Britain's most successful and best loved actors ... the long awaited story...' *Independent*

'It really is a life story, I thoroughly enjoyed it.'
Matt Baker, The One Show

'He comes across as hugely likeable and approachable.' *Daily Mail*

'Touching, funny and warm-hearted.' *Sunday Mirror*

'Touching and funny ... it really is a top read.' *Sun*

'Written with real charm.' *Guardian*

'Affable, humble and unpretentious.' *Metro*

'Lovely-jubbly.' *ES Magazine*

'An engaging and entertaining read.' *Daily Express*

DAVID
JASON
My Life

arrow books

Published by Arrow Books 2014
6 8 10 9 7

Copyright © Peglington Productions Ltd., 2013

David Jason has asserted his right under the Copyright, Designs
and Patents Act 1988 to be identified as the author of this work

All images are courtesy of the author and his family with the following exceptions:
©BBC; ©ITV/Rex Features; ©Freemantle Media/Rex Features

The author is grateful to quote from the following poem:
'Under Milk Wood' by Dylan Thomas © Orion

Map illustration © Darren Bennett

Every reasonable effort has been made to contact all copyright holders, but if there are errors or
omissions, we will insert the appropriate acknowledgement in subsequent printings of this book.

This book is a work of non-fiction based on the life, experiences and recollections of the author.
In some limited cases names of people, places, dates, sequences or the detail of events have been
changed solely to protect the privacy of others. The author has stated to the publishers that,
except in such minor respects not affecting the substantial accuracy of the work, the contents of
this book are true.

This book is sold subject to the condition that it shall not,
by way of trade or otherwise, be lent, resold, hired out,
or otherwise circulated without the publisher's prior
consent in any form of binding or cover other than that
in which it is published and without a similar condition,
including this condition, being imposed
on the subsequent purchaser.

First published in Great Britain in 2013 by
Century
Random House, 20 Vauxhall Bridge Road,
London SW1V 2SA

www.randomhouse.co.uk

Addresses for companies within The Random House Group Limited can be found at:
www.randomhouse.co.uk/offices.htm

The Random House Group Limited Reg. No. 954009

A CIP catalogue record for this book
is available from the British Library

ISBN 9780099581161

The Random House Group Limited supports the Forest Stewardship Council® (FSC®), the
leading international forest-certification organisation. Our books carrying the FSC label are
printed on FSC®-certified paper. FSC is the only forest-certification scheme supported by the
leading environmental organisations, including Greenpeace. Our paper procurement policy
can be found at www.randomhouse.co.uk/environment

MIX
Paper from
responsible sources
FSC® C016897
www.fsc.org

Typeset by Palimpsest Book Production Limited, Falkirk, Stirlingshire
Printed and bound by CPI Group (UK) Ltd, Croydon CR0 4YY

To my lovely wife and daughter, my family and everyone who has helped me on this journey; this book is for you.

ACKNOWLEDGEMENTS

As well as the family members, friends and colleagues who appear in this book, there are some additional people I would like to thank for their support, advice and friendship:

Rod Brown; Ray Cooney; Bob Cutler; Les Davis; Jack Edmonds; Ray & Gloria Freeda; Suzi Freeda; Don Gatherer; Saleem Goolamali; Lady (Mary) Hatch; Keith Marzetti; Jimmy Mulville; Dave Rogers; Lynda Ronan; Alan & Linda Smith; Giles Smith. A special thanks to Meg Poole.

And anyone else who knows me!

INTRODUCTION

By way of greeting, a brief recounting of my time on a desert island with no discs.

Which near-death experience shall I begin with? The one involving the thirty-foot drop at Ronnie Barker's house? The one with the pair of pliers and the bare electrical wire? The one in which the giant polystyrene sugar lumps rained down on me from a great height? Or the one caused by the rogue Flymo in Crowborough?

Actually, let's get to all of those later. For now, as our little appetiser here, ahead of the death-defying feast beyond, let's cover the one where I almost cop it on a desert island in the middle of the ocean.

We're talking 1996 – my first holiday with Gill, who was then my wonderful girlfriend and is now my wonderful wife. I'm fifty-six years old at this point, and we're in the paradise which is the Virgin Islands, in a lovely remote spot, and I have decided to go diving. (I am proud to be able to call myself a qualified Dive Master, a fact I may mention in the following pages more than once.) A bad hurricane has hit these parts in the preceding stormy season and very few of the tourist operations are back up and running as yet. However, in the little town I drive to, there's one diving place open and the girl in the office, who is an instructor, says she'll get a boat together and take me out for a dive.

So off we go, puttering miles out into the beautiful blue open water, entirely alone there, and the instructor drops anchor and we strap on the masks and tanks and plunge in.

And it's bliss, as diving usually is. My two favourite activities in the world: diving and flying. I am rarely happier than when deep in the water or high in the sky. Psychiatrists: help yourselves.

Bliss, then. Bit of a strong current down there on this occasion. But even a few minutes at forty feet below – I'd recommend it to anyone. We clamber back into the boat and get ready to head for home, but the anchor has caught and won't come up. I volunteer to dive back down and free it.

All good. The anchor is now loose and I surface. Except that, while below the water, I must have got sucked into the current at some point without realising, and when I come to the top, I discover I have lost the boat. Or perhaps the boat has lost me. It makes no difference. I'm in high, pitching waves and twisting my head around in a state of increasing disorientation, and the boat is nowhere to be seen. Indeed, nothing is anywhere to be seen. Just miles of pitching waves, and me.

Panic, at this point, is obviously a decent option. But I try not to. There's a motto we Dive Masters know well: 'Stop. Breathe. Think. Act.' I had that thoroughly drilled into me by my instructor in the Cayman Islands, Ray 'Taffy' Williams, a former soldier with plenty of stories to tell who became a great friend. 'Stop. Breathe. Think. Act.' Any minute now, I think, a wave will lift me and I will catch sight of the boat, or the boat will catch sight of me.

The waves do lift me. But I don't see a boat. I appear to be alone in the ocean, miles from land, under baking sun and, as I am gradually realising, with increasing dawning horror, at the mercy of a current drawing me ever further outwards.

2

It's at this point, anxiously swivelling my head from side to side, that I notice a tiny island. At least, I think it's an island. It bobs in and out of my view. It's some distance from me, but it might just be swimmable. Is there any other option? I don't think there is. I start to swim.

The swim is exhausting. It seems to last for hours and saps all the energy from my supremely fit (obviously) and (if you don't mind me saying so) highly shapely fifty-six-year-old limbs. But, dragging myself onward, I do eventually reach the island. Relief!

Except not. Perspective has played a foul trick. When I get there, it isn't really an island. It's more a broad, high, steep rock. No gently shelving sand to fling myself onto then, like in the movies. Instead, a tall, jagged cliff face, slapped by waves.

This inhospitable crag remains, though, my only plausible saviour. Assuming I can get onto it, obviously. By now my arms and legs are heavier than they have ever been. I have to use the waves to lodge me halfway up the rock. I try twice and fail and get washed back. If I don't get on this next time, I'm not sure I'll have the energy to try again. One last desperate effort . . .

I ready myself, ride the wave onto the rock, and this time manage to cling on and climb up. At the top of the rock is a small dip containing a shallow puddle of seawater flung up by the waves. I lie down in this puddle. And then I pass out.

I don't know how long I'm unconscious for, but when I come to, I sit up and discover that – well, what do you know, and isn't this just typical? – it was all a dream and, flooded with relief, I'm waking up back in bed with Gill in the safety of the apartment.

No, I don't. Because it isn't a dream. The bit about it being a dream was a dream. I am actually and indisputably on a rock in the middle of the ocean, under the still-baking sun.

But hang on. My eyes focus and there, out to sea, is the boat, plainly visible in the distance. The boat! The instructor is still out there, on the bright blue water, looking for me. I wave and shout. But the wind carries the sound away and she's looking down into the water. She's not looking at the rock.

I'm over here! It's OK. She's got to see me in a moment, hasn't she?

I watch numbly as the boat completes a few more silent circles. And then, with a sinking heart, I see it turn and motor away, growing smaller and smaller, towards the thin ribbon of the coast on the distant horizon.

Abandoned. She's given up on me.

Well, now I truly am stuffed. Washed up, a castaway. What would Robinson Crusoe do? Seek a source of food among the vegetation, no doubt, and begin to build a shelter. Yeah, well, cheers, Robbie. I'm on a flipping rock. There is no vegetation, nothing with which to build a bijou shack and start a cosy bonfire, and very little altogether in the way of possibilities, short of beginning a new life as a cormorant.

Again, I don't know how much time now passes. But I do know that, as I sit there, staring mournfully across the wide expanse of totally unpopulated water, I have time to reflect. Just suppose it did end here. Just suppose the clock was now running on my final few hours, the reaper donning his terrible cloak and getting the scythe from the umbrella stand in his hall, prior to setting out. Just suppose I was, indeed, about to die. Well, you'd have to say, it had been a pretty good innings. Cut short, maybe. But a pretty good stretch. A lot of luck in there. A lot of good times, with some truly great people. And some really amazing success. *Only Fools and Horses*, *The Darling Buds of May*, *A Touch of Frost*, a few BAFTAs on the mantelpiece – not too shabby as CVs go. If it should all come to a halt right now, in a hot puddle, well, at the very least you would have to argue that it had been a busy and fulfilling life, and not bad at all for a working-class lad from north London who –

Oh, stuff all that. Here's the fact: I don't want to die alone on a rock. I don't even want to die in company on a rock, given the choice. I want to be alive. I've got stuff I still want to do. I've got Gill somewhere back on that shore. Reasons to live.

But what's this? A dot on the horizon, growing larger, getting closer. The instructor has returned to the shore for help, that's what she's done. There are figures in the boat. They're searching for me. I wave and shout and wave and shout. Someone in the boat lifts his head and sees me. Now the people in the boat are shouting and waving and the boat is coming to the rock. I'm saved.

True story, dear reader. And like the tale you're about to read, not one I have told before, though now, looking back at seventy-three, seems as good a time as any. Looking back, I should say, in a state of boundlessly grateful and sometimes puzzled wonderment at the unlikelihood of the journey that took me from where I started to where I've got to.

It's a story of immense good fortune, I have to say. But with scrapes, and a few things worse than scrapes, along the way. For, as we'll see, that day in the Virgin Islands was not the only time in my life when I thought the boat had gone and the boat came back.

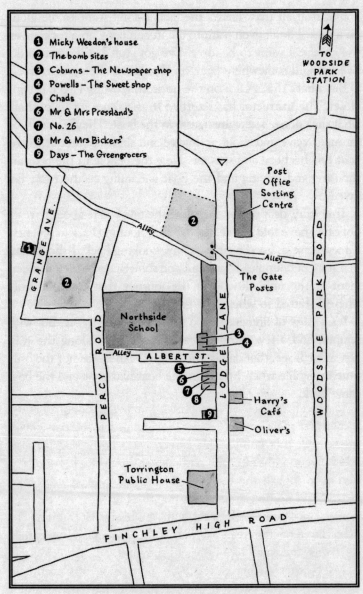

1 Micky Weedon's house
2 The bomb sites
3 Coburns – The Newspaper shop
4 Powells – The Sweet shop
5 Chads
6 Mr & Mrs Pressland's
7 No. 26
8 Mr & Mrs Bickers'
9 Days – The Greengrocers

TO
WOODSIDE
PARK
STATION

Post
Office
Sorting
Centre

Alley

The Gate
Posts

GRANGE AVE.

Alley

Northside
School

PERCY ROAD

Alley   ALBERT ST.

LODGE LANE

WOODSIDE PARK ROAD

Harry's
Café

Oliver's

Torrington
Public House

FINCHLEY HIGH ROAD

AROUND LODGE LANE c.1950

CHAPTER ONE

Life during wartime. A long-standing mystery resolved. And sundry near-death experiences, one involving a tomahawk.

What I remember is being extremely young and hearing thunder and feeling the walls of the house shake and the floor beneath us tremble and fearfully asking my mother what was going on. And my mother holding me close and saying, 'It's nothing to worry about. It's just God moving His furniture around.'

It wasn't, in fact. It was Hitler moving London around – something the German Chancellor seemed to be particularly keen on at that point in his career. I was born on 2 February 1940, five months after the outbreak of the Second World War, and even though those five years of global conflagration quite clearly had nothing to do with me, the Luftwaffe nevertheless pursued me from aeroplanes, with impressive enthusiasm, for all of my tenderest years. Which is why I associate my earliest days with the smell and taste of brick dust.

My brother Arthur, seven years my senior, was eventually evacuated to the safety of the countryside, like half a million other London children. But I was too young for that, so my infancy was spent in war-torn north London, where, upon the sounding of the air-raid sirens, I was periodically strapped into a government-issue gas mask, an infringement of my liberty which, apparently, I bitterly resisted. Then I was made to lie down with my parents in the Morrison shelter – essentially an indoor wire-mesh cage which doubled as a stout dining table and which gave you a fighting chance of surviving in the event that your house collapsed around your ears. As the printed letter that had come round from Mr G. Beach, Air Raid Precautions Officer for the Borough of Finchley, had kindly explained: 'Protection in your own home is an excellent alternative to communal or public shelters, and it conforms to the principle of dispersal which experience has proved to be a wise one.' Excellent and wise, indeed. So, there, amid the distant and not-so-distant crumps and crashes and all the awesome noises of destruction, my mother would lie with me, dutifully honouring the principle of dispersal, and doing her level best not to transfer her fear. It was just God, moving His furniture around.

We kept my infant gas mask in the house for many years; it was like a rubber deep-sea diver's helmet, but designed to hold the baby's entire body, with drawstrings at the bottom. Long afterwards, I used to get an eerie feeling just looking at it.

We were the White family and for some reason the target of Hitler's frustrated anger included our tiny terraced house at 26 Lodge Lane in Finchley – so tiny that when you opened the front door, you almost fell up the stairs, which were right in front of you. It was a three-up, three-down. There was a front room, which we were never allowed to go into except at Christmas and, presumably, in the event of a member of the royal family happening to drop in, although, in my recollection, this rarely happened. Beyond that was the middle room, where the open fire was and where the whole family sat and listened to the wireless – and where, much later, we gathered to watch the television. Beyond the middle room was the kitchen, and beyond the kitchen, out in the backyard, in a lean-to, behind a latched wooden door, was the lavatory – all mod cons. But no electricity, of course: electric light didn't come to Lodge Lane until the early 1950s. Until then, it was gas lamps, with their fiddly mantles and constant hiss.

And then upstairs were three bedrooms, although one of them was really just a box room – a box room suitable only for a very small collection of boxes. That was where my sister June slept, after she came along, seven years after me, in 1947. I shared with Arthur, a cosy arrangement which prevailed for nearly a decade until he left home.

My mum, Olwen, worked as a maid in a big house in the well-to-do suburban part of Finchley. Her employer, always spoken of with great reverence in our house, was Mr Strathmore, a portly judge. Mum had found work with him when she left Wales as a young teenager, fleeing her drunken and violent father – not a passage of her life that she was much inclined to speak about. At first Mr Strathmore employed her as a live-in maid, and even after she met my dad, married and began renting a house of her own, she still went there in the day to clean.

She took me with her to work one day and I remember, as she unlatched the gate, being staggered by the grandeur of this place – a detached house in its own garden, of all things, with its own drive. I went back and looked at it many years later, and, comparatively speaking, it wasn't all that grand. But at the time, to a kid from Lodge Lane, it was a place of unimaginable richness – something from another world entirely. When my mother eventually retired, Mr Strathmore gave her a Japanese silk print of cherry blossoms – again, a rare and exotic item in our terms. It hangs in my house to this day.

There were no books in the family home, but my mother was a bright and talkative woman who loved a gossip and a story, embellished or otherwise, and was given slightly to malapropisms: family lore has her leaning over the fence and solemnly informing Mrs Pressland from next door that the woman over the road had gone into hospital to 'have her wound out'. And she was Welsh so, of course, she sang. One vivid vignette in my mind: being cuddled up with her on the sofa in the dining room on a dark winter afternoon, just the two of us in the house, the fire lit, her singing me Christmas songs as snow fell into the yard. In truth, physical affection and displays of emotion were rare, and moments of intimacy, too. But that wasn't just my parents: that was how people were. It didn't feel like a lack. We knew we were loved.

My father, Arthur, was a porter at Billingsgate market. His brothers were butchers – indeed, if you climb back through my family tree, butchers crop up a lot. It turns out that I come from a long line of people who knew how to wield a meat cleaver. There was a notable exception in the form of my great-great-great-great-grandfather (roughly speaking), back in seventeen-hundred-and-frozen-to-death, who owned a brick-making business in Sussex and was apparently an extremely wealthy man. But no sooner had the White lineage finally come into some money than one of the sons immediately blew the fortune away – drink and women, no doubt, and the rest of it, I'm sure, he wasted. And after that, everyone went back to being butchers again.

Anyway, my father had courageously stepped to one side of the family tradition of butchery and he was a fishmonger – firstly at Billingsgate and later behind the counter of the Mac Fisheries fish shop in Camden Town. He moved on from there to serve in another Mac Fisheries branch, in the Jewish community in Golders Green. A practical and resourceful man, he knew how to save a bob or two. He cut up an old bike tyre and stuck lumps of it around the front of his work shoes to form an improvised bumper against wear and tear and the cold water that fishmongers spend their lives sloshing around in. Thus rubberised, and making sounds like a pantomime horse, he would be up at four and trot off to work on his bike. Of course, 1940–45 were the years of the wartime blackout, making night-time cycling a potentially risky business. Sure enough, one dark morning soon after my birth, so the story goes, my father, his shoes and his bike dropped into a freshly made bomb crater. The bomb had dropped on the London side of the bridge at Archway, right in the middle of the road. It was so deep that it must have stunned him momentarily. He was down there for some time until the morning light dawned and some passing air-raid wardens heard his cries for help. They hauled him up to the surface, whereupon, as he stood dusting himself down, they could only express their astonishment. 'Look at this bloke: he's had a bomb drop right on top of him, and he's still alive!' My father did not correct them. He straightened the front wheel of his bike, smoothed down his hair and rode on to work.

By all accounts, my father was something of a showman in the workplace, joshing with the customers, whom he loved, giving them a bit of a routine as he wrapped the haddock and the hake, messing about with the scales and the weights. It was probably his way of making the job tolerable, because a lot of the time he'd have been frozen and wet and on his feet for hours on end. (Arthritis would punish those feet for a lifetime of exertion when he was older.) In any case, piss-taking seemed to run on his side of the family. The term he and his relatives used for it was a piece of obsolete market trader's slang: chi-iking. At work, and socially, my dad was forever chi-iking – bantering, winding people up. At home, though, the showmanship tended to go away and he was a rather broody, forbidding presence whom you did your best not to cross. He occasionally gave the impression that he didn't much want us kids about. He adored my mother, though, and respected her, entirely aware that she was the brains that made the family work.

So, to Mr and Mrs White, in the particularly cold February

of 1940, a further son. Two further sons, in fact – twins. But only I emerged alive from the womb (or, as my mother would have put it, 'the wound'). I was healthy, but my companion for those nine months simply hadn't thrived. In the family version of these events, passed on to me as a child, I had been too greedy and eaten all the food. (Note how even this potentially sensitive area was not spurned as an opening for mild chi-iking.) The fact that I was originally one half of a duo would eventually give rise to a theory, much propounded in newspaper profiles over the years, that all my life since then has been a desperate effort to compensate for that stillborn brother. It's a grand idea, though I fear the truth may be a lot more prosaic. After all, this incident, sad as it was, was something that dated back to the day I was born, about which my memories are bound to be a bit patchy. From my point of view, it was a distant curiosity, a piece of passed-down history. It was hard to feel it as a loss – or even as an event in my life.

Still, the legend surrounding this biographical detail and its psychological meanings gained a further layer of decorative gilt after a pair of journalists visited my mother at home, late in her life, with flowers, warm smiles and open notebooks. Whereupon, over a pot of tea, my mother garrulously told her friendly visitors how delighted she was that I had taken the stage name 'Jason' in my twin's honour. Furthermore (and here one can imagine the journalists' biros starting to scribble especially quickly), the stringencies of the war, which saw so many public services suspended, had denied my twin the opportunity of a traditional funeral and so my mother had had no option, had she? She had buried him herself in the backyard.

Well, I did mention that my mother liked to embellish a tale. I should also point out that she was, shall we say, well into her anecdotage by the point at which she gave this interview. (I remember her telling me over the phone, 'I had a lovely chat about you with some journalists today,' and thinking, 'Uh-oh.')

So, just to straighten the record: I and my ill-fated twin weren't born at home; we were delivered at North Middlesex County Hospital, as declared on my birth certificate. My mother, to the very best of my knowledge, buried exactly no bodies in our back garden, during wartime or any other time. And my twin, being stillborn, was unnamed. I owe my stage name to another source of inspiration altogether, as I shall relate.

Now, it may well be that my parents were troubled by the baby they lost, and the life that never was, in ways that I wasn't, and in ways that I never knew. I assume, at least, that they weren't preparing for twins: in the absence of ultrasound scanning, the first they would have even known about my mother carrying two babies, rather than one, would have been at the birth. Did that make it easier to accept? I don't know. I can only say that they always seemed entirely sanguine about what happened. Perhaps the times taught them to be so. After all, there was a war on. There was a lot of death about. People like my mother and father did what they could, and got on with being alive. And so did I.

*   *   *

No bad turn-up, of course, to have a fishmonger in the family during wartime. And no bad thing, either, to have an uncle who was a butcher. The war brought food shortages and strict rationing. Apparently, as a baby – in the absence of anything sugary or even a traditional dummy – I was given a carrot as a pacifier, so they must have been cheap and readily available. But like everyone else, my parents had to scrape and scratch to get what provisions they could, and anything extra was welcome. Which is why, one morning, after an air raid, Mrs Pressland called across the fence to my mother in a state of some excitement. 'Mrs White,' she shouted, 'you've got a dead chicken on your roof.'

Now this was quite a coup. The unfortunate piece of poultry had obviously been flung up there during the night's destruction – manna from the skies. It seemed unlikely that the chicken had been innocently blasted from a nearby coop – this was London, after all, where not a lot of people kept chickens. But maybe a butcher's shop had copped it, or just some unfortunate household's larder. Didn't matter, really. The point was, a whole chicken would provide our family with at least two decent meals, and stew from the boiled-up bones – and with no resort to the ration book. (My mother, incidentally, made the world's greatest stews, sometimes from almost no recognisable ingredients whatsoever, and proudly and defiantly took her recipe's secrets to the grave with her.) So my mother eagerly rushed upstairs to the room my cot was in, looked out and begin to devise a plan to get this heavenly delivery down.

Except, as closer inspection from my bedroom window revealed, it wasn't a chicken. It was part of a human arm. I'm not sure even the Presslands would have been hungry enough to boil *that* up.

I was too young to know, but I often wonder what must have bulked larger in my mother's mind at the moment she realised what had come to rest on the tiles: the sheer horror, or the disappointment at not getting a free roast. In any case, the local Air Raid Patrol was called and the warden turned up with a ladder and quietly bagged and removed the offending limb.

The Luftwaffe never did manage a direct strike on 26 Lodge Lane, but they did manage to take out a stretch of three houses down the road. The assumption was that a German plane had got hit, and the pilot dumped his load in desperation as he struggled to get back across the Channel. There were strikes on Nether Street, Percy Road, Lodge Lane – you could follow the track of these discarded bombs across a map. Two hundred yards to the right and the despairing bomber would have taken down, at the very least, our outside toilet and anyone who happened to be in it.

A narrow escape for the Whites, then, and a cautionary illustration of the thinness of the thread by which all of us held our lives in those dark and tremulous days. Although, of course, had the bomb dropped two hundred yards the other way, it would have been nowhere near us. But that's not as good a story, nor as good a cautionary illustration.

So, the German armed forces failed to get me, and so, too, did my seven-year-old brother, although he also had a go. My mother checked on me one night, when I was just a few months old, and found Arthur slumbering in the cot on top of me and in grave danger of smothering me. He said he'd got frightened of the dark and had clambered in for company.

A few years later, Arthur was again almost successful in seeing me off, this time by using an old canvas army shoulder bag, which we normally used to hold wooden play bricks, to strap me to the coat hook on the rear of the back door in the kitchen – with my compliance, I should add, because we both agreed that if he spun me round in this position until the bag was tight, I would then, when released, spin back and amusingly resemble a tangled parachutist up a tree. (Look, I was seven, right? I was just delighted to have my older brother condescending to play with me.)

Actually, we were wrong about the parachute impression. As it turned out, my proximity to the door prevented me from spinning and unwinding in any way, and, accordingly, having turned blue, I didn't resemble a parachutist at all, but, more closely, a hog-tied Smurf. Kids: don't try this at home. The entertainment continued when, in what could almost have been a scripted moment, my mother entered from the other side of the door on which I was hanging, and obliviously asked, 'Where's David?' At which point, my brother straightforwardly reported, 'He's on the back of the door.' My mother shut the door to reveal me, bright blue, gasping my next-to-last breath.

Obviously Arthur had some productive impact on my childhood, too. He spent a lot of time wheeling me around the streets in a wheelbarrow, like some kind of nobleman in an eighteenth-century litter. And he was the source of my early wardrobe – lots of hand-me-down clothes that I was sincerely assured I would 'grow into'. In fact, I was assured I would 'grow into' a lot of things, including the large bike I received for Christmas, aged ten, to the pedals of which my father had to attach wooden blocks so that my feet could reach them. For a while there, I was touring the neighbourhood on what was, in effect, an orthopaedic bike. I didn't exactly look suave and sophisticated. Then again, I had a bike: the joy of that fact overwhelmed any embarrassment.

As it turned out, I was to get most of my growing done by about the age of fourteen when I reached five foot six and my body decided it had had enough of lengthening and left it at that. We shall have cause to return, periodically, to the advantages and disadvantages of my less than statuesque height in the course of this narrative.

Around the age of eight or nine, though, I did become the proud owner of a pair of perfectly fitting wellington boots – a fantastic breakthrough if only because this meant I could now clamber down into the brook without soaking my socks. The brook was in the nearby park, and my big childhood mates Ronnie Prior, Ray Jeffers and I would head there to spend long afternoons building dams, prior to appointing ourselves fighter pilots and bombing those dams to bits by throwing stones and making all the appropriate noises while we did so. The war was over by then, but it lived on in our imaginations and our games – how could it not?

Incidentally, in case, dear reader, you still have the appetite for this kind of thing: find a building site that has a large pile of soft sand – not sharp sand, but soft sand. Then push some house bricks around the sand to form a network of mountain roads. Then wet some of the sand and mould it to form tank turrets. Push twigs into the turrets to make guns. Now position these sand-tanks on the mountain roads and, from a distance of fifteen to twenty feet, attack the tanks with thrown stones. Hours of amusement can be yours. And no batteries needed.

Lodge Lane when I was growing up was a quiet backstreet, mostly made up of houses, though it also included Smith's the cobblers, and a greengrocer's run by a family called the Olivers, who owned a horse and cart and would deliver the fruit and vegetables door to door. Every year they would decorate the cart and dress up the horse and set off for a rally in Hyde Park and would often return with prize rosettes, to the widespread pride of the neighbourhood.

Also using a horse and cart, but to less popular effect, was the window cleaner, a largely cheerless soul who, as was the tradition, carried a bucket with him to collect up anything the horse left behind on its way through. I often found myself wondering – as you do – what would happen if you were to insert a firework into that bucket, when it was full, and then if you were to light the touchpaper on that firework and retreat. And one day, entirely in the interests of science, I found out.

What would happen is this: there would be a muffled bang, followed by a really quite magnificent fountain of horse shit, much of it eventually attaching itself to both the window cleaner and his recently completed work. A splendid result. Except for the window cleaner, obviously. And I don't suppose the horse was all that happy, either. Still. Nobody much liked that window cleaner. Or his horse, frankly.

Lodge Lane also had an off-licence, Chubbs, where jugs of beer could be filled from taps. The railings outside the shop had been commandeered for the war effort and you could easily climb up and lean over into the backyard. If you were lucky, there would be a crate of empty pop bottles within reach and, with a willing accomplice behind you on the pavement, you could lift a few of them out and pass them back, and then take them into the shop to claim (or, in fact, re-claim) the deposit – though I think Chubbs wised up to that little racket eventually and started stacking the crates further from the wall. It was from Chubbs, incidentally, that I got my first Jubbly – a pyramid-shaped carton of frozen orange juice, and a complete treat. As the advertising slogan used to say, 'Lubbly Jubbly.' I would get to hear those words again, a lot further down the line.

Then there was the street's tiny shop-cum-cafe with four tables and chairs and, on its little counter, a battered tea urn and a dingy stove with a greasy, blackened frying pan. It was run by an ancient bloke called Harry, who was forever in a pair of exhausted, shiny-kneed corduroys and who had a wounded foot which prompted him to go about with a proper shoe at the end of one leg and a carpet slipper at the end of the other, held on by half a dozen elastic bands. I used to go into the shop on an errand to buy my mother's cigarettes for her and find Harry grimly making tea and egg-and-bacon sandwiches for the local builders – salmonella on legs, you would have to assume, and unlikely to pass muster with the hygiene inspectors these days, but a key community service in any case.

I was also responsible for bringing back my father's *Daily Mirror* and, on Sundays, his *News of the World*, and running round to Radio Rentals, the electric appliance shop, to swap the battery for his radio set. No electricity, remember. For my father to listen to the Home Service of an evening, he required two electric 'accumulators' – unwieldy glass jars which enabled you to peer in at the metal plates, steeped in their mysterious liquid. You'd have one accumulator wired up to the radio, and the other on charge at Radio Rentals. For my part, I would eventually acquire a crystal radio set, which miraculously required neither batteries nor electricity. I kept it in my bedroom, twitching the whisker of wire to find voices or music, and lying in bed in the dark, me with one earpiece, Arthur with the other, listening to the great wide world.

There wasn't much to keep us off the streets in those days, although when I was about seven, my mother took me to church a few times – or, as she referred to it, 'the House of God'. She wanted me to be religious. She wasn't particularly religious herself, but she clearly believed it would be nice if I was. Perhaps she thought of it as an accomplishment, like playing the piano – something her son might do to make her proud. Anyway, on none of those trips to the House of God did she stay. She pushed me in through the door and left me there for the service while she walked home. One Sunday, after depositing me, she had just got into the kitchen and was probably about to make herself a cup of coffee (or Camp chicory essence, more like, which was what passed for coffee in our house in those days), when lo and behold I turned up behind her. (This was easily achieved as the key to the front door always dangled on a string, fixed by a nail to the back of the front door, so you could simply reach through the letter box and pull it out. This was as good as asking burglars to come in and help themselves. But as there was very little for burglars to help themselves to, it didn't seem to bother us much.)

Seeing me, my mum said, 'What happened? Why didn't you stay in church?'

I said, 'I've come home. I've had enough.'

She said, 'What do you mean?'

I said, 'Well, I've been going to the House of God all these weeks, and every time I go He's never at home.'

To my seven-year-old mind, it stood to reason. Why wasn't He home? If you went to Auntie Win's, my dad's sister's, as we would for Sunday tea sometimes, Auntie Win was actually there. And you'd get a piece of cake if you were lucky. God, on the other hand, was never in. And as for a piece of cake, forget it.

On top of that it was always so cold in there. So why would you go? Disillusion with religion set in right there.

I probably figured my time was better spent playing Knock Down Ginger – that classic game where you rap on someone's front door and run away, a sport, alas, with very few takers these days, in the PlayStation and Xbox age. A shame, really, because clearly Knock Down Ginger promotes a healthy, active lifestyle, especially if – as once happened with me – you have barely finished knocking when a bloke throws open the door and comes out after you.

I promptly turned and scarpered, only to swivel my head and discover that this bloke was still coming. Normally blokes would just open the door and shout. So I put my head down and ran a bit faster. He was still on my tail. I went over a wall. He was still there. I ran and ran. He ran and ran. There was no losing him. Finally – at a point where London began to give way to open countryside, or so it seemed to me – I realised that I simply couldn't run any more. I had to stop. This would mean getting a belt round the ear, I knew, but at least I wouldn't die an agonised death by exhaustion, which seemed to be the alternative. So I leaned against the wall, trying to recover, and awaited my fate. My pursuer soon reached me and I braced myself for the clobbering that would surely follow. In fact, he leaned there too, breathing heavily for a while. And eventually, when he had composed himself, he said, 'Well run, son. Bloody good run.' And then he turned and walked back the way he had come – followed, eventually, at a slightly bemused and wary distance, by me. Needless to say he was taken off the list for Knock Down Ginger.

The strike on Lodge Lane had left a handy bomb site. It didn't occur to us kids to think of it as a place where people had suffered and died or to consider the gravity of the scene in any way. Rather it seemed as if the war had gifted us the perfect playground. We had all the bits of bricks we could possibly desire for throwing around and building things, and an absolutely brilliant location for bonfires. Percy Road had their bomb site and we at Lodge Lane had ours. Every autumn, in the run-up to Bonfire Night, we'd go out in the evening and raid the Percy Roaders' bomb site, because they might have a stash of rubber tyres or bonfire-building materials, or some other treasure they had collected. And then the Percy Roaders would come and make a revenge raid on our bomb site, usually in the dead of night.

Then there was the mob from round Downing Street way (not that one, another one). Our site faced the opening to the alleyway which led to Downing Street, so it was strategically well placed to see off invaders from that direction – especially given that someone eventually came up with the ingenious idea of tying an old rubber bicycle inner tube to the gateposts, which were still conveniently standing, and using the resulting machine as a catapult with which to ping half-bricks across the street into the alley. We had a stack of broken masonry ready as ammo at all times, in case of attack. The real heavies in the gang were the ones who pulled the rubber back. I was too slight for that duty, but I saw active service as one of the loaders, passing up the bricks. The Downing Streeters didn't used to know what had hit them. Well, actually they did: it was house bricks.

House bricks and, on one occasion, worse. Ernie Pressland, my next-door neighbour, who was a bit older than me, was the leader of the Lodge Laners – all boys of course. Girls might as well have been another species for all that we had to do with them at that stage. Under Ernie's instruction one day, we used bits of slate – still lying around the place from the bombed roof – to construct tomahawks, made with a wooden chair leg, split at the top, with the slate, cut into the shape of an axe head, slotted into it and bound round with string. Hey presto – the classic American Indian hand-held scalp-taker.

The next time the Percy Roaders raided us, out we sprang from our hiding places. Mine, I remember, was a galvanised water tank. We chased them into an immediate, screaming retreat, brandishing our tomahawks. Unfortunately one of our number, getting slightly too much into the western spirit, threw his weapon. It arced meanly through the air and bounced against the back of some poor kid's head, causing the kid in question to fall to the ground. Those of us in the pursuing pack instantly put the brakes on and ran the other way. Whatever happened after that, I genuinely know not. I assume the poor chap managed a full recovery, because we would have heard about it fairly quickly if he hadn't. Nevertheless, slate tomahawks were quietly withdrawn from our armoury from that day forward.

As 5 November was shortly to arrive, we decided to build ourselves the mother and father of all bonfires. We collected rubbish from all over the neighbourhood and stacked it high into the air. Ernie, again in charge of the operation, had the genius idea of constructing the bonfire with a low tunnel into its core so that, when it was finished, someone could still crawl into the centre of the pyre and light it from within. This made sense because, given the late-autumn weather, the bonfire was likely to get soaked by rain, but this approach left a dry centre, ready for ignition.

Because I was the smallest, I was given the duty, come the appointed hour, of crouching down and burrowing deep into the mound with the matches – a duty which I regarded as the utmost honour. However, as I was within, getting it lit, some prankster – by the name of Ernie, I'm fairly sure – decided it would be most amusing to light the outer end of the tunnel. I think it had been Ernie's plan all along: he thought it would be great fun to see an incandescent White exit, or not, from the centre of the fire. From outside came the noise of uproarious laughter, followed by acrid smoke and flames. Somehow I managed to push my way out, not best pleased.

Still, at least I wasn't hospitalised in that particular incident – unlike the time when a lump of brick, thrown by my brother's mate Jimmy Bickers, created an opening in my forehead which required closing by qualified medical staff. And unlike the time when the top of my skull broke the flight of a rusty paint tin flung by, of all people, my brother Arthur – his third significant attempt on my life. And unlike the occasion when the back of a parked-up welder's truck into which I happened to be scrambling proved to contain a six-inch nail which cut a long, deep groove in my thigh. Blessedly, Mr Bickers, Jimmy's dad, the owner of the only car in Lodge Lane, was at home and prepared to play the part of the ambulance driver. I needed anaesthetic while that particular gash was healed, and in those days that meant chloroform dripped onto a gauze mask. Really, if the wounds didn't get you, there was a decent chance the treatment would. It's a wonder I made it through this period at all. But such was life as a Lodge Laner – lived under the permanent risk of death to ourselves and others.

Eventually, to our immense chagrin, when I was about ten years old, the council levelled the bomb site and built a small block of flats in its place. And with that we lost our playground. The flats are still there, and the alley too, and many of the old houses, but sadly not number 26, which at some point became a car park. But times have changed, of course, and customs with them, and you'll look in vain nowadays for children throwing handmade tomahawks at each other. Maybe they're doing it on the internet, instead. That would be far safer.

With our playground gone, we had to seek other venues for our amusement. But the world of entertainment was itself moving on rapidly. There was untold excitement round our way in the summer of 1953 when Ronnie Prior's dad acquired the neighbourhood's first television set. He had it installed for the Coronation of Queen Elizabeth II that June and then invited everyone within about a three-mile radius to come and share the experience. You've never seen such a crowd gathered in a single sitting room. People were hanging from the light fittings.

The technological marvel we were all straining to see had a glass screen, the thickness and approximate shape of a standard goldfish bowl and affixed to a teak wood cabinet large enough to conceal several bodies. Yet the apparition on that screen of these silvery figures, going about their regal business in Westminster Abbey, seemed utterly miraculous. The only thing you'd ever seen like it was the movies. But this was the movies in the corner of a room – unthinkable levels of magic.

Two years later – just in time to catch the launch night of Associated-Rediffusion, the first ITV channel, in September 1955 – we had our own set at 26 Lodge Lane, on hire purchase. You put a sum down, paid a weekly fee, and then two years and half a dozen new tubes later, the television was yours. That opening night for Associated-Rediffusion included a variety show, a boxing match and an advert for Gibbs SR toothpaste. But never mind the fact that the tubes kept going and that my father was never entirely happy with the positioning of the aeriel on top of the set, I rather liked the look of television. My hunch was that it had a great future ahead of it, if it ever managed to catch on.

CHAPTER TWO

The cockerel from hell. Something called acting. And the law feels my collar.

Every summer Mum would take me and my brother and sister to stay with her family in Wales, going on the train from Paddington, which was a stunning scene of noise and smoke in those days. It's hard to convey, now, the excitement in the build-up to those trips. Sleep the night before would prove nearly impossible. Then there would be the ride on the Underground, taking our cardboard cases; and then, at Paddington, the walk down the ramp that led into the station, with the unutterably exciting sound and smell rising out of the place and beginning to envelop you. I remember us working our way across the thronging concourse, seeking out our train, utterly trusting my mother to find the right platform – completely in her hands in that wonderful, literally carefree way of childhood, which goes eventually and which you can never get back.

I would spend the entire train journey with my head out of the window – not too far, for fear of getting decapitated by another train coming the other way or the arm of a passing signal, but part of the way out. There was something magnetically compelling about catching sight, on bends, of the rest of the train that you were in, and I positioned myself where I could see this magic whenever it happened. By the time we got to Cardiff, where we changed for the valley train and Pontlottyn, half my face would be blackened by the steam, like some kind of peculiar London-born Pierrot doll. At which point my mother would have to spit into her wadded handkerchief and clean me up. The first time we travelled up from Cardiff on the Merthyr line, I thought I was in fairyland. The line ran along and through mountains so green they hurt your eyes, and the river wove in and out of the valley like a blue ribbon. I was a young lad who had lived among the bricks and mortar of London. Here, you could virtually smell the colour green.

In Pontlottyn I had two uncles – Uncle Llewellyn and Uncle Idris, known as Uncle Id – and a batch of cousins, large and small. Uncle Id had two sons, my substantially older cousins, Cyril and John. John was a miner whose leg was badly injured when a tunnel he was working in caved in on him. Some weeks later, he came out of hospital. It didn't stop him riding a bike, though, with his broken leg stretched straight out in a plaster cast and his other foot doing all the pedalling.

You might think Cyril, meanwhile, had taken a blow to the head, because during some possibly over-lubricated evening or other, with a few of his beer-drinking mates, he had taken a bet that he wouldn't drink a glass of petrol. On the plus side, I guess he must have won the bet. But the petrol did untold damage to his digestive system, put him in hospital for quite a long time and, essentially, crippled him for the rest of his life. Kids: don't do this, either.

Obviously a fairly deep streak of eccentricity ran through this part of the family generally, as evidenced by the fact that, sometime around 1940 or 1941, with the Blitz in full swing, a party of them had come up to London to stay with us in Lodge Lane in order, basically, to have a look at the war. I guess they must have thought it was the kind of thing that wasn't likely to happen all that often and that you might as well get a sight of it while you could. So up they came. And they were, apparently, thrilled when a doodlebug obligingly cut its eerie mechanical path above our roof in broad daylight, bringing the excited Welsh visitors rushing from the backyard, through the house and into the street in order to track its course, while my mother tried and failed to convince them that it might be better if they joined the rest of us under the kitchen table at this point.

Anyway, the general trend was for the London part of the family to visit the Welsh part, rather than the other way round. Sometimes we would stay with Mum's friend, Mrs Rogers, who lived on the hillside in a place called Abertysswg, in a big house that I was very impressed with. Other times, though, we would stay with Uncle Id, which was a different experience. Uncle Id had been a miner, but had retired in order, it seemed, to be able to spend more time doing what he principally loved, which was drinking. He lived very poorly in one of a network of tiny workers' cottages in the heart of Pontlottyn. The houses had no gardens but backed on to a little square of wasteland, partly given over to stinging nettles, in the middle of which was a string of toilets – about half a dozen cubicles, each one shared. This less than magnificent emporium was known as the House of Commons. Each cottage had its ascribed cubicle – Id's was number four, as I recall – but you shared it with five or six other families from the square. By these standards, the outdoor privy by the back door at Lodge Lane, cramped and draughty as it was, came to seem almost Roman in its luxury. As for the smell that routinely greeted you as you gingerly eased your way into the House of Commons . . . well, let's just say that, on a hot summer's day in Wales – and, just occasionally, you did get one of those – the aroma rising off that block would have been enough to stop two advancing legions of the Spartan army.

Uncle Id had a pet cockerel with only one working eye, called (naturally enough) Nelson. The other eye was missing, presumed lost in some long-forgotten dust-up with another cockerel. And whether it was because he still bore a grudge about that, or for other reasons, Nelson had what we would now call 'issues'. In fact, he was essentially a Rottweiler in a cockerel outfit. This battered bird had appointed himself protector of Uncle Id's property and its chief guardian against invasion, not just by other animals but also by humans. Indeed, the only human Nelson was prepared to tolerate was Uncle Id – to the extent of coming to sit on his shoulder at breakfast, where Id, who appeared to love Nelson as much as he loved anyone or anything, would feed him bits of bread. You can imagine the wonder I had for Id, who appeared to possess the powers of Dr Dolittle.

Mostly, however, Nelson would adopt a sentry position on the window ledge out the back, flicking his head around and flexing his neck to scope the surroundings with his one good eye. To know Nelson's fixed monocular gaze was to know fear. Deep fear. Coming in or out of the house, your best chance was to hope that he was asleep, when you just about had a chance of tiptoeing quickly around him. What you didn't want to do, however, was to get caught between the back door and the House of Commons. Because then Nelson would attack.

Dear reader, I don't know if you have ever been attacked by a cockerel, but if you haven't, then allow me to tell you that it's an experience with very little to recommend it. Sometimes a cockerel, defying physics, has the uncanny ability to come at you low, hard and seemingly out of nowhere. Or Nelson did, anyway. Occasionally, you would peer tentatively from the rear threshold of the house and establish that the horizon was clear. Then, just as you were marooned in the middle, he would materialise aggressively at your ankles, chasing you into the House of Commons. And then you'd be stuck there, looking out through a knothole while he paraded up and down outside the door, daring you to come out again. What was it with that bloody creature?

There wasn't a time that I returned to London from Uncle

Id's without a pair of legs peppered with beak wounds below the knee. Moreover, this double jeopardy – the aroma of the toilet block plus the chance of getting pecked to ribbons by a violent half-blind cockerel – meant I spent an awful lot of the summers of my childhood determinedly crossing my legs and clenching my buttocks, evacuating my bowels and bladder only as a very last resort.

Despite the battles with Nelson (and perhaps a little bit because of them), Wales was a magical place to my boyhood self. With my cousin Derek, who was roughly the same age as me, and his gang of mates, I would go out all day clambering around those mountains, drinking water from the springs and playing in disused mines, among the overgrown railway tracks and abandoned wheel-houses. One year Cousin John, who after his leg injury had healed had been given a job 'at the surface', as they called it, organised for me and my mate to take a tour of a working mine. I would have been about fourteen. I remember us both climbing nervously into the lift with John and the mine safety officer, and then descending slowly through the cold and wet to where no man or beast should go. In the cage of the lift on the way down, the darkness was so thickly black that you couldn't see your hand in front of your face. I know that's a familiar expression, but I experimented, bringing my fingers right up to touch the tip of my nose and even touching my eyelashes, where I still couldn't see them.

Eventually we reached the bottom, where the pit ponies stood mournfully in their stalls. We were shown around and taken halfway to the pit face. All I can say is that those men who worked there, in that wet, dusty, close environment, were heroes.

On the return journey to the surface, it seemed to take an eternity to reach the top and we were more than a little relieved when the doors finally clanked open and we stepped out into the light and the warmth of the day. John then took us over to the winding house, where the man who operated the lift said, 'Did you enjoy that, boys?' We must have looked a little uncertain, even as we politely nodded, and he burst out laughing. 'I had you going up and down that lift like a yo-yo,' he said. He was bringing the cage up and then gently sending it down again, then up again, then down again, just for a laugh. He knew that it was so dark that we had no point of reference, and no way of knowing which way we were going. The secret, and his expertise, was to make the lift change direction so smoothly and gently that you never noticed it happening.

At the end of the day, I used to sleep on the couch in Id's front parlour – a battered horsehair chaise longue with its stuffing spewing out. But I used to love this bed because it put me in prime position to experience the sheer wonder of the local train. This house had at one time in its history been a shop, so it had a big front window looking out over the road to the embankment that carried the railway line. At about four in the morning I would be woken by the noise of the Merthyr-bound steam engine, pulling out of Pontlottyn, leaving in its wake the local miners who had finished their night shift. Then, as it would shunt past, I could raise my head from the pillow and see the glow of the firebox, lighting up the figure of the fireman shovelling in the coal, and hear and even feel the tremendous rhythmic thunder of the engine from where I lay. Hard to better the romance and excitement of that, for a young boy. Then I would hear the miners on their way home, clanking down the pavement in their steel-capped boots, and sometimes, when the mood took them, they would sing, their voices rising gloriously through the pre-dawn summer air, singing for the sake of singing. They call Wales the land of song, and on many of those holiday mornings, I knew why.

*   *   *

HOLIDAYS BEAT SCHOOL, of course. I attended Northside Junior School and then Northside Secondary Modern, as they called it, without noticeably raising the bar, scholarship-wise, at either

– and certainly not at the former. At primary school, Miss Kent read us the Greek myth of Jason and the Argonauts in daily instalments, and that fired my imagination. But that was pretty much where my interest in the classroom started and ended. Learning wasn't really my thing, and it was fairly clear from an early stage that I would be unlikely to be troubling the scorers at Oxford. In tests at primary school, I routinely finished third from bottom of the class. If I told you that the person who finished second bottom was called Richard Moron and, moreover, that Richard Moron devoted the best part of his school days to drinking the ink out of the inkwells and chewing reflectively on sticks of chalk, then you might begin to get a sense of where I stood.

Bottom of the class? That was Pidgy Saunders, who, bless him, couldn't write his own name. Not even with a stick in the ground. So, there you have it: the line of descent went White, Moron, Saunders, strictly in that order – and that was also the case after the test to decide which stream (A, for the intelligentsia, and B, for the rest of us) we would go into at the secondary school.

Being in the B-stream wouldn't have mattered much to me, except that Tony Brighton, my best friend throughout primary school, and a fellow Lodge Laner, scored high enough to go into the A-stream. That hit me for six. I thought we should have been together, me and him, fighting the world. But suddenly, he was the brains and I was the laggard. It was very divisive, and not a little irritating. (I should add that Tony and I did continue to fight the world together, despite this academic wedge so cruelly driven between us. At fourteen, the lucky benefactor of a cigarette machine at Finchley ice rink that had a fit and disgorged its entire contents of Capstan Full Strength into his waiting hands, Tony gave me my first cigarette, thus commencing a habit which was to stay with me for many happy years.)

My main problem was that I lacked confidence – couldn't

stand the thought of thrusting myself forward in lessons. And that inadequacy continued for some time after I moved across from the primary school to the secondary school. With my male peers, self-assurance was less of a problem. If anything, I was a touch on the cocky side. I made two particularly firm mates in these years – Micky Weedon from two streets away in Grange Avenue, and Brian Barneycoat – and all three of us were the same height. The Shorthouses, we used to call ourselves. Otherwise, though, in a social hierarchy where power and influence naturally gravitated to the big and the strong, I sought to compensate for the relative slightness of my physical presence by the classic method of being the clown. I don't recommend this as a fail-safe scheme for the avoidance of bullying. Sometimes it's the short ones trying to be funny that get picked on worst of all. But it worked for me.

My comic speciality was mimicking the teachers. There was a teacher at Northside Secondary Modern called Mr Winter who was tough – not nasty, but tough, and when he talked, you listened. He had quite a deep voice and was very well spoken, but I could do a very convincing Mr Winter. So when there were children monkeying around with the caretaker's equipment in the bike shed at break time, I would wait my moment and shout: 'You, boy! Get off those ladders!' People would freeze, jump away – much to everyone else's hilarity and increasing my own kudos.

Academically, though, I struggled and was quite close to useless for a very long time. Because I couldn't do many of the things I was asked to do, I was gripped by the thought that I couldn't do anything at all. That kind of attitude feeds on itself very quickly and is the curse of many a school career. What mainly turned it around for me was the arrival, as my form teacher, of the appropriately named Mr Joy – the new, all-singing, all-dancing, fresh-out-of-the-teacher-training-school-showroom Mr Joy. Mr Joy was also the school gymnastics master. And gymnastics was the one area of school life where I genuinely could do things – and do them better than others. Maths might have been a problem, but if you wanted someone who could stand on his hands, or execute a perfectly rounded somersault, I was your boy. The epiphany came during a rope-climbing lesson in my early teens, when, for the first time in my school career, I was singled out as an example: 'White – show them how to do it,' said Mr Joy.

For a moment, I looked around on the assumption that another White had turned up in the class without me knowing. But no. He meant me. So I was up that rope like lightning. If Oxford had offered a degree in rope-climbing, they would have been begging me to come – and I would have been weighing their offer against a number of attractive and equally firm propositions from the top-ranking American universities. But they didn't.

Mr Joy, though, through many such moments, gave me the confidence that I could do things. And that confidence started to filter through to other areas. I'm not saying I became Harvard material overnight – not unless Harvard is particularly drawn to students whose final school report relates that they have 'considerable ability' in woodwork – but I did OK, even blossomed a bit, and won some prizes for my work. That same report for English says: 'Reads with intelligence, fluidity and understanding.' I owe that to Mr Joy because I think he did something no one else had thought to do: he told me I was good at something.

And let's not knock woodwork, in any case. At home, I still have, and use to this day, the magazine stand that I made in that Northside woodwork class with Mr Bradshaw. That's craftsmanship: built to last. Eat your heart out, IKEA.

As for school drama, I wouldn't have touched it with any length of bargepole you could have found, had not a special set of circumstances contrived to force this alien subject upon me. Northside Secondary was readying itself for its annual production. This was a new idea, courtesy of the new headmaster. The chosen play was set in Cromwellian times and entitled *Wayside War*. However, a week away from curtain-up, the boy in the leading role went down with the measles. Panic for all concerned, of course – but not for me. I couldn't have cared less, having nothing to do with the production whatsoever. At least, I had nothing to do with it until the headmaster, Mr Hackett, approached me in the corridor one afternoon and told me they needed a volunteer to replace the bloke with the measles – and that, moreover, I was the volunteer they had in mind.

Why me? Perhaps my playground reputation as the world's leading mimic of Mr Winter preceded me. Perhaps I just happened to be in the wrong corridor at the wrong time. Whatever, fate's finger had pointed. Or certainly Mr Hackett's had.

'What do you say, White?'

Now, I wanted to act the lead in the school play about as much as I wanted to poke myself in the eye repeatedly with a burnt stick. My mate Micky Weedon had somehow got himself caught up in this production, and he had heard nothing but ribbing about it from me. Acting was, to my feckless, boyish mind, girly, sissy, highly likely to involve the wearing of embarrassing clothing, and completely certain to bring down on one the sniggering scorn of one's peers. Having worked so hard to counter the effects of my diminutive stature and ensure at least some degree of social standing among my larger fellow students, the last thing I wanted to do was blow it all entirely by revealing myself to be, of all ridiculous things, a thespian.

'I'd really rather not, sir,' I muttered.

At which point the headmaster said, in a quiet but distinctly steely tone: 'Don't make me have to tell you to do it.'

It took me quite a while to unpack that sentence. But I eventually got the gist of it: in simple terms, I had no choice. I was volunteered, whether I liked it or not.

I should stress that, at this point in my life, the full extent of my theatrical experience amounted to exactly one primary-school production, at around the age of nine, playing a monkey. The drama in question was a piece of vaguely organised chaos entitled *Around the Town* – one of those plays written to involve as many children in the school as possible. When I say I played a monkey, in fact what I played was an actor who was trying to get to his theatre, but who was running late and becoming sidetracked and needing to ask for directions all the time. None of which would have been all that remarkable but for the twist that, in this play-within-the-play, the actor was due to represent the aforementioned monkey and had, for unexplained reasons, chosen to spurn the changing facilities at his intended theatre and don the full monkey outfit at home, prior to setting out. As you do. Consequently, the people he meets along the way, 'around the town', think he actually is a monkey . . . with predictably hilarious consequences.

I'm sure there was some wholesome message at the heart of it all, about appearance and reality and accepting people for what they are, or some such – or perhaps a simpler moral about the virtues of punctuality and the general inadvisability of going about dressed as a monkey in a built-up area. But my abiding memory is of wearing what was, in effect, a baggy brown fur bag, poking my head through the window of a badly painted paper backdrop and asking, 'Can you tell me what the time is?' – and thereby causing mass, and badly acted, panic.

This, you could convincingly argue, was scant preparation for the more serious proposition of a leading role in *Wayside War* – a one-act play about espionage during the English Civil War, featuring exactly no people dressed as monkeys. Nevertheless, my part required me to wear the full regalia of a seventeenth-century cavalier, including a giant foppish hat with a feather in it and floppy boots – a prospect which pretty much froze my liver with embarrassment.

But, of course, I was without a choice in this matter. My number had been called and there was no time to wish otherwise. I got my lines learned in short order and, come the night, drew a deep breath and clumped out onto the school stage, reasoning that if I was going to die, then at least I would die with my floppy boots on. Ditto, my foppish hat.

As it happened, though, I didn't die. On the contrary, under the lights and with the attention of the room upon me, I found I rather enjoyed myself. I found I enjoyed, too, the accolade of the audience afterwards. OK, so a roomful of parents at a school play isn't the hardest audience to wow, even in north Finchley on a Friday night. Nevertheless, it felt good. And the headmaster coming up afterwards to tender his congratulations . . . well, that felt good, too.

And what felt even better was when two West End producers, who happened to be in the audience on the second night, came round to the dressing room afterwards, said the show had absolutely knocked them to the floor, and positively begged us to allow them to transfer the production to the Theatre Royal, Drury Lane, just as soon as a slot became available.

OK, not really. But there was, at least, a consensus in the school that we should enter *Wayside War* into the East Finchley Drama Festival – a totally new concept on me, and not an event to which I would previously have given the time of day: a drama competition where, over the course of a fortnight or so, local schools and amateur groups vied for supremacy by running their best efforts past a panel of judges. And blow me down if *Wayside War* didn't get through to the final Saturday, where it faced off against two other productions for prize play of the festival – and won. Glory upon glory. Not only was drama a bit of a lark, I now realised, it was a competitive lark, and that certainly appealed to me.

And through all this, my peers didn't spurn me and cast me out into the social wilderness, never to return: on the contrary, they turned up to see the play with their parents and watched and applauded. Also, along the way, it was impossible not to notice that the rehearsals were getting me off a few lessons, and that could hardly be accounted a bad thing. We even had to leave school one day and travel into London to Nathan's, the costumiers, for our outfits – and then take them back when the production had finished. Permission to travel out of school on a school day . . . this was living very high on the hog.

All things considered, then – the larking around, the applause, the bunking off – I came quite rapidly to the conclusion that I rather liked the cut of acting's jib. Superficial of me to see it in those terms? Actually, I would stand by that summary of the theatre's advantages, as a profession, even now: it's quite fun, people applaud if you're lucky, and it gets you off work.

* * *

THE LETTER WAS dated 1 April but it was not, sadly, a prank.

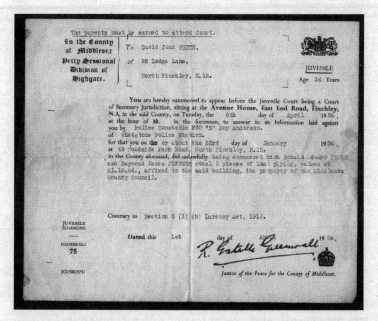

Nothing I could do but hold my hands up. Just like in Cluedo: it was me, in Woodside Park Road, with the lead piping.

Our defence, m'lud: the resale value of the said and formerly affixed piping was of no interest to us, the juveniles in question (Masters White, Prior, Jeffers), being not so much unlawfully concerned with the making of a quick ten bob on the sly, but rather with the melting down of the aforementioned lead and the forming it thereafter into soldiers to play with, in all innocence, as young boys, if it so please the court.

Was that true? Both the passage of time and due respect for the processes of the law insist that we draw a veil over this element of the proceedings. Let us merely note, before moving swiftly on, that, after a morning in court with a very tidy head of hair, a very well-knotted tie and a decidedly less than impressed father, I was 'discharged, subject to the condition that he commits no offence during the period of twelve months next ensuing'.

So, was I, at this point in my life and about to leave school, on the slippery slope towards a life of petty crime? Or was I just a north London lad with a little bit too much time on his hands who needed occupying?

Either way, it didn't matter. I had found something to keep me off the streets and out of mischief. I had a new hobby.

CHAPTER THREE

*Going Incognito. Adventures in electricity. Further lasting
scars. And why you should never go in the lift shaft of an
incomplete block of flats.*

Immediately after the historic victory of *Wayside War* in the
hotly contested East Finchley Drama Festival of 1954, my mate
Micky Weedon and I were standing around, soaking up the glory
and generally feeling rather smug about ourselves, when a man
in a cravat came up. His name was Doug Weatherhead and he
was the director of one of the other plays that we had defeated
in the final. He offered his congratulations and said a few kind
words, roughly amounting to 'Darlings, you were marvellous'. And
then he asked us if we would like to join his amateur theatre club.

This would have been the Incognito Theatre Group, based
not far from Finchley in Friern Barnet, for which this bloke
Doug ran the junior section. And, clearly, his offer was of no
interest to us whatsoever. Less than no interest. Do amateur
dramatics outside school – in your own time? This man must
have taken us for fools. Micky and I smilingly declined.

'Well, that's a pity,' Doug said. 'We could do with a couple
of boys. We've got about twenty girls and no males so it's getting
hard to find plays we can cast.'

Imagine here, if you will, a short silence in which the sudden whirring of cogs in the minds of two fourteen-year-old boys is almost audible. Imagine too, perhaps, the sight of those two fourteen-year-old boys exchanging a look of dawning comprehension.

An abundance of girls? A shortage of boys?

'What time does this group of yours meet?' I asked.

A week later I became an active member of the Incognito Theatre Group and stayed that way for the best part of eleven years until I became a professional.

Would amateur theatre have lured my boyhood self eventually, of its own accord, without this additional 'abundant girls' aspect? Perhaps, with enough encouragement and enough prodding from external sources. But what I can say for sure is that Doug Weatherhead had caught me and Micky at a very vulnerable moment. By this point in our lives, puberty had begun to wreak its steamy havoc. Yet, of course, in those days, in 1950s Britain, puberty had an extraordinary amount of difficulty wreaking anything at all. Even on into my later teens, sexual activity was an exotic, remote and highly tentative thing. Girls, assuming you had access to them, tended to be extremely reluctant to help your puberty along its way, and the opportunity to get even as far as 'first base' seemed like the rarest of blessings.

Some of us Lodge Laners in those sensitive, budding years were fortunate enough to be smiled upon by a neighbourhood girl who, in and around the bomb site playground and just occasionally down the side of the Salvation Army Hall, would uncomplicatedly enable curious male acquaintances to touch her breasts. However, lest you get the impression that this was a woman of woefully loose principles, let me make clear that you could only ever feel those cherished parts a) briefly and b) through the thick insulation supplied by her jumper and bra. One's gratitude was boundless, of course. But in such a context, the idea of eventually consummating a relationship and having something that we had heard called 'sex' was a dream, entirely fantastical – about as connected with reality in our minds as an episode of the Dan Dare comic strip in *The Eagle*.

The morals of the day, certainly in working-class communities, had set themselves firmly against sexual experiment, and certainly against experimental intercourse. A terrible stigma was attached to getting pregnant outside marriage, and that stigma extended also to children born out of wedlock. Unwedded conception spelled nothing less than social ruin, for you and your family, not to mention the poor soul that you brought into the world. Girls had to bear the most formidable brunt of that, of course, so if they came across as cautious, or even prim and proper, who could blame them? Boys, for their part, trembled in the knowledge that, nine times out of ten, a slip-up would mean marriage. And marriage was forever, and forever was a very long time.

However, the idea of using a condom was fraught with complication to the point of impossibility. There was the difficulty of acquiring such a thing, for a start, which would require a staggering act of face-to-face boldness in a chemist or a barbershop. And, in any case, they were joke objects – invented, so it seemed to us, not for the serious purposes of birth control, but entirely so that boys would have something about which to make smutty, but somehow ceaselessly amusing, jokes involving the word 'johnny'. Encounters were kept to petting – in various weights up as far as 'heavy', if you were lucky, which you probably weren't – and no further. Small wonder that a brief touch of entirely wool-encased and cotton-packed breast was something both prized and glorious. Meanwhile, if amateur dramatics could guarantee to put Micky Weedon and me in a room where girls, with all their distant promise, regularly abounded – well, then Micky Weedon and I were automatically in favour of amateur dramatics, and all power to its elbow.

And so it came to pass that, on a Monday evening in the

early summer of 1954, Micky and I leaned our bikes up against the wall of the former lemonade factory which was the head-quarters of the Incognito Theatre Group and, rigid with self-consciousness, shuffled to a position narrowly inside the door. Just as Doug had forewarned, the gathering that met our eyes in that room was almost exclusively female. Did we therefore immediately glide, swan-like, into the centre of the throng and begin to turn on our nonchalant and yet somehow irresistible charm? No. We clung together and refused to let one another out of each other's sight for the rest of the evening.

That first Monday, I don't think we took any active part in the proceedings at all – just watched as Doug put the others through their paces, getting them up onstage in little groups and cooking up scenes in which they could improvise. Slowly, though, over the course of the following weeks, Micky and I thawed enough to get involved. And, clearly, even setting aside purely demographic considerations, we couldn't have been more fortunate in where we had landed up. The Incognito Group had been running since 1938 and had the exceptional advantage of operating out of its own theatre. That small, red-brick factory, set back from Holly Park Road, had been acquired after the Second World War, and had then been renovated and fitted out with rows of seating bought from a bombed cinema to make a small but perfectly serviceable auditorium. OK, the facilities might not have been West End standard – the upstairs dressing rooms were fairly dingy and what the theatre offered by way of lavatory facilities, to actors and audience alike, was a set of Elsan portable chemical toilets down an alleyway at the side of the building. Inconveniently, there were no lights out there so, on play nights, ladies who desired to powder their noses (such as my mother and my aunts and various family friends, who became unfailing patrons of any Incognito production that I was involved in) were offered a torch to guide them on their way.

Still, the priceless advantage of having this dedicated space, rather than sharing a hall or a public room somewhere, as most amateur groups had to, was that sets for a production could be built and left up for the run of the play, rather than dismantled every night or partly packed up so that the local Mothers' Union, or whoever, could have the run of the place the following morning. It gave the Incognitos a bit of an edge.

The other thing the group was clearly blessed with was Doug Weatherhead, a man who was, I came to realise, tirelessly dedicated to the organisation and to the cause of amateur theatre in general, and someone to whom I would end up owing an awful lot. In due course, Doug coaxed me onto the stage and began to set me those little improvisations. 'I want you to come up with Janet and Rita,' he would say, 'and pretend that you are the husband of one and the boyfriend of the other. How are you going to cope with that?'

How indeed? But Doug was an excellent coach, who would always say afterwards, 'That's very good, but what about the possibility of this? Or what about considering it this other way?' What he was doing was building our confidence to stand up in front of the rest of the group and let go a little.

Fat chance of that with me, though, in the beginning. I found those initial improvisational set-ups purgatory. They didn't just make me uncomfortable: they made me want to shrivel up and post myself down a crack in the floorboards. But when Doug eventually handed out some sheets of paper and we started to run through a bit of a play, things were totally different. Then I had something to grab hold of and I felt less exposed. I discovered that if I could add the confidence I had found as a freelance impressionist in the school playground to some written lines, then I was away.

Pretty soon after this, I went to see the company compete at a local drama festival. Another group there put on a play called

Dark of the Moon – a strange, alluring piece about witchcraft and superstition and all manner of weird goings-on in the Appalachian Mountains. I remember feeling enthralled, loving the oddness of it. The Incogs won a prize that time, which was quite inspiring, too. My own Incog debut came when Doug put me in a one-act play set in the Far East; as I recall, I played opposite a girl called Rita Chappel, but otherwise memory has drawn a gauzy veil over this production's majesty and the sensation it no doubt caused across the theatrical world. However, I more sharply remember doing another early show – a one-acter for a drama festival, a piece about crooks taking over a ladies' hairdressing salon. The crooks in question had hopped into a hairdresser's to evade the police and then had to pretend they were running the place. As one of the crims caught up in this farrago, it was beholden upon me at one point to call out, primly, 'Louise – the telephone please!' Comedy gold, I'm sure – but an uncommon foray into that area for the Incognito Players.

Indeed (and this might seem odd, given what I would eventually go on to specialise in), comedy was rarely on the bill for the Incogs. Where possible the group liked to go in for pieces of serious drama – with the emphasis on serious. In 1959, for example, we treated Friern Barnet to a production of *Easter* by August Strindberg. Two hours of furrow-browed Swedish angst in a theatre with an outdoor toilet . . . it doesn't really get much more cerebral than that, drama-wise. I'm not sure how much of that play I understood at the time, at the age of nineteen, and I'm not sure how much of it I understand now, to be perfectly honest. But I can certainly tell you that at no point did this production require anyone to go for a big belly laugh by falling through the open flap of a pub bar. Permit me to reproduce the introductory note from the programme for the occasion (handwritten in ink on a sheet of plain A4 and xeroxed, as was the way):

> The play is set in Lund, a small provincial town in
> Sweden. It was in this town that Strindberg spent the
> winter of 1896 recuperating after his mental break-
> down. Here he watched the spring return and was
> moved as never before by the sufferings of Holy Week.

And a happy Easter to you, too.

Even closer to the cutting edge, I played Cliff Lewis, the
Welsh lodger, in an Incognito production of John Osborne's
Look Back in Anger, put on soon after the play's professional
debut at the Royal Court Theatre in 1956 – where it had caused
no little shock and horror in certain quarters for its unadorned
portrayal of working-class life. That was quite a hot item for an
amateur group to dare to pick up on so quickly, but the Incogs
knew very little fear in these areas. We also put on Osborne's
Epitaph for George Dillon. We did Tennessee Williams's *The Glass
Menagerie*, too, and I also remember playing a shell-shocked
soldier in the trenches of the First World War – no bag of
laughs. And in an adaptation of the biblical story of Noah, I
played Ham, the bad 'un among Noah's sons. Again – not much
in the way of pratfalls here.

But this was where I cut my teeth – the first stages of my
acting journey. I was in the Monday-night juniors, but I was
very soon starting to get called over into the senior group, which
met on Wednesdays and Fridays. There was a consensus that I
was useful – to the point where I even got headhunted, as it
were, by another local amateur group called the Manor Players.
They performed out of a church hall in Church End, Finchley.
One evening, I was back from work, stripped to the waist and
washing at the basin in the kitchen, when there was a knock
at the door. I casually opened it, still half naked, to be confronted
by two tall, imposing gentlemen, one of them with a drooping
moustache. I assumed I must have been in trouble with the
police again, but in fact it was Chris Webb from the Manor

Players, wanting to know if he could have a word. I put a shirt on and took them into the front room, where they explained they were looking for someone who could play a teenager in a production of *Escapade*, a very witty play by Roger MacDougall, who wrote many of the Ealing Comedy films.

And that was the play for which I received my first review. The notice in question was under the byline of W. H. Gelder, the theatre critic of the *Barnet and Finchley Press*, whose reputation went terrifyingly before him. Gelder clearly fancied himself the Butcher of Barnet and struck terror into local actors' hearts. He was a tough man to please and wasn't inclined to go easy on a production just because it was amateur and contained teenagers. Indeed, the sentence 'Gelder's in', passed around backstage before curtain-up on an opening night, was enough to cause buttocks to clench and voices to rise by half an octave, right across a cast.

Anyway, Gelder, this choosy arbiter of dramatic taste in the north-west London area, somehow found it in his heart on this occasion to commend me. All these years later, obviously, I don't recall exactly what he wrote, but it was something along the lines of how 'David White looked like a young James Cagney and played, though only 16, with the ease of a born actor'. (OK. That's exactly what he wrote.)

A young James Cagney? I was ready to accept the comparison. The ease of a born actor? I didn't object to that bit, either, though I did, eventually, when I had finished glowing, laugh it off. It seemed like such an unlikely idea.

I was co-opted into the senior group of the Incogs permanently after that and, from then on, was expected to play across a broad range. And I was growing in confidence, warming to this business of finding characters to hide behind – coming to know the pleasure of losing yourself in a role. Amateur dramatics offered me an opportunity to escape which I increasingly found myself hurrying towards.

As for the abundant girls – well, suffice to say that I found myself stepping out with three members of the Incognito Group, on various occasions, in those early years. Innocently and demurely, of course, as the times dictated: a date at the pictures; possibly an arm around the shoulder (a painfully incremental process which, in the planning and nervous execution, could consume as much as seventy minutes of a ninety-minute feature); maybe some hand-holding on the way home; perhaps, if the stars and the planets aligned, as sometimes they did, a kiss goodnight. So, amateur dramatics delivered on that promise, as well.

Incidentally, the Incognito Players are still in operation – thriving, in fact – with a membership of around 130 actors and staging six week-long productions per year. Furthermore, the place has proper toilets now and in 2010 the building even acquired a foyer. Because of my connection with the place, they asked me a few years ago to become a patron, which I was pleased and proud to do.

And they're still setting the bar sensationally high. Not that long ago I went along to see a production of *Equus* – a play which famously calls on its male lead to be uncompromisingly naked for a while. And, of course, if you're in the front row at an Incog production, even these days, you're very tight in on the action . . . so . . . well, what can I say? It practically dipped in your box of Maltesers as he walked around.

I'm not sure Micky Weedon or I would have been on for that – and certainly not on our first Monday night. But well done to the lad in question. And it shows you how far amateur theatre has come since my day.

* * *

I LEFT SCHOOL at fifteen with no idea what I wanted to do for the rest of my life – or, really, with any clear concept of 'the rest of my life'. That's not a notion a fifteen-year-old boy can very easily get his head around. At that age, it's rare that you find yourself thinking, on any given morning, much further ahead than lunchtime.

However, one thing I thought I knew was that my options were limited. In the world I came from, your aspirations weren't likely to be grand. We were never encouraged to aspire. Maybe it's different now. But I don't remember anyone at my school in 1955, as I headed out of the gate for the last time, saying to me, 'White, the world and all its wonders are out there: which glorious bit of it are you going to try and grab a hold of?' The assumption was, pretty flatly, that the world and all its wonders weren't out there. Not for you. So you'd get yourself a decent menial job and that would be that.

True, my brother Arthur, seven years ahead of me, had somewhat flown in the face of convention. He had started off straightforwardly enough, by training, in the family tradition, as a butcher when he left school. But then, in 1951, when he was eighteen, he was called up for his statutory two-year period of national service. (I was to escape this duty. The scheme was winding down by the time I was old enough and was halted altogether in 1960, so, alas, the British armed forces were never to witness what I could have brought to the battlefield.) Arthur soon discovered that, during national service, you were encouraged to develop interests – perhaps because, with the war being over, they didn't know quite what else to do with you. So, based in Colchester, he had begun to act, taking up with the repertory company there – quite casually at first, and then more seriously, to the extent that, when he emerged, in 1953, he had resolved to seek himself a place at drama school.

I still vividly recall a weekend, during his service, that he came home from Colchester in the company of a beautifully dressed, immaculately coiffed actress with whom he was friendly at the time. She sat on the sofa at Lodge Lane, appearing to fill the room with her poise and sophistication, while my father did his best not to look at her too closely and only narrowly failed.

Anyway, just because my older brother had broken the shackles and cracked open the door to another, more colourful world, it didn't automatically follow that I could do the same. Quite the opposite, in fact, on the theory of lightning and its well-known general reluctance to alight twice in the same location.

I duly reported to the jobcentre. There I queued up at a window, filled out a form, and then sat around waiting for someone to call 'Next'. At which point I was summoned through to a featureless little grey-painted room and given a preliminary interview. The whole set-up felt fantastically, bowel-liquidisingly intimidating to me. 'What kind of thing do you have in mind for yourself?' I was asked. To which my less than helpful answer was, 'I don't know.' The only previous work experience I could claim was a brief spell at fourteen as a grocery delivery boy for the Victor Value supermarket on the high street at the top of our road. Hours: two evenings per week, 4.30 p.m.–6.30 p.m., and Saturday mornings. Pay: almost nothing, but if you were lucky you might get a threepenny-bit tip from the housewife you delivered to. Skills: well, those front-loaded delivery bicycles are quite tough to handle, you know, especially if the carrier at the front is stacked so high that the tyre is squeezed down to the rim. (Little did I know that the ability to handle a delivery bike would serve me well thirty years later in a television series.)

Still, it emerged, in the course of this hobbled conversation at the jobcentre, that I liked mechanical things and that I was quite practical. (Did I already mention in these pages the magazine rack that I made in woodwork at Northside Secondary Modern, the joints of which continue to be crisp and lock-tight to this day?) And, after some riffling of index cards on the part of my interviewer, it further emerged that they had an opening in a garage. And not just the door.

Popes Garage, to be specific, on Popes Drive, Finchley. I was employed as the 'boy' – which is to say, essentially, that I made the tea. But occasionally they'd let me get underneath the cars and be a proper grease monkey and do some fixing. The business was run by a bunch of London-born brothers, and the one in charge of the workshop was known to us as Mr Len – a right hard nut, it seemed to me, although that might have had as much to do with my own continuing nervousness in front of anyone who represented authority.

Even so, at first I was happy enough in my new employment and actually rather enjoying myself because I was learning about mechanical things. My fellow mechanics – all older, all taller – were largely welcoming too, although I paid a price for trying to impress them during one of the lunchtime games of football that were played with a tennis ball in the yard between the garages and workshops. All down one side of the improvised pitch was a tall stack of corrugated iron. Demonstrating the tactical acumen and shrewd footballing brain that has served me so well during my long years in the game (or would have done, if I had ever really played football, which I haven't), I thought that if I could take the ball down the gap between the corrugated iron and the garage wall (and I was sure I was small enough to do so), I would be able to pop out at the other end and score before anyone had really figured out what I was doing.

It worked a treat. The tennis ball barely left my feet as I burrowed down the narrow passageway, suddenly invisible to teammates and opponents alike. Squeezing out at the other end of the stack, I moved inside and deftly side-footed the ball into the far corner beyond the goalkeeper's despairing dive. And then, with a loud cry of 'Yeesss!', I turned to celebrate both the goal and my extreme cunning with my no doubt enormously grateful teammates.

Except that everyone in the yard was staring at me in open-mouthed horror – or, more particularly, staring at the river of blood flowing from the head wound I had just unknowingly sustained by clonking my temple against the sharp edge of a sheet of corrugated iron at the far end of the stack. Off I went to the hospital for stitches – yet again. I think I probably only needed to go one more time to qualify for my own set of needles.

Still, thirty-seven years later, this latest scar would outdo all the other ones by coming to star in its own television series. In 1992 I began playing Inspector Frost in the series *A Touch of Frost* for ITV. In the books by R. D. Wingfield, on which the series was based, Frost is given to fiddling ruminatively with a scar on his cheek, a wound sustained in a gunshot incident. It was a little character detail that we were keen to use. But instead of getting make-up to apply a fake cheek scar, I pointed out that I might as well save time and effort and use the real one by my eye. So it came in handy in the end.

Blood loss and permanent disfigurement aside, my early days at the garage passed happily enough. I'd jump on my push bike at Lodge Lane in the morning and set off to work with a perfectly light heart. And come the end of the week, I'd return home with some money – give a bit to my mother for my 'keep', set some to one side for the Post Office savings account, and have the remainder for going out with. For years, I had been watching my dad come home from work on payday and hand over the brown paper envelope with his money in it. And my mother would take out the housekeeping, then the bit that was going towards the holiday savings, and then the little bit that was set aside for emergencies, and hand the rest back to my dad for his beer money. I felt some pride in being able to do the same. (And that little scene stayed with me. In later days, when I became an actor, I was used to setting money aside. It had become a discipline with me, so, unlike certain of my less fortunate brethren, I was never caught out when the taxman called.)

So my contentedness at Popes and in the world of paid labour endured for a couple of months. But then winter came, as winter will. The temperature in Popes' workshop now dropped to somewhere around the level of a beach on the Orkneys in mid-January. There were a couple of square electrical heaters mounted high on the wall, which worked as hard as they could but really only ended up providing a thin layer of warmth for the ceiling. The big wooden front doors were closed against the elements, but there was a gap underneath them which was probably big enough to squeeze a cat through, if you pushed it hard enough. Accordingly, as you lay flat on your back under a car, getting dripped on by oil or water, the wind would come howling through that gap and find its way unerringly up the trouser legs of your overalls. I'm not sure that even Captain Oates would have been ready to withstand discomfort at these levels for very long. And call me a fair-weather mechanic but it entirely sapped my enthusiasm for the job.

When the winter came to an end, Mr Len came in to see me and offered to upgrade me from garage boy to apprentice mechanic – a five-year deal, at the end of which I'd be fully qualified and ready to crawl under any car that would have me. I thanked him for the offer and asked for a short period in which to think about it. Back home, I told my parents, and they were delighted: I'd got a job and the chance to acquire a set of skills – I was sorted for life. Pats on the back all round.

So when I told them that I wasn't going to accept Mr Len's offer, they weren't just disappointed, they were completely baffled. My mother, in particular, couldn't get her head around it at all, and spent a long time trying to get me to see sense.

But I resisted. I don't quite know where I found the certainty to do so. It wasn't like me at that time to be so sure of myself and swim against the tide – I was quite timid in those years and tended to do as I was told. But I just knew I couldn't spend five years working like that. And it was mostly the memory of that long winter in the Arctic-cold workshop that did it for me. I declined Mr Len's offer, and was back at square one.

Coincidentally, my accountants, who were in Paddington when I first started using them, eventually moved into an office on Popes Drive, not far from the site of that garage. If you'd told me, when I was a wannabe grease monkey with barely enough money in his pocket for a pint of milk, that one day, just along the road, would reside the company I had had to appoint to look after my finances because they had become too complicated for my brain to handle, I would have accused you of indulging in a not particularly subtle or amusing piece of chi-iking. Yet it came to pass. The accountant I appointed was Raymond Freeda, of FMCB, who became a good friend and is still a good friend, and my accountant, today. Does anybody's accountant periodically send them entire sheets of Jewish jokes? Mine does. Here's a couple of them.

'I just got back from a pleasure trip: I took my mother-in-law to the airport.'

'Someone stole my credit cards. I won't be reporting it. The thief spends less than my wife did.'

Come 1957, though, and seventeen years old, I was off down to the jobcentre again, and again without the faintest clue what I wanted to do with my working life. And this time there was no immediate solution. I checked in at that jobcentre every week for a number of months and they dangled various opportunities in front of me, none of which managed to float my boat, until one day the woman behind the counter said, 'The Electricity Board are hiring apprentice electricians.' This at last seemed like something I might find an interest in. There ensued another harrowing and mumbled interview. And two weeks later, I got a letter to say I'd been accepted.

The Electricity Board took on ten of us as apprentices in our area, which was known as 'North Met' and encompassed a large slab of north London. We were sent on day release to Enfield Technical College to learn electrical theory. The rest of the week, we would be assigned to on-site jobs or, on the days when that kind of work wasn't available, drafted into the Electricity Board showrooms to fix broken electrical appliances – vacuum cleaners, cookers, heaters. These days, if your iron breaks, the chances are you'll be throwing it away and buying another one the same afternoon. At the back end of the fifties, you got it mended. I was to spend a lot of time nipping about in an electric van, collecting broken irons and equipment from EB showrooms, and rewinding the elements from toasters back at Fortis Green works.

We clearly had a restless need to entertain ourselves. One time we were sent out to wire tubular heaters into the pews of a huge and terrifyingly cold church in Muswell Hill – a straightforward enough task but clearly not sufficient to absorb our imaginations entirely. Among our number on that job was a little bloke called Dougie – even smaller than me, and therefore officially at the bottom of the pecking order. So, we lured Dougie up to the church's wooden gallery and used brass nails and buckle clips to tack him to the floor through his overalls. We abandoned him there, stapled to the floor, for a whole day. Cruel? Perhaps it was. But note we had our limits and that a sense of basic human decency prevailed: we didn't leave him overnight.

I fear it may also have been Dougie who was the victim of some equally childish and regrettable deviousness involving a bogus mission at the bottom of a lift shaft and a swiftly removed ladder. If you're building a block of flats, and you're high up and you need to relieve your bladder, do you climb all the way down and use the appropriate facility? Not when there's a convenient and as yet empty lift shaft to hand you don't. Which makes the bottom of a lift shaft in an incomplete block of flats somewhere to avoid if at all possible – as Dougie would no doubt have eagerly confirmed after spending a dank afternoon up to the rims of his rubber boots in unpleasantness.

Apprentices were made to work pretty hard in those days, and the jobs we had to do were very varied. For example, we wired a block of flats in Golders Green which, strange as it may seem, still stands today. In that block, we put in underfloor heating and I was told to oversee the pouring of the concrete floor, to make sure the builders didn't trample over our beautiful handiwork and muck it up. (Underfloor heating in those days was done with copper cables, which were both fragile and really expensive.) So it came to pass that I was alone on the sixth floor of this partly completed building, when an Irish navvy, who appeared to share the dimensions, more or less, of a bungalow, climbed onto the service lift at ground level, along with two wheelbarrows fully laden with cement, and called out, 'Bring her up.'

Now, I wasn't technically speaking the world's most experienced operator of the service lift, but I had seen it done, and knew what the routine was. Basically, there was a rope and you gave that rope a big old tug and it let the clutch in on the motor below and sent the lift's platform shuddering upwards. Then, at the appropriate moment, when the lift had risen to the desired level, you gently and gradually relaxed your grip on the rope and brought the platform slowly and smoothly to a halt. This could be done at any floor as the lift was rigged up to pass the semi-finished balconies all the way up the building.

So I duly pulled on the rope, and the large Irishman and his barrows began their groaning and rickety ascent. I, meanwhile, readied myself with the rope to perform the slightly trickier stopping manoeuvre. As the critical moment neared, and when the builder had risen to the point where his knees were level with the floor, I used my skill, judgement and considerable hand–eye coordination to begin to relax my grip on the rope and brake the lift's upward motion – only to mess up completely and lose control of the rope.

I watched the navvy's eyes widen as it dawned on him that the bottom could be about to drop out of his world in the most literal of ways. As the platform abruptly went into reverse below his feet, I saw the Irishman's face disappear earthwards and I let go of the rope altogether, thus bringing the lift to a shuddering stop. The abruptness of the halt bounced the wheelbarrows and the navvy in unison a couple of times and then tipped the barrows' contents off the edge of the platform. Only the navvy's irate head was visible above the floor. Fortunately, a suitably qualified floor-layer was on hand to take over the operating and bring the platform up to the right place. Or perhaps unfortunately: did my large Irish friend tip his head back and laugh with the simple joy one feels when one has narrowly eluded death? No. Boiling with fury, he chased me all over the building, calling me every name I had ever heard and several that I hadn't, and would have probably lobbed me off the roof if I hadn't found some cement bags to hide behind. I still wonder to this day whether that falling cement ended up permanently encasing some innocent builder who chose the wrong moment to walk below. Apologies to his family, if so.

This wasn't my only brush with an ugly and premature ending during those times. Electricity is a powerful and dangerous force, as I learned at college, of course, though perhaps more clearly while rewiring a girls' school in Highgate. My superior on the job, Johnny Cole, said, 'Get up that ladder and undo those wires in that distribution box.' In this case, it was a three-phase one at 415 volts. The normal working voltage was 240, so I asked the obvious question: 'It is off, isn't it?'

'Of course it's off,' said Johnny. So I climbed up as far as I needed to go and plunged my pair of standard issue pliers into the void to obey my master's voice.

The next thing I know is a flash of light as bright as the dawning of time. And the next thing I know after that, I am lying on my back against the wall on the other side of the corridor, flung the width of the place by the reaction of apprentice's metal on 415 volts of flowing electricity. Johnny was pale with horror because his initial thought was that he had just accidentally killed me. He was wrong – not far wrong, but wrong. I was dazed and slightly hollow but I very quickly mustered the energy to produce the traditional line: 'I thought you said it was off.' The pliers, incidentally, were never seen again. They probably landed in Clapham.

Volt meters and phase-testers were, of course, available for use, but the standard test for live circuitry for lazy buggers who couldn't quite be bothered to go and fetch the appropriate piece of equipment was to lick your finger and bring it closer and closer to the wire until you did, or didn't, get a little shock. Really, it's a wonder none of us weren't permanently fried.

I'd always cycle to work, and most days I would cycle home for lunch as well. I could be on a job down at Hornsey, about four miles away, but, come the lunch hour, I'd be back on my bike, pedalling like fury up Muswell Hill to scoff down lunch at Lodge Lane prepared by my long-suffering mother, and then pedalling all the way back to be on the job sixty minutes later. This behaviour made no sense whatsoever, but it just seemed to be what one did. It also kept me trim at about eight stone and with a rather svelte, if I may say so, 29-inch waist.

On the days when I really was too far away to cycle home – the other side of Highgate, say, which was a prohibitive six miles distant – lunch would be a bag of chips, at 3d (one and a half pence in today's money), half a bottle of milk and a couple of rolls from the bread shop. The idea was to fill yourself up as cheaply as you could – and, take my word for it, the combination of fried potato, starchy white bread and full-fat milk will do that for you every time. If I was feeling rich, I would also trouble the fish and chip shop for a pickled onion – a big white thing, the size of a tennis ball, found floating in vinegar in a glass jar on the counter and looking ominously like a biological specimen from a medical school. But that was only for when I felt flush. In general, the question was: how much could you not spend? And then, wadded with chips and milk, I would head back for the afternoon shift.

* * *

WE'RE TALKING NOW of the late 1950s – a period I remember with great affection. On Sunday evenings in those days, I would go round to Micky Weedon's little terraced house and his mother would make us high tea – cold meat and salad, followed by cake and sandwiches. It became a sort of tradition. And then we would listen to *The Goon Show*. Other radio entertainments had drawn me in, such as *Riders of the Range*, the western adventure series, and *Journey into Space*, the sci-fi drama which started when I was thirteen and had me immediately hooked. There was *Dick Barton, Special Agent*, too, although my interest in that was mostly in the galloping theme tune. But the big and lasting passion, above all of those, was *The Goon Show*. That was the number one. The sheer madness in the show's sense of humour, and the general sense of chaos from which the programme appeared to rise, completely got to us – me, Micky Weedon and Prince Charles alike. 'Why don't they make them like that any more?' the three of us would no doubt shake our heads and ask each other.

At the end of the show, the BBC's continuity announcer would regularly say, 'And if you would like tickets to see *The Goon Show . . .*' and give out an address you could write to. And, extraordinarily, these tickets were free – yours for the price of a stamped addressed envelope. So I sent a letter, assuming that pretty much the whole world would be doing exactly the same, so my chances were non-existent. But in fact the whole world must have been doing something different because two tickets for a recording duly arrived.

This was a pretty sophisticated night out for Micky Weedon and me, who had been known, when we were nine or ten, to entertain ourselves, of a winter's evening, by getting the cheapest return fare from Woodside Park for the London Underground and then spending the whole evening down there. You could run around the system, changing trains and switching lines, without ever emerging above ground at any point. Somehow, whole hours would happily pass in this manner, with us chatting, people-watching, generally mucking about and not getting up to very much at all. Then eventually we would make our way back to Woodside Park and surrender the return portion of the ticket to the guard at the barrier, who little suspected that we had made something like a thirty-mile round trip for three hours in the meantime, as the guests of London Transport. Talk about budget entertainment. It was perfectly warm down there too, even in winter, at no extra cost, increasing the bargain element. Who needed the internet?

But now we were grown-ups. We took the Underground from Woodside Park and rose to the surface at Camden Town, where we had to find our way to the Camden Town Theatre – not somewhere we had ever been before. And once there, we queued up in the street and then were finally let into the auditorium – the first time I had set foot in a proper theatre. Obviously, at this point it was set up for a radio recording, but it had once been a music-hall theatre and it seemed kind of musty and yet vividly grand to me.

We were buzzing with anticipation. The Goons lived in the radio, as far as we were concerned. We knew what Spike Milligan and Harry Secombe looked like, but we had a less clear image of Peter Sellers. To watch them doing the show was therefore going to be revelatory in all sorts of ways. I remember things starting with Milligan and Secombe bringing on a large sign saying 'The Goon Show' and placing it carefully on the stage. Of course, it was upside down, which set the tone. Milligan was in an old sweater, Secombe was in a sports jacket and trousers. There seemed to be no sign of Peter Sellers at that point. The Ray Ellington Quartet struck up the music and then the show started. It began with Secombe, as Neddy Seagoon, pretending to spot a figure off in the distance and saying, 'Who would be stupid enough to stand right on the edge of a cliff?' And at this point a slim man in an immaculate suit stepped forward from the rear of the stage and, script in hand, said, 'Hellew, my dellings.'

Here, finally, was Sellers. And it was such a contrast – this ridiculous, high-pitched comic voice coming out of this elegantly dressed, sophisticated man. And it's still one of the most impressive entrances I've ever seen in a theatre. The interplay between the three of them from that point on was magical. One of them would come across a joke and corpse. ('To corpse': theatrical term meaning to be overcome by laughter at an inappropriate moment. Said to derive from the ancient sight of an actor shuddering while pretending to play dead.) Then he would try to get back to the script, and the more he tried to get back, the more the other two wound him up further, and the more the other two wound him up, the more the audience laughed. Micky and I were ecstatic afterwards, totally wired by what we had witnessed.

My fandom endured. In 1963, I went to the Duke of York's Theatre to see Spike Milligan in *The Bedsitting Room*, the satirical play he wrote with John Antrobus. I had never seen anyone come out of character onstage and address the audience, as Milligan did that night. I was in the fourth row of the stalls and Milligan spotted a girl at the front, eating sweets. He broke off to ask her what she was eating and whether he could have one – which she gladly gave him. He leaned forward over the footlights and took a sweet from the box she offered up to him. He bit into it and held it up to his ear, saying, in a squeaky voice that might well have been coming from the sweet, 'Help! I'm a prisoner in a Malteser factory!' It was the most avant-garde thing I had witnessed. Afterwards I went and hung around in a small knot of people at the back of the theatre, until Milligan came out and sat on the steps for a while, when I was able to get his autograph on a scrap of paper. That autograph meant a lot to me for years after.

Another seminal theatrical experience: in late 1958, my good friend Bob Bevil and I found ourselves putting in some sockets in a flat in Hyde Park Square Gardens and getting into conversation with the American guy who was renting it. And he said he was appearing in a show in the West End and asked us if we would like a couple of tickets. The show was *West Side Story*. It had opened on Broadway the previous year, and then transferred to London, with some of the original American cast. And, of course, it was stunning, especially for two working lads from north London – the songs, the choreography, the sets, the sheer punch of the orchestra coming out of the pit at you. It blew my mind away, and is still my favourite musical to this day.

And the bloke whose sockets we did? That was David Holliday, who starred as Tony. Holliday would go on to play many distinguished theatre roles, singing and non-singing, and (truly impressive, this) to be the voice of Virgil in the first series of *Thunderbirds*. But I'm sure he would concede that he would have been nothing without Bob's and my sockets at that pivotal moment in his career.

Back at work, Bob and I found ourselves doing a rewiring job on a big house in Highgate that was being renovated. This substantial and well-appointed property, we came to realise, was the home of Billy Wright, the footballer, and Joy Beverley, one of the Beverley Sisters singing group. They had married in 1958 and that union of ultra-famous England captain with ultra-famous pop singer made them the Posh and Becks of their day. Of course, I wasn't expecting to meet either of the residents in the course of these labours, realising that both of them probably had better things to do than stand around watching an electrician run a length of copper wiring up the side of their yet-to-be-decorated sitting room.

But that only goes to show how wrong you can be, because one day, while I was up to my shins in wiring, in walked Joy Beverley. And not just Joy, either. She was accompanied by one of her sisters – either Teddie or Babs. I didn't know which one it was. But that's the tricky thing about identical twins, of course: what you've got to understand is, they look alike. It's why we call them twins. Still, whether it was Teddie or Babs, or Babs or Teddie, just to be in the presence of these people – just to be said 'hello' to by them, as they crossed the room – was excitement beyond words. I think my eyes must have become dinner plates. I felt like I had come into contact with a world as far removed from mine as it was possible to imagine, a world of glamour and stardom and wealth.

Opposite the cul-de-sac that the house was situated in was a little park on the edge of a hill, with a bench in it, and come lunchtime, I sat there on my own with my chips, my milk and my bread and stared out across London.

* * *

IN 1958 I was in trouble with the law again – this time for riding a motorbike without learner plates. Or, rather, as the summons put it, 'without displaying in a conspicuous position on the front end or the rear of such vehicle the distinguishing mark'.

Stood to reason, though, didn't it? If you hadn't passed your motorbike test, you weren't allowed to carry anyone with you. Therefore, if you wanted (as I frequently did in those days) to sling your mate Micky Weedon or Brian Barneycoat on the back and zoom off to Southend for a day on the beach, there was nothing for it but to get rid of the L-plates.

Result: a steep, ten-shilling fine. But no ban, fortunately.

I had always planned to have a motorbike. Cars were an unattainable dream at this point – way out of our price range. It was the motorbike that was the working-class man's vehicle of escape. And as soon as I had a little money coming in, I could make the motorbike plan a reality. But even then, for me, it remained a luxury item. When Ernie Pressland from next door was called up for national service, he flogged me his drop-handle push bike, and that's what I continued to go to work on. The motorbike was for weekends and for pleasure.

In 1957, when I was seventeen, a cousin's boyfriend had a friend whose friend's friend was friendly with a friend who had a cousin whose boyfriend had a repair shop up at Muswell Hill, and he pointed me the way of a bloke who was selling a bike from his garage at home. It was a 350cc BSA B31 – a bit of a beast, in all honesty, and certainly a much more powerful machine than I was looking for. But the bloke selling it was very persuasive. He said, 'You'll only want a bigger one when you get used to it. You might as well start with a proper bike that's going to really look after you.'

He had a point. Besides, the bike had taken on a romantic lustre in the half-light of the garage and I was already smitten. I parted with all the money that I had been stashing away in the Post Office and took him up on his generous (and quite cunning, as it would turn out) offer to ride the bike home for me.

Nobody taught you to ride a motorbike in those days. You gleaned what you could from people who already had bikes, and the rest you discovered for yourself by trial and error. And if you happened to be a little short in the leg, your trials and errors were made no easier. You had to learn how to climb aboard, and how to throw your full eight stone down onto the kick-start. If it didn't kick back, the bike started. If it started, you rocked it forward off its stand. If you could get it off its stand, you could start feeding the power in as you let the clutch out. And then you could stall it and start all over again. And once you'd mastered that end of the business, all that remained was to discover how to travel forwards on two wheels without falling off. (The almost total lack of traffic on the roads in those days definitely played into one's hands here.)

All went swimmingly for a few days, my pride surging as I coolly piloted my new machine around the neighbourhood, fancying myself very much the liberated bachelor – until one morning, at the bottom of our road, a worrying noise started up, as if someone were clinging on to the bike's underside and attacking the engine with a hammer.

I climbed off to have a look. The downtube that came from underneath the petrol tank and held the engine in beneath the crossbar had come apart and the engine was waving about like a flag in the wind. In a state of nearly tearful distress, I wheeled the crocked bike back home, and then returned to see its former owner for an explanation – or, better than that, the return of my hard-earned savings. He was, as you might guess, less than helpful. 'Nothing to do with me, guv,' he said. 'Sold as seen, mate.' And with that, the door closed.

I was mortified. All my savings! Gone! Evaporated! Stolen! After a few days of wandering around in despair, I lashed the engine on with wire and pushed the thing to a repair shop on the high street, where I was told that I'd been flogged a grade-A pup. The bike had been in an accident which had entirely broken its frame, and the owner had welded it back together and painted over it. It would take weeks to make the thing roadworthy again. Collapse of super-stud's ego.

Still, that was my first motorbike – little beloved by my mum, who naturally feared, as mothers will, that I was destined to end up killing myself on it, and who also deeply resented my habit of stripping the engine down and performing running repairs in the kitchen. She certainly didn't like the way I would boil up the chain in a lubricating solution of molybdenum disulphide in a saucepan on the stove, while de-coking the cylinder head on the dining table.

A year or so later, with some more hard-earned money salted away, I was able to trade up, chopping in my historically damaged B31 at Slocombe's on the North Circular Road at Neasden. What I swapped it for was a long-coveted 495cc BSA Shooting Star – sometimes known as a Star Twin and the first BSA model to go into production after the war. That wonderful piece of machinery was to take me all over Britain – east to Clacton, west to Cornwall and north to the Lake District. I still have a copy of it which I have restored to look like the original – again, after salting away some hard-earned cash.

In the summer of 1960, I used that bike to head out to Essex. We North Met electrical apprentices were dispatched to a training centre at Harold Hill for a month-long course on metalwork and welding. I was put up in digs with a family nearby for five nights a week, and went in each day to the brazing shop, where I found myself in a class of lads from all over the south of England, all sent to learn metalwork and its associated arts, including one or two East Enders who looked like they would have your innards out with a welding iron, if you weren't too careful. Still, we all seemed to rub along well enough. In fact, a camaraderie swiftly developed, with the trainees ranged against the instructors, who wore brown coats and were largely stern and humourless, patrolling the workshop and barking orders: 'Stop talking! Back to your station!'

You were in a big hall, with two long rows of desks, lathes to one side and, behind glass screens, the brazing area, with its forges and giant anvils. Everyone had his own station, where he had a vice, a metal block and a drawer full of tools. It was a scene ripe for undermining and for nefarious practices of all kinds, and my good friend Bob and I rather ended up running the place in this regard. We'd send the word around: 'At eleven o'clock, two minutes of banging.' Come the moment, the room would abruptly explode into a cacophony of ringing hammers, while the instructors buzzed around in confusion: 'What's going on? Stop this!'

We came to think of ourselves as prisoners of war, with the instructors as the prison guards. At lunchtime, we would solemnly form up in two lines, and, on the command from Bob and myself ('Atten-shun! By the left . . .'), march across the tarmac to the canteen – or, as we preferred to think of it, the cookhouse – whistling 'Colonel Bogey', just as we had seen it done in the movies, although, in this case, watched by the girls from the secretarial course, who would come to the windows to see what the noise was about.

Incidentally, the canteen had two sets of doors, sandwiching a small box-like entry hall to keep out the draught, about six feet square and eight feet high. It was the tendency of our febrile minds to imagine that this area was an airlock, and that you could only open the inner doors when everybody was inside the foyer and the outer doors were closed. So, at the conclusion of our march from the brazing shop, and on the command 'Fall out!', we would open the outer doors and then squeeze into the hallway before advancing. How many apprentice electricians can you fit in the entrance to a technical college canteen? This was a question we answered most lunchtimes – the answer being, a lot more than you'd think, especially if you double up and hoist a few onto your shoulders.

We eventually had a mock judicial system up and running, too. Offenders – those perceived to have acted in ways contrary to the ethos of the workshop – would receive a summons from

the Brazing Shop Court, and be required to attend a hearing
at the appointed time during a given lunch hour. At first we
hand-wrote the summons, but as the judicial system grew more
sophisticated, we had them typewritten by a girl on the secretarial course in her spare time. (Think of it as our version of
prisoners of war forging passports.) I still possess one of these
documents, issued, it would appear, to a Mr J. Davies.

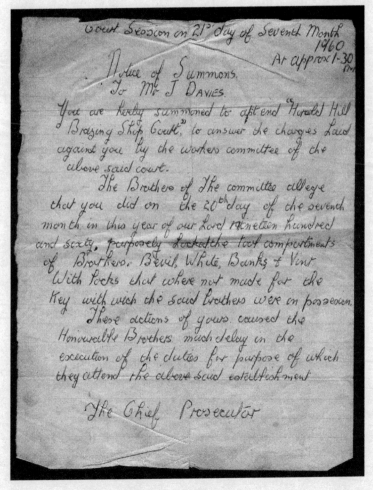

In court, we would hear from the prosecution and the defence, with me frequently playing the judge, deploying my metalwork hammer as a gavel, and handing down such sentences as 'last in line for the canteen next Thursday'. This managed to keep us entertained until the course ended, although I should prob- ably point out that we did find time in our busy day to learn a few things as well.

All in all, my life seemed to be coming together in this period – or, at any rate, settling into a rhythm. I was learning a steady trade. I had some steady money coming in. I had a steady hobby – the amateur theatre. I had a steady motorbike. I had even started seeing a girl quite steadily – Sylvia Cunningham, whom I had met at a party in 1959. During our apprenticeship with the Electricity Board, Bob and I had been doing some wiring in a flat opposite the swimming pool in Finchley. The daughter of the people who owned the flat was going to be engaged to a guy called Tony and was throwing an engagement party. She invited Bob and me along. There, I was smitten from across the room by the sight of a beautiful woman with jet-black hair and a figure to die for, whom I eventually managed to pluck up the courage to speak to, and whom, by the end of the evening, I was desperate to see again. It turned out that she lived with her parents, on the other side of London from north Finchley, in Lee Green, south of Blackheath – a fifteen-mile trip. But, of course, that was no barrier to an apprentice electrician with ardour in his heart and his own motorbike.

And I must have been serious about Sylvia because I took her to the West End on occasion for a wide-screen Cinemascope film presentation – and not just that, but also a meal afterwards at the Golden Egg on Tottenham Court Road. The Golden Egg was a chain restaurant, and a rung or two down from the Angus Steakhouse, I will admit, but it still served notice of a man's firm and reliable intent. As the name would tend to indicate, it allowed you to have any form of egg – egg and chips, double egg and chips, omelette and chips, double egg omelette and chips, double egg omelette and no chips, and even egg with no chips. And it had window seats where you could sit and look out at the world going about its business, and the world could look in at you going about your business – eating egg and chips. In terms of high-living, this place clearly took the egg and chips.

Sylvia and I ended up going out for a number of months, and she was, it seemed to me, at the oh-so-experienced age of nineteen going on twenty, the love of my life. That said, in conversations with her during the course of our relationship, when I once or twice gently floated the notion of perhaps one day devoting my life to acting, it never went down particularly well. Sylvia made it abundantly clear that she didn't want to end up with a thespian. She found it a very unsettling thought. She wanted, as she put it, a 'steady' man. And fair play: no actor, to my knowledge, has ever been described as 'steady' – at least, not in the opening sentence.

Sylvia had her own ideas about the future, and she often voiced them: a nice little house, two-up and two-down, with a Morris Mini Minor in the drive. That was the dream. She was quite specific about the Mini, which was brand new then, and all the rage. And, to a large extent, I could see the appeal of it all, and shared it. It was the comfortable, conventional place towards which our relationship was probably headed. The electrician and his wife, their house and their car and, no doubt, in due course, their kids.

And then, one night in July 1960, during the month I was staying in Harold Hill on the Electricity Board's welding course, Sylvia invited me over to her place. Her parents were going to be out – off at the cinema. The house would be empty for a couple of hours – just the two of us. I can't deny it: heading south by motorbike and anticipating this extremely rare evening of isolated togetherness, visions of intimacy danced in my head. Alas, though, those visions were not realised. The house was, indeed, achingly void of all others for the evening. It was a bungalow as well, so we wouldn't have had to go far to get to the bedroom. But the telly was on in the sitting room and we watched it in near silence, pausing only to sip tea. There was no intimacy, rare or otherwise, nor any mention of the possibility of intimacy. Not so much as a peck on the cheek, let alone a snog on the sofa. Sylvia, engrossed by the telly, sat in her father's large and comfy chair while I was marooned in misery on the sofa. What seemed like an ocean separated us.

Time wore on. Her parents were due back. Disconsolately, I got up to leave and stood by the sitting-room door.

'Well, I'd better be going. I've got a long ride ahead,' I said.

A pause.

'Goodbye, then,' I said.

A pause.

'Goodbye, then,' said Sylvia, not moving from her chair. I don't think she even moved her eyes from the television.

I went out into the hall and completed the fairly lengthy task of re-donning my motorcycle gear. No expensive leathers for me, alas, but, rather, some cheapskate protective kit of a plasticky rubber construction. These items weren't the best for insulation either: in the winter, you had to stuff an extra layer of newspaper down your front to protect your stomach from icing over in the wind. The trousers ballooned, the shoulders were uncharismatically square. I looked like a miniature Darth Vader.

Thus rubberised, I reappeared in the door frame of the sitting room.

'Aren't you going to kiss me goodnight?' I said, sounding somewhat plaintive.

There now ensued an odd kind of Mexican stand-off. Sylvia clearly felt that if I wanted a kiss I should go over to her chair to receive it. My feeling was that if Sylvia deigned to get up and cross the floor, it would at least partly make up for the evening's unexplained coldness, and its failure to serve up those visions of nirvana that had been with me on my long bike ride over.

A perhaps not especially adult impasse followed.

'You come over here,' said Sylvia.

'No, you come over here,' I replied.

'No, you come over here.'

This was threatening to go on for quite some time.

'I'll meet you halfway,' I said diplomatically.

'OK,' she said.

There were about six paces between us in total. I now took three of them.

'So now you come your half,' I said.

'You've come halfway,' she said, still not moving. 'You might as well come the whole way now.'

'No, you come halfway.'

'No, you come the rest of the way.'

We'd probably still be there now if I hadn't turned round, unkissed, and walked out.

I headed down the garden path to the little gate, as purposefully as a man can who's wearing several pounds of cheap black rubber. There at the kerb stood my faithful steed, my BSA 495. I mounted up. By this point, Sylvia had come out of the house and down the path.

She said, 'But what's the matter? You didn't even kiss me goodnight.'

I said, 'You didn't seem to want me to.'

And with that, I kicked the bike into life and drove away.

What a journey that was. Hell hath no fury like a man spurned and on a motorbike, and on the long ride back to my digs in Harold Hill, frustration and humiliation duly boiled up. Yet somehow, instead of yielding blind anger behind the handlebars, leading to a dangerous lack of lane discipline at roundabouts, it appeared to produce clarity and conviction and a whole new self-certainty. Accordingly, I may be one of a very limited number of people to have experienced a Damascene conversion in the Blackwall Tunnel. At least, it's that portion of the journey home that I particularly recall – things clicking into place, a firmness of purpose cohering in my mind despite the noise of the bike cannoning off the walls. I swear that in that unlovely, grubby and actually rather unsuitably narrow passage beneath the Thames, under the electric lights, the scales fell from my eyes.

By the time I got back, I was fully and absolutely resolved. Stuff it all. Stuff the steadiness. Stuff the two-up, two-down and the Mini on the drive. Stuff the conventional path I'd slowly been drifting up. That wasn't my future. I was going to do the unsteady thing. I was going to become an actor. I didn't know how, but there had to be a way, didn't there? And even if it took me a while (which it would – several more years in fact), I was going to find it.

While on the course, I had been loyally phoning Sylvia from the phone box opposite my digs. Now I stopped. After a few more days, I returned to Finchley and I didn't phone her from there, either. It was as abrupt as that. It alarms me now to think how easily my twenty-year-old self shut down on someone. But it was like a thrown switch. Some moments alter the course of the rest of your life, and that was one of them.

CHAPTER FOUR

The rejection of a promising career as a pirate. Some slightly questionable business involving bongos. And a change of name.

In late 1959 the period of my apprenticeship with the Electricity Board came to a finish – and not, alas, a triumphant finish. The EB informed me that they were declining the opportunity to take me on into full-time employment. They declined the opportunity to take on Bob Bevil too, so at least I wasn't the only one. Was that because the pair of us had spent such a large part of our apprenticeships mucking about, forcing ourselves into imaginary airlocks, staging mock trials, stapling people to the floor through their boiler suits, etc.? I wouldn't care to speculate. All I know is, when our term had run its course, the Board somehow felt able to let us go.

But I had at least got some training and a certificate under my belt. So, Bob Bevil and I decided to go into business together as electricians. We must have been serious because we had our own business card printed up – one with a fold in it, none of your cheap nonsense. On the top flap was my name – David J. White – and then the card opened up to reveal the legend 'B. W. Installations & Co. – Electrical Contractors, Intercommunication

Engineers', along with the address and telephone number of our head office: my parents' house at Lodge Lane, Hillside 3526. (Finally, regular use was found, beyond Christmas and royal visitations, for that neglected front room, which became our headquarters.)

David J. White

B.W.
Installations & Co.
26, LODGE LANE, FINCHLEY, N.12

Intercommunication Engineers? Oh yes, most certainly. In the course of going about our business, Bob and I had met an Irish subcontractor who was installing door-answering equipment imported from Italy – the buzzer and two-way intercom system which is absolutely standard and unremarkable now but represented an exotic leap forward for technology in those days. 'What? You mean I can lift this receiver and find out who's at the door without coming down thirty-four flights of stairs? Why, it's an electric-powered miracle.' And loads of blocks of flats were going up in the holes left by the Luftwaffe, so this was something of a boom area at the time, meaning that our Irish contractor friend had lots of work to pass on to me and Bob – ripping us off royally in the process, we would eventually work out, but for the time being we were absolutely delighted. B. W. Installations & Co. was up and running. Which wasn't acting, of course. But it was a living.

Meanwhile, the acting was going well and my reputation in the small but slowly expanding corner of amateur dramatics that I occupied was continuing to grow. And my attitude towards it had decidedly changed. When I looked around at my fellow amateurs at the Incognitos, and in the various other am-dram companies that I was hooking up with in the early 1960s, I realised that there were distinct groups. There were some doing it because they loved it and because it was sociable. These were people who would probably have taken offence if you had asked them whether they had further aspirations in the theatre – like you had accused them of having some kind of ulterior motive, when, in fact, they were in it for pure fun and pleasure. I could sense that, although I had been a part of that group in the beginning, I no longer was.

Then there were others who wanted to be professional and were hoping for a break – that some day they would be discovered. It was only a matter of time. Someone from the West End or the movies would find their way up to Friern Barnet and be utterly staggered by what they saw from the old cinema seats. Then they would be waiting for you with a contract at the stage door, and the following day, or certainly within the week, they would make you a star. It seemed to me that, for quite a while, I had been quietly moving into that group. I had been one of those people who didn't quite have the courage or the know-how to take the future into their own hands, but who were waiting for it to happen – waiting to be discovered. And waiting to be discovered wasn't necessarily going to work. You needed to find some way to make it happen, or you needed something, or someone, to give you a shove.

In my case, a big old push came in 1962. I was twenty-two and I represented the Muswell Hill Players at the Hornsey Drama Festival. I won Best Supporting Actor that weekend

– the first time I had ever won an individual award for my acting. I still have the trophy – a medallion of an angel waving some laurels around, attached to a simple wooden plaque, about four inches tall. The head judge at the festival was André van Gyseghem, a very distinguished man of the theatre who did lots of television work in the sixties. (Among many other things, he appeared in *The Saint* with Roger Moore and was Number Two in the great Patrick McGoohan series *The Prisoner*.) And in his commendation during the prizegiving, he stood up and told the room that, hesitant though he always was to encourage people to take up acting for a living, he would have absolutely no hesitation recommending me for a career as a professional. Such a public endorsement from such a qualified source really boosted my confidence.

Who would have thought that twenty-five years after André van Gyseghem gave me his blessing, I would know the glory of hearing my name called from the stage of the Grosvenor Hotel ballroom, of rising from my seat, dressed in black-tie finery, and of working my way through tables crammed with the great and good of British entertainment? And then of climbing the steps, with my legs almost giving way underneath me, to receive the 1987 BAFTA TV award for Best Actor, for my role as Scullion the Head Porter in the drama *Porterhouse Blue*?

Yet that simple small plaque, presented in those far humbler circumstances in Hornsey, will always mean . . . well, quite a lot less, actually, now I come to think of it.

But you've got to start somewhere – and to be honest, it was a good start. That prize in Hornsey was definitely another coin-drop moment.

After the festival, the Muswell Hill Players returned in glory to the town hall at Friern Barnet for a reception in our honour – a cup of tea and a piece of warm cheese on a stick. And there, as I stood about, rather self-consciously cradling a saucer and trying to look as though receptions in my honour were given at town halls most weeks, a tall, neatly suited woman who was among the occasion's hosts introduced herself.

She explained that she had a prominent job on the local council, and asked me what I did. I told her I was an electrician. She then asked me if I had ever considered going to drama school to study. I told her I hadn't given it much thought, principally because it wasn't something I ever imagined being able to afford. She said that money didn't necessarily have to be a barrier. There were such things as grants. If I ever applied, she felt very sure that, in the circumstances, the council would be able to provide me with one.

Now, this set my brain whirring. I had been getting all these nudges that I should take acting seriously – and it could hardly get more serious than going to drama school, could it? No doubt many people would have prescribed this as the best way forward. An acting qualification would give me a proper grounding to lift off from.

So it was with much enthusiasm that I reported my conversation with the councillor to my mum and dad, back at home. 'I think I should do that,' I said. 'I think I should apply for drama school.'

Their reaction? They couldn't have been less enthusiastic if I'd just proposed setting up a commercial newt-breeding operation in the bathroom.

It wasn't that my parents had anything against actors. They already had one of those in the family, remember – my older brother Arthur. Arthur had delighted Mum and Dad by settling into a respectable, steady job as a butcher – only to come home after his national service and declare that he fancied being a thespian instead. He had then duly won a scholarship to go to the Royal Academy of Dramatic Arts in London and, to my parents' gradual relief, his gamble had paid off. He was making a living as a professional actor. He was finding plenty of theatre work and, moreover, had played Caradoc Owen in *Mrs Dale's*

Diary, the long-running drama serial on BBC radio. I can remember the family crowding round excitedly at home to listen to his debut appearance. Shades of the scene in front of the television at Ronnie Prior's house for the Coronation a few years earlier, although, of course, on this occasion, being personally involved, we were that much prouder.

Still, there was no question that my mum and dad had been made uneasy by the sight of their cherished firstborn swapping a steady trade for a wildly unpredictable one. And now here was their second son threatening to do exactly the same thing. It was déjà vu. (Not that that's the expression my parents would have used.) By now they were used to having a bit of extra income on the table from the keep that I provided. If I jacked in work, I would once more become a financial burden to them – one they really couldn't afford.

My parents weren't unreasonable about it. My mum made it abundantly clear that, if this were my heart's desire, I could apply to become a student, write off for a council grant, abandon my job as an electrician and head off for any drama school that would have me. But there was no way I would be able to live at home 'sponging off us', as my father might gently have put it. I'd be on my own. And as I was a person who rather liked his home comforts, that rather kiboshed my little plan.

So how did I respond? I was too old to go stamping up to my bedroom and slamming the door, of course, though I'm sure the thought occurred. I was extremely frustrated. I was trying to be young and thrusting and my young thrustingness had been thwarted. On the other hand, I knew my parents would have found the money if they could, but the money genuinely wasn't there. So what could I do? Get on with being an electrician was probably the best idea, and come up with another plan for the acting.

Did I resent my brother? How could I? He got there first, seven years earlier – at a different time and in different circumstances. And I would have cause to be extremely grateful that he did. As we'll see in due course, it was my brother who got me my first proper break.

In the meantime, Bob and I got on with building our electrical business. For the first two years, it was quite a struggle. There were some periods when we couldn't find work and were obliged to sit around at home, scratching ourselves and staring out the window. But we didn't give up. We kept at it. We became very industrious about seeking jobs, going round to builders' yards, and even builders' houses, and knocking on the door and trying to beg, blag or charm a contract out of them. Eventually, through a bloke called Derek Hockley, we latched on to quite a bit of work with Ind Coope breweries, doing the electrics in refitted pubs. We also got a contract to do the Redbridge Hotel at Redbridge, and we found we could get quite a lot of business rewiring private houses.

That was often quite grubby and uncomfortable work. Getting wires from one side of a room to the other could require cutting two trap doors in the floor and then climbing down into the claustrophobic cavity under the floorboards and sliding across with the wire in your hand. Just to make it more complicated, you might have to cut a further hole through a dwarf wall along the way. You found all sorts down there: dust, spiderwebs, rat droppings, mice piss and, just occasionally, the rat who left the droppings and the mice who did the piss. You soon learned the key tricks: buttoning your overalls to the neck and tucking your trouser legs into your socks to keep out unwanted intruders. At the end of the day, I was quite often entirely blackened, like some poor Victorian kid who'd been sent up a chimney.

I had eventually traded my motorbike in for my first car – a second-hand Ford Zephyr 6 saloon with crimped fins and shiny chrome wing mirrors. I thought that was going to be the passport to international jet-set pleasure with members of the opposite sex. In fact, I mostly ended up playing taxi driver for all my carless male mates, ferrying them around London and beyond. But the Ford soon had to go, anyway, because Bob and I needed a more practical vehicle for the business and for tool-carrying purposes. I swapped it for a Standard Companion, the magnificently named estate version of the Standard 10 and essentially a chunky van with windows. That served us well enough until some wally ploughed into the back of it at traffic lights on the North Circular at Ealing. I glimpsed this car, thundering towards us, in the rear-view mirror and just had time to say to Bob, 'Brace yourself.' A split second later there was an almighty crunch and a lurch and we were lying on our backs staring at the car's ceiling. On impact, the Standard's tubular metal seats had collapsed underneath us like deckchairs. I got out and went round to the other side to help Bob, whose head had taken a bit of a thump on the windscreen. He was able to clamber upright, and stood, dazed, on the road. He was wearing this wonderful cheapskate car coat at the time, far too tight for him, with four big leather football-style buttons on it. 'Are you sure you're all right?' I said. Bob nodded gently and drew in a deep breath to compose himself. At which point, one by one, the buttons popped off the coat – pop, pop, pop, pop – like something in a cartoon. We laughed about that for years afterwards.

Goodbye, Standard Companion, however. The car was a write-off. Still, we got the money from the insurance and put it down on a pair of Mini Vans – one each, kind of 'his and his', if you like. Bob's was black with a white roof, and mine was grey with a white roof. I loved that Mini Van. It was just the job for work, and just the job for whipping up to the Athenaeum Ballroom in Muswell Hill of a Saturday night, as was our wont. The Athenaeum was an old cinema which had been converted into a giant dance hall, spread over two floors with a huge bar. Only Colin Quinton, among our number, really knew how to chat up a girl. The rest of us just did a lot of standing around, stretching out a pint and watching the girls dancing with each other. I do remember one monumentally bold occasion when the night wore on and Bob and I stepped towards a pair of dancers to make our move. 'Can we break you up?' said Bob. One of the girls looked at me, and then looked at Bob. 'Nah,' she said, flicking a dismissive thumb in my direction. 'He's too short.' Bob, bless him, was most put out on my behalf. 'You can't say that in front of him!' Frankly, my dear, comments about my height were water off a not very tall duck's back by that point in my life.

On the nights when we did get lucky (and, reader, I profess that, despite our general lack of proficiency in this area, there were one or two of those), the Mini Van came in handy for lifts home and for moments of privacy, especially if halted by the kerb in the appealing, sylvan quietness of Gypsy Lane in Barnet.

My twenty-first birthday came and went during this busy period, marked by a zinging party at Lodge Lane – sandwiches, cake, a keg of beer and a soundtrack of Buddy Holly and Lonnie Donegan hits which I had painstakingly taped off the telly and the radio onto my valve-operated Grundig reel-to-reel tape machine (bought on the never-never, of course. If you played it for a long time, the rubbers got hot and stretched, and everything, even Lonnie Donegan, started sounding like Hawaiian guitar music).

Well, I say the party was zinging. It would have been a darned sight more zinging if my mother hadn't come down in her dressing gown at midnight, crossly shut the music off and turned everyone out into the cold February street. The humiliation of that stung for a long time.

By 1964, B. W. Installations was doing pretty well. We had taken Johnny Dingle on board as a permanent assistant. Joyce Dodd from down the road was coming in to type up our estimates. (Joyce had a crush on Bob, if the truth be known, but, alas, much to my puzzlement, Bob wasn't interested.) The work was flowing in, nice and steadily. But I knew, and Bob knew, that the real dream for me was acting. I felt time creeping on. I couldn't bear the idea of getting to thirty-five and not having given it a shot – and then maybe living with the regret and the sense of 'what if?' for the rest of my life. And at least the electrical business was solid now, so it wouldn't be like leaving Bob in the lurch. It was as good a moment as any. Late in 1964, I told him I was going to quit.

He couldn't have been more magnanimous about it, nor more encouraging. We did a deal whereby, in exchange for giving Bob my share of the business, I could keep my prized Mini Van. He also promised me that if the acting didn't come through, or there were periods of downtime with no money coming in, he'd give me work to do. It was a nice bit of security to fall back on.

And so performing what we might call a reverse Nelly, I unpacked my trunk, metaphorically speaking, and said hello to the circus.

* * *

I HAD RESOLVED to turn professional. Now all I needed to do was find someone who was prepared to pay me to act. How hard could it be?

Quite hard, as it happened.

I hadn't been to drama school. I hadn't been to university and acted there, which was another widely used route into the business. I had no relevant qualification behind me, unless you counted crawling under people's floors, looking for electrics, which people tended not to. I mean, sure, if the lights fused, mid-production, I was always going to be another pair of hands. But that didn't necessarily guarantee my ability to carry a play.

I had attended no classes on vocal projection and stage

positioning – no seminars, no workshops. I only had what I had learned two evenings a week in amateur dramatics. Otherwise I was running on instinct. And, no doubt, that absence of formal schooling not only troubled me in the early days, but planted a legacy which has stayed with me the whole of my life. All actors are a mix of confidence and doubt – of bulletproof self-belief one minute, and trembling insecurity the next. It's what makes us such a joy to be around – albeit sometimes unsuitable as domestic pets.

But the self-taught among us have, I think, our own particularly strong strain of the common actors' virus – and somehow no amount of success and acclaim ever quite squeezes it out of you. You know what you know – but, at the same time, you carry with you the shadowy sense that there might, unbeknown to you, be a *proper* way to be doing this. It's as if you are waiting to be found out. It's like a koala bear that sits on your back, its face alongside yours – endearing, in a way, and yet possibly a problem in the long term.

Whatever, it was certainly clear to me, at the very beginning, that I had a lot to learn – and, moreover, that I would have to learn it on the job. But that was assuming I could find a job to learn on. Like countless novices before me and since, I would pick up the *Stage*, the theatre and entertainment industry's newspaper, every Friday – in my case from WH Smith the newsagent on Finchley High Road. (I had to get them to order it in specially for me because, funnily enough, there wasn't a big call for the *Stage* in Finchley. Most copies probably went to Hampstead, or somewhere similar.) And I would take it home and intently comb the back pages where the adverts for upcoming auditions were. And then I would send off a simple letter (I couldn't include a CV because I didn't have one) and apply for absolutely anything and everything. Small plays by first-time writers, seaside entertainments, stunt extra in a piratical seaside entertainment involving jumping off diving boards (seriously – we'll come on to that), children's shows, second spear carrier from the left in provincial Shakespeare productions – I wasn't fussy. I just wanted to act.

Unfortunately, the people I applied to *were* fussy. The letters of rejection were soon flooding in. For one thing, many of the advertised jobs turned out to require prior membership of the actors' union, Equity. But, of course, you couldn't get into Equity without having a job as an actor. I was in the traditional catch-22 that traps so many performers when they first set out on their fumbling way towards a career: you can't get any work unless you've acted before, and if you haven't acted before, you can't get any work.

But one thing which I definitely had in my favour was determination. I kept on writing. And finally, after countless applications and countless refusals, and at the expense of what would now be a rather fine collection of first-class stamps, I hooked one: an audition for a place with Margate Repertory Theatre, who were looking for actors to add to their general company.

I could have hooted with relief and delight, and, indeed, did, several times. At last someone had opened the door. And now it was up to me.

The auditions were held somewhere off the bottom of Devonshire Street, in central London. The requirement for each actor, as explained in the letter from Margate, was to offer a rendition of a piece from Shakespeare, a piece from a modern play and then a piece of your own choosing. At the appointed hour, I climbed some dingy stairs to a dusty little anteroom, where a person took my details and invited me to sit and wait. I duly did so, in the process noticing two things: first that my heart now appeared to be playing some kind of drum solo behind my ribcage; and second, that my fists were bunched so tightly that my nails were digging into my palms. Welcome to the world of auditions.

In due course a door opened and the preceding actor passed

through on his way out, giving me a fleeting moment in which to read the expression on his face. Horror? Delight? Mortification? Relief? It was hard to say. Then, after a few more clenched moments – and not only my fists – I was called through.

It was a big, high-ceilinged room with a wooden floor, entirely unfurnished, as I recall, but for a table at one end of it, behind which was seated the Margate Rep audition panel – two women and a man. I introduced myself, as best I could, although my tongue now seemed to have taken on the thickness of a can of Spam.

'So, what are you going to do for us . . .' The man paused and looked down on a sheet of paper which I suspected had hundreds of names on it. '. . . Mr White?'

'I'm going to do *Richard III*,' I said, stiffly. 'The opening speech.'

'Very good,' said one of the faces at the table. 'In your own time.'

In the context of the expectant silence that then fell, the project I had announced suddenly seemed more than a little daunting. Indeed, the full difficulty of acting, and its basic absurdity, descended on me all at once. Basically, I was going to have to transform myself, at the click of a finger, from a jobbing electrician who has decided to give the theatre a go, into a vengeful, unscrupulous, blood-crazed monarch with a hunched back. Moreover, I was going to have to do this while on the edge of a personal nervous breakdown and in front of three complete strangers in an otherwise empty room.

I drew a deep breath, stooped slightly, to convey the all-important hunched back ('That'll impress them,' I thought), and kicked off.

'Now is the winter of our discontent / Made glorious summer by this son of York.'

OK so far, but I was still far from relaxed. Moreover, as I continued, I began to hear a rapid tapping noise coming from somewhere in the room.

'*And all the clouds that lour'd upon our house . . .*' tap-tap-tap.

The noise was light, but persistent, a bit like rain on a window, and more than a little distracting.

'*In the deep bosom of the ocean buried . . .*' tap-tap-tap.

By now I could see a look of consternation on the faces of the three people at the table, who could hear the tapping too.

'*Now are our brows bound with victorious wreaths . . .*' tap-tap-tap.

And that look from the table, in combination with the still increasing volume of the taps, caused me to dry, mid-line, and come to a halt.

Tap-tap-tap.

The noise continued in the otherwise quiet room. And I was slowly drawn to the gaze of my interviewers, all three of whom seemed to be directing their puzzled eyes at the floor below me. I looked down and was surprised to discover that the tapping was coming from the ends of my own legs. In my clenched state, the muscles in my calves had tightened, I had gone forward onto the balls of both feet and my heels were trembling rhythmically on the floor.

End of audition. 'Thank you very much, Mr White. We'll let you know.'

Now I had to recover my legs and make an exit. It was dead man walking – one of the longest walks I'll ever make.

Out in the street, full of embarrassment and self-loathing, I felt about as foolish as I have ever felt. If I couldn't even pull myself together to audition, how would I ever get anywhere?

Even when I overcame the shaky legs, I wasn't immune to other humiliations. I got an audition for another repertory company – I think it could well have been in Basingstoke – and successfully kept my legs under control throughout, only to be told, 'I'm sorry – you won't match up to our leading lady.'

Match up? What – in terms of acting ability? No. What they meant was, their leading lady was five foot ten. Being four inches south of there, I would never match up to her in height. What they were saying, ever so politely, was, 'You're too short, mate.'

It wouldn't have been an issue in the movies, of course. Many of the world's leading film stars are shorties, mentioning no Tom Cruises. Mentioning no Alan Ladds, either. Ladd was one of my earliest cinema heroes. He was reputedly only five foot seven – but that didn't stop him forming a convincing screen relationship with Veronica Lake. But in film, you could stand on a box, dig a pit, shrink a doorway, lower a door handle, manipulate the perspective. In the theatre – no such luck. If the male actor only comes up to the female actor's waist, you've got yourself a problem. I was made to realise very early that, however this acting life of mine panned out, romantic leads were probably going to be hard to come by.

In the end, I owed my first big break, as I've said, not to those endless letters, but to my brother. (I could have saved a fortune in postage if I'd known.) Now moving smoothly in the world of theatre, Arthur had forged a particularly good friendship with an actor and director called Simon Oates. Simon was one of those irritating men who are tall, handsome and extremely popular with women. Indeed, girls seemed to fling themselves at him on sight. It will tell you something about the style and panache of the man that he auditioned for the film role of James Bond in *Dr No*, came through a number of screen tests and got down to the final three for the part before they ended up giving it to someone called Sean Connery. I wonder what became of *him*. Really it might just as well have been Simon smoothly driving Aston Martins away from exploding warehouses as anyone else. That was pretty much how he was in real life.

Anyway, in the early spring of 1965, my brother brought Simon and his girlfriend along to see me in an amateur production of *The Teahouse of the August Moon*, with the St Bride's Players, based in Fleet Street. This was the John Patrick play, based on a novel by Vern Sneider, about a clash of culture between Pacific Islanders and occupying American officers after the Second World War. (I'm pretty sure I was playing Captain Fisby. At any rate, I'm fairly confident I wasn't playing Lotus Blossom, the geisha.) I don't know how thrilling a prospect this must have been for Simon, but he came anyway. And afterwards we went to the pub and Simon was good enough to tell me that he thought I had come across well – and also good enough to give me the impression that he wasn't just saying this because he was there as a mate of my brother and felt he ought to be encouraging.

Eventually Simon asked me what I was going to do next, and whether I had any plans. Now, as it happened, I was in a position to tell him that I did. My scattershot mail-outs to the small ads in the back of the *Stage* had just opened a highly promising avenue.

'Well, actually, Simon, yes,' I said, adopting all the nonchalance I could muster. 'I've got the chance to be a pirate in Southend.'

I still have that letter, dated 10 March 1965 and typed on the headed notepaper of Leon Markson Limited. The ad had asked for actors who could take part in a ship-based theatrical extravaganza at the seaside. Mr Markson, the producer of said extravaganza, had replied to my application as follows:

> *Dear Mr White,*
>
> *Thank you for your letter.*
>
> *Would you be kind enough to let me know if you are able to use diving boards at 5 and 7 metres?*
>
> *Also would you let me know the lowest salary you would accept for a 15-week season?*
>
> *As you will know, the fight scene on the ship may call for some of the cast to fall over the side and while we have experienced divers for this purpose, accidents can happen.*
>
> *Yours sincerely,*
>
> *Leon Markson*

My mother Olwen looking radiant in Wales in her youth.

My dad, 1930, doing his bit for King and Country.

The White clan, circa 1947. I'm the ugly mug in the front, third from right. Mum behind me to the right, Arthur behind me to the left and Dad the short one in the middle at the back. June still to come.

Me, sister June and brother Arthur in the backyard at 26 Lodge Lane.

Me and my big brother – even then a vent act.

Christmas with the Whites, circa 1950. How we laughed.

Post-war knees-up for the children of Lodge Lane. At least it kept us from throwing tomahawks at each other.

Me at 14. Note prefect badge and Brylcreemed hair.

Cousin John wearing the latest après-mining gear.

Me being a minor miner. On holiday in Wales, circa 1955.

Dad (left) at work in the fishmonger's. A song, a dance, a pound of hake.

At 14, proudly wearing my costume for the school production of *Wayside War* – my breakthrough moment.

June, sophisticated and with beehive at 17, posing casually, holding the wall up by our outside loo.

Brian Barneycoat and me, Jack the Lads on our most prized possessions. Note absence of cars.

Arthur in his twenties, playing Puck in Regent's Park. He's still got those horns.

Micky Weedon and me, at 16, suited, booted and ready for international jet-set pleasure.

Aged 18, outside the builders' yard opposite our house, trying to look like a film star.

Micky and me modelling cheap waterproofs and enjoying a brief gap in the rain en route to Cornwall, late 1950s.

Val Doonican goosing my mother and my Aunty Ede. Val was a good friend of my brother Arthur and this was taken at Arthur's house.

Arthur and I audition for the Mafia at somebody or other's wedding, circa 196

By the way, just to complete the indignity, the letter was addressed to 'Daniel White'. Close, I suppose.

Anyway, I would, indeed, have been able to reassure Mr Markson regarding my ability to dive off boards at five and seven metres. That kind of stuff was like falling off a log to me – except higher up, of course. As for the dangers involved, well, sometimes you take your life in your hands just walking up the street. I was all set to write back to Mr Markson with a full declaration of my competence and bid him have the eyepatch ready and waiting. After all, whatever else you want to say about this project, it was an offer of work in the absence of any other. To that extent, then, my ship had come in – with the twist that I would be expected to fall off it every night for fifteen weeks for the lowest salary that I would accept. And in the full awareness that 'accidents can happen'.

When I had explained all this to Simon, he did his best to nod soberly – but then gave up and fell about laughing instead. When he'd finished laughing, he told me he thought I should probably be aiming a bit higher. (And, no, he didn't mean the ten-metre board.)

'I've a proposal for you,' he said. He was going to be directing a play at Bromley Rep, in south London, beginning at the end of April. 'I may have a very small part for you,' he said.

I was already nodding like mad when he added that there was one potential drawback. 'It might mean blacking up,' he said.

Even then, in 1965, this was an uncomfortable notion. But I didn't care. If I was prepared to risk death on the ocean waves in order to get into the theatre, I was certainly prepared to endure a fortnight in politically incorrect make-up. Fault me if you will, but I just wanted a break.

'I'd like that very much,' I said.

You will understand how buoyed up I was by this offer over the ensuing days – and, equally, how deflated and anxious I became as two weeks went past without any further mention of it. I was beginning to think I might have been better off going away to sea with the pirates. But then, on a Thursday when I was upstairs getting ready to go out to the pub, the phone rang, and it was Simon.

'Are you still serious about wanting to be an actor?'

My heart sped up here, and my breath started to come – as in my youth – in short pants.

'Yes, I am.'

'Then you come to the New Theatre, Bromley, next Tuesday morning, 10 a.m., and you start rehearsals. You happy?'

God, yes, I was.

'It's a Noël Coward play and you'll play the small part of a butler. Are you all right?'

'Yes.'

'Good. See you Tuesday.'

By now I could barely breathe at all, in any kind of pants, short or otherwise. This was it, at long last: a professional role.

That Tuesday, the first day of the rest of my life as an actor, dawned optimistically bright and clear. Or was it ominously cloudy? You know what? I can't remember. But what I do recall is that I set off from Finchley in the Mini Van sometime around dawn, so as to remove all possibility of being late. As a result, I got there at least an hour too soon. I found somewhere to park, and then walked around outside the theatre until five to ten.

The New Theatre wasn't among the capital city's most gilded or most storeyed venues. In fact, it was a converted swimming pool. But it felt like a temple as far as I was concerned. I went in through the front door and a woman in the box office pointed me in the direction of the swing doors through to the auditorium. And I'll never forget the magic of that – walking down the aisle between the velvet seating towards the stage on my first day as a professional actor. I could hardly breathe with the thrill of it.

I was introduced around the cast. Everyone seemed to me to be rather grand, but that was probably my insecurity. They were so elevated in my estimation because they were professional actors and I was the lowest of the low.

Scripts were handed out: Noël Coward's *South Sea Bubble*. My part: Sanjamo the butler.

Let's say it wasn't a big role. In fact it was completely tiddly. The play was mostly people sitting around talking in a terribly thirties, terribly upper-crust manner. And every so often, I got to come on and serve the drinks. Still, Simon had decided that the piece was a touch stuffy in places, and he wanted to liven it up a bit. So every time I appeared, he gave me bits of business to do and built up this butler's character until he was far more important than he was written to be.

In particular, there was a moment near the end of the play when there was a set of bongo drums lying vacantly on the stage. Simon had me come on quietly to do some clearing away in the background of a scene. While other actors were in conversation at the front of the stage, I was to look longingly at these drums, clearly wanting to play them but knowing that it isn't really the place of a servant. But then I had to yield to temptation and pretend to play them – only to end up accidentally hitting the things, causing the other actors, in conversation at the front of the stage, to jump and spin round.

Again, one winces to reflect on this: a blacked-up actor, yearning to play the bongos. What can I say? Such were the times. Let me at least speak in defence of the routine's purity as comedy, though. It was a Laurel and Hardy thing at root: you know someone is going to do something; what you don't know is when. The comedy lies in how you draw out that time and fill it – edging gradually closer, almost committing, backing off, starting again, and hoping to pull the audience in and out with you.

Nevertheless, for all its grounding in the established practices of the greats, this business with the bongos did not entirely delight my fellow cast members in the scene – those at the front of the stage trying to carry on with their dialogue. As far as they were concerned, this little fart of a waiter was doing stuff that he shouldn't have been doing and upstaging them. But that only dawned on me later. At the time, I was completely green and oblivious. As far as I was concerned, I was simply doing what the director told me.

And whatever else you want to say about my portrayal of Sanjamo, it made an impression. They liked their theatre in Bromley in those days, and we played to full and supportive audiences. Moreover, when the play was reviewed in the local paper, I got a mention. On 30 April 1965, in the *Bromley Press*, under the less than promising headline 'BUBBLE RUNS INTO TROUBLE', the production, and in particular its pacing, was greeted with really quite stunning levels of indifference. However, readers who got as far as paragraph eight (and I was one of them) will have discovered and no doubt digested the following:

> A small but well-acted part is that of David White as the native butler of the governor.

A small but well-acted part! OK, so no one was ever likely to lift that line as the title for their autobiography or get it printed up on T-shirts. But I was more than happy at the time.

My contract was for two weeks' rehearsal and two weeks' performance. At the start, I bought myself a little hardback notebook for my accounts, and duly noted in biro my salary for the two weeks of rehearsals (£7 and 5 shillings per week) and for the two weeks of the production (£15 per week. In 2013 terms, £15 would be the equivalent of about £110. Not great, even for a waiter).

And now that I had an official signed contract I could get

into Equity. I rang up straight away, and said I wanted to join. The woman on the phone said, 'What's your stage name?'

'David White.'

A silence followed while she checked the records. There was already a David White.

'Would you like to choose a different name?'

Free-associating wildly, I said, 'David White . . . *head*?'

There was already one of those, too.

This was harder than it seemed. As I dithered and cogitated some more, the woman said, 'You could always call back, you know.' But I wanted to get in quick, fearful of losing my chance. And for some reason my mind, casting around in desperation, fastened on to the legend of Jason and the Argonauts, burned into my imagination forever by the afternoon readings of Miss Kent back at primary school.

'David Jason?' I said.

The woman at Equity checked.

'No, there's no David Jason,' she said.

There was now.

CHAPTER FIVE

Unrecommended behaviour at weddings and airports. Some business with a porter's trolley. And the night that Hector from Hector's House tried to seduce me.

The first public appearance of David Jason – henceforth to be regarded as standing in permanently for the artist formerly known as David White – was on 24 May 1965 at the Vanbrugh Theatre Club in London. And the person who lined up the work for me? My brother, again. Nepotism has its critics, but you probably wouldn't have found me among them at this stage in my career. Hey, it's just nature's way of keeping things in the family.

How it happened was that Arthur had been asked by the actor and producer Malcolm Taylor to be in a stage production of the great Dylan Thomas poem for voices, *Under Milk Wood*. Unfortunately it clashed with something else Arthur was doing, but he told Malcolm that his little brother was also very good at Welsh accents and suggested he give me a listen. Malcolm would have been well within his rights to say, 'Your little brother? Yeah, what do you think I'm doing here – running a nursery?' and then go back to his list of phone numbers. But fortunately he didn't. He agreed to see me.

So I went along to meet Malcolm and auditioned for him in the front room of his flat in Randolph Avenue, Maida Vale. This was another buttock-clenchingly intimidating prospect because Malcolm had a very serious thespian background. He had trained at RADA, in the same year as Diana Rigg, Susannah York and Albert Finney; he had appeared onstage with Laurence Olivier in a Royal Shakespeare Company production of *Coriolanus* – and, OK, he was only a spear carrier, but it still counts; he had acted at the Royal Court in Tony Richardson's production of *Luther*. He was altogether someone who knew his theatrical onions. So here I was standing in front of the door to a basement flat in Randolph Avenue. I took a deep breath and pressed the doorbell. I heard it ring somewhere deep inside the flat. I rang again and suddenly the door opened and there, standing before me, was a small, rotund fellow with a huge mop of curly black hair and a cherubic face. 'Hello,' he said. 'You must be Arthur's brother. Come in.'

I followed him down a small dark passageway and into his warm and bohemian-style flat. He took me into the living room, which had a low, marble-topped coffee table and a large sofa, and Malcolm sat down opposite me in a comfortable armchair. He asked me what I'd done – and it didn't take me long to tell him. He then asked me to read from *Under Milk Wood* – the opening speech of the narrator first, then some of the other parts, the Reverend Eli Jenkins and Mog Edwards. And, of course, the Welsh voices that the words asked for came very easily to me, being half-Welsh and having spent all those summers in Wales.

Malcolm gave me the job there and then. It was going to involve a couple of days of rehearsals, back at his flat, beginning in a fortnight's time, and then a week of performances at the Vanbrugh Theatre, which was RADA's own auditorium, with no set wages, but a split of the takings.

In that cast was the terrific Ruth Llewellyn, subsequently

better known as Ruth Madoc (and also as Gladys Jones from *Hi-de-Hi!*), and the imposing Windsor Davies, who would later do a lot of Welsh-accented shouting as Battery Sergeant Major Williams in *It Ain't Half Hot Mum*. So I was among some properly rich Welsh vocal talent here.

The resulting production wasn't so much a play as a semi-staged reading. The narrator was on his own, stage left, and then there were eight actors in two rows of four, with music stands in front of us holding the scripts. The show began blacked-out with the rough outline of our figures and a pin spot on the narrator: 'To begin at the beginning: It is spring, moonless night in the dark town, starless and bible-black . . .' At the end of the narrator's speech, the backcloth would start to lighten with the morning. And now the sound effects were fed in: the dog barking in his sleep, 'farmyards away', and so on.

Playing Reverend Eli Jenkins required me to get my tongue around a litany of Welsh waterways without biting it clean off:

> 'By Sawdde, Senny, Dovey, Dee,
> Edw, Eden, Aled, all,
> Taff and Towy broad and free,
> Llyfnant with its waterfall,
>
> Claerwen, Cleddau, Dulais, Daw,
> Ely, Gwili, Ogwr, Nedd,
> Small is our River Dewi, Lord,
> A baby on a rushy bed.'

You try saying that after a couple or three pints of Brains SA. I thought it was fantastic – just the best stuff to read aloud. It was the start of a big love affair for me with that Thomas piece. I've been able to recite large chunks of it ever since.

It was also the start of a great alliance with Malcolm Taylor. He was only three years older than me and we clicked straight away. Indeed, Malcolm subsequently became one of my closest friends, and eventually a business partner. (We founded Topaz Productions together in the late 1980s.) We were to share many nights of London-based, bachelor-style carousing and, in the mid-to-late 1960s, fancied ourselves rather dashing, I think, in our open shirts and casually knotted silk scarves – two actor-laddies about town. This phase came to an end when Malcolm was fortunate enough to marry the lovely actress Anne Rutter, with whom he spent the rest of his life and with whom he brought up two lovely and talented girls. I was his best man. I was more than happy – nay, merry – to be so and delivered the conventional poor-taste speech. I no longer recall the exact text of my sermon, but I do remember that I wore my hired top hat throughout it (indeed, I refused to take it off all day) and that something I said caused a relation of Annie's, in full Scottish regalia including kilt, to leave immediately in a huff. Sorry, Scotland.

Afterwards, still merry, I gathered up a bridesmaid and drove to Heathrow Airport in the MG Midget sports car that I owned at the time, so that we could wave the newly-weds off on their honeymoon. Driving plastered? This is not behaviour that one would, in all conscience, recommend to anyone today. Furthermore, Malcolm was intending to evade the then rather strict regulations on the import and export of currency by wedging some extra notes into his socks. Thus the departing honeymooners were waved through passport control by a well-oiled figure in loosened morning dress shouting, 'Look in his shoes! Look in his shoes!' This is not behaviour that one would, in all conscience, recommend today, either. The bridesmaid and I then returned to central London, with the Midget's top down and the wedding festivities gloriously continued.

When *Under Milk Wood* finished its week-long run and the takings were divvied up, we each received the slightly shrivelled sum of £6 and 6 shillings – but so much more came out of this venture than mere pecuniary reward. Five years later, in 1970, Malcolm restaged the production at the Mayfair Theatre where it ran for a month, to quite a lot of acclaim. Also, very significantly for me, there was a party after one of the Vanbrugh Theatre shows, at which I was approached by someone called Ann Callender, who said she was a theatrical agent. I believe I was filling a paper plate with sausage rolls from the buffet table at the time.

'Do you have an agent?' she asked.

'No,' I said.

'Would you have any interest in acquiring one?' she said.

'Not really, thanks,' I said and went back to my more pressing interest at the time, which was in acquiring another sausage roll.

I think Ann must have reported this rather truncated exchange to Malcolm Taylor. At any rate, Malcolm now came up to me, mid-sausage roll, and explained that, actually, an agent was no bad thing for an actor to have, and that Ann was no bad thing as an agent. I sought her out.

'Can we start that conversation again?'

So now I had an agent.

An agent, but, at that exact moment in time, no work. Bob Bevil had promised me, when I left our electrical business, that, whenever the acting dried up – as it does for the best of them from time to time – he would try to hand me a job or two to put a bit of money in my pocket. So it was that, with my glamorous theatrical career but recently ignited, I set off, along with my mate and fellow sparky Johnny Dingle, to wire a block of flats in Borehamwood. (Johnny's real name was Dorman but he answered only to the nickname Dingle.)

Back to reality. On that particular job, as I recall, tea was brewed in a garage used for storing building materials. When I say brewed, I mean brewed. The technique was to take a galvanised bucket, fill it three-quarters with water, bring it to the boil over a Calor-powered gas ring, and then add tea bags, condensed milk and sugar. At 10 a.m. precisely, and again mid-afternoon, you would hand your mug over to the chief brewer, who would solemnly dunk it into the bucket and hand it back to you, now filled with a dark brown and strangely creamy liquid. It was, without question, the worst cup of tea you could possibly imagine that hadn't been deliberately sabotaged.

Also on that job, Johnny and I took to breaking the monotony of electrical work by staging mock fights with one another. We'd start by swearing, then chuck stuff about and slap each other with bits of conduit, banging and roaring and basically making as if in the middle of the barney to end all barneys. Well, it passed the time. One of the things to look forward to was lunch. Johnny's mum used to send him off to work with the most delicious liver-sausage sandwiches. If he was in the right mood, I could easily persuade him to swap me one for some of the chips I would have popped out in the van to acquire from the local chippy, as was my culinary delight.

This was the pattern for the first three or four years of my acting life. I would pick up parts where I could. And when there were no parts to be picked up, it was back to the overalls, the pliers, the pointless mucking about, the stodgy lunches and the extremely dodgy tea.

It kept my feet on the ground, I guess. It definitely kept the lining of my stomach on the ground.

* * *

ANN, MY BRAND-NEW agent, called. She had some work for me. Visions of Hollywood movies danced in my mind.

'You can be an extra,' she said.

'Oh,' I said.

'In a crowd scene,' she added.

'Oh,' I said.

'In an advertisement,' she concluded.

'Oh,' I said.

Hollywood would have to wait.

The advertisement was for something so important that I can't now remember what it was. But I do recall that I was required to form part of the crowd at a racetrack and cheer as some racing cars shot past. That wasn't an especially onerous piece of acting, you would have to say. I went along, I stood, I cheered, I went home. But hey. It was all work, as far as I was concerned.

One good thing came out of the experience. I ended up standing in the crowd next to a bloke called Tony, another jobbing actor from London like me, trying to get a foothold. We hit it off – to the point where, at the end of the day, Tony asked me if I wanted to go to a party he was throwing at his place at the weekend. I was more than happy to accept.

Tony gave me his address. He lived in a flat near the Edgware Road. Off I went, on the appointed evening, bottle in hand. (I was well versed, by this point, in the classic partygoer's trick of taking the cheapest bottle you could find, putting it among the other bottles on the drinks table, somewhere near the back, and making sure you drank from another bottle altogether, hopefully superior. Reader, if you haven't already adopted this tactic, do so immediately.)

The party was fun. Tony had some nice friends, including a number of extraordinarily beautiful women. I consumed a smattering of wine over the course of the evening and felt quite relaxed. However, come about 1 a.m., everyone was sitting around the living room, and someone got out some tobacco and some cigarette papers and started to roll a joint.

It was the first time I had ever been in the same room as a real live funny-fag. It was a total novelty for me. I'd never seen it done, and I have to admit, it rather fazed me. Alcohol I could happily entertain the concept of. But the thought of illicit substances made me nervous. The joint, which, by the time it had been stuffed and rolled, ended up being roughly the size of a roll of carpet, was ignited and passed round. Again, as a complete novice, I didn't really know what the etiquette was, but I happened to be smoking a cigarette, so when the joint reached me, I said, as casually as I could, 'No, you're all right – I've got one on.' I then took the sweet-smelling roll of carpet and passed it to the person next to me.

This happened a couple of times – the joint going round, me, somewhat anxiously, not participating. Bill Clinton asked us to believe that he didn't inhale. Well, I'm asking you to believe that I didn't even get the thing near my lips. Eventually the roll of carpet was finished, and not long after that everyone around me was away – giggling and laughing and having (literally) a high old time. Feeling left out and altogether surplus to requirements, I decided to go home, thanked Tony and left. As I walked back to the car, I remember feeling like a bit of a stiff – not exactly Mr Cool or Mr Sixties. Not exactly in with the in-crowd. One of the out-crowd.

And there, I have to say, through the period of hectic cultural change and hitherto unprecedented revolutions in personal freedom, I remained. I wasn't out to spoil anyone else's good time. Dope just wasn't (as we would have said in those days) my scene. Credit me, at least, with a bit of gumption. When there was so much stuff flying around, it took quite a lot of willpower to be yourself and not just go with the flow. I remember the peer pressure being such that, if you said no, the partygoers thought you must have just landed from the planet Zuton – or were maybe a police officer in disguise.

Still, some curiosity must have lingered. Flash forward with me, if you will, to the early 1980s, and an evening in the flat I eventually took in Newman Street, central London. Present: me, my mate and his wife and my girlfriend at the time, Myfanwy Talog. Either him or me had got hold of a couple of joints – I really don't recall which one of us or where from. We decided, in the interests of science and human understanding, to carry out a little experiment: to smoke them and see if we could find out what the fuss was all about.

Both the girls declined to participate. But neither of them seemed averse to the idea of me and him having a go. So the pair of us passed the lit joint backwards and forwards for a while, smoking it as if it were a cigarette, and we waited for the effect to take hold.

Periodically I would peer through the fragrant smoke and say, 'Nothing yet. What about you?'

He replied, 'Nothing whatsoever.'

A few more puffs went by.

'Anything yet?'

'Nope. Not a sausage.'

Some more puffs.

'What about now?'

'Nothing, mate.'

We concluded that it was hopeless.

Fifteen minutes later, someone at the table said something completely anodyne – along the lines of, 'Are you sure they're your shoes? They don't look like your shoes.'

And that was it. Though we didn't know it at the time, we were off.

It was as if this line about the shoes was the funniest thing anyone had ever said, about anything, ever. We laughed until the tears streamed down our faces and the breath drained from our lungs. We were just about recovering ourselves when one of the girls said, 'What's the matter with you two?' And off we went again. Because that was hysterical, too. Everything was hysterical. It's strange – even after all these years, I can remember it reasonably clearly.

Time became rather flexible. Everything seemed to be happening at quite a woozy distance. It appeared to be taking about twenty minutes to answer a simple question. I could hear what I was being asked, but getting the words together for a response was becoming an increasingly time-consuming process. And the fact that it was difficult was, in itself, funny. The girls, far from amused, grew more and more disgruntled and impatient. And the more disgruntled they got, the more amused we became.

It seemed to go on for days, although it was probably only about an hour and a half, at most. At some point in that period, the two girls gave up trying to get any sense out of us and left us to it. They left and went over to my friend's flat. Much beyond that, I don't recall, though I must have stopped laughing and found my way to the bedroom eventually. That was where I regained consciousness the following morning.

So, now I'd tried it, at least. But that was it for me. Once was enough. It had been funny, and even euphoric. But at the heart of it was the thought that I didn't have control, and that aspect of it I found frightening, rather than liberating. Obviously it's about the kind of person you are. Some people are good at letting go, and some people aren't. But perhaps it was also something about being involved in comedy. If you're a comic actor, the idea of people laughing at absolutely anything is actually rather worrying. You want to know why people are laughing. You want to be in control of the reason they laugh. You want to know it's coming from something you've done – something you could do again if you had to. The idea of relinquishing control of the laughter to a substance . . . I couldn't get on with that at all. Call me timid or old-fashioned if you must, but me and drugs didn't mix, and from that moment on, I made a pact with myself: sink or swim, it had to be me.

* * *

WHILE WE'RE ON the subject of artificial stimulants, I should perhaps relate how me and alcohol learned to be careful around one another as well. Tales of tippling actors are legion, of course. Many, I'm sure, are the greats (and even more numerous the not-so-greats) who have found that, while out onstage, it helps to have a little something coursing through the system. I was lucky to get a salutary lesson in this area very early in my career.

It happened in the mid-to-late sixties, while I was on tour with a theatre production in Glasgow. Brian Izzard, a flouncy and flamboyant television producer with a large amount of hair (certainly at the back, if not at the front), happened to be in town and, having seen the show I was in, he invited me to meet him for lunch the next day so that we could 'discuss a few projects'.

I was more than happy to join him. The idea of going to lunch in order to 'discuss a few projects' still seemed fabulously romantic to me then, and almost chic – a highly desirable feature of this new life as an actor that I had signed up to. Plus, when you were on tour, the offer of a free meal was never to be declined. It was one of the reasons why, in those early days, I was always delighted when my agent came out to see me in far-flung places around the country, which she loyally did. I knew she'd take me to dinner afterwards and I'd be living high on the hotel restaurant's hog for once – choosing roast beef and all the trimmings, most likely, and not stinting on the starter and the dessert. Not forgetting, it goes without saying, her warm and exceptional company and her tender concern for all areas of my professional and personal well-being.

Anyway, the producer and I met at some suitably appointed eaterie and, while I browsed the menu for roast beef, he called for a bottle of wine. 'Oh, why not?' I found myself saying, as he heartily charged my glass, prior to heartily recharging it barely a few moments later. Before long, over the main course, bottle number one had been drained and my amiable companion was ordering another. 'Very nice,' I agreed. Bottle number two also seemed to go down rather smoothly. The occasion had now taken on a warm and comforting glow, which by no means receded with the arrival of bottle number three. Come the pudding course, the producer suggested that maybe a glass of dessert wine would round things off most pleasantly, and I didn't disagree with him – even though I had never heard of dessert wine and had no idea what it was.

Somewhere around three thirty in the afternoon, I emerged from the restaurant, followed soon afterwards by my legs. The producer and I shook hands and vowed to meet again to take our discussions about projects further – though, to be honest, the details of those discussions and those projects were already beginning to be a blurred and misty memory, as of something that happened in a far-off place, to someone else entirely. I then turned and, relying almost entirely on instinct, made my way back to my digs.

It was about four by now. I lay down on the bed and watched the overhead lampshade begin to perform sickening circles around the room. Clearly there was no way sleep could come to me in this state, so I sat hunched forward on the edge of the bed, rising occasionally to walk the room's tiny perimeter when the dizziness became too much.

At five, not noticeably more sober, I headed to the theatre where, in just two and a half hours, I would be required to take to the stage and play a part which, alas, could not, by any scope of the imagination, allow me to pass myself off as shit-faced. I asked for a big jug of black coffee to be brought to the dressing room and swigged it down, while pacing up and down. In make-up, I passed the time breathing deeply, hoping the make-up girl would interpret this as some kind of vocal exercise rather than as embarrassing evidence that I was as pissed as a newt.

By curtain-up, I had gathered enough self-possession to step into the lights – and although portions of the ensuing evening seemed to vanish without me really noticing what was going on in them, I was able to leave the stage at the end of the play (and the theatre almost immediately afterwards), congratulating myself on my inner strength and resourcefulness in having got away with it. But, of course, what else is the gift of acting, if not the ability to convince other people that you are something other than what you actually are?

Except I hadn't. The next day members of the cast came up to me with worried expressions on their faces and said, 'What was up with *you* last night? Were you pissed?' I had missed cues, interrupted speeches, stumbled over lines, and over my own feet, not to mention the feet of other people, and generally turned in a complete and utter howler.

Consider me well and truly warned of the perils of mixing drink and acting. Never again.

* * *

IN JULY 1965, mindful of my glowing and almost certainly box-office-boosting reviews for 'a small but well-acted part' in Noël Coward's *South Sea Bubble*, Bromley Rep re-employed me – this time in *Diplomatic Baggage*, a farce by John Chapman. My role? Hotel porter. (Porters and waiters: a theme was very quickly emerging in my early work. Lots of actors wait tables while 'resting' between jobs. Not me. I did electrics while 'resting', and waited tables while I was working.)

But I was a lot more involved this time – a greater part of the plot, without any artificial or controversial expansion of the character by the director. Being a sixties farce, and typical of the genre, the play was all about going through doors and in and out of windows and cupboards – very much of the classic 'oops, here comes the wife, better climb in the wardrobe with the mistress and the vicar' school of theatre. And it got me involved in one bit of business in particular that, in many ways, set the mould for much of my early career.

What happened was, I wheeled a trolley of room-service food into a hotel room, where our philandering protagonist was busy entertaining his mistress. And then I exited. Soon after this, and at the most sensitive moment in the ensuing seduction scene, of course, the philanderer's wife calls up from reception. (I did say this was typical farce material.) Now in a flap, the philanderer resolves to conceal the mistress in the trolley, hidden by the tablecloth – as you would. Or certainly as you would if you were a character in a British farce. And then he calls up the porter (me) to take the trolley away.

So, in I come and grab a hold of the trolley, ready to whisk it out – only to discover that, for some reason unknown to me (although known to the audience), it is now unexpectedly, almost unbudgeably heavy. What I worked up for this moment was a huge pratfall – one in which, clinging to the trolley's handle, I appeared to be entirely horizontal at one point, hovering briefly in the air before crashing completely to the floor. Then I got up and began to inspect the trolley suspiciously for the cause of its additional burden – nervously circuiting it, tentatively lifting the lid off the silver salver resting on top of it, and so on, but, of course, never looking in the obvious place.

All this stuff got a big reaction from the audience. It also got a big reaction from the local paper. 'For me David Jason stole the show,' reported the drama critic of the *Bromley Press*. 'The physical demands made upon him are tremendous and one wonders whether he can keep it up to the end of the fortnight's run. As the Paris Hotel porter his acting is superb and the round of applause he received on Monday was thoroughly deserved.'

I did, indeed, survive the physical demands of the fortnight, I'm pleased to be able to report – and with little more than superficial bruising across about 85 per cent of my body's surface area and some mild hip ache. And, to an extent, the die was cast by that routine. It's what I became known for: introducing additional physicality into farces. If you wanted an actor who could fall over while trying to move something – or even fall over while not trying to move something – I was a pretty decent bet. If you were looking for someone to play Hamlet, on the other hand – well, it might not be too much of an exaggeration to say that the chances of my career setting off down that path were quietly extinguished the minute I showed I could fall trying to move that trolley in Bromley.

My agent, Ann, came along on one night of the run with her husband, a television producer, director and writer – a certain David Croft, later associated with *Dad's Army*, *Are You Being Served?*, *It Ain't Half Hot Mum*, *Hi-de-Hi!* and *'Allo 'Allo* or, to put it another way, more than three-quarters of the most successful sitcoms made for British television in the seventies and eighties and an extraordinarily high proportion of the greatest comedy hits of all time. David saw me in *Diplomatic Baggage* and that piece of business with the trolley chimed with him. He bore it in mind for later, as we'll see.

* * *

As HER MAJESTY the Queen so rightly put it, in her Christmas broadcast to the nation in 1965: 'Every year the familiar pattern of Christmas unfolds. The sights and the customs and festivities may seem very much the same from one year to another, and yet to families and individuals each Christmas is slightly different.'

That was certainly true for my family that year. All the usual sights, customs and festivities were in place: the chicken (cheaper than turkey), the tree, the decorations. But it was the first Yuletide season when, in addition to all that, they had been able to gather together and see one of their own kith and kin on the television, dressed in a policeman's outfit, hanging from the ceiling. Slightly different, or what?

The location for this once-in-a-lifetime Christmas scene

was the BBC pantomime – my first ever appearance on the small screen, and clinched while I was still a nobody, just eight months after my professional stage debut, a turn-up which must have been down to some pretty smart work by my agent. She must have really upped her game since getting me the part as an extra in the advertisement at the racetrack. It was the habit of the BBC in those days to organise a pantomime for Christmas – in this case, *Mother Goose*. They would sprinkle the cast with TV favourites, and film it, as live, in a traditional theatre, in front of an audience, and then broadcast it on Boxing Day, so that viewers at home could feel they were getting the full panto experience without leaving their armchairs. In the mid-sixties, the BBC panto could expect to get an audience well in excess of 15 million people. (You're going to tell me, perhaps, that there wasn't a lot else on. I'm not here to argue. I'm simply setting down the figures.) Accordingly, I was pretty thrilled to get the nod – and still thrilled on the morning of 17 December as I headed for the Golders Green Hippodrome (very handy for those of us who lived just up the road in Lodge Lane).

The big stars of the show that year were Terry Scott and Norman Vaughan. Vaughan had taken over from Bruce Forsyth as the host of *Sunday Night at the London Palladium* – just about the biggest show on television at that point in time – and would later have a stint as the presenter of *The Golden Shot*. His catchphrases at the time were 'Swinging!' and, its opposite, 'Dodgy!' It was still the case, in the mid-sixties, that a comedian had to have a catchphrase, just as it had been in earlier times for Tommy Trinder ('You lucky people'), for Arthur Askey ('Hello, playmates!'), for Arthur English, ('Mum, Mum – they're laughing at me again') and countless others.

Terry Scott was a giant star at this point – and, bless him, a fairly sizeable pain in the . . . well, let me put it another way: he didn't suffer fools. It seemed to me that fame had temporarily exhausted his patience with lesser mortals, as fame sometimes will. He was certainly way above little people like me.

Someone I warmed to straight away, though, was Jon Pertwee – later, of course, one of the greatest of the Doctor Whos, but then most famous for his part in the BBC radio series *The Navy Lark*. We chatted and he gave me some very sage advice about avoiding productions with too many comedians in them. Jon had been in the 1963 London stage production of the musical farce *A Funny Thing Happened on the Way to the Forum*, with Frankie Howerd and Kenneth Connor. Apparently, partway through rehearsals the director had called the cast together and told them, 'If you carry on at this rate, you'll be acting in the theatre next door.' Members of the cast were constantly moving themselves into a position just behind the shoulder of the last person to speak – it being the comic's instinct to take the dominant position upstage. Eventually all the action was taking place against the backcloth. I filed this away as something to watch out for.

Jon also ended up showing me some photographs he had of himself in the swimming pool at his place in Spain. I remember thinking that was pretty swish – having a place in Spain. On Jon's shoulders in one of these photos of sun-drenched bliss was his young son, Sean. The next time I saw that little chap he was a full-grown man, standing on no one's shoulders, playing a villain opposite me in *A Touch of Frost*. Sean Pertwee turned out to be a very fine actor.

Also present for the BBC panto was Lauri Lupino Lane, the son of the great music-hall actor Lupino Lane, and the undisputed living master of the legendary wallpaper routine – that eternal homage to DIY gone wrong, which could be shoehorned into almost any show, via some subtle line such as, 'Ooh, I think the kitchen needs redecorating.' Then out would come the wallpaper, the buckets of paste and the decorating table, and slapstick chaos would duly ensue. There's a climactic moment where Lauri Lupino Lane's bowler hat gets filled with wallpaper paste and the hat has a hole in it, so that when he forces it down on his head, the paste fountains out of the top of it. Never fails.

And then there was Kay Lyell, who played Priscilla the Goose. Kay was, perhaps, the most celebrated panto goose of her generation. It was her speciality, and, indeed, the work of her lifetime. She had her own outfit, or 'goose skin', which was magnificent and came, of course, with full, top-of-the-range egg-laying capabilities, which I'm sure gave her the edge in this particular marketplace. Kay was said to live in a tiny top-floor flat in Covent Garden and to keep the goose skin in the bath – the only place big enough to store it unfolded. Every time she wanted a bath she had to whip the goose out and lay it somewhere else temporarily. And then, when she had finished, she would dry out the bath and return the goose to its rightful storage place. Personally, I think I might have found that rather tiresome after a while, but, I guess, if you work as a pantomime goose for long enough, you eventually acquire bombproof levels of patience, and Kay seemed to find the arrangement perfectly acceptable.

In rehearsal, she wore only the bottom half of the outfit, which rather let the light in on the magic, I suppose. She waddled about the place in what was essentially a pair of fluffy pyjama bottoms ending in rubber gaiters and big webbed feet. I have to say, she was very adept at walking in those feet without making them flap and smack the floor like a diver in flippers, which would have spoiled the effect. I have to say, also, that the work of the Goose Woman was of more than merely passing interest to me. Not many months before this, at the Incognito Theatre Group, I had had the rare distinction of playing the part of a raven – a role in which I had immersed myself by going to study the ravens in situ at the Tower of London. Executing a passable raven, you might be surprised to learn, is actually quite complicated and physically demanding, particularly in the way they scuttle forwards. There's more buttock-action than you might think.

Now, I have no wish to run down posthumously an undisputed legend of British pantomime. But, if I may be frank, her obvious skill with the feet aside, I was a little disappointed with Kay's goose. From the legs up, she played it very straight, in my opinion – very much a no-frills, no-nonsense kind of goose. She did exactly what it said on the feathers. But I'm probably quibbling uncharitably. It obviously hadn't hindered her career.

I, meanwhile, played the King of Gooseland, that marvellous, if quite negligible role. And, along with Terry Scott and Jon Pertwee, I ended up in a section of the show called 'The Flying Policemen'. We were attached to harnesses in Kirby's Flying Ballet, and we all swung about, hung from the grid, dressed as coppers, flying around and bumping into each other to a piece of music that was so well known at the time that I can't remember it. Nothing more to it than that, really, but somehow the sight of fully uniformed police officers solemnly flying above a stage seemed to garner a big laugh.

Can I just mention the sheer agony of the Kirby harness? It featured two leather straps, which were passed under the groin area and up the sides of the legs, and, after a while, the weight of your body hanging from its wire would cause those straps to close in on one another, in a slow scissor-like motion. Pain of a rare and intimate order would be felt and, imperceptibly, your voice would begin to rise through the octaves. Words can't express the joy and relief you felt when your feet touched earth again and the feeling began to return to your nether regions.

Reflect on it from my point of view, though: for those brief moments in-harness, plucked from the obscurity of a very early career in repertory theatre, I was quite literally rubbing shoulders with the greats. And also arms and knees. And even, in some of the more extreme collisions, thighs.

The fee I was paid for rendering these services over the course of three days, incidentally, was £74 2s 8d – an exponential leap from the £15 I had earned for a week's theatre at Bromley. If I hadn't already known that television was where the money was, I certainly did after that. If one could get by in the theatre on £15 a week, £74 was no slap in the face with a wet lettuce.

That Christmas, at Lodge Lane, the family gathered around the box to witness my broadcast debut. There was my mum, my dad, my sister June, my mum's sister Aunt Ede and my cousin Ken. I'm sure they were as made up as anyone could be to see a close relative of theirs swinging from a cable, in uniform. Mind you, you have to bear in mind that TV was very unsophisticated at the time, and that the only close-ups you saw were of the stars. The rest of us were in rather blurry long-shots. Afterwards, I gave my parents a relaxed, smiling look, designed to convey the message, 'You see – it seemed like a big risk at the time, but I told you I'd be all right, career-wise.' And they gave me a look back designed to conceal their probably still raging anxiety.

That wasn't the only time in my career that I bumped into Terry Scott. Not long after this, thanks to David Croft and his memory of my trolley business in *Diplomatic Baggage*, I got a one-off part as a waiter in *Hugh and I*, the very popular comedy series that Scott starred in, along with Hugh Lloyd, before he went on to even greater sitcom glory in *Terry and June*. My part involved a couple of lines and some of the aforementioned funny business from the stage play. Before this piece of business there was some dialogue exchanged between my character and a couple in the restaurant. In rehearsal, the crew were clearly enjoying it – often the first sign you get that something is going to work. It was at that point that I noticed Scott taking the director aside and having a little whisper in his ear. And the next thing I knew the director was coming over to me and saying, 'You know what? I'm not sure that line works particularly well there. I think we'd better give it to Terry.' Of course, I had to do as directed, and got on with it, like the diligent new boy that I was. But inside I was thinking, 'Ah, so that's how it works, is it?' – and other much less charitable things.

* * *

MEANWHILE, AT BROMLEY Rep, the Christmas pantomime was *Aladdin* – and once again a police uniform was called for. I played Flip, from Flip and Flop, the comedy policemen. Flop was Robert Fyfe, who much later played Howard Sibshaw, the funny old fart on the bike in *Last of the Summer Wine*. Fyfe was a Bromley regular who lived locally enough to walk into the theatre.

I'm not sure that the roles of Flip and Flop necessarily drove either Robert or me to our best or most complex work. Indeed, if there had been an award for least funny comedy policemen in a pantomime setting, my feeling is we would have stormed it that year. Then again, being so unfunny that you almost came back round the other side as funny was part of what panto was about and a big reason people bought tickets. I don't think we sold anyone short.

Anyway, my happy reward for these efforts was that David Paulson (who ran Bromley Rep and was known, broadly across the company, as 'Poofy Paulson' on account of his fine head of wavy hair) put me on a year-long contract – one of the last such contracts that Bromley offered. Shortly after that the idea of contracts went out the window, because they realised it was more economical and flexible to recruit actors piecemeal.

Fortuitous timing, then – and wonderful training. I was playing a different character every two weeks and being met head-on by all sorts of different challenges. In *Murder at the Vicarage*, for example, adapted from the Agatha Christie whodunnit, I had to play the part of a haemophiliac vicar who, on his first entrance, discovers a dead body slumped over his writing desk and utters the immortal line, 'Blood! Blood! Blood!' Every time I did this, the audience laughed. It didn't matter what inflection I put on it, whether I shouted it or muttered it, whether I gave it the full Shakespearean welly or spoke it without a flinch in my finest stab at Eastern European minimalism – a titter ran through the auditorium. It drove me nuts. I ended up asking senior members of the cast, 'What can I do to stop them laughing?' The reply in each case was, 'Nothing, love. You're stuffed.' For as long as the play had been staged, it seemed, that line had got a laugh.

But there wasn't much time to dwell on it, of course. Soon after that I hung up the dog collar and pulled on a pair of cut-off trousers to play the lad Jack Hawkins in *Treasure Island*. The part of Long John Silver in that production was occupied in high style by the great Paul Bacon. Paul was a wonderful actor with a real, deep, actorly voice, a great fop of grey hair and a more gloriously theatrical manner in real life than you could have scripted. He had achieved a degree of fame in Australia, where he had been on television in a soap opera. But he had come to London to become famous globally, because, in those days, that was the route you took. And thus the trajectory of his career had brought him from Sydney to Bromley Rep – and made him quite the local star. Sometimes, in a break from rehearsals, I would pop up the road with Paul to a cheap tea room for a pot of tea and a bun, and every now and again he would be stopped on the street by Bromley theatregoers. He was the darling of the rep and elderly ladies would say to him, 'Oh, Mr Bacon, I do enjoy your work.' And he would say, 'Oh, my dear, how very kind of you to say so . . .' and courteously give them five minutes of his time. I was agog in his company.

He was also extremely committed to his art. To achieve plausible one-leggedness, as the role of Long John Silver required, Paul had his leg strapped up tight behind his thigh, which almost crippled him in reality. Every time he came offstage, there were two people waiting in the wings to unstrap him and ease his leg down, so the circulation could start returning to his foot.

Our *Treasure Island* also nobly refused the option of a stuffed parrot in order to go for a real one instead – a huge macaw, a wonderful creature, hired from the local pet shop. However, sometimes it would play, and sometimes it wouldn't. It was quite compliant about sitting on Paul's shoulder – and extremely compliant about shitting all down the back of Paul's costume. Some nights, though, the parrot would get bored and express its boredom by turning round and showing its arse to the audience. Alternatively it would launch an attack on the big hooped gold earrings that Paul was wearing, sometimes managing to yank them out altogether. And sometimes it would go for the earring, miss, and get Paul's ear instead. Paul would frequently end the night with big lumps taken out of his lobes.

Of course, for as long as the bird was onstage the audience would be watching it, rather than the play, so the entire cast knew the indignity of being upstaged by a parrot. But Paul knew that indignity most keenly of all. There was a moment where he had to perch the parrot on a balustrade for a while, and then later collect it by putting out his arm. If the parrot was in the right mood, it would walk up Paul's arm and back to his shoulder again, earning a giant round of applause. If the parrot was in the wrong mood, it wouldn't budge – much to Paul's increasing irritation. But he was a pro, and he got on with it, bloodied ears or no bloodied ears – an example to us all, whatever our walk of life.

Those Bromley days were a fiery old baptism altogether, because while you were doing your current production at night, you were rehearsing your next one during the day. New scripts were constantly having to be learned – something which I have always found very effortful – and the threat of accidentally and ruinously dropping a passage from *Treasure Island* into a Saturday matinee of, say, *Hay Fever* was ever-present. Or, perhaps even worse, dropping a passage of *Hay Fever* into a Saturday matinee of *Treasure Island*.

Rehearsals generally ran from ten fifteen until four in the afternoon, when you would break for tea and then get ready to be onstage for curtain-up at seven thirty. And given that I was still living with my parents at Lodge Lane when this contract began, by the time I had driven home it was about eleven thirty or midnight and I'd have to be up again at eight fifteen to be ready to drive back down to south London for the next morning's start.

Eventually, to be nearer the theatre and to start growing up and being a normal adult-type person, I moved into a flat above a hairdresser's in Thornton Heath. The hairdresser's in question belonged to my brother Arthur and his wonderful new wife, Joy, whose own towering beehive hairdo in those days was an absolute work of art. The business was named, without fear of confusion, 'Joy's'. Arthur and Joy had decided they no longer wanted to live above the shop and, with things going well for both of them, they had put a deposit down on a place on a new housing estate nearby. They offered me the flat at a generously low rent. It was the first rung on the ladder to independence. Every night I would unlock the front door, head through the darkened salon, past the big dryers and, amid the sticky scent of lacquer and shampoo, climb the stairs to bed. At last, no doubt to my parents' intense relief, I had flown the nest – and at the age of twenty-six, probably not a moment too soon.

In *Aladdin* I had acted with an actress called Frances Barlow. She was only five foot four, so even I was a bit taller than her. I had seen her in a musical and had been smitten with her and when we acted together I finally plucked up the courage to ask her on a date. We went out for quite a long time in the mid-1960s. She lived with her father, out near Heathrow Airport, so, again, my Mini Van clocked up quite a few miles. Our relationship ran along very easily and pleasurably. Then one day, when, quite by coincidence, we had both been auditioning in the same building, we went for lunch. Somehow the conversation ended up with us discussing the possibility of us moving in together and things becoming more permanent. And the more I thought about it, the more it terrified me. At that stage in my life, I thought of myself as wedded to my career and I was paranoid to an absurd degree about getting tied down and trapped and stopped. Moving in with someone would have scuppered my future – or so my panicked mind thought. So we finished.

This was a pattern which was to repeat itself several times during those early years when I was struggling to get a footing in the business. I went out with girls and became close to them, but at the first sign of anything more permanent or of the emotional connection strengthening, I would break away and flee, as fast as I could. I wasn't just phobic about commitment, in the traditional male way, I was phobic about wrecking my chances of making it as an actor, a project from which I rarely relaxed in those days and which preoccupied me to the exclusion of pretty much all else – including, I can only confess, the feelings of the woman I happened to be with at the time. (Frances went on to work as a singer on a Greek cruise liner. And the ship's captain, who was obviously no fool, invited her to dine and they were wed, I'm very happy to say.)

Back at the theatre, I found myself cast in Sheridan's *The Rivals*. I played Bob Acres and the aforementioned grand thespian, Paul Bacon, played Sir Anthony Absolute. Paul and I ended up sharing a dressing room. He would have been in his forties at this time, and I was twenty-six – but a young twenty-six, and knowing very little, really, about the ways of the world. I certainly had no idea what homosexuality was. I just thought he was very theatrical and a lovely man who could hand down his experience to me. For example, the Restoration was a period that Paul knew well and for *The Rivals* he taught me all sorts of tricks – how to bow and how to stand and how to shape your hands in the appropriate style. He was a great and generous teacher and I loved him for that.

What I didn't realise was quite how much he liked me.

One day Paul said, 'You must come round for supper and we can go through our lines together.' And I said, 'Yeah, that would be a great help – lovely.' He turned out to be residing in the less than grand circumstances of a tiny Bromley bedsit, and apparently living out of a suitcase. Still, there was a stove in the corner on which he cooked us a wonderful meal, and we talked about the play, did a reading, and sat in the room's two armchairs having a glass of wine or two. And then, as the hour wore on, Paul rose from his chair, came and sat on the floor in front of me, put his arms across my knees and gazed up at me.

I thought, 'This is odd. This is what you'd do if you were a girl. Or certainly if you were a girl in a movie.'

At that point, Paul started to run his hand up my leg. At this, the hairs rose on the back of my neck. I remember feeling that it was very important to keep talking – to keep talking and, almost as if not noticing, push away that hand. Which I did. But back the hand came, creeping further along my thigh. So I, still talking fast, pushed it away again. Back it came.

Eventually, Paul said, 'You know you want this, dear.' To which, I replied, 'Actually, I should probably be getting off home.'

I stood up and stepped round him towards the door. But in that instant he had somehow leapt between me and the exit. I still don't know how he did that – how he got from a reclining position on the floor to a standing position at the door in the click of a finger. It was like magic – the sort of thing David Copperfield might have done, in his 1980s pomp. I thought there must have been two of him – perhaps a body double, working as a plant.

And then he put his arms around me and started to kiss me.

I remembered at that point an expression I had heard girls use: 'His hands were everywhere.' Now I knew exactly what they meant. No sooner had you taken one hand out of here than another one went in there. He was like an octopus.

Pressed back against the door, I eventually got a decent hold on both his forearms, held them tight and said, as firmly as I could, 'Paul, I don't want to lose your friendship, but I really must go home. Thank you for a nice evening.'

We never mentioned it again and our friendship, blessedly, continued to thrive. Paul died in 1995, without reaching the level in the profession that he desired and deserved. In the late 1960s and early 1970s he found household-name fame at a remove, as the voice of Hector in the hugely popular children's glove-puppet show *Hector's House*. I was really pleased for him, although, thanks to that night in a Bromley bedsit, I could never hear that floppy-eared dog saying 'I'm a great big dreamy old Hector' in quite the way I was intended to.

CHAPTER SIX

A short stay in a cheap motel. The Book of Genesis, revisited. And how I did eventually become a pirate.

It's important to demonstrate range and flexibility in your early years as an actor, so it's with some pride that I now relate how, within a month and a half of launching myself onto the nation's screens for a few seconds as a harnessed policeman, I was back again, appearing for a few seconds as an unharnessed criminal.

This was in February 1966, during the first series of *Softly Softly*, a CID-oriented drama serial, spun off from the BBC's popular cop show *Z-Cars*. *Softly Softly* starred Stratford Johns, freshly promoted to the plain-clothes force as Detective Superintendent Charles Barlow – not that the star of the show was anywhere near the scene that I was in. My second moment of nationally broadcast action saw me play the part of the co-driver of a getaway van – a character imaginatively named 'Smith'. Actually, the verb 'play' might be a bit of an exaggeration here. I'm not sure I was that convincing. I was meant to be dozing in the van's passenger seat and to be startled awake by the arrival at the window of a policeman with a torch. When I watched it back later on the television, I almost died with mortification. I woke up in that van quicker than any human has ever awoken anywhere. It wasn't as if someone had shone a torch on me: it was as if someone had connected my privates to the torch's battery. I should like to point out, though, that I was used to directors helping an actor to draw the nuance out of a character, as tended to happen in the theatre. In television, clearly, you were supposed to know all that already.

Anyway, given the absence of wires and the fact that absolutely no one in the cast, so far as I can remember, was wearing a goose outfit, I guess we would have to call this my first venture into serious televised drama. Incidentally, the actor who was sat beside me, playing the driver (and perfectly convincingly, with dialogue and everything), was Brian Wilde, whom I would later come across as Mr Barrowclough, the ineffectual prison warden, in *Porridge*.

After my abrupt wake-up on *Softly Softly*, I wasn't entrusted with another television role for six months – until August. And even then, critics of a harsh frame of mind might have said the words 'role' and 'television' were something of an overstatement. The appearance we're talking about was in the soap opera *Crossroads*.

Ah, the Crossroads Motel. Even now, just the mention of the word can cast a chilly hand around an actor's kidneys – and not only his kidneys. 'The actors' graveyard' they used to call it – a hole into which many a promising career disappeared, screaming, and where you were actively encouraged to bring your own shovel. The motel had opened in November 1964 and already, by the summer of 1966 when I checked in, it had become a byword for low production values and – I'm sorry to relate – iffy acting. Of course, that's a terribly sweeping generalisation about a series in which a lot of the performances and a lot of the storytelling were really good. In defence of both the production staff and the cast, most of the show's failures to hit the mark were the result of doing everything in a blind hurry. The series was running at the heart-attack rate of five half-hour episodes per week. In 1967 the producers admitted partial defeat and scaled it back to four episodes in order to give themselves – and everyone else – a bit of breathing space. Three episodes per week was perhaps a more reasonable proposition, but that didn't happen until 1980, by which time everyone was completely knackered and the programme only had six more years to run. But no one was making allowances for that. *Crossroads* had become an open goal for satire.

And yet, for all that, it was a big hit, a television juggernaut – massively popular, the ITV network's second most-watched show after *Coronation Street*, and sometimes even capable of nudging ahead of *Corrie* in the ratings. (It was also, let us not forget, the favourite programme of Mary Wilson, the wife of the then prime minister, Harold Wilson. Could this be the same Harold Wilson who tried to stop my dear mate Malcolm Taylor from running down the country's currency supplies by leaving Heathrow with more than £50 about his person? I believe it could.) All in all, the show must have been getting at least as much right as it was getting wrong. I wasn't in a position to be snooty about the offer of work on *Crossroads*, but, more to the point, I wasn't inclined to be, either. To me, it meant continuity of work and also an invaluable opportunity to learn about working in front of television cameras, which is such a different discipline from acting in the theatre. I would have been mad not to seize it.

So, off I went on the train to Birmingham, the home of ATV. Rehearsals were held in a couple of rooms in a backstreet, on the second floor of an unprepossessing building, up a flight of concrete steps with a metal handrail. The assistant stage manager met me at the double doors. These opened into the main rehearsal room, all laid out as a bare but full-scale mock-up of the set. Masking tape on the floor marked the edges of the rooms, posts indicated doors. The motel reception desk – which, as for so many characters, would be my point of entry into the series – was represented by a couple of planks on a pair of trestles. I was shown into a smaller side room, containing a jumble of chairs around the edge, including one rather comfortable-looking armchair which I proceeded to plonk myself down into. Other cast members slowly began to arrive. Sue Nicholls, who played Marilyn Gates the waitress, was very warm and welcoming. She came up and said hello straight away. Everyone else, though, seemed to go a bit on edge at the sight of me. I couldn't for the life of me work out why, and assumed it was just me, as a nervous novice, judging the atmosphere wrongly. So I carried on sitting there, with my head buried in the script, and waited.

In due course, the star of the show, Noele Gordon, arrived. Noele was TV royalty, even then, and I was a bit starstruck. It wasn't really my place to jump up and introduce myself and I thought if I kept my head down, she wouldn't notice me and I wouldn't have to have an embarrassing, nervous exchange with her. Out of the corner of my eye, I was aware of her slightly pausing in the doorway. Then I heard her say good morning to the other regulars and she went and sat on the other side of the room.

All a little unsettling – but the explanation soon came. Some of us, including me, were called for our scene and as we made our way out of the green room, one of the others (and I'm not at liberty to tell you who that was, because I can't remember) hissed, with some urgency, 'You sat in Noele's seat.'

Great start. And thanks for telling me now, I thought, rather than when I walked in. Maybe it was some kind of test for the new boy. 'Let's see if he sits in Noele's seat!' Frankly, that was exactly the kind of thing I would have done if I had been in the regulars' position. It might sound a bit pathetic, but little things like that can be a major source of entertainment to the cast of a production and brighten a routine day. Whatever, when we came back out from rehearsing (and on every other occasion from then on), I made sure to park myself somewhere else.

Noele – or Nolly, as I learned to call her, like everyone else did – actually turned out to be perfectly approachable. She was a big gun, powerful, hugely experienced and carrying this enormous show, and she was pretty aloof. She could certainly make people quake in their boots but I got off pretty lightly. She had an amazing capacity to be faultless with her lines – 'DLP', as we used to say: dead line perfect. This was no matter how much she had to say, which, in any given week, was an enormous amount. When someone like me came along, who had so much less to say than her, but still struggled to get it all learned, it was a little embarrassing. She had a reputation for being mightily fierce and difficult, and to have a touch of the Gorgons about her, but I was never on the end of any of that. In any case, you have to be careful with rumours about people's reputations. It's like the story that made the newspapers about Tom Cruise, and how people on the set of one of his movies had been instructed not to look at him. Well, of course they were. It's the first thing extras are told: 'When the star walks into this scene, don't look at him.' The scene is hardly going to look natural, is it, if everyone is craning their necks to get a look at Tom? But, of course, that story gets out and becomes evidence of starry preciousness and absurd grandeur on Cruise's part. So you learn to be wary.

When rehearsals were through (and let's say they were not extensive), we moved on to ATV Studios for the recording. The show had no film unit for location shooting. The budget didn't run to that. Everything was filmed within one small studio. The motel reception area, Meg Richardson's office, the sitting room, the kitchen, Kitty Jarvis's shop – all the sets interlocked in a single cramped space. A cat, swung carefully, could have orbited the entire world of *Crossroads* in a single revolution. None of the sets was lavishly appointed, either – and least of all the shop. You'd have been pretty disappointed if you'd popped out to Kitty's to pick up a few essentials. It basically ran to a couple of boxes of soap flakes, some packets of cereal and that was about it. It was like Russia before the fall of communism. In fact, I think the shops in Russia were better equipped.

Nor did the budget run to editing – except of the crudest kind. Tape (which is what the show was recorded on) was expensive, and therefore at a premium. Or so we were told. Scenes were shot in one extended take, 'as live', meaning that all sorts of slips, errors and fumbles made it to air. I was once in a scene set in the kitchen, with an Australian actor, an extremely nice chap, and all was going along well enough until, suddenly, he dried – completely forgot his lines. My stomach dropped to the floor in sympathy for him because this was the worst thing that could happen on the *Crossroads* set. It wasn't live television, but we were instructed to behave as though it was.

However, in the corner sat the continuity girl, with the script in one hand and, in the other, a handset with a button on it, which, when she pressed it, would cut the microphones in the studio. With the actor looking over to her for help, she now pressed the button, gave the actor his cue and let the button up again. He took the cue, recovered his speech and we battered our way onwards to the end of the scene. I think both of us were expecting to hear the director call 'Cut!' at any moment and send us back to the beginning. But the call never came.

The next week, when this episode was broadcast, I made a point of tuning in at home. The whole escapade went out, exactly as it happened in the studio: you saw the actor lose his words and freeze, you heard the soundtrack go completely silent for a couple of moments, and then you heard the soundtrack come back up again and saw us carry on. Amazing stuff. I don't think you'd get away with it today. Actually, they didn't really get away with it then, either.

Everyone connected with the programme – crew, cast, writers – was in a rhythm, and tightly locked into it. They had to be, because of the time constraints. Anything that interrupted the schedule was potentially ruinous and therefore not to be countenanced. Normally they had a number of staff directors that they would call on in rotation. So, in fact, it was a bit of a closed shop. But on one of the episodes I was in, all the staff directors were unavailable for some reason, which handed an outsider his chance. So in came a new director who, unfortunately, made the cardinal error of trying to be a bit creative. He eased himself in by playing according to the rules for a couple of episodes, and then he decided to push the boundaries. He wrote out his camera plot – his plan for all the camera moves – handed it to the crew and retreated to the gantry to command the camera run-through from there.

Now, the director's half of the conversation that ensued was inaudible to me because it was conducted through headphones to the cameramen and sound crew. However, I was on the set, waiting in another portion of it for my scene, so I could hear what the crew were saying back to the director through their microphones, and it went something like this:

'I won't be able to.'

Pause.

'No, it's in the way.'

Pause.

'But I won't be able to.'

Pause.

'You really want me to go in that close?'

Pause.

'But what about the carpet?'

Pause.

'All right, all right, whatever you want.'

Time for the camera run-through. The camera – a big old lump of metal in those days, on a substantial set of wheels which had to be wrestled around by hand – does indeed, despite the cameraman's declared reservations, go in 'that close'. But, as it does so, it catches on the edge of the carpet and forces it up ahead of itself. As a result, the actors on the set are suddenly confronted by this giant wave of carpet coming towards them – a kind of Wilton tsunami.

Cue a humbled director: 'Er, OK, let's try that without moving in.'

Camera crew 1, Director 0.

You had to hand it to the bloke for wanting to try something different. At the same time, he picked the wrong show. You didn't think outside the box on *Crossroads*. You thought entirely within the box. The box was king. After four episodes, that director was gone – I thought forever. But, blessedly, he survived. I saw his name come up on many shows in the years after this and he became quite a successful producer. Good manners forbid me to name him.

My character was called Bernie Killroy. Did the scriptwriters get the surname from the famous Second World War-era shipbuilder who always left his moniker on the ships he worked on – 'Killroy was here'? Perhaps they did. What's certain is that the gradual creep of madness into the storylines (madness which would eventually give the world the one where Meg's new husband attempted to murder her; the one where Meg ran over someone in the car park; and in perhaps the signature moment of desperation, the one where the motel was blown up) was even now beginning to stir. In fact, I like to think I was at the cutting edge of that eventually famous tendency in the show's plotting. Bernie began life as a crooked boxing manager. The boxer I was managing was played by John Hamill, a fit, handsome man whose fame and general desirability had brought him an excess of female attention. (John once boasted to me that he had enjoyed some careful ministrations from a female accomplice while doing 100mph on the M1. Talk about going too fast.) And what do you know? Bernie Killroy turned out to be a complete and utter rogue, a thief, a cheat, a liar and, apart from that, a bit of a cad, not to mention completely unreliable. I might have seemed to have John's best interests as a boxer at heart, but all the while I was hatching an outrageous plot to steal a whole fistful of money from the motel.

And what do you also know? Meg discovered my dastardly plot just in the knickers of time, saved the day and sent Bernie on his way with an instruction never to darken her motel sheets again. On your bike, Bernie. And on your bike, me. Without further ado, I trousered a handsome fee and waved goodbye to *Crossroads* forever, because all new actors and actresses were brought in on three-month contracts and your storyline was likely to last exactly that long and no more.

Except it didn't. A couple of months later, in the autumn of 1966, Bernie was back, bringing me with him. At the end of an episode, by way of a cliffhanger, an unsuspecting Nolly, in the middle of organising a dinner party, had to enter from the kitchen, catch sight of someone, or something, and drop a tray of crockery in shock. Cue theme and end credits.

Cut to the next night's episode. We see Nolly do the thing where she drops the tray of crockery in shock again. Cue me, standing at the head of the table: 'Hello, Meg.'

Unutterably shocking for Meg, of course, and for fans of the show across the nation – but good news for me, because it meant another well-paid week or two. Oddly, though, Bernie was no longer the feckless, light-fingered reprobate who had almost brought Nolly's business to its knees on his last appearance. Suddenly, he was a sunny, life-enhancing chappy, in whose mouth butter would remain unspreadable. Alas, I can't exactly recall the storyline by which this personal transformation was explained. Over the precise details, time has drawn its kindly net curtains. It's perfectly possible, though, that Bernie's change of heart wasn't explained at all. Characters were undergoing personality transplants in *Crossroads* all the time, as new scriptwriters came and went.

However, I do recall that, at the end of that stint, the producer took me aside and told me they wanted to make Bernie a fixture – a regular character.

'How would you feel about joining the show full-time?'

That pulled me up pretty sharp. It was quite an offer. My contract with Bromley Rep had come to an end by this time. Working on *Crossroads* was obviously going to mean good money (£76 per week, to be specific), and steady money, at a time when I couldn't guarantee myself either of those things. It would also mean relocating to the Midlands – but when you considered the professional certainty on offer, that could have been an upheaval worth enduring. I asked for some time to think about it, back at home in London. And then, after much thought over the next few days – carefully mulling over such key aspects as the money, the security, the money, the fame, the money, the opportunities to open supermarkets, possibly for even more money – I decided to take the risk.

'No thanks,' I said.

Now that was quite bold of me, if I may be allowed to say so. Regular television work was nice, obviously, and it's always good to be wanted. To be offered a part on one of the nation's most popular television shows only one year after making the decision to turn professional as an actor was quite a result, too. The thought process was maybe naive, but it went something like this: I wanted to be an actor, meaning I wanted to play different characters in different things. I think if you'd asked me in that period where I saw myself headed – and if I'd given you an honest answer – I'd have said the National Theatre. In my mind, that was the pinnacle. If you could rise there, you were clearly an actor of weight and substance. Lofty ambitions aside, though, what I loved about acting was the chance it gave you to adapt. The idea of playing one character, and one character alone, for the foreseeable future, maybe forever . . . well, as lucrative and comfortable as that would have been, it had the slight look of a trap to me. I bit my lip and moved on.

* * *

WHAT I MOVED on to wasn't the National Theatre, as it happened. It was to an audition for a new musical. Now, this really was going to be a big departure for me, for the very good reason that I can't sing. Never have been able to, never will be able to. And not being able to sing is, for fairly obvious reasons, likely to limit your opportunities, when it comes to musicals.

My agent thought I shouldn't be discouraged, though. She said she knew a good singing teacher and she reckoned that, with one decent session with him, I probably ought to be able to knock up a passable version of 'If I Were a Rich Man' from *Fiddler on the Roof* – enough to pass muster at the audition, at any rate. And then we could take it from there.

Well, it was my duty to be up for absolutely anything at this crucial formative stage in my professional life, so I duly went off and had a lesson with the prescribed music teacher. It was a fairly rough session, all things considered, one in which I perhaps surprised the teacher with the full extent of my incompetence. Certainly, when I opened my mouth for the first time, I don't recall his eyes lighting up in a way that suggested he'd found a new Pavarotti. We pretty quickly discovered that I had problems with pitch and timing – especially timing. Nor did I have a natural tone. And my phrasing wasn't much cop, either. But apart from that, I was fine.

So, less than confident, I attended the audition on the appointed afternoon. They called me and I came on from the wings. There were four or five people on the auditioning panel, sitting in the stalls. I believe one of them was Ned Sherrin. 'Do you have a piece of music for us?' one of them said. I did indeed: I was carrying in my sweaty mitts the sheet music for 'If I Were a Rich Man'. There was a pianist in the stalls. When he stood up, I could just see his head. I handed him my music, and then he sat down and disappeared. The next thing I heard was the sound of the piano starting up, and then continuing for a little bit, and then stopping.

Up came the pianist's head.

'Everything all right?'

'Yes,' I said.

'Can you hear me OK?'

'Oh yes,' I said. 'I can hear you fine.'

'OK,' said the pianist. 'It's just that I played the intro and you didn't come in.'

'Didn't I?' I said.

'No,' he said. 'But let's try again.'

His head went back down and the piano started up once more. I waited for what I thought might be my moment. (Problems with timing: the teacher wasn't wrong about those.) And then the piano stopped again.

Up came the pianist's head.

'What happened?'

I said, 'Did I miss it again?'

He said, 'I'm afraid so.'

The pianist thought for a moment. I could sense some restlessness coming from the panel in the stalls.

'I tell you what,' the pianist said, 'I'll nod.'

'OK,' I said.

So, the pianist's head disappears again, the music begins and then, after a few bars (I believe that's the technical word), he jumps up from his seat so that his head appears briefly in my line of vision above the edge of the stage, nods and then drops down again. And, on that more than faintly comical cue, I was away.

I have no idea how that rendition of 'If I Were a Rich Man' went. I only know that eventually the piano came to a dramatic finish and that, shortly after that, so did I.

'Thank you,' was, I think, as much as they had to say about it in the stalls.

After that they made me do a bit of acting, which I was a lot more comfortable with. And then there was one last test.

'We just want to see what your range is,' somebody said.

I wasn't expecting this. This wasn't in the script.

'My . . . range?' I said.

'Yes. You know – how high you can sing, how low you can sing?'

'Right,' I said.

'Do you know the song "Somewhere Over the Rainbow" from *The Wizard of Oz?*'

I said, hesitatingly, 'Er, yes . . .'

They said, 'Could you just give us a couple of lines from the beginning?'

I said, 'Bloody hell. Must I?'

Actually I didn't say that. But it was what I was thinking. You don't have to know much about music to know that 'Somewhere Over the Rainbow' starts with a big sweep, from low to high. The first word of the song is 'Somewhere' and the distance from the 'some' to the 'where' is not a journey for the faint-hearted. It's quite a test, even in the privacy of your own bathroom, let alone on a stage in front of someone who was possibly Ned Sherrin.

The pianist gave me a note. I went for it, missed, and found a clutch of other notes instead which I then chased as hard as I could in the approximate direction of the song. I must have sounded like a leaf-blower.

'Thank you,' they said, again.

I didn't get the part.

But I did learn an important lesson about myself. I can't sing.

Hang on, though . . . didn't I already know that?

*   *   *

I HAD A better time at an audition for a production of *Peter Pan* that I went for in late 1966. There was no singing involved, nobody asked to test my range and I ended up landing a part as one of the pirates. That might not sound much, but this particular *Peter Pan* was a pretty prestigious production. It was booked to open on a glorious set (a towering mast, a multi-decked pirate ship, the works) at the Strand Theatre in London – my first experience of playing in the West End. And then, after a three-week run, it was scheduled to tour the country – my first experience of that, as well. I was in starry company, too. Peter Pan was Julia Lockwood, the daughter of the famous film actress Margaret Lockwood, and the owner of one of the world's most wonderful smiles. Captain Hook was Ron Moody.

This was a bit of a dream for me. I was already a big fan of Moody. I had been to the original London stage production of the musical *Oliver!* and seen him play Fagin. (The film version, which made him enormously famous, came later, a year after the *Peter Pan* production, in 1968.) A wonderful bit of business he did onstage that night was lodged in my mind forever. It was a scene where Fagin was counting money on a table, very quickly sorting these coins into piles and slapping them down on the surface so that, as well as being a mesmerising piece of quick-handedness, the whole routine had this brilliant noise and rhythm to it – chik-chik-chik-chik, slap! chik-chik-chik-chik, slap! Superb.

Watching him work from close up was a real privilege. The same goes for working with Julia Lockwood, though she could be quite sharp. I was in the wings alongside her one night when

Ron made an exit after a scene with his manservant, Smee. The scene had ended with Captain Hook grandly putting out an arm for his cloak – but Smee is standing behind Hook, dutifully holding up the cloak on the other side. So Smee meekly jumps round to take the cloak to the extended arm. But by the time he gets there, Hook has put that arm down and extended the other one. There was a little bit of toing and froing like this, and some knockabout stuff, with Hook getting more and more huffy and Smee wincing and getting into more and more of a mess, before Hook snatched the cloak, and off they both came.

As Ron passed Julia backstage, I heard her say to him: 'There's a round there.' Meaning she thought the moment could get a round of applause, if it were done properly. People had laughed, but they hadn't applauded. 'Donald always got a round there,' she added. She was referring to Donald Sinden, who had played Hook in another production of *Peter Pan* that Julia was in.

This clearly got to Ron. He didn't like coming off worse in a comparison with Donald Sinden. He interpreted it as a challenge. Over the next two or three performances, he really began to work at that moment with Smee and the cloak – expanding it and eking the maximum amount of humour out of it. Sure enough, at around the fourth attempt, he left the stage to applause. He had got his round.

Ron was a sensational performer altogether and a terrific improviser when things went wrong. One of Hook's props was a tin lamp, meant to look like a candle behind glass, which was actually battery-operated, for convenience purposes, with a switch on it. At one point Ron was supposed to enter in the darkness with the lamp switched off and shout, in despair, 'Something blew out the lamp.' One night, unfortunately, something hadn't blown out the lamp. It was still on. The audience began to laugh. Ron looked very slowly from the lamp to the audience and said, 'Something *tried* to blow out the lamp.' He got a round of applause for that, too.

You couldn't help but learn from the experience of being around people like that. Indeed, this whole period was a huge learning curve. One very important lesson I picked up by observation during that production: never be rude, arrogant or otherwise objectionable to the member of the backstage crew whose job it is to fly you on the wire. One of the Lost Boys came to understand this the hard way. He had begun to get above himself, as the production wore on, and he was being a bit high and mighty with the crew – bossing people about, complaining if things weren't exactly as they were meant to be. Big mistake. When you're all harnessed up and ready for a flying scene, you're in a very vulnerable position. You're basically a puppet – attached to strings that someone else is in control of. Even when you were getting on perfectly well with the crew, they would often muck about and put the fear of God into you. You would be standing in the wings, wired up and waiting to go, and the person responsible for hauling on the wire would just gently lift you up onto your toes, making you panic and think he was about to send you flying out onto the stage before your cue. And then he would equally gently set you back on your feet. And then he would put you up on your toes again, and set you back on your feet again – just twitching the wire, messing with your mind.

The point is, the Lost Boy with the attitude problem had upset the wrong people. One night, for the scene where the Lost Boys flew onto the ship and fought a battle with the pirates, a member of the crew gave that guy's wire the most almighty tug. He took off like a rocket. Instead of landing gently where he was supposed to land, he went smack into the mast and fluttered down like a smashed butterfly. He then had to sit on the deck in a heap, gathering his senses, while the rest of us fought around him. He was very careful in front of the crew after that.

After the West End run, the show packed up and, with a

Me and Micky Weedon in Tony Brighton's backyard playing horseshoes because we thought it made us look like cowboys.

With Bob Bevil on holiday in Jersey. London boys, ladykillers, electricians.

Early thesping in *The Glass Menagerie* with the Incognito Theatre Group at Friern Barnet at the beginning of the sixties.

With Brian Babb and Vera Neck in an Incognito production of *Epitaph for George Dillon*.
Already working the sofa for business.

Early 1960s. Having a lovely war in *Journey's End*. The Incogs took up more and more of my evenings.

Weedon and White roll up their shirtsleeves and get down to some serious acting. Rehearsal for the Incogs' *Noah*.

Me on the phone to my agent during *The Teahouse of the August Moon* in the mid-sixties.

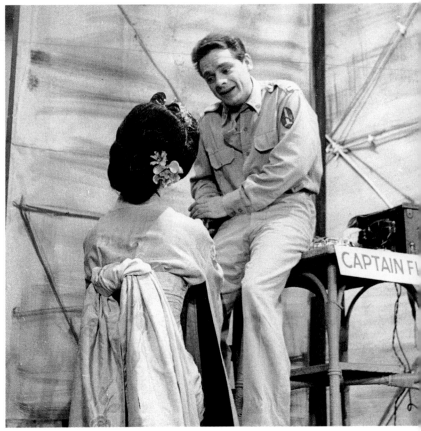

The Teahouse of the August Moon again. I was on loan to the St Bride's Players of Fleet Street.

Best man at Malcolm Taylor's wedding. This was the only time in the whole day that I took off the top hat.

With the inimitable Leslie Sarony in *Peter Pan*, 1966. Pirates ahoy.

Return of the vents. Arthur and I give it some gottle of geer in the late sixties.

Clockwise: Denise Coffey, Eric Idle, me, Terry Jones and Mike Palin before the operation.

Serious business. Touring *The Norman Conquests* with Roger Hammond and the Oxford Theatre Company, late 1960s.

With Lynda Bellingham in some exciting knitwear. *The Norman Conquests* again.

Buttons in panto. To the left of me, Sylvester McCoy, warming up for Doctor Who. To my right, David Rappaport warming up for being David Rappaport.

First big West End role: the hapless Brian Runnicles in *No Sex Please – We're British*, Strand Theatre, 1973.

Touring *No Sex Please* in the Far East with Helen Gill and Geoffrey Davies.

slightly scaled-down cast, set off on tour. I was enormously excited at the prospect. Indeed, I was so excited that I used it as an excuse to treat myself to a thick fur coat I'd seen hanging in the window of a boutique called Lord John, quite near to the fire station on Shaftesbury Avenue. It was a caramel-coloured coney, with buttons the size of a baby's head, and it was so huge on me that it had to be taken up at the back to stop it dragging on the ground. When it was buttoned up, I, to all intents and purposes, disappeared and became, instead, a walking teddy bear.

I can't recall now what I paid for this stately garment but I do know that I flushed as I handed over the cash. I had persuaded myself, though, that, at least to some extent, this was a practical purchase. I reasoned that a big chunk of fur wouldn't go amiss while out on tour, especially in the colder climes we were set to visit up north, and that it would even service me with an additional bedspread to supply the overnight insulation not provided by certain landladies' pitifully thin sheets. And I wasn't wrong about that. Many were the winter nights when sleep was made possible for me in such places as Aberdeen and Newcastle by the primitive method of lumping an animal skin on top of myself.

Deep down, though, I knew that I had bought the coat as a statement. Clothes never really meant all that much to me and, even in the ragingly fashion-conscious sixties, and even though I was located right at the heart of swinging London, were nothing I particularly bothered about, beyond the odd fancy addition of a jauntily tied silk scarf. But I fancied myself very much the sixties gentleman in that coat – more than that, an actor about town. I wore it until it was completely denuded of fur around the buttons and until the bits of fur that hadn't dropped off were dry and stiff and only lightly rooted in its cracked leather. That fur served me handsomely as coat and impromptu bedding up and down the British Isles, not just during *Peter Pan* but for quite a while after. By the end of its life, I looked like a teddy bear that someone had had for eighty years. (And probably smelt a bit like one, as well, but let's not dwell on that.)

On tour, the atmosphere of a school trip prevailed. The cast travelled together in a hired coach – although not the stars. Julia and Ron went separately. They also stayed in hotels, whereas we had to find our own digs in each city. Transport was provided, in other words, but not accommodation. You would ask around among your fellow actors for tips on the best and cheapest bed-and-breakfast places in which to stay. If that failed, there was always a list of landladies at the stage door. I was to do a lot of time in B&Bs as a touring actor in the early seventies, and I will come on to some of the drawbacks, and even the horrors, in due course. This first time, though, the whole touring life was new to me and I found it all positively romantic.

Julia Lockwood remained a little apart from the more humble among us, even on tour. You would get a 'Good evening' as she passed through the theatre, but that was about it. Mostly she spent her time in the company of her travelling female assistant. Ron, on the other hand, was happy to muck in and often came out with us all for a meal after shows. We usually ended up in Indian restaurants because they combined the virtues of being cheap and open until late. It was Ron, I believe, who decided to take decisive action against the amount of random flatulence that seemed to beset our social group, particularly on the way back to digs after these curried meals. Wherever we were, Ron took it upon himself to nominate what he called 'the flatting post' – which might be a pillar or a lamp post or a postbox, according to his whim. Subsequently, anyone wishing to vacate themselves of accumulated wind had to be touching the post when they did so or else a punishment would be levied. Ron was good company – always ready with a joke or an impression. He did the best impersonation of Alastair Sim I had ever seen.

On other nights, a few of us pirates would take ourselves out to a nightclub in a forlorn attempt to meet girls. You might get as far as opening a conversation in which a girl asked you where you were from and what you did. 'I'm an actor,' you would say, as suavely as you could. 'I'm up from London.' That was it. The girls as good as turned their backs and fled. It didn't sink in with us for ages that, if you came out and said you were a visiting actor, a girl immediately knew you were only there for a week, and were most likely only after one thing. It seemed to be just about the worst calling card you could present. Better by far to say you were an electrician, frankly. Accordingly, we couldn't pull girls to save our lives when we were on tour. By contrast, the gay members of our fraternity seemed to be having a high old time. It didn't matter which city we were in, they always seemed to know where to go to find willing company. That used to really wind us up. They would come in the next day with their tales of exotic conquests and exhausting nights of passion, and we'd be spitting feathers.

Frustrations aside, this was a happy time, darkened by only one moment. My piratical prop in one scene of the show was, for some reason, a bugle on a lanyard, which I used to sling around my neck. All the props used to be gathered on the props table backstage, so that you could collect what you needed just before your entrance. I always seemed to be beaten to the props table by a particular pirate who thought it was amazingly amusing to say to me, 'Do you want your prop?' And then he would toss the bugle towards me but hold on to the lanyard so that, just as the instrument was reaching me, he could tug it back to himself, out of the air, and catch it. It was quite funny at first, I suppose, but slightly wearing after the twenty-third time. Alas, one night this pirate went through his usual bugle-lobbing routine, but accidentally let the lanyard slip.

Result: I was caught smack on the eyebrow by a big lump of brass trumpet.

A wound immediately opened and began to bleed copiously

down the side of my face. The pirate was stricken with remorse. Someone grabbed a cloth, which I wadded up and pressed to my eye before heading off to the stage to complete the scene I was due to play, with one hand held to my eyebrow. After curtain-down, I was straight off to hospital for stitches – and not for the first time in my life, as you may recall. I thought the plaster might present a problem. You don't see too many pirates with Elastoplast on their faces. Conveniently, however, I found I could draw an eyebrow on the plaster in make-up and nobody was any the wiser.

Lesson: the show goes on, even if someone has just brained you with a musical instrument.

Call us opportunistic, but a number of us pirates, looking ahead in the schedule, noticed that our production of *Peter Pan* was due to perform onstage at Stratford – the home, of course, of the Royal Shakespeare Company, the very pinnacle of acting excellence. Well, here was a chance which a young pirate with ambition in his heart and an Elastoplast on his eyebrow could surely not miss. Four or five of us duly hatched a plan to call the RSC, mention we were going to be in town, and ask if we could come in and see someone about the possibility of joining the company.

Flaming brass neck, I think you would have to call this. But it's always been true that if you don't ask, you don't get. So one of us rang up – I can't remember who, but we were all in on it, and very much a team in this respect. To our surprise, the RSC's response was not 'Go away and stop wasting our time, you horrible little pirates'; it was 'OK, then, come in and see us one afternoon when you're in town'.

General excitement plus much back-slapping ensued. So, come the appointed hour, each of us was seen in turn in a room at the RSC by a kindly young casting director who had taken the time out of her afternoon to meet us. And I, of course, was immediately offered Hamlet, starting that night.

All right, I wasn't. I couldn't have done it anyway because I was otherwise disposed, giving my Gentleman Starkey to Ron Moody's Captain Hook. After a bit of a chat, I was gently sent on my way with the casting director's very best wishes. All of us were. And fair enough: we were just pirates. But I think we were heartened that the RSC, of all places, had taken the trouble to see us and at least give us a chance. We were all taught an important lesson: big doors aren't always as locked as they appear to be, not even to pirates. You might as well give them a rattle and see what happens.

The name of that casting director, incidentally, was Meg Poole. There's an old saying: 'Be nice to people on the way up because you never know whether you're going to meet them on the way down.' And it almost applies in this case. Meg eventually left the RSC, became an agent, joined the Richard Stone agency and, many years after this, ascended to a partnership in the company, where she ended up very skilfully and very patiently looking after the career of . . . me. Which she continues to do today. It's a small world, piracy.

Anyway, even if the RSC had turned me down, the future was bright. I knew as much because a psychic told me. Another little on-tour excursion found me in the front room of a council house in Birmingham, having my destiny foretold for the price of a few pieces of silver – or probably a note, actually, allowing for the effects of inflation. I was led this way in a taxi one morning by two excited actresses who swore by the prescience of this famous psychic and insisted I go along with them for a visit.

I regret to say that memory, and the Random House legal team, have erased this august seer's professional name from my recollection. Let's be content to call her Mystic Mavis.

To be honest, this kind of thing was more my dear sister June's area than mine. Nevertheless, when it was my turn, Mystic Mavis ushered me into her humble parlour and, while the girls waited out in the hall, I sat opposite her at a small table. She was a neat, middle-aged woman in civvies – no headscarf or spangled shawl, or any of that nonsense. She didn't use a crystal ball or cards, either. She simply worked from your presence – which is a good trick if you can do it, and very much cheaper on props.

'You're in the theatre,' Mystic Mavis told me.

'I am,' I said, because she was right: I was. At the same time, she wouldn't have needed to be a genius to work that out, would she, with the three of us trooping in, all with London accents? One of us could have let something slip, even if our appearance, manner, underslept demeanour and perhaps even vague but persistent smell didn't betray us straight away as travelling players.

'I see sparks around you,' Mavis went on. 'Are you possibly an electrician?' She paused. 'In the theatre?'

Blimey. Now, hold on. That wasn't bad. That was quite impressive. I mean, wrong about me being an electrician in the theatre, but right about me being an electrician. Maybe I still bore the aura from that time I got electrocuted while rewiring the girls' school in Highgate. Mavis then moved on from telling me things about my present that I already knew and began to explore the bigger topic, from my point of view: my future.

'I can see your name in big red letters,' she intoned, 'above the title of a play in the West End of London.'

Yeah, well, nice idea, obviously, and thanks for your time. But dream on, Mavis.

* * *

IN THE LONDON cast of *Peter Pan*, playing a squaw, was Carol Collins, a dancer and a skater who also worked on ice shows. She was very attractive, a great girl, and eventually she and I started going out – in as much as people working in the theatre could be said to 'go out'. The hours you worked didn't make that easy. You really only had Sundays to spend together.

Carol lived with her mother just off the North Circular, near the Hanger Lane gyratory, one of London's premier congested junctions, made eternally famous by radio traffic reports. Carol had a brother called Phil, I remember, who fancied himself as a bit of a drummer. When I went round to the house to pick her up, he would often be in his bedroom, thundering away like a loony. I don't think he particularly took to me at first – but then I was the idiot walking out with his sister. However, one day, when he was coerced down from his eyrie, maybe to partake in food, he took a shine to the leather jacket I used to wear. I let him put it on and he had his photograph taken wearing it.

Nice lad. I wonder what happened to Phil Collins. It would be good to think that it had worked out for him and that he'd had some success somewhere down the line.

Carol and I went out together for two years and then we broke up. There was no particular reason; it just happens like that sometimes. Then one afternoon in 1972, when I was working in the West End in *No Sex Please – We're British*, I bumped into her. I was walking to the Strand Theatre – something I loved to do in those days, ambling through the London streets, anticipating the show ahead and feeling generally glad to be alive – and there she was. We hadn't seen each other in ages and I invited her to see the show. We talked afterwards and almost straight away I was right back where I used to be with her and we were off again. I was on my own at the time, and she was as well – two lost souls.

And, actually, I do know what became of Phil. Carol took me to the Theatre Royal, Drury Lane, to see Genesis. I had never been to a rock concert. But Carol was the squeeze and this was her brother, so along I went. It was an eye-opening experience – and very theatrical, actually. Tremendous lighting, deafening sound, high production values. In one of the numbers, they had the singer, Peter Gabriel, strapped to a cross and, with smoke billowing and lights flashing, they slowly flew him out to the flies and away. I thought, 'How do they get away with that?' Everybody in the audience went potty. I'd never seen anything like it. The ringing in my ears took forty-eight hours to clear.

Soon after this, Carol and I separated again. Nothing to do with Genesis, I hasten to add, or the night they crucified Peter Gabriel. The split was my fault. I began to feel I was getting in too deep. I was immature and once again I got frightened about going down a road that would lead to responsibilities – responsibilities that might, in turn, take me away from the theatre. I think that was what drove the wedge. There could have been no other reason.

It happened a number of times. It happened with Fanny Barlow, who wanted us to shack up together. It happened before that, with Sylvia. When the person I was with got too close or I felt that I was getting too involved, I drew away. I was very adept at snuffing out the spark, I'm sorry to say. An absolute expert at it.

I don't suppose it exactly helped me to develop long-term relationships in those days I was away from home so much, on the road with touring plays. Touring was a peculiarly Victorian experience in that period – the late 1960s and early 1970s. You travelled on Sunday, when any journey of any length took all day because there would be work on the railway line and a replacement bus service would be in operation much of the way. All routes passed through Crewe, and on Sunday at Crewe station, everything was closed, so you couldn't get anything to eat. You would have to leave the station and try and find a bun somewhere. Sometimes at the station you would run into other little groups of actors heading off in another direction, and exchange a grudging nod of sympathy.

Eventually you would arrive at your next location, for the

next week or two of work, and the search would begin for digs. Sometimes, if you were lucky, you would have a tip-off: 'If you're going to Birmingham, you must get in touch with Mrs So-and-So.' There were a few famous landladies whom you tried to get to stay with because they had a reputation for being nicer and more tolerant than the others. They would give you a key to let yourself in with, for instance, whereas others would stick to a strict curfew and lock you out if you missed it. Or they might have a reputation for offering cotton sheets and pillow-cases, as opposed to the usual cheap Bri-nylon bedding, which either caused you to slip out of bed altogether during the night, or sent a static surge through your system that left your hair standing on end for the next fourteen hours.

Even the nicest and most liberal establishments, though, operated a firm 'no overnight guests' rule. This, too, could be overcome, though only, one keenly felt, at the expense of grave personal risk to both parties. More than once was the occasion when I returned, extremely quietly, to the room of a female colleague, only to be woken in the morning by the inquisitive tapping on the door of the landlady. At which point I would be obliged to take cover by scrambling, partly clothed, into the wardrobe. Farcical, I suppose you might call it. Let no one say that life never imitated art, or vice versa.

I tremblingly recall staying in one establishment which offered not only a strictly enforced curfew, an unbreakable 'no overnight guests' rule and Bri-nylon sheets, but also the presence of the landlady's four cats, meaning that most of the surfaces were lightly coated in moulted fur. I came down in the morning to a breakfast of bacon, egg and beans, and hungrily raised my knife and fork above the plate, only to look down and notice a cat's hair floating on the yolk of the egg.

Didn't mean I didn't eat it, though. I picked the hair off and tucked in. Well, you had to, didn't you? Otherwise you'd starve.

Indeed, the trick was to find out what the latest possible time was for breakfast, and then to time your run so that you hit it exactly. Then, if you ate as much as you possibly could, it might mean that you didn't have to spend any money at lunchtime. Smart thinking.

It was a terribly frugal existence, then – and also, from time to time, a properly depressing one. The conviviality of the cast and crew and the sense of being part of the travelling circus couldn't always be relied upon to sustain you. Despondency would creep up and seize its moment to lay you low – often, in my case, during free hours and while availing myself of a brief opportunity for tourism. Up at Hadrian's Wall was one such occasion. I remember staring at a section of that ancient monument one day and feeling bleaker than if you had asked me to rebuild it.

But, most memorably, I recall sitting on a bench one afternoon, looking up at the outside of Lincoln Cathedral, and feeling about as far from home and as unutterably lonely as I had ever felt. At that point, the thought uppermost in my mind was, roughly speaking, 'Why am I doing this? What kind of way is this to spend your life?'

CHAPTER SEVEN

A problem with sugar lumps. A mess made with some yogurt. And a monumental coming-together at the end of a pier with Dick Emery.

In those early days, in the mid-to-late sixties, my agent sometimes rang me up and asked if I fancied appearing in a commercial for television or cinema. I invariably did fancy it. Anything that might lead to something else, was my general philosophy of employment back then. And, as a result, I am one of a very small number of actors who can say, in all honesty, that they have dived into a giant teacup in order to outline the unique merits of Tetley tea bags.

And don't knock it: it sounds unlikely now, but that may actually have been one of the most dangerous professional appointments I ever took on. The reason I got the job was not just on account of my diminutive stature but also because, as my agent was well aware, I was one of a very small number of actors who was a trained diver. Now, you don't get many of those in a tea bag.

(My diving experience at this point: I had some proper lessons with Wood Green Civil Defence Association, on the recommendation of a friend, at the age of about eighteen. We followed up with some open-water diving sessions in a gravel pit in Hoddesdon. It was winter and you had to break the ice to get down. The water was so murky that, frankly, you might as well have been suspended in tea, so this was doubly good training.)

The set-up required me to squeeze into a white wetsuit and then plunge down into an enormous cup of tea. Then I had to swim to the surface to report that the flavour had, indeed, flowed out of the tea bag, via its cunning perforations, and into the enveloping water, and not got stuck inside, which I suppose could plausibly have been the concern of potential customers in the early days of the tea bag, when the magic was still new. And then, in the visual pay-off, having set everyone's mind to rest, I had to look above me, say something to the effect of 'Uh-oh', go wide-eyed with panic, and then duck to spare myself getting clobbered from above by a pair of giant sugar lumps.

No CGI in those days, of course: no noodling this scene together on a computer afterwards; no jumping up and down in front of a blue screen for a few minutes and then going home to let the pixel-boffins do the rest. In the mid-sixties, if you wanted to be filmed diving into a cup of tea and then being pelted with sugar lumps, you had no option but to build a cup of tea big enough to dive into, and a pair of sugar lumps big enough to be pelted with. And then the diving and the pelting actually had to happen. Accordingly, on the day, I arrived to find cup, tea bag and lumps of an appropriate scale ready and waiting, along with a suitable quantity of brown-coloured water. And, of course, that tight white wetsuit.

Incidentally, the problems they had with that brown water – trying to get the shade of brown right, to the satisfaction of the people from Tetley, who were obviously very fussy about how their product was going to be portrayed. It went through many phases – from puddle to wet dog. It was ages before everyone was happy.

So we went for a take. And all went well, until we got to

the end. There was a problem with the sugar lumps: they floated, and remained floating for about ten minutes before they sank. Sugar lumps, as practical experiment in domestic settings has long since proved, don't do that. Sugar lumps sink. So a means had to be devised of causing the sugar lumps to go under. They were made from wire mesh, coated with plaster of Paris, and the method chosen involved splitting the lumps open and putting weights inside them. Big weights. Stage weights, to be specific – the blocks of steel they use to hold stage flats in place, a number of which happened to be hanging around near the set. They started off putting one of these weights inside and then going for a take to see what it looked like. Now it sank – but not in a realistic enough way. So they continued adding weights until everyone was happy that the lumps behaved as sugar lumps might. By the end of this incremental weight-increase process, I looked up from my position, treading brown water in the teacup, and noticed, to my alarm, that it was now taking two props boys to manhandle each one of these cubes.

I now found myself dressed like a sperm in Woody Allen's *Everything You Always Wanted to Know About Sex* and dodging an artificial sugar lump weighing about the same as a baby elephant. As it whistled past me, it felt like I had been blasted full in the face by a strong wind. There is no question that, if I hadn't managed to flip aside as the sugar lump narrowly slipped past the skin on the end of my nose, I would have been splattered all over the teacup by the second one. Forget the tea bag; the flavour would have ended up flowing out of me. Health and safety: where were you then?

With a considerably more slender degree of danger, I also did a commercial with my brother Arthur around this time. Arthur and I had a little ventriloquist act that we had worked up for special occasions. He would be the ventriloquist and I would be the doll – an extremely disobedient doll. We got a very small pair of trousers, stuffed the legs with socks and rags and attached small wellington boots to them. I would tie these altered trousers around my waist using a belt, and then stand behind a chair, flopping the wellies over the chair back, and Arthur would stand alongside me, as the ventriloquist, and pretend to work me. If I put make-up on so that my jaw looked hinged and my mouth seemed unnaturally large, the effect was quite amusing.

A friend of Malcolm Taylor's was a casting director for commercials and she had seen us do this routine, so one day, when she happened to be looking for a vent act for a yogurt advertisement, she asked us if we fancied having a go. We thought, 'Nothing ventured.' So we went along to the audition and ended up sitting in a waiting room with about half a dozen genuine vent acts, all holding their dolls – a slightly awkward scene, as you might imagine. Eventually, it was our turn. The director sat us down and had us do some business with a yogurt pot. I was supposed to conclude the skit by putting the spoonful of yogurt in my mouth. Instead, by way of a final flourish, I took the spoonful of yogurt and rammed it in my ear. It was just something I thought of on the spur of the moment. This seemed to clinch it. We got the job.

Such were the things I was prepared to do in those slightly unfocused early days. I dreamed of being an actor, and I'd stick yogurt in my ear if I thought it would get a laugh and advance my cause.

* * *

IN APRIL 1967, I got a small part in *The Dick Emery Show* on BBC television. Dick was a damn good stand-up comic and also a drag act, and he was a huge star at the time. His catchphrase entered the language: 'Oooh, you are awful – but I like you.' He turned the affectionate but over-forceful whack with a handbag into an art form, and nobody stumbled in heels while walking up a street the way Dick Emery did. People loved him.

My moment on the show, basking in the light cast by his skirt-wearing glory, came and went in the blink of an eye, but I seemed to make an impression on him. Dick was booked to do a summer season at the Pier Theatre in Bournemouth that year, and when my name came up as a possible cast member, he was instrumental in getting me the job. I spent May in London, rehearsing the two shows we were taking down there, a pair of farces whose names, perhaps, betray their nature: *Chase Me, Comrade* and *Honeymoon Bedlam*. And then I packed my suitcase, slung it in the back of my new car and set off for the seaside.

New car? Yes, I had chopped in the trusty Mini Van for a Mini without the van bit – new, dark blue, found at a showroom in Finchley and bought, of course, on the never-never. I was very proud of that car.

That was my first taste of the joys of a summer season in an end-of-the-pier show – and I probably couldn't have found a better comic to undergo my initiation with than Dick Emery. Dick was formidably good at his job, and very serious and diligent in the way he went about what he did. After a while, though, when he got settled into the play and everything was up and running, the comic in him would re-emerge and he would get up to all sorts of nonsense.

Most of the contents of the plays now evade my memory's grasp, but I particularly remember a scene set in a hotel bedroom in *Honeymoon Bedlam* where I had the role of a young policeman sent to interview the hotel manager, who was played by John Newbury. Dick entered, dressed (surprise, surprise) as a woman, and at one point he would have to walk down to the front of the stage and then turn his back on the audience and address John and me, upstage centre. As soon as Dick knew the audience couldn't see his face, he'd start gurning at us, pulling the most horrendous faces – faces in which his lower lip seemed to pass up over his nose, faces wherein his eyes seemed to grow to the size of tennis balls and his chin to drag along the ground, faces which seemed to express the most alarming of sexual intentions towards us . . . the worst faces you have ever seen. This was all done, of course, with the intention of getting us to crack up and muff our lines. Dick was merciless. It wasn't enough for him to see you starting to go. He would keep at it until you went completely. It reached a point where even the audience could sense that he was up to something. They could hear the tremble in our voices and see that we had turned puce and were doing our best not to look at him. The audience didn't mind, of course. They loved that kind of stuff, coming from Dick, and, after all, this was seaside fare – people on holiday who were out for a good time. This was not the West End.

Dick was married to a dancer and a choreographer called Josephine Blake. This was his fifth marriage of five. However, there was a girl in the company who was very attractive. She turned Dick's head, and he decided he had to have her. So he set himself the task. He was quite brazen about it – very open about his courting of her. I couldn't believe his audacity, in a way. He came in with huge bunches of flowers and chocolates for this girl, wined her and dined her. He was a very charming man and she was powerless to resist. When Dick's wife came down from London, as she did from time to time, the rest of us had to put our heads down and pretend that nothing was going on. The affair lasted for the season – because that's all it was, for Dick: a season's affair. But I think the girl got quite broken-hearted about it at the end. She had taken it more seriously.

It's a wonder Dick had the time and energy for all this. When we were in Bournemouth he would do the stage show six nights a week and two matinees, and then on a Sunday, which was supposed to be his night off, he'd drive off to do a stand-up routine at a seaside joint somewhere else. I went with him one night to Swanage Pavilion. It was a revue show for the holidaymakers, with Dick top of the bill. He was on a percentage of the box office, so he was pulling down some tidy money for those appearances. And because it was a slightly different setting, he could do more risky, close-to-the-knuckle routines – be a bit more 'blue', as we used to say. The place went mad for him. I count Dick as one of the great British comics of that time. In my opinion, he was right up there with Bob Monkhouse as a gag-teller.

I loved that summer season. I was on £29 per week, which seemed relatively princely to me. I shared a dressing room at the theatre with John Newbury and on a nice day we could open its door and go out onto a small balcony and smell the briny sea. Of course, when the weather was rough, the entire play took place against the background roar of waves thundering against the legs of the pier. You often wondered whether, by the time the curtain fell, you would be halfway to France on a lump of wood.

To save a bit of money, I rented a little three-bedroom cottage in a leafy suburb with the actress Doremy Vernon, who later played the canteen manageress in *Are You Being Served?*, and a young actor who was my understudy. We worked out that it would be much cheaper than going into digs, and it also left us completely free to come and go as and when we pleased. On the occasions when we needed to pop back to London, I would cram Doremy and John Newbury into the Mini and give them a lift, dropping them off in Chiswick before I headed on back to my flat in Thornton Heath. Doremy had to travel in the front seat because she had been a dancer and her legs were too long to go in the back. It was John who had to hunch up back there, much to his chagrin and lasting discomfort.

Mostly, though, we stayed in Bournemouth on our days off and entertained ourselves there. David Browning was our company manager and also played a small part in *Chase Me, Comrade*. He was a keen fisherman and would often be down by the sea with his rod. He informed me that there were a lot of mullet in the water near the pier. That rather inspired me. I hired a speargun, a face mask and some flippers and spent a day spear-fishing under Bournemouth Pier. I ended up spearing half a dozen mullet, and then emerged from the water like Ursula Andress with the fish swinging from my belt. We took them back to the cottage and cooked them for supper.

It's no exaggeration to say that summer in Bournemouth was formative for me – and not just because it enabled me to observe Dick Emery from close quarters. It was where I forged a connection with the man who would shape the course of my career in so many ways and link me eventually with Ronnie Barker.

Humphrey Barclay was a television producer, not long out of working in radio. Rediffusion, the London ITV station, had put him in charge of creating a new comedy show for children. It was meant to be a revue show, with sketches and music, which I don't think children's television had gone in for before. Humphrey was partway through recruiting for it, and had already found some interesting and very talented, though as yet unknown, writers and actors who were recently out of university. Their names were Eric Idle, Michael Palin and Terry Jones. Humphrey was looking for another ingredient to add to the mix – someone who could do physical comedy.

Initially, his thoughts turned to my great friend Malcolm Taylor – known to you already as the director of the stage version of *Under Milk Wood*, and as a man who attempted to smuggle currency out of the country in his socks. Malcolm auditioned for Humphrey – and Humphrey gave him the job. Malcolm then did a remarkably selfless thing. He told Humphrey he should have a look at me. When I talked to Malcolm about this afterwards, he just said that he thought the work would be perfect for me – more perfect for me than for him. That's not the kind of thing that happens in our business very often. Most people cling to whatever opportunity they're given, and understandably. But not Malcolm. I was always enormously touched and grateful to him for that.

In order to have a look at me, Humphrey made the journey down to Bournemouth, and took his seat for an evening performance of *Chase Me, Comrade*. Now, Humphrey was a classics graduate from Cambridge, and a rather scholarly and intellectual man. I'm not sure that sitting among a crowd of lairy holiday-makers watching Dick Emery camping about the place in drag was naturally his first choice for a good night out. It didn't help either that, in *Chase Me, Comrade*, I didn't make my big entrance until the start of the second half of the play, so Humphrey had endured quite a lot before I even showed my face. Humphrey later confided to me that I came very close to playing to his empty seat. During the interval, he was right on the edge of cutting his losses, walking out into the good Bournemouth night and going back to plan A.

A fortuitous piece of timing, then. I owe so much of what subsequently happened in my career to Humphrey that I shiver to think what might have become of me had he not overcome his better judgement and forced himself to endure a few more minutes of end-of-the-pier farce.

So, at last, on I came. The first half of the play had concluded with everybody else running around after Dick Emery, who, unless my memory is deceiving me, was dressed up as a Russian ballerina. (I don't wish to accuse Humphrey of being fussy, but what's not to like about this set-up?) The second half opened with me arriving in an empty house, letting myself in through an ajar door at the centre of the set, and shouting, 'Anyone home? It's Bobby Hargreaves. I'm your new neighbour.' The stage remained empty. In the middle of the set, positioned at the foot of some steps, was a large ship's bell. During the play, this bell was used to summon everyone to dinner. The deal was that I'd ring the bell to find out if there was anybody home and, at that point, everyone would come back onstage.

However, I had the stage to myself. And, as the production went on, I sensed an opportunity and started to pad this little moment out. I'd taken to casting a good look around the place to ascertain that there was nobody around – I'd go from one side of the stage to the other, catch sight of this bell, move on, go back to it, gradually growing more interested in the bell, developing a longing to ring it, but behaving as if I didn't quite have the nerve . . . And I found I could take the audience right along with me, have them cracking up at my indecision and get them willing me to ring the bell – to the point where people would actually start shouting out from the stalls, 'Ring the bell! Ring the bell!'

It was like that business with the bongo drums, back in that Noël Coward production, my professional debut – the old Laurel and Hardy principle again, of knowing what's going to happen, but not knowing when. But it wasn't like that first time in Bromley, when I built my part up with the full blessing and collaboration of the director, Simon Oates. This was a hijack, pure and simple – the equivalent of an air steward wrestling the pilot aside and taking over the aeroplane.

The cast would all be in the wings, waiting for their cue, and I would be drawing this piece of business out for ages – not amusing all of those backstage, I have to admit. A couple made their displeasure known to me. Even the director asked me if I wouldn't mind reining it in a bit. And for the one and only time in my career, I flagrantly disobeyed the director's orders. If it hadn't been working, I'd have seen his point. But it *was* working, gloriously. In other words, I was doing what I enjoyed doing best, and that was making people laugh. And perhaps that business never worked more gloriously than the night Humphrey came to see me, when I pushed it as far as I'd ever dared to push it, working the crowd into a noisy frenzy of frustration.

156

And among those shouting 'Ring the bell!' that night? Cambridge classics graduate and reluctant end-of-the-pier show attendee Humphrey Barclay. (He admitted this to me afterwards.)

Which is how I came by a part in *Do Not Adjust Your Set*.

CHAPTER EIGHT

Children's entertainment beckons. I become a superhero.
And a couple of little things that got away.

It amuses me that the conversation which gave rise to so much of my career in television took place in the tiny, run-down bar of the Bournemouth Pier Theatre – not the world's ritziest watering hole, nor a venue that seemed to have much connection with the glamorous world of major broadcasting deals. Indeed, it was somewhere you would only have gone for a drink if you had been . . . well, marooned at the end of a pier with no other options.

Nevertheless, this was the place where Humphrey Barclay waited for me after the show, and we spoke for a while over a drink or two before he drove back to London. He was an impressive guy – clearly very bright. He was actually a year younger than me – twenty-six to my twenty-seven – yet I felt very much the junior party in the conversation. He was terribly well spoken and socially way above me, in class terms. And, as I mentioned, he had gone to Cambridge, where he had been in the Cambridge Footlights. He was part of that 1964 gang – with Tim Brooke-Taylor, Bill Oddie, John Cleese, Graham Chapman, among others – who put on the revue show *Cambridge Circus* and ended up taking it not just to the Edinburgh Festival but also to New Zealand and then, triumphantly, to Broadway. When he worked at the BBC, he was one of the founders of the comedy show *I'm Sorry, I'll Read That Again*. Now he had been given this brief to put together a children's sketch show for Rediffusion.

Humphrey told me how much he'd enjoyed what I did that night on the stage and how he thought I would be perfect for this new project. He said, 'When you get back to London I'd like to put you together with the others I've got lined up.' He mentioned these three hotshot writer-performers that had come out of Cambridge and Oxford. He said he wanted to add another actor and an actress to give the team a bit more comic breadth. He said, 'I'd love it if the actor was you.'

This sounded interesting to me, although it struck me as strange that Humphrey didn't want to use Bill Oddie, whom he obviously knew well and who was my age, small like I was, and a bit of a knockabout comic, the same as me. I never got to the bottom of why Humphrey passed over him, and I didn't trouble to ask. I simply agreed to meet up with everyone when the season was finished in Bournemouth.

Back in London, Humphrey brought us all together. The actress he had invited along was Denise Coffey. Denise was intelligent, friendly, eccentric and very funny. She would have been about thirty years old at this point, and had cut her teeth in repertory theatre and had worked as an interviewer on BBC radio. She was a good theatre actress, too. I remember, some time after this, going along to see her when she was in a production at the Young Vic and being really impressed by what she could do.

And then there were the three lads: Eric Idle, Mike Palin and Terry Jones. They were three years younger than me – just twenty-four – and my initial reaction to them was that they seemed a bit posh. They were certainly very confident – absolutely sure of themselves in a way that I could never have imagined being in those days. Eric had been to Cambridge, the same as Humphrey, but in the year below him; he had been president of the Footlights. Mike and Terry had known each other at Oxford and had written and acted for the Oxford Revue, which was Oxford's equivalent of the Footlights. They were highly educated, very articulate and quite experienced – whereas I, of course, hadn't been to university and hadn't even been to drama school. They were very chummy with each other and, dare I say it, a bit cliquey. The one that immediately seemed the nicest – and also the most talented, to my mind – was Mike Palin. I felt that there was less of a boundary with him. Even so, I was a little short of self-esteem in their company. Also, as they'd known each other for a while, they were already, to some extent, a team, whereas Denise and I were the additions, in a sense – the ones drafted in by Humphrey. That probably set the dynamic between us from the beginning – created a slight division in the team that was always there. Not that there were ever any fallouts or major disagreements.

Over the eighteen months that we worked together, we didn't socialise very much, and when we did, I was never entirely comfortable. I remember Eric inviting me to a party at his flat one weekend. It was on a Saturday afternoon, to celebrate his birthday. He was living with his girlfriend at the time in a first-floor apartment in Beauchamp Place in Chelsea. Dead posh: certainly posher than a flat above a hairdresser's in Thornton Heath. I walked into this grand square of beautiful white stucco Georgian houses and looked around, thinking, 'How can someone in our business afford to live here?' I thought I must be in the wrong place until someone on a balcony spotted me and called down, 'Are you looking for Eric's?'

The voice came from a very attractive young woman. 'Yes,' I called up. 'I'm one of his guests.'

'I know,' she said. 'I recognise you. It's the door on the right. I'll buzz you in.'

I was thinking, 'Blimey. This could be my lucky night.' Wrong, though. She was Eric's girlfriend.

The flat was beautifully decorated, with oil paintings on the walls, and soft velvet furniture. Champagne was served, which I hadn't seen very much of before this point. Mike and Terry were there, and Terry Gilliam, too. The party was a rather bohemian scene – pretty hip people, pretty intellectual conversation. Everyone was very nice and very friendly, but I felt I fitted in like a pork chop in a Jewish salad. I was out of my depth.

Still, the five of us rubbed along perfectly well at that initial meeting and it was clear that we would be more than capable of working together – assuming this project ever got off the ground. Apparently there was someone at Rediffusion who still needed persuading of its value. Humphrey told us, at that first gathering, 'We've got to go and sell this idea to Lewis Rudd.' Rudd was the head of comedy at Rediffusion.

So, that was the next step. At this point, remember, the show really was just an idea in Humph's head – and a fairly vague one at that. We had no scripts to read from, no sketches to show anyone. I don't think we even had a title. We just had . . . us. On the way up to his office, Humphrey urgently told us, 'When we go in, you've got to impress him with how funny you are.'

Which is, of course, just about the worst thing to tell anyone. Be funny! It's a recipe for disaster and I was already gritting my teeth as I walked in. The others were too.

Our anxieties did not diminish when we got our first sighting of Lewis Rudd. He was not the kind of bloke whom you would have identified as the head of comedy at a broadcasting company. You would more likely have put him down as some terribly old-fashioned bank manager. When we walked into his office, he was behind his desk in a collar and tie – impeccably strait-laced. And now we were going to have to be funny. In a crazy, impromptu way. In front of a bank manager.

It was a disaster. There were chairs lined up in front of Rudd's desk for us to sit on, so the first thing we did was to squabble like kids over those chairs, stealing them off each other, sitting on top of each other, pushing each other over. Eventually, when we were all seated in a line, Terry decided to fling himself off his chair, onto the floor. Then he got up and sat down again. Then he flung himself onto the floor again. Seeing this, the rest of us decided to fling ourselves off our chairs over and over again, too – except for Denise Coffey, who got up on Rudd's desk and walked up and down it for a while. Denise was a very talented actress of the short and serious kind: a leggy, sex-bomb kind she was not, so to watch her try and vamp old Lewis was quite an experience.

It was excruciating. I still shiver with embarrassment to recall it. Did Rudd find it amusing? I couldn't really tell you because I was on the carpet most of the time, completing my latest hilarious fall off my seat. But I guess all this forced anarchy showed that we were, to some extent, mad, or at any rate fearless – fearless enough to be the cast of a children's sketch show. Lewis Rudd signed us up. Whether he did this purely in order to get us out of his office and end the nightmare, I simply don't know. But the upshot was, by the time we left we had a commissioned show.

So that was the start of *Do Not Adjust Your Set* – a title which was one of Humph's brainchildren. The phrase will mean almost nothing to modern generations but it was on a notice frequently screened on television in the fifties and sixties, whenever the signal failed, which it quite often did. Humph thought it would gain the show some free publicity. Now all we had to do was create the show. The writing fell chiefly to Mike, Eric and Terry. Mad or fearless ideas seemed to flow from them very easily. I guess we thought we were making a kind of visual *Goon Show* – unfettered and bonkers. An early skit featured government inspectors going to find out how the boffins are getting on with building Concorde – and the boffins, who appear to have misunderstood the plans, turn out to be building a ship rather than an aeroplane. Pure, simple idiocy.

Or take the sketch that Eric came up with, in which he played a salesman in a home-appliances shop. A couple come in looking for a fridge and a heater. 'Step this way,' says Eric. First of all he shows them a fridge, opening the door and saying, 'This is a lovely one – top of the range. Feel that? Loads of heat. You'll certainly be able to warm your toes on this one of an evening.' Then he shows them a radiator. 'Very cold, this one – one of the coldest on the market. Keep everything lovely and chilled, this will.' That was it. I didn't think this would ever work. It just seemed so bluntly stupid. But it did work. Sometimes, just turning something on its head seemed to be enough.

As the first episodes came together, the director, Daphne Shadwell, who was experienced in putting the cameras on more traditional forms of children's television, and possibly found aspects of this show a bit of a step sideways from her comfort zone, said that she wanted to have a character running through the show, done as a filmed insert. I think it was Eric who came up with the idea of Captain Fantastic – a greengrocer with superpowers, who didn't do anything particularly fantastic. As it was obviously going to be a physical role, and as I was always the member of the team who got hit by the frying pan (or hit by whatever else a character needed to be hit by in order to get a laugh), it was always going to fall to me.

As superheroes go, Captain Fantastic was something of an everyman figure. No capes, tights or pants worn over trousers. His signature uniform was a long brown raincoat, buttoned to the neck, and a bowler hat, and he carried an umbrella (a token of normality), and boasted a large and more than faintly implausible black moustache. It was pretty quickly clear that he needed an arch-enemy – someone dastardly to do battle with and save the world from. So Denise became the dreaded Mrs Black, the force of evil who was always trying to blow everything up, including the world. Eric and Mike wrote the first two or three adventures in the life of this new, patently inadequate superhero and Denise and I were sent off with Daffers (as we had come to know Daphne) to shoot them. We decided to film them at twenty frames per second. Film runs normally at twenty-four frames per second and taking those four frames out just gives it a slightly quickened edge when you play it back at the right speed – not sped-up, Benny Hill-style or to the extent of a Charlie Chaplin film, but just slightly off, enough to add an extra dash of oddness. (As it turned out later, Ronnie Barker was very fond of this method, too.)

So Captain Fantastic became a fixture in the show. Daffers, Denise and I used to go away in a coach for a couple of days and record a set of these little films. We normally worked from a rough storyline and improvised the rest. The production manager used to accompany us and bring along a big wad of cash. We'd have lunch somewhere – out would come the wad. We'd have an overnight in a hotel and need to settle up in the morning – out would come the wad. Everything seemed to get paid for by the wad. It was great. We were out, being paid to make films and behave like idiots, and wherever we went, the tab was being picked up. I couldn't have been more blissfully happy, really. There was a wonderful freedom to it all as well. I was doing something I loved, but also doing it under no pressure. I was an unknown actor, so nobody had any expectations of me that I had to live up to. No one was expecting me to deliver. That kind of pressure came later. At this point I was simply free to bury myself in the work and enjoy it. I learned from this why so many people find solace in painting and drawing, such as my dear friend Brian Cosgrove, the animator, and my very talented wife, Gill.

Like everything in *Do Not Adjust Your Set*, the Captain

Fantastic films were about all sorts of nothing much. One episode was devoted entirely to the arrival of a giant box in the middle of a field – truly stupid stuff. (Diving about on the grass in that field brought my face out in hives – my first allergic reaction to pollen.) Humph had the idea that Captain Fantastic should arrive in the Land of the Backwards People. The Backwards People had coats on back to front, buttoned up at the rear, and gloves, and masks on the backs of their heads, and walked with a bizarre gait. Captain Fantastic encountered them on a beach – it was all rather bizarre and eerie in a *Doctor Who*-like way. Humph also found this wonderfully twitchy piece of classical music called 'March of the Heroes' and that became the films' soundtrack, binding it all together. I thought that, in some small way, I was following in the path of my heroes, Laurel and Hardy and Buster Keaton, and it made me very happy. I felt that, if I did nothing else in my career, I'd always have Captain Fantastic.

Series one ran to thirteen half-hour episodes, the first of which went out, as a kind of appetiser when the biggest audience was likely to be watching, on Boxing Day in 1967. This was turning into a bit of a tradition for me. Two Christmases previously, you'll recall, I had been able to gather the family to watch my blurred and distant figure swinging from the ceiling in a policeman's costume in the BBC pantomime. This festive season, I proudly brought my kin together to see me muck about in some mock-Shakespearean nonsense, appear on triangle with the popular German group the Eric Von Tuthri Players – formerly the Eric Von Tuthri Four – and fail to get served by Michael Palin's bafflingly obstructive grocer. They also got to witness a deafeningly discordant performance of the theme song from *The Sound of Music* by the Bonzo Dog Doo-Dah Band, the surreal pop-jazz group featuring Neil Innes and Vivian Stanshall, and a skit in which an entire gang of criminals turned out to be undercover policemen. (The Bonzos, incidentally, were a crazy bunch of way-out musos, and we were all dedicated fans of theirs, especially after hearing their hit song 'I'm the Urban Spaceman'. When they performed that number in the studio for the show, the entire crew were going around singing it, and carried on for weeks afterwards.) Plus, of course, they were privy to my starring role in the first episode of the adventures of Captain Fantastic – ending on a fairly typical cliffhanger, voiced sonorously by Mike: 'Who is the mysterious tree? Who was in the exploding lunch box? Who was the first man to drink the Channel? Will Captain Fantastic survive the horrors of the boating park? See next week's exciting adventure. Or don't as the case may be.'

Did the room rock with the White family's delighted Yuletide laughter? I'm not sure that it did. Just like with *Crossroads*, the programme was filmed as-live because Rediffusion was reluctant to spend money on tape-editing, so the quality of the production was not exactly cinematic. The broadcast of the first episode also included a four-minute passage of blank-screened dead air, where someone had forgotten to put on the advert reel.

Still, never mind how it played at 26 Lodge Lane. *Do Not Adjust Your Set* was an immediate smash hit with its target audience. Kids got it straight away. Whatever else you wanted to say, there was nothing like it on the television at that time and suddenly all the kids locked on to it. It spoke directly to them – to the point where they could feel proprietorial about it. It was their humour: none of the adults got it. The mums and dads would say, 'I don't know what you're watching this rubbish for' – and that just elevated it even higher in the kids' estimation. It was mad.

The funny thing was, none of us knew much about kids. Certainly none of us had kids at that time. So it wasn't as though the show was based on close observation of what makes kids laugh and what doesn't. This was the exact opposite of market-researched comedy. Maybe the secret was that, at some level, we simply *were* kids. Otherwise, I can't explain it. All

I know is, the sketches had to make us laugh, or they didn't get in.

The show began to develop. Terry Gilliam, an American friend of Mike's and Terry's, who had a lot of hair and pitched up in an enormous Afghan coat, contributed a couple of sketches and then, in the second series, did some animations for the show – one about a Christmas card, and another which was a strange chain of consciousness, called 'Elephant'. (I still have a drawing Terry did of me, in 1968, during another Humphrey Barclay television sketch project called *We Have Ways of Making You Laugh*. Frank Muir was the star of that show, and Terry would sit in the studio with a pen and pad, sketching away, and then, at the end of the programme, reveal what he had drawn. One time he turned his pad to the camera to reveal . . . my head on a pig's body. Well, thanks for that, Terry. But I wonder what a Terry Gilliam original is worth now? I could probably sell it and buy a place in Barbados.)

Though nearly all the writing was by Mike, Terry and Eric, Denise and I chipped in a little bit too. Denise invented a moment where the camera finds her sitting in a cardboard container and she looks into the lens and says, in a very upper-class voice, 'Whenever I go to the theatre I always take a box.' (OK, it doesn't necessarily spring off the page, but to see a full-grown person in a posh dress cramped up in a box was very funny.)

The sketch what I wrote, as Ernie Wise would say, featured a sedan chair, carried by four flunkeys, all in seventeenth-century costume. We see these flunkeys running along with the chair, very primly and properly, in a park. Suddenly the flunkey holding one of the rear corners of the chair starts to wobble. The sedan drops and he comes off and rolls away down into the ditch. At this point, complete with powdered wig, I lean out rather haughtily from inside the curtained sedan chair to see what's going on. Then I climb out, open up the back of the sedan chair

– the boot, as it were – and take out the spare flunkey, folded away in there. I attach him to the rear corner, check his calves briefly for road-worthiness, climb back in, and off we go again.

A work of profound comic genius. Clearly, I missed my vocation.

Anyway, never mind that: suddenly I was a budding star of children's television. It wasn't the route I'd particularly imagined going down when I set out – and I'm sure the same was true for Mike, Terry, Eric and Denise. But none of us were complaining about it.

* * *

EARLY IN 1968, I was summoned to the BBC Television Centre – the high church, the Mecca of the TV world. To get an audition in those hallowed halls at the time, you either had to be God or one of His disciples. David Croft asked me to read for a part in a sitcom that he had co-written with an actor and writer called Jimmy Perry and which they were trying to get off the ground. Michael Mills, the BBC's head of comedy, was, apparently, very keen on the show and determined to see it made. David was perfectly upfront with me: he, Jimmy and Michael had wanted another actor for this particular role, and this actor had desperately wanted to oblige them, but he was unavailable because he had already signed up for another show. They'd love me to try out, though.

One morning, at about ten, I went in to see David, Jimmy and Michael in a room at the BBC and read for them from the pilot script of this proposed series. It was pretty good stuff, I thought: set in wartime, funny, character-driven. Then I went home, where Ann, my agent, phoned me at about twelve thirty. 'Good news,' she said. 'They want you for the part.'

I hung up. I was so excited. I was going to be in a BBC comedy series; I was going to be rubbing shoulders with the movers and the shakers. I couldn't wait to tell people – specif- ically my mother. I felt enormously pleased with myself.

At about three in the afternoon, the phone rang again. It was Ann once more. 'Look, I don't know how to tell you this,' she said, 'but I think you'd better sit down. I'm afraid they don't want you for that part any more.'

Well, that knocked the wind right out of my sails while, at the same time, removing the bottom from my world. The explan- ation went something like this. Apparently, David and Jimmy had gone to lunch in the BBC canteen and bumped into Bill Cotton, who famously went on to be Controller of the BBC but at this point was a producer of light entertainment shows. Cotton said he was pleased he had run into the pair of them at precisely that moment because he'd just spoken to this rather well-established actor – the one Jimmy and David had originally wanted for the part I had read for just that morning. And he'd had to tell the actor how sorry he was, but the next series of the Spike Milligan show that he had signed up for some time ago had been cancelled – but at least, by way of compensation, he had Jimmy and David's show to do instead.

So that was that. Jimmy and David had got their original choice for the part after all – and they didn't even know it. So David, who had been put in a difficult position, had to explain the mix-up to Ann, and Ann had to explain it to me.

All of which is another way of saying that, for two and a half hours, I was Corporal Jones in *Dad's Army*.

'Ah, well,' I consoled myself, after I put down the phone, 'bet that show doesn't come to anything, anyway.'

* * *

IN LATE 1968, between making *Do Not Adjust Your Set* and not making *Dad's Army*, I did at least manage to add an item to my growing CV of vanishingly small roles in television shows that people might have heard of. I made an appearance in *Randall and Hopkirk (Deceased)* – though not before enduring an embarrassing experience which can still dampen my palms today.

Randall and Hopkirk (Deceased) – in case you haven't heard of it – was a detective series, featuring the traditional pair of cop buddies, with the twist that one of them (Hopkirk) is a ghost whom only Randall, his partner, can see. (Just to be clear, we're talking about the original version here, with Mike Pratt and Kenneth Cope, not the much later remake with Vic Reeves and Bob Mortimer.)

I read for the part of an illusionist's assistant in what I thought was a rather good script, or certainly a rather good plot. The illusionist's act involved giving a gun to a random member of the audience, getting them to fire it in his direction and seemingly catching the bullet in his teeth. (Kids: this is another of those moments where I must urge you not to attempt any kind of imitation with your guns at home.) However, a woman in the audience, who for reasons of her own did not wish the illusionist health and prosperity, was going to produce her own gun and, using both the darkness of the theatre and the noise of the trick gun as cover, pop him off.

My proposed part in this moment of deathly intrigue? Merely to stand on the stage and be a kind of music-hall barker on behalf of the illusionist, saying something along the lines of, 'And now, ladies and gentlemen, I must call upon you to be as quiet as you possibly can as we reach the moment in the act requiring the utmost concentration.'

Anyway, I went home after the audition and heard nothing for several days and assumed the director had found himself someone who could bark louder or better. But then, late on Thursday afternoon, my agent rang: 'The *Randall and Hopkirk* people just wanted to check that you've got the script for tomorrow.'

Well, no, I hadn't got the script. In fact, I didn't even know I'd got the part.

After some more phone calls of a rising urgency, and amid apologies for crossed wires, the script was sent straight over to me at home, strapped to the leg of a pigeon – or possibly using a courier on a motorbike, I now forget which.

By the time it arrived, I had just the evening to learn the lines before getting up at dawn on Friday morning and going over to Watford Theatre, which was the location for the shoot. Really, one evening ought to have been enough to get those lines straight in my head – even for me, who has always found line-learning quite hard. It wasn't as though this was the longest or most complex soliloquy in the history of scripted drama. Yet something about the words, combined with the general sense of last-minute panic, meant that I couldn't say these lines smoothly any more than I could have threaded a bit of cotton through the eye of a needle by throwing it. I found I was getting to a certain point in the speech – the same point every time – and then tripping up and collapsing. I spent the whole evening working at it, with no improvement whatsoever. At which point I went to bed, hoping that I could rely on sleep's magical balm to carry the problem away.

Alas, sleep's magical balm didn't do anything at all. Early the next morning, I stood, with extremities tingling, on the lip of the stage at the Watford Theatre and awaited the call of 'Action!' The theatre was stacked full of extras, so, essentially, I was playing to a full house. It was a slightly fancy shot. I had to stand there and the camera was pushed down the centre aisle, through the stalls, in between the audience, so that it closed in on me as I began to speak.

We went for a take. The camera came sweeping down the aisle and, on cue, I launched into the speech – only to hit the sticking point and completely dry. The theatre fell eerily silent.

'Go again,' said the director – rather coldly, I felt.

Back went the camera up the aisle. Everyone readied them-selves again.

'Action!'

Down came the camera, off I went – and again hit the sticking point and stopped.

'Go again,' said the director – even more coldly.

Back went the camera . . .

This little ritual went on for what felt like the best part of a morning. Every time I would reach the same point in the speech, fumble it and dry, and the camera would beat a weary retreat and the extras in the audience would mutter to each other conspiratorially. And, of course, the more it happened, the worse it got. I was like a nervous horse approaching Becher's Brook in the Grand National. I'd see the tricky moment coming up ahead of me, looming larger and larger, and then stumble into it and end up with a mouthful of twigs.

From the director came no words of comfort or encourage-ment, no arm around the shoulder: just an icy 'Go again'. And the camera would have to be dragged back up the aisle once more, and everything reset.

Finally, just shy of double figures, and sweating like a hippo in mud, I cracked it. I got an enormous round of perhaps slightly ironic applause from the audience of extras, bowed (also ironi-cally) and left. Then I went home and waited several days for my ears to stop being hot.

No wonder I drove my agent into an early retirement around this time. OK, not exactly. Ann Callender's broader desire to spend time with her highly successful husband, David Croft, and their family of (eventually) seven fabulous children may also have had something to do with her withdrawal from the business. Either way, I now became, at the recommendation of my friend Malcolm Taylor, a client of Derek Marr. Ann and David remained a part of my life so I have more than merely professional reasons for being permanently grateful to her for

introducing herself to me over the sausage rolls after that production of *Under Milk Wood*.

*   *   *

THE SECOND SERIES of *Do Not Adjust Your Set* – thirteen more
half-hour episodes – went out in February 1969 and finished in
May. Where the first series had been thrown together in a by
and large cheerful and liberated spirit, the mood changed during
the making of the follow-up. Terry, Mike and Eric started getting
a little frustrated that some of their material was getting edited.
There were tremendously strict rules in those days about what
was acceptable for children's TV and it put a very tight strait-
jacket on the writers. They put up with it at first, but then they
began to find their humour expanding – getting, perhaps, a little
more adult.

I could see where they were coming from. You couldn't, for
example, show a couple in bed – by which I don't mean you
weren't allowed to attempt portrayals of sexual activity, though,
of course, you weren't. But you couldn't show a couple in bed
at all, even if they were just reading or having a conversation.
That, despite its innocence, was considered inappropriate. The
lads were beginning to find that a lot of the stuff they were
submitting for the show was getting the red pencil – being cut
out by the censors. Society seemed to have liberated itself but
television hadn't, and Eric, Mike and Terry really chafed against
that and felt very thwarted by it. It didn't affect me and Denise
Coffey so much, because we weren't really major parties in the
writing and were, in any case, mostly off on our own doing
Captain Fantastic. But for Eric, Mike and Terry, the Three
Musketeers, this was a constant battle and an increasing source
of conflict with the powers that be.

In the course of fighting that battle, they began to wonder
about the nature of the show. Mike and Terry in particular were

thinking that perhaps inside *Do Not Adjust Your Set* there was a grown-up programme waiting to get out. They talked about proposing a late-night version of the show, one in which their adult material would have a chance. In the end they said they wanted to go late night, get out of children's television altogether. They went to see Lewis Rudd, the head of comedy. They asked him if they could take the show late night so they could open up the script content. Rudd absolutely put his foot down. 'No way,' he said. 'You're the most successful show we've ever had on children's television, so why would I put you anywhere else? We want more of the same – the same being *Do Not Adjust Your Set*.'

Mike, Terry and Eric then decided to throw down the gauntlet: if you don't let us do the show late night, we won't do the show at all. Rudd still said no. So, when the contract came up for renewal, they didn't sign it. That meant Denise and I were out, too. To say we were disappointed about that is an understatement. I was also disappointed about the way the others went about it. Mike, Terry and Eric didn't discuss it with us; they just told us that this was what was happening. They weren't going to pick up their contracts. The next thing we knew, they were gone, and so were we, because without them, clearly, there was no show. I minded that.

What happened after that, of course, is a matter of historical record. Mike, Terry and Eric went away and continued to plot their move into adult television, and a year later they regrouped with John Cleese and Graham Chapman, and brought Terry Gilliam back on board to do animations, and *Monty Python's Flying Circus* was born. Basically it was a more grown-up version of *Do Not Adjust Your Set* – but without me and Denise.

'Did that rankle?' I hear you ask. 'Yes,' I hear myself answer. It rankled a lot. I can't speak for Denise but I know my nose was out of joint. Dear reader, the chances are you will have come across *Monty Python's Flying Circus* at some point in your life and will be aware how big that show became and how important in the history of comedy. It was as though the band had broken up and then re-formed without us. Denise and I were part of the original group, but we got sidelined. Or that's how it felt to me.

After Mike, Terry and Eric left, Rediffusion did talk to me about possibly developing Captain Fantastic into a series of his own. They thought the character had enough life in him to stand up separately. I agreed with them about that, but I wanted to know how the show would be shot. For me, it was obvious that it would only work if film was used, as we did in the original inserts – with the speeding-up and the silent-era trickery. If you tried shooting it on tape, in a studio, without the filmed stunts . . . well, I couldn't really see where that would go. But, of course, shooting an entire series on film would have been expensive. Rediffusion said they wouldn't run to that. If there was going to be a Captain Fantastic series, it would have to come indoors and be made on tape. But the whole point of Captain Fantastic, it seemed to me, was that it was a fond parody of the silent era. If you lost that, you lost everything about it. It had to be made on film, or it was nothing. So I walked away from the idea.

What an extraordinary little phase that was, though. A brush with *Monty Python*, a brush with *Dad's Army* . . . it was as though everything I touched turned to gold – but only after I'd stopped touching it and gone to another room. It was Clive Dunn, of course, who got the role of Corporal Jones – and what a superb job he made of it. Would I have been anywhere near as good in the role? Who knows? But also, if I had ended up in *Dad's Army*, would I have been able to do *Open All Hours* and *Only Fools and Horses* and *Frost* and all the other things that my career opened out into?

Afterwards, of course, and all these years later, it doesn't matter: I went on to do other things and to be extremely happy doing what I was doing. At the time, though, when you're out of work, and unsure where you're headed, or even if you're headed anywhere at all, and you're looking at the success that people are having without you . . . well, I was pretty bitter about it.

I had to sit back and watch *Monty Python's Flying Circus* and *Dad's Army* ascend to the skies without me. It was like the Beatles all over again, and I was Pete Best. Twice.

Incidentally, I bumped into Eric Idle many years later. It was after I had done *Only Fools and Horses*, so all the dust had long since settled. He must have been over from Los Angeles, where he had gone to live. I had a lunch arranged with someone in London, and when I walked into the restaurant, there was Eric at a table. We greeted each other warmly and did the usual how-are-yous, it's-been-ages and how's-it-goings. I was struck by how transatlantic his accent had become.

'I see you're still fucking about on television,' he said, brightly.

'Er, yes,' I said, less brightly.

And then we said our fond farewells and got on with our respective lunches.

CHAPTER NINE

A shaggy dog story. How I delivered Bob Monkhouse's babies. And the West End finally beckons properly.

Captain Fantastic and Mrs Black might have been out of work, after the demise of *Do Not Adjust Your Set*, but Denise Coffey and I were very quickly offered the chance to revive our partnership in a television show that featured a dog. Unfortunately for both of us, the show didn't just feature a dog. It also was a dog. Indeed, if you'd been asked, at the time, which was the bigger dog – the show or the dog – I don't think you'd have picked the dog.

I'm not sure where the finger of blame should ultimately point for this little pothole in the path of our careers. Maybe it should point at everyone involved, because we all, more or less cheerfully, went along with it. But my first connection with the project was a meeting at what was now Thames Television (formerly Rediffusion), with Daphne Shadwell, the former director of *Do Not Adjust Your Set*, with whom by now both Denise and I were quite close. Daffers referred to us as the 'G'nommies' – a contraction of 'garden gnomes'. (Denise was even smaller than me, at five foot two.) It emerged that somebody had come up with an idea for a script for Denise and me – and for a third party, of a canine nature.

At the time, just about the most famous dog in the world, after Lassie, was the Dulux sheepdog. He was certainly the most famous dog in Britain. His extremely fluffy work in widely broadcast advertisements for household paint had ensured him that status. Why, in the early 1970s, there was barely a person in the country who hadn't been inspired by that dog's example to paint their sitting room magnolia. He was really packing them in, down at the DIY shops.

So somebody came up with the idea of using the Dulux sheepdog in a television series for children. The theory was that the show was bound to be popular because almost everybody loved the Dulux sheepdog, or, at least, were prepared to give him the time of day. Therefore the people at Thames got in touch with the Dulux sheepdog – or, I should say, they got in touch with the Dulux sheepdog's people. (When you're as famous as the Dulux sheepdog was, you don't pick up the phone yourself: you have handlers for that.) And the word from the Dulux sheepdog's people was that the Dulux sheepdog was very keen on the idea – provided, obviously, that his personal terms could be met, regarding fee, basket, water bowl, supply of Boneo, etc., and, of course, provided no better offer came up in the meantime. (That's always a risk with the really big names.)

Here's the thing, though. The Dulux sheepdog (and I can say it now because he's not likely to be reading this) wasn't a trained dog. By which I don't mean he wasn't house-trained, because he was. I mean he wasn't trained as a performing animal. He wasn't a circus act. He didn't have a set of tricks up his sleeve. He was just a dog that looked lovely and had an unusually keen interest in interior decorating.

Actually, thinking about it, even in the Dulux ads, the Dulux dog didn't do much, did he? Not even decorating. You certainly didn't see him paint the rooms, as I recall. Mostly he just walked through them, or sat in them with his tongue hanging out and his hair over his eyes. Mind you, there are a lot of actors who have got away with less.

Anyway, in that meeting at Thames, we talked about the possibility of a set of stories involving a brother (me) and a sister (Denise) who would go about the place, solving mysteries and bringing criminals to justice, all the while accompanied by a dog (Dulux). There was no title for this show at first, until I rather brilliantly came up with one – *Two D's and a Dog*.

Do you see what I did there? David and Denise both start with the letter 'D', you see, and so does the word 'dog', which means it sounds nice coming after 'Two D's'. Put the whole thing together and you get 'Two D's and a Dog'.

That blinding flash of inspiration on my part was greeted in the room with . . . well, almost no enthusiasm at all, actually, until it became clear that no one was going to come up with anything better. So, for better or worse, *Two D's and a Dog* it was.

After that, some scripts were written and before long Denise and I found ourselves on-set in the actual presence of the Dulux dog – a huge moment for us, as you can imagine. I think we were both a little nervous, being around a star of that magnitude, and especially given the size of his jaw. If I could confess something, though (and it's not an uncommon phenomenon, this), I thought he looked slightly smaller in the flesh. But then people often say the same about me.

However, when it came to working with the Dulux dog . . . well, I'm not going to beat around the bush here: he was a total nightmare. We had a lot of problems getting the dog to do anything that the script required – which wasn't much, frankly, but we did at least need him to be along with us a lot of the time, if only in a vague 'I'm here too' kind of way, and even that proved problematic.

For instance: because I could drive a motorbike (and was now, unlike in 1958, legally entitled to carry a passenger without attracting the raised eyebrows of the authorities), someone had the cute idea of putting the three mystery-busting stars of the show on a bike-and-sidecar set-up – me at the front, Denise riding pillion and the Dulux dog in the sidecar.

Thinking about it, me at the front, Denise in the sidecar and the Dulux dog riding pillion would have been funnier. And me in the sidecar, Denise riding pillion and the Dulux dog doing the driving would have been funnier still. Or maybe it should have been Denise driving, me and the dog riding pillion and no one in the sidecar. Or perhaps all of us should have been in the sidecar and nobody should have been driving. But you can see why we didn't try it.

Now, it took forever to get the dog into the sidecar. He wasn't keen on the idea at all and was, I felt, several times on the verge of storming back to his trailer, slamming the door and refusing to come out for the rest of the afternoon. Finally, though, after much soothing and enticing by his handler, he overcame his inner demons and agreed to go in there, on cue, when the door was opened for him. And then I had to spend a long time gently driving up and down until he got used to the motion and we could trust him not to fling himself from a moving motorbike in fear, which would have been embarrassing for all of us, and a nightmare for the insurers.

Eventually we could get the dog into the sidecar relatively smoothly and trust him to stay there. However, getting the dog out of the sidecar was another matter. We discovered this while filming an episode in which the three of us resolved to go into a haunted house to find out why it was haunted. (Scooby-Doo, eat your cartoon heart out. You too, Shaggy.) Denise, the Dulux dog and I roared up to the front of the haunted house in question, and Denise and I jumped off the bike, full of purpose and ready to go charging through the front door and demystify the place forever – and the Dulux dog just sat there like a lump. Which rather drained the moment of its dramatic intensity.

The cry, as usual at such times, was 'Cut!' followed by words which, if my daughter should read them in this book, I would struggle to explain. The director, the props boy, the handler – they tried everything: coaxing, calling, dangling treats, offering a pay rise. Still the dog sat there. Finally, the handler lost his patience and shouted, '*Will* you come out?!'

At which point, the dog snapped at him – 'Rrrough!' – and nearly had his hand off.

Honestly, if I'd gone to the press with that story at the time, I could have ruined the Dulux dog's career in show business forever. Think of the headlines: 'TOP DOG IS REALLY ANIMAL SHOCK', 'THE DULUX DOG: THE TRUTH ABOUT HIS DARK UNDERCOAT'.

Two D's and a Dog lasted for one, faltering series, broadcast in 1970, after which, to no public outcry whatsoever, it was cancelled. The show does not appear to feature prominently in the archives under 'Golden Children's Television' – and I have to say I'm quite glad about that. Indeed, I quite hope the tapes have all been scrubbed, Dulux dog and all, so they can't come back to haunt me.

Didn't someone once say something important about the perils of becoming professionally associated with children and animals? Indeed, they did. But nobody ever listened to them.

* * *

MEANWHILE, MY FRIENDSHIP with Humphrey Barclay, the producer of *Do Not Adjust Your Set*, grew. We spent a lot of time together and became good mates. We were part of a small gang who met up every now and again for meals at the Ark in Notting Hill, where we would quaff wine and have merry interludes. One time Humphrey invited me to join him at a chalet in Switzerland for a skiing holiday. Also there were Suzy Miller, who was Humphrey's secretary, and Suzy's boyfriend, who quickly earned the nickname the 'Spider of the Piste' on account of the figure he cut, from a distance, on the slopes in his all-black clothes.

Apart from a holiday in Jersey with my old business partner Bob Bevil, this was the first time I had been abroad and only the second time I had ever been on an aeroplane. I flew into Geneva and then, following the extensive instructions written out for me by Suzy, took a train to Les Diablerets, where Humphrey picked me up. I was wearing, needless to say, my monumental fur coat. I took a few skiing lessons, venturing out onto the piste in my normal clothes, having none of the specialist gear. I absolutely loved it.

Back in London, Humphrey said he wanted me to meet an old friend of his called David Hatch, who was a radio producer at the BBC. The three of us got together in the bar of the Langham in Portland Place, opposite Broadcasting House. When I walked in, David was already at the bar, standing in a pose that would become very familiar to me, holding his beer glass up at his chest, as if it were an extension of his lapel.

Hatchy and Humphrey had been in the Cambridge Footlights together. I liked him immediately. During the course of our conversation he said, 'Well, David, have you ever done any radio?'

'No,' I said.

'Why not?' he said.

'Nobody's ever asked me,' I said.

To which he replied, 'Well, I'm asking you now.'

He had taken over a late-night sketch show – one which he felt was a bit linear and not a little boring. He wanted to give it a kick up the backside, and make it a satirical sketch show, sending up Parliament and the powers that be. He put together a collection of young writers, keen to cut their teeth in the comedy business, and a small company of actors, including Bill Wallis, David Tate, Sheila Steafel and me. Together, from 1970 onwards (and, in my case, on and off, all the way through to 1991), we began to make *Week Ending*.

We'd get together at the BBC on a Friday morning, and the half-hour show would go out at eleven that night. I played roles in sketches and did voices and impressions. My Jim Callaghan, for example, was unshakeably in office between 1976 and 1979. I also doubled as Tony Benn and a variety of newsreaders. I loved the immediacy of the programme and the way it forced you to apply your skill as an actor so quickly, across so many different parts. I'd find myself playing, for example, the aide to the Minister of Defence (played by David Tate and always, for some reason, portrayed in his bath, with a rubber duck), or perhaps sending up a royal wedding, or maybe reading some of the one-liners that formed 'Next Week's News', the show's regular sign-off. This was basically an excuse for the writers to show off their punning skills. Thus I found myself musing, in the firm voice of a newsreader: 'If Evita has got Juan Peron, what has she done with the other pair?' (This joke requires some Spanish pronunciation. Also some knowledge of Argentine political history. Ask a teacher. If you're still struggling, try saying 'one' for 'Juan'. If you're still struggling . . . oh, let's move on.)

The atmosphere on *Week Ending* was very egalitarian. We sometimes had to audition among ourselves for parts in sketches. We'd all have a go at doing the necessary political voice and whoever was best at it and made the rest of us laugh hardest got the part.

Hatchy went on to be one of the big cheeses in BBC Radio – although not before he had been hauled up to the BBC's ivory tower himself on occasions, and given a dressing-down because there had been complaints about a perceived bias against the reigning government. David would point out that it wasn't bias at all. The fact of the matter was, the ones who happened to be in power were the ones making the decisions, so they happened to be more available for satire than the ones in opposition. It wasn't political, then, so much as practical. I don't think the big people had an answer to that. In any case, the government changed numerous times during my years on the show, without the jokes drying up. We let them all have it, indiscriminately. Funny how politics works: one lot comes in until we get fed up with them, and then we sack them and bring in the other lot. It reminds me of this great verse:

> Little fleas have littler fleas
> Upon their backs to bite 'em
> And littler fleas have smaller fleas
> And so on, ad infinitum.

One Friday Hatchy invited along to the recording a young, quiet, bespectacled cub reporter from the *Luton News* who, off his own bat, had been sending in material of a consistently high standard to the show. That was my first meeting with David Renwick, who became a good friend of mine, and went on to write for *The Two Ronnies* and *Not the Nine O'Clock News* and, latterly, to create the sitcom *One Foot in the Grave* and the drama serial *Jonathan Creek*.

In 1977, my work for *Week Ending* resulted in me being given a spin-off solo sketch show, *The Jason Explanation*. It was the beginning of many things for many people, myself included.

One day, early in our acquaintance, Hatchy announced that he had got some tickets to see Alastair Sim performing in *The Magistrate*, by Arthur Wing Pinero, at the Chichester Festival Theatre. We drove down to Sussex – Humphrey at the wheel, Hatchy and me in the back, relentlessly and mercilessly taunting the driver, as I recall. ('He's turned left. I would never have turned left there.' 'He's made a mistake, of course.' 'We'll be lucky if we get there before midnight.') What a thrill to see Alastair Sim, though. I had been a huge fan ever since I saw him play Scrooge in the 1951 film version of *A Christmas Carol* – the definitive Scrooge, in my humble opinion. In *The Magistrate*, he was Mr Posket, and I will always remember the brilliant routine he did with a pair of braces, in a scene where he was getting ready to go out. These braces were hanging down his back and he had to wriggle to get them up onto his shoulders, one at a time. Every time he got one side up, the other pinged back down. Eventually he got them both under control and stood up – at which point they both flew off at the same time. The amount of business he got out of a simple pair of braces! Years later, I was offered the Mr Posket role and, remembering Alastair Sim and the braces, I thought, 'Great.' Then I thumbed through the acting edition of the play, hoping to find a description of the business with the braces. But it wasn't in there. I would only have had my memory to go on, and I didn't know exactly how he had constructed it. So I didn't do it – I turned the role down. I didn't want to do the play without this thing Sim did. That business would have been the high point for me.

In 1970 Humphrey offered me a piece of work which, it's no exaggeration to say, changed the course of my professional life. It was just a tiny thing, really, yet it set off a whole chain of reactions – though not before it had cost me my relationship with my agent.

It all began one day when Humphrey rang me and said, 'You've seen *Hark at Barker*, haven't you?' Of course I had seen it. It was Ronnie Barker's comedy series for London Weekend Television, with Ronnie playing a bumbling but forthright old aristocrat, Lord Rustless, and delivering pricelessly out-of-touch lectures on life from his ancestral home at Chrome Hall. I loved it. Indeed, I had sat and watched it and thought to myself, 'Now, that's a programme I would love to be in.'

'There have been some references in the show to a character called Dithers,' Humphrey went on. 'He's Lord Rustless's gardener. So far we've only seen him zip past the window on a lawnmower. Well, Ronnie wants to bring him into the show properly. Ronnie thought about playing the part himself but we all think it would be better if someone else did it. What do you reckon about taking it on?'

'I'd love to do it,' I said.

'Great,' said Humphrey. 'We reckon Dithers is about a hundred years old, and the way we see him is, he's covered in hair and has a floppy hat, and the only thing that sticks out is his nose.'

'I'd definitely love to do it,' I said.

I had always wanted to work with Ronnie Barker, ever since I had seen him on *The Frost Report* in the sixties. He was already a legend in the business. This was a dream offer as far as I was concerned.

I told Humphrey to talk to my agent and arrange it all, as per usual, and hung up feeling rather giddy and very pleased with life in general.

A bit later, though, Humphrey phoned back.

'Listen,' he said, 'I've got to tell you, as a friend: I know you deserve it but your agent is asking far too much money for that part. He's asking for money I haven't got. Seriously. I can't afford you.'

I was shocked to hear that. I expressed to Humphrey again how much I wanted to take this chance to work with him and Ronnie, and I asked him to keep the part open while I had a word with Derek.

I then rang Derek straight away. I said, 'Look, I really want to do this part.' He said, very bluntly, in the crisply enunciated manner that Derek had, 'They're not offering you enough money.' I said, 'But I really, *really* want to do this part.' He said, again, 'They're not offering you enough money.' I said, 'Can I come and see you?'

I went straight round to Derek's office. I can still picture the scene: me standing rather tremblingly like an errant schoolboy in front of Derek's desk, Derek seated with, as ever, a cigarette going. Derek smoked for Great Britain at Commonwealth and Olympic levels – and smoked flamboyantly too, holding the fag aloft in his fingers, sucking on it with pursed lips, exhaling tightly. A fag wasn't just a fag with Derek: it was a five-minute drama.

I explained again that I wanted to do the part. Derek, who clearly felt he was being crossed, said, 'I advise you not to.'

I said, 'But I'm not interested in the money. I want to work with Ronnie Barker.'

I was quite choked up about it. Derek looked at me silently for a short while. Then he said, 'Right.'

He picked up the phone receiver and inserted his finger into the dial. (Rotary dials in those days, my children.) Then he waited while the line connected. And then he said, 'Give me Humphrey Barclay's office.'

A pause.

'. . . Hello? Is that Humphrey Barclay?'

And with that Derek handed me the receiver and sat back, staring at me.

Rather stunned by this behaviour, I put the receiver to my mouth and spoke to Humphrey. 'Er . . . it's David. I've just . . . well, I've spoken to my agent and . . . I told him to accept and . . . I want to do the part.' Humphrey could tell from my voice that I was a bit tremulous. He said, 'Great. Thank you.'

I handed the receiver back to Derek and he dropped it onto its cradle and said, rather tartly, 'Anything else?'

And I said, 'No,' rather sotto voce, and turned and left.

That was the beginning of the end for me and Derek Marr – and a pretty salutary lesson for me, I guess, about doing the things you want to do. If I had followed the money and not my heart, I wouldn't have got to work with Ronnie B. I simply couldn't turn that opportunity down. It didn't concern me what

I was getting paid. In truth, the way I felt about it, I would have quite happily paid ITV for the privilege. I'm sure Derek thought he was only protecting me from myself, and looking after the interests of his client. But in this case, I knew myself and my interests better than he did. I have never been a naturally assertive or confrontational person. But right then I knew what I wanted and I made sure I stood firm and got it.

I'll talk about working with Ronnie B. later. Suffice to say for now that I went ahead and did the part of Dithers and had a fantastic time, making a connection with Ronnie that profoundly affected the course of my life thereafter. So I'm quite glad I took the trouble to go round and face up to Derek.

I did need a new agent, though. On the set of *Hark at Barker*, I met a very attractive actress called Moira Foot, who was playing Lord Rustless's maid, Effie. (She went on to feature in *Are You Being Served?* and, perhaps most famously, to play Denise Laroque in *'Allo 'Allo*.) Moira and I went out together for a while. Her father, Alistair Foot, was the co-author, with Anthony Marriott, of the play that was about to do big things in the West End, called *No Sex Please – We're British*. (We'll have cause to come back to that play.) Before he turned his hand to writing, Alistair had been a civil engineer who had worked on the construction of the M1, Britain's first motorway. Not a lot of playwrights can say that, nor that they have a bridge named after them. (The engineers used to take the liberty of loaning their surnames to the bridges they were planning. So Alistair's allotted bridge – either fortunately or unfortunately, depending how you look at it – was the Foot Bridge.) Alistair and I got chatting one day and I told him about the situation with my agent, and he said he thought he might be able to get me a meeting with someone called Richard Stone, who handled a lot of the top comedy talent at the time – Terry Scott, Hugh Lloyd, Dave Allen, Bill Maynard, Jon Pertwee and a host of people way bigger than I was.

Alistair was indeed able to get me that meeting, and I did indeed meet Richard Stone, and, 4,013 years later, the Richard Stone Partnership still represents me today.

I remember that first meeting with Richard. I was shown into his office and he sat behind his desk where – for carefully calculated psychological purposes, I don't doubt – his chair was higher than the guest's. He asked me what I wanted to achieve most. I said to him, 'I want to work.' Which was the right answer; some time after, Richard told me that if I had said I wanted to be rich, or I wanted to be famous, he probably wouldn't have taken me on. As it was, he put me on contract as his client for a year. I never signed another contract with him after that, because I never needed to. Our relationship was understood.

With a new agent looking after me, it seemed a pretty good moment for me to take stock. In 1970, I was thirty years old and I had been an actor for five years. Five years was the period I had set myself when I took the decision to give up electrics. I had told Bob Bevil, my partner, I would give it five years, and if it still wasn't working out, I'd jack it in and come back to the tools. I didn't mean I'd give myself five years to become a big star; I meant I'd give myself five years to see if I could get regular enough work as a paid actor. That was the full extent of the master plan. It's so tempting, when you look back over careers that have worked out OK, to assume that every twist and turn was shrewdly calculated to bring about the desired end. I wonder whether that's ever really true. It certainly wasn't true in my case, where things owed so much more to happenstance – to one thing turning up after another. There was no strategy, no graph, no sheet of paper with a carefully thought-through mathematical equation on it. The idea, as I saw it, was to get work, lose myself in it and enjoy it while it was there, and then, when it was over, look for the next thing.

In those first five years, I ended up surprising myself. There had been a couple of months early on when I'd been twiddling my thumbs. But apart from that, I seemed to have done a fair old amount of stuff. There was the year with Bromley Rep, the production of *Under Milk Wood*, the BBC panto with Terry Scott, *Crossroads*, *Peter Pan* in the West End, the summer season with Dick Emery, a couple of appearances in *Doctor in the House*, the two series of *Do Not Adjust Your Set*, *Week Ending*, *Hark at Barker* . . . And that's before we even mention the crowning career glory of the children's series with the Dulux dog. If you had offered me all that on day one . . . well, I think I would have bitten your hand off faster than the Dulux dog would have done.

One thing slightly nagged at me, however. All the work I was getting – with the exception of *Week Ending* on the radio, obviously – was very much of a specific kind: physical comedy. In the theatre and the television work that I was being offered, I was doing a fair amount of swinging from wires, and an awful lot of falling over, not to say quite a bit of jumping across soft furnishings. Now, don't get me wrong, swinging from wires, falling over and jumping across soft furnishings were things I very much enjoyed doing. At the same time, though, swinging from wires, falling over and jumping across soft furnishings hadn't necessarily been – how shall I put this? – they hadn't necessarily been the dream at the outset. When I had started out along this road, the dream, really and in all honesty, had been acting: the proper stuff. Five years in, looking back over what I'd been up to, there wasn't much sign of that. Shouldn't I now be thinking about changing it up a little bit, and getting involved in a bit of . . . acting?

I expressed this little doubt to Richard Stone. I explained how it had entered my mind that, just once in a while, it might be nice to be in a play where there was a sofa on the stage and I didn't necessarily have to jump over it or end up under its cushions. Or (and here was one from left field) perhaps every now and again I could be in a play that didn't have a sofa in it at all. You know – something like *King Lear*. (*King Lear* doesn't have a sofa in it. I just checked.)

I suppose what I was saying, in a roundabout kind of way, was that I was wondering about broadening myself, pushing for some serious roles. Richard thought very hard about this. Or if he didn't actually think very hard about it, he did a very good impression of someone who was thinking very hard about it. Then, his ruminations complete, he told me, 'Don't swim against the tide. Go with the current. If this is the work that's coming your way, accept it and go with it. Later, there may come a time when you have established yourself and you can change direction. But don't start heading upstream when you've got something going for you.'

He also, in a manner of speaking, stood up for falling down. 'People want you because you can do comedy,' Richard said, 'and that's not necessarily an easy thing to do. Actually, it's probably one of the hardest.'

I took his advice. I haven't lived to regret doing so.

So, I again set aside those National Theatre aspirations, girded my loins, bolstered my nethers and, with a spring in my eye and a twinkle in my step, went back to comedy in the theatre – farcing around, I guess you could call it. In 1971, Richard got me an audition for a part in a play called *She's Done It Again!*, originally written for Brian Rix's company by Michael Pertwee, Jon Pertwee's brother, and due to be staged at the Playhouse in Weston-super-Mare. The star of the show was to be Bob Monkhouse. It was a piece about a vicar whose wife has sextuplets, delivered one by one over the course of the play. I appeared as a daft old seventy-year-old professor with a white wig and a white moustache, who becomes involved in the delivery of the babies. It was quite demanding, I suppose, although, after Dithers the hundred-year-old gardener, this character was a veritable spring chicken. The part involved lots of throwing myself around and a nice bit of business with (of course, and why the hell

not?) the sofa, where I jumped on it and got a foot trapped
between its cushions. In the process of disengaging the trapped
foot, I would normally manage to get the other foot stuck and
draw the action out as long as I dared.

One time, somewhere in the middle of the action, I sat down
on the sofa with one leg tucked under myself, and I noticed
that this made the leg appear to stop at the knee. So I converted
this into another demonstration of the professor's general ditz-
iness: he now became confused about the whereabouts of the
rest of his leg, and made a great show of believing he had lost
it somewhere. Then I rolled up a sofa cushion to use as an
artificial leg. The play, of course, had to wait while I got up to
all this. To put it briefly, I was getting away with murder. But
hey: it was a summer season in Weston. The audience didn't
seem to be complaining.

Bob Monkhouse and I became good friends in those weeks.
We enjoyed each other's company enormously. I was very
impressed by him: by his professionalism, by his knowledge of
comedy, which was vast. Eventually, he and his wife Jackie
started inviting me over for dinner at their place near Luton.
Bob's house was even more vast than his knowledge of comedy,
and beautifully decorated, hung with an amazing array of paintings. Bob had a cinema in the basement where he screened
silent-movie reels from his collection. He had a deep respect
for the physical comedy of the silent stars and it was a source
of frustration to him that he couldn't do physical comedy
himself.

Our friendship grew out of our attempts to wind each other
up and make each other corpse during that absurd farce in
Weston-super-Mare. I would have to rush in with the sixth and
final newborn baby in a blanket and present it to Bob, who was
playing the vicar. The part of the newborn was, of course, played
by a doll but because the contents of the blanket weren't strictly
visible to the audience, I was able to make little additions to

its burden offstage. One night, Bob found himself staring down at a baby that had been rather rudely adorned with a sausage. Another night, it was wearing a fright mask. A third night, I thrust Bob a blanket containing no baby at all, but just his pants, which I had retrieved from his dressing room.

Bob would have his revenge at the moment in the play where I was required to look offstage through a window in the set and remark on the weather. And there, meeting my gaze where the audience couldn't see him, would be Bob waving . . . well, all sorts of things at me. Or I might see him bent over and scandalously in flagrante with the wind machine. Or there would be Bob with his flies open and the sausage would be . . . But enough. Silly and puerile these antics no doubt were – yet things like that kept up the energy of the show, and I'm sure that energy transferred to the audience, somewhere along the line.

Doing *She's Done It Again!* with Bob was a happy experience altogether, and only slightly marred by what eventually happened to my toes. A few of us in the cast decided to fill some spare time in the day by taking riding lessons at a nearby riding school. We thought it would be fun, and also riding is no bad skill for an actor to have on the CV, especially if the makers of a cowboy film come calling. (Casting director: 'Can ya ride a hoss, kid?' Jason: 'Yes, siree.')

So my riding lesson went fine: I familiarised myself with the controls and fairly swiftly worked out such niceties as how to change gear and which end was the front and which was the back. Afterwards, I climbed out of the driving seat and my instructor showed me how to loosen the bridle and then told me to lead my horse to water to see if it wanted a drink. Well, there's a famous old saying in this area, isn't there, and I was about to appreciate the full force of it. The famous old saying is: you can lead a horse to water, but you can't stop it standing on your foot. As we moved towards the trough, I discovered what it felt like to have two tons of steaming animal passing its entire weight through my size-seven toes. And what it feels like, in case you're wondering, is painful.

So, I was straight off to A&E for, by my calculation, the 741st time in this book alone. Diagnosis: two dislocated toes. Remedy: a bit of exquisitely painful manipulation to get the toes back to roughly where they had started, followed by the binding of the affected area in a substantial white bandage. My foot now bore the size and approximate appearance of an adult Yorkshire terrier. I could only wear an extra-large slipper over the bruising and was afflicted with a heavy limp, both of which inconveniences seemed to threaten my continued participation in the play. But, of course, the farce must go on, so we had some lines written into the play giving my character the professor a touch of gout. I saw out the rest of the season in a carpet slipper, like the trouper I was and remain.

Bob was a cartoonist – a really rather good one – and every night you'd find another drawing of yourself pinned to your dressing-room door. After my upset at the riding school, I found a caricature captioned roughly as follows: 'D. Jason, desperate for attention, has his foot broken by a horse to garner sympathy.' I took the drawing inside and put it on the dressing-room wall with the others. By the end of the run I had two strips of Monkhouse cartoons, Sellotaped to the wall, from the ceiling down to the floor – and nearly all of them insulting.

Was it true that, on account of my capering, I often got a bigger round of applause from the Weston audiences at the end of the show than Bob, the star they had paid to see? Modesty forbids me from saying so.

Actually, hang on a minute . . . No, I've just been on the phone to modesty, and it appears that modesty doesn't actually forbid me. So, yes, it was true. I did often get a bigger round of applause at the end of the show than Bob.

But here's a measure of the man: was he bitter? No. Even though Bob was the lead, he decided to come down at the curtain call before me, take his bow, and then gesture to me to come on and take my bow. Which was very generous of him. I can't think of many big stars who would offer an unknown actor his moment like that. Then again, after the first week, Bob started staying on the stage after the rest of us had gone and giving the audience ten minutes of stand-up material. So note how he made sure he had the last word.

For the next three years, I worked on Bob's radio show *Mostly Monkhouse*, appearing in sketches and doing voices. With regard to comedy, he was a student as much as anything else, and a collector of it. If any new comic came along, Bob would be in the audience with a notebook and pen, writing down anything new. That's why he became known as the 'Thief of Bad Gags'. He was the first person I knew who had satellite television, getting this ridiculously large dish installed on his property – presumably so that he could plunder the airwaves of the entire world for gags twenty-four hours a day.

Actually, Bob was a bit of an early adopter of new technology all round. We once stepped out of the theatre together and he said to me, 'Look at my glasses.'

I said, 'What about them?'

He said, 'They're tinted, right?'

I said, 'Er . . . yes, they are.'

He said, 'But when we were inside, just now, they were clear.'

I said, 'Were they?'

'Yes. They're these new reactolites. Indoors, they're clear, so you can see. But when you go out in the daylight, they automatically darken to protect your eyes. They react to the light.'

'They don't, do they?'

Honestly, what would they think of next? I didn't know. But I was pretty sure Bob Monkhouse would buy it before anyone else did.

For me, the best of Bob never came across on television. Some part of him just didn't travel down the camera and into the living room. In the flesh, though, he was just superbly, supremely funny. You had to be there, and I consider myself fantastically fortunate that I was. We had this fond scheme that one day we would make a silent movie together. We walked round and round his garden one summer evening, hatching plans for it. I wish those plans had come to something because I think the film could have been funny. But Bob's workload as a comic was enormous. He was constantly on the road, and he wasn't hungry to do other things.

While I was delivering babies in Weston-super-Mare, my pal Malcolm Taylor was continuing to plot and scheme, as ever. Somehow, in the course of this plotting and scheming, he had convinced the powers to let him put on a play at Sadler's Wells. It was Sheridan's *The Rivals*, which I had already appeared in, five years earlier, while starting out at Bromley Rep. Again, I played Bob Acres, the country bumpkin who comes into some money and is then thrown right out of his depth into the middle of high society – a bit like me at Eric Idle's birthday party. This time, though, rather than Bromley, I was in the somewhat more salubrious surroundings of the legendary Sadler's Wells Theatre. They were trying to resurrect Sadler's Wells as a place for plays. Joseph Grimaldi – the greatest comedy actor of his time and possibly the most famous man of his age – trod the boards there, back in seventeen-hundred-and-frozen-to-death. But, by the beginning of the 1970s, it had long since gone dark, theatre-wise, and had become mostly famous for ballet and dance.

The Rivals worked well there, and I got some really good notices. One night, Richard, my agent, turned up in the audience with a theatre producer called John Gale – a typical, larger-and-louder-than-life producer figure. I don't think he was actually wielding a fat cigar and wearing a fur coat the size of a car, but you felt he ought to have been. Gale was the producer of *No Sex Please – We're British*, the aforementioned comedy by Alistair Foot and Anthony Marriott, which had opened at the

Strand Theatre in 1971, with Michael Crawford in the lead. This was just before Crawford really became a household name with the British public as Frank Spencer in *Some Mothers Do 'Ave 'Em*.

Now, the critics had torn *No Sex Please* to shreds. They thought it was terrible and gave it an absolutely filthy time – quite unfairly, really. The play wasn't Shakespeare, or Ibsen, it's true, but it was a very funny play and a very funny piece of entertainment. Not for the first time in history, the critics and the people who actually pay for their own tickets had to agree to differ. People were flooding to the play and stuffing it full nearly every night. It had become the West End's must-see show – a massive success, albeit by no means an overnight one. The cast had toured it around the country for three months before-hand, doing the spadework and getting it right.

Still, Crawford had now done a year in the West End in what was an incredibly physical role, involving all sorts of knockabout stuff, and he had decided to move on – leaving John Gale with a bit of a dilemma. The success of *No Sex Please* had been significantly down to Crawford: much of what was truly funny about the play only existed in the bits of physical business he was doing. When people came out of the theatre, they weren't talking about how wonderful the play was, they were talking about how wonderful Michael Crawford was. The obvious fear was that, without him, the show would go limp and the gold mine would dry up.

The producers wanted a name, really, to replace him – an established star. But they couldn't find anyone famous who could do what Michael Crawford was doing. Which was why Richard had persuaded Gale – with some difficulty, as I understand it – to come and have a look at me in *The Rivals* that night. I met him briefly after the show and let him run an appraising eye over me. He was very non-committal, although he said he liked the production. I didn't hear anything more for a few weeks.

The problem that Gale had was that I was virtually unknown. I had a bit of a reputation in the business, maybe, but there was no way that I was a name you could put up outside a theatre and expect it to bring in the crowds. At the same time, I think Gale had reached the point where he was running very low on other choices. The bigger names they had in mind for the role had gone to see the play and, perhaps feeling a bit overawed by Crawford, decided it wasn't for them. So, when all the other options had run dry, it came down to me.

Finally, long after I had given up expecting to hear anything, Gale got in touch and invited me and Richard to meet him at his office in the Strand, where we had a long discussion. I got the feeling that Richard had been doing a big persuasion number on Gale – but that Gale still wasn't completely persuaded. Eventually the deal was that he would put me in the show for three months, while he continued to hunt for someone else. At any time within that three months, if someone better turned up, he could replace me and I would just have to sling my hook. As for pay, word had it that Crawford was on 12 per cent of the box office, which meant he was earning very nicely, thank you. By contrast, I was to be given a flat rate of £100 per week, for the first three months, and £150 after that, as long as the box office didn't go down.

Scaled-down money, replaceable at any time . . . you will appreciate that these weren't the most flattering of terms for me to be entering the show on. But I wasn't arguing. In fact, I was delighted. For one thing, £100 a week might not sound a lot today, but in 2013 terms, that was about £1,000 a week – a more than handsome enough wage, it seemed to me. For another thing, I was going to be the lead in a major West End show. (As long as I didn't cock it up, obviously.) This was a huge result for me.

In due course, Richard said, 'You must go and see the show.' And I, in some entirely misguided, fancy and highfalutin way, said something along the lines of, 'No, no – I don't want to be influenced. I want to make the role my own – come at it afresh, make it my own creation.'

What a plonker.

Fortunately, I was persuaded to see sense: I went to the show. Strangely, I had met Michael Crawford fleetingly, just to shake his hand, a year or so prior to this. I went out with a dancer called Melanie Parr, who had a close friend in the dance troupe Pan's People, whose weekly chiffon-clad appearances on *Top of the Pops*, interpreting the chart hits of the day, made them the object of much wistful reflection among male adolescents and beyond. Crawford had been persuaded to open a summer show with Pan's People in Sussex, quite near Melanie's parents' house, which is how Melanie and I ended up going along. Crawford was quite the ladies' man and I think the opportunity to spend a little quality time with the country's leading all-female dance troupe might have influenced his decision to say yes to this particular gig. And why not? He was a good-looking, highly talented actor – a bit like me, only taller.

Anyway, now here I was in a box during a matinee at the Strand watching him in *No Sex Please*. And my God, he was good. Intimidatingly so. He had been in the show for a year and he had worked this stuff until it was absolutely honed, and very, very funny. As I sat there, listening to the reaction he was getting from the audience, my plan to begin anew with the play and style it entirely according to my own whim (whatever that was) began to recede. And in its place came a far better plan: to copy as much of Crawford's performance as, in my opinion, worked – which was all of it – and to introduce a way of playing the character that suited my height.

A brief run-through of the plot of *No Sex Please*, lest you were unfortunate enough to have missed it: the play is basically about a bank manager who starts to receive, unexplained, vast shipments of sex books, all of which, to spare him embarrassment, have to be hidden upstairs in the flat above the bank where he lives. The area manager of the bank is coming to take out the bank manager's mother – which might sound a bit contrived but, of course, it enables the bank manager to be at risk of embarrassment in front of not just one but two rich sources of mortification: his boss and his mum. Crawford's character was one Brian Runnicles, the hapless, put-upon bank clerk, who gets lumbered with the task of getting rid of the dirty books on the bank manager's behalf, and sparing his boss's wrongful and potentially ruinous exposure as a pornographer.

I did say it wasn't Ibsen, didn't I? But I did also say it was very funny. And it was funny because of what Crawford was doing. For example, the set incorporated a serving hatch. This got used on and off, as the play developed. At one point, for example, unnoticed by the characters onstage, Runnicles got his arm trapped under the hatch, from the offstage side, and then drew attention to his plight by twisting his fist around and knocking on it. The hatch was used several more times for bits and pieces, building to the climactic moment where Runnicles, now trouserless (obviously), had to go running across the stage and take a flying leap right through the open hatch. And as he committed himself to the dive, the hatch broke and dropped, so that he ended up crashing through it. These were pieces of business that Crawford had perfected and was pulling off with, it seemed to me, military timing.

Then there was a wonderful sequence where the area manager was allegedly on his way up the stairs, and the flat was still crammed with piles of dirty books. Runnicles and the other two characters onstage at that time formed a kind of panicked chain gang, the other two picking the books up and throwing them along the line until they reached Runnicles, who hid them, one by one. And every time Runnicles turned back, the next book was already in the air, flying straight at him. It was like a circus routine. Yet somehow all the books got tidied away and exactly as the last volume disappeared, the door opened and the area manager came in. I loved mastering that routine when the role was mine and we used to get a round for it every night, because it was so beautifully designed and performed.

The important lesson I learned that night, watching Crawford at the Strand, was this: don't be such a fool as not to use things that work when they're offered to you. If someone has blazed a trail, don't muck about in the long grass: follow them up it. If it works, and has been proved to work, you'd be an idiot not to help yourself.

Soon, when I had settled into the role, I began to add a few things of my own, on top of Crawford's stuff. I invented a piece of business with some brown wrapping paper. Having rid the flat of its burden of filthy books, Runnicles takes delivery of a box, again addressed to the manager. This, to his dismay, turns out to be full of filthy photos. There was some lovely business about being terribly offended by these pictures, but then picking them up and actually becoming rather interested in them. Imagine, if you can, an innocent character, obviously a virgin and likely to remain so, picking up individual photos and trying to decide which way up they're meant to be. Anyway, after I had unwrapped the parcel, there was brown paper all over the floor. One night, charging about with the photos, I put my foot on the brown paper and realised that it moved beneath you. It was shiny on one side, like ice. So I thought, if I start treading on it, I could slip and fall flat on my face. The next night, I tried that, and it worked. Then I built it up further, so that I could walk away from the paper as if deep in thought, and then I could rush back, jump onto the paper and slide to the front of the stage, as if on a snow-board. With a slight and invisible motion of one foot, I perfected a braking motion so that I'd seem to be about to go flying into the front row, but then, just as people were readying themselves for the arrival of an actor in their lap, I would turn my ankle and come to a dead stop, right at the lip of the stage. Business à la Jason.

There was also some nice à la Jason business with a Pakamac – that classic piece of cheap and cheerful rainwear which was essentially a plastic bag with buttons. Runnicles was in and out of this less than fetching garment claiming that it was a disguise he wore while getting rid of the books. The pakamac was a good visual gag in itself but I used to come in, take it off and park it on the single newel post at the foot of a little staircase that ran down onto the stage. Then, later on, in one of my numerous panics to hide, I would take the pakamac off the newel post, drape it over myself and pretend to be another newel post on the other side of the steps. And then I worked up a bit of business out of that, too. When the danger was clear, I would pretend to be trapped in the pakamac, and would breathe in so that the plastic got sucked tight to my face, then stagger around and pretend to be on the verge of fainting. (Adults: don't try this at home – a) it's dangerous, b) it's copyright.)

Perhaps my favourite stunt, though (and this was one of Crawford's), came at a point where Runnicles was at his lowest ebb, fed up with everything and saying, 'I'm not doing this any more.' At that moment, the area manager starts to come through the door and Runnicles isn't meant to be there, so his boss, Peter, the bank manager, simply picks him up and throws him out through another door. The bank manager was played brilliantly by Simon Williams, who was already beginning to make it big on the television as James Bellamy in the drama series *Upstairs Downstairs*. We had to arrange it so that Simon grabbed me by the arm and I performed a kind of jump. But it looked exactly as though Simon had picked me up off the ground, tilted me through ninety degrees and thrown me off horizontally before crisply slamming the door. It was all in the bending of the legs, ladies and gentlemen, and the timing of it, and diving while appearing to be thrown. I landed on a mattress on the other side of the door, carefully placed there at the right time by the stage crew, who were faultlessly brilliant in this area – thankfully, or I would probably have broken my arm the first time we did it. That moment was totally theatrical, in the sense of things happening physically in front of you. In a film you would think very little of it because you would know it had been tricked. Here, in the flesh, it was very imposing, and also a complete hoot. There were many moments in the play like that. It was related to the work of magicians, in a way: with them, it's sleight of hand; with us, it was sleight of body.

By opening night, I was fully rehearsed and raring to go. It was a huge moment for me, obviously, and I was abuzz with nerves and excitement – to the point, in fact, where you could probably have used me as a generator to illuminate the marquee outside the Strand. On which, incidentally (and I'm sure you'll understand my thrill about this), stood my name in red lights above the title of the play. I truly felt I had arrived. Remember Mystic Mavis, the Birmingham psychic, and the prediction she made for me in her sitting room all those months and chapters previously? Well, reader, it all came true, exactly as she foretold, right down to the colour of the lights. It's why I'm someone who won't hear a word said against psychics. (They know that about me already, obviously.)

That first night was going well. Most of my nerves had tamed themselves the moment I stepped onto the stage and quickly started to get laughs, which soon banished the rest of them. But then came a bad moment with Simon.

It was at the clinching moment for a scene, right before the interval. Simon's bank manager had to hold his arms out wide in a gesture of resignation and say, 'What are we going to do?'

Standing opposite him, I found myself making the same gesture with my own arms, exactly mirroring it.

When we came off, Simon stormed up to me, right up close.

Simon is six feet tall, so he was able to impose himself upon me from a relatively great height. He said, 'Don't you *dare* ape me.'

He had thought I was copying the gesture to take the piss out of it.

I said, 'I wasn't aping you. I was responding to you in the way I thought my character would.'

I went to my dressing room and shut the door, feeling shaken and a bit sick. I'd never had an eyeball-to-eyeball confrontation with another actor offstage in the middle of a play before. I was thinking, 'Is this how it is in the West End? How am I going to last three months?'

We battled on through the rest of the play, got an ovation and took our bows. I still felt a bit tense about what had gone on earlier, though. However, in due course there was a tap at my dressing-room door and in came Simon. He apologised profusely for going off on one. The way I understood it, he had felt very tightly controlled while playing opposite Crawford and, in that little misunderstood moment between us on the stage, he had had a vision of it all happening again with me. Anyway, from that moment on, the two of us started to have fun without even a flicker of a cross word. Which is just as well, really. When someone much bigger than you is in charge of chucking you through a door every night, you want to get on with them.

Of course, all the throwing and diving made the role very athletically demanding. Fortunately, the show had its own osteopath – a man called Paul Johnson, one of life's good people, who used a room in the theatre as a surgery for the cast and crew and for a lot of the West End theatre dancers in particular. He used to pay the production a visit on Wednesdays between the matinee and the evening performance and sometimes he'd be there on a Saturday afternoon as well. I was quite often in with him, asking him to see off the worst of the physical damage inflicted on my frame by chucking it through a closed serving hatch on a nightly basis. Paul was a big man, in all directions, who could massage pulled muscles back into life – a saviour for dancers but also, as I frequently discovered during this period, a saviour for a knockabout comic actor.

I remember one period where, every time I finished the show, I would be in agony with my foot. The pain would subside completely overnight, only to climb back to agony-pitch again the following night. Paul took a look at me and said, 'I'm not surprised. You've dislocated your big toe.' Click – back it went. Did this ever happen to Gielgud? I ask myself. He didn't make much fuss about it, if it did. Mind you, I do believe, in his younger days, Laurence Olivier was asked to name the best attribute an actor could have. He replied, 'Stamina.' That was certainly the best attribute an actor in *No Sex Please – We're British* could have had. You and me both, Lozzer.

After a year in the role, I was presented with a very nice lighter and an engraved brick with a hole hollowed out of the middle of it, which sits on my desk to this day with my pens in it. I was in *No Sex Please* for eighteen months, and I think I only had two nights off for illness in that whole period. (I was laid low by a throat infection, the traditional occupational hazard for the theatre actor. All the dust and germs of a thousand nights gather up high in the flats and then, when someone slams a door in the set, the spores of ages shower gently down around you and into your vulnerable passages.) For sixteen of those months, I had the greatest time, but as the end of my contract loomed, when I was asked if I wanted to sign up again and continue, I realised that it was time to move on. I had done as much with the role as I was ever going to do with it. I couldn't see it developing in a different direction if I stayed in it, so, much as I loved it, I decided to opt for change. To my relief, the box office didn't go down on my watch. In fact, it started to go up. John Gale saved himself a stack of money by having me in the role. After six months, we were packed out and he was paying me peanuts, relatively speaking, so he got to go laughing all the way to the bank. Did I burn with resentment about it, though? I can't say I did. I was having too good a time.

It was one of the friendliest casts I had ever been in, a proper team even as people came and went: people like Richard Caldicot, who was a brilliant foil; and Evelyn Laye and Jean Kent, who eventually took over from Evelyn – both big stars who knew the business inside out; and Simon Williams, of course, and Belinda Carroll, who was Simon's wife in real life, and whom I could get corpsing like nobody's business. Belinda eventually left, to be replaced by Liza Goddard, who was famous for being in the legendary kids' TV show *Skippy the Bush Kangaroo*. Before Liza's arrival, the cast solemnly marked Belinda's last night in the show by filling her knickers with shaving foam. During the play, that is. There was a moment when she had to come offstage, stay a beat or two in the wings, and then go straight back on. In that pause, fleeting though it was, her fellow thespians offstage nonetheless found time to squeeze a large helping of Gillette's finest grooming product into the rear of Belinda's underwear. Back out she went, of course, destined to play the rest of the scene and the rest of the play with a pair of silently frothing pants. A memorable final performance, I'm sure.

Belinda, Simon, Richard . . . these were bigger and better actors than I had earned a right to be moving among. I was completely energised by the experience. I had that fabulous, liberated feeling that only comes at the start of your career, when you don't have a reputation to lose, you only have a reputation to make.

It wasn't the greatest play in the world, but it wasn't meant to be. It was a vehicle to make people laugh. It was a moment in the culture, too. Despite the sixties, sex was something most people couldn't quite bring themselves to talk about, and here was a play about exactly that reticence and awkwardness and shame. People recognised themselves in it. And you had to be there on a Friday or Saturday night, when the place was packed with people absolutely in fits. You'll know, I'm sure, the expression 'rolling in the aisles'. Up to that point, I'd always assumed it was figurative – an exaggeration. At *No Sex Please*, I saw it happen. People actually laughed so hard they fell out of the chairs and into the aisles.

Indeed, more than once we had people carted out with heart attacks. I'm not saying that's something to be proud of – and all sympathies, of course, to the people concerned and their relatives. At the same time, it's a sort of backhanded compliment.

In the audience one night: Ronnie Corbett. He was getting ready to play Brian Runnicles in the film version of the play that was made in 1973. 'But why him and not you?' I hear you loyally cry, your voice thick with affront and tremulous outrage on my behalf. 'After all you had done for that production,' I hear you loyally add, dabbing tears of hurt from your appalled eyes.

The answer is simple, actually. Ronnie was already a star. They couldn't have raised the money for a film on my name. They could raise it on his. That's how it works.

In the audience another night: a coach party from Leeds including a student called Gill Hinchcliffe. Not that I knew her, or knew she was there at the time. It was something I found out a couple of decades later when she told me – not all that long before I married her.

*   *   *

I HAD BEEN living all this time in the flat above my brother and sister-in-law's hairdressing salon in Thornton Heath, still jostling past the free-standing hairdryers on my way in at night.

Then one day, Josephine Tewson, a brilliant actress I knew well from *Hark at Barker* and *Mostly Monkhouse* (she was later very successful in the nineties sitcom *Keeping Up Appearances*), told me she was moving out of her flat – a rent-controlled, one-bedroom apartment in a Peabody Estate building on Newman Street, just behind Oxford Street and right in the middle of London. She asked me if I knew anyone who might want to take it over. I told her I definitely did know someone: me.

The day I moved in, I was fumbling in the doorway with my key and suitcases, when the door to the flat across the landing opened, exposing a man in a pinny, in the middle of doing the hoovering. This was Micky McCaul, a bookmaker turned estate agent, who with his wife Angie became firm friends and the best neighbours an actor in search of late-night drinking companions could wish to have.

I loved that bachelor pad and I loved the neighbourhood, too, and the sense of being deep in the beating heart of the city, which was not a sensation that was always available in Thornton Heath. I liked the fact that everything was just a short walk away – Tottenham Court Road, the One Ton pub in Goodge Street, Macreadys, a private club at Seven Dials, run by Ray Cooney, among other people, where highly detaining graffiti covered the wall of the Gents. One day the landlord had it painted over. Within moments a solitary, neatly written line had appeared in the fresh paint: 'Where has all the graffiti gone?' Sometimes I would drift up Oxford Street to watch the street hawkers at work, flogging their dodgy watches and perfumes off the pavement, or doing cup-and-ball trick routines on milk crates – and bundling everything away and legging it at the first sight of a policeman. It all had a sort of edgy romance to me.

On Sundays, though, my only day off from *No Sex Please*, I would sometimes decide to get out of the city for a few hours and would drive out to Dunstable Downs in Bedfordshire with

Carol Collins, park up and sit there watching the gliders float around in the sky. It was a wonderful way to relax and get away from the job. One day when we were there, Carol said, 'You're always on about flying, and how fabulous you think it is. Why don't you go down and ask how much it costs?'

Always keen to look after the pennies, I said, 'No, it'll be far too expensive.'

But my curiosity was piqued, and eventually I did go and ask, and it turned out that learning to glide was not nearly as wallet-stripping as you might have imagined. Indeed, it was clearly the cheapest way to get into the air, and clearly within reach of an actor with a job in the West End. So I started going out to Dunstable every Sunday and learning to fly a glider, and in due course I was flying solo and studying towards my Silver C qualification. I loved it – to the extent that I ended up in partnership with a couple of guys at the airfield and bought myself a share in a glider. I was now the part-owner of an aircraft. Admittedly it was the cheapest kind of aircraft money could buy, and I only owned a third of it. Still, this would have seemed an entirely fantastical development in the days when I was a callow lad, acquiring my first second-hand motorbike.

Back on land in London, socialising after work was inherently complicated. In the early 1970s, the pubs closed at ten thirty, which meant no further service and that achingly familiar cry, 'Ain't you got no 'omes to go to?' The cry was the same in any pub in the city. I sometimes used to wonder whether it was the same bloke, going round to them all on his bike and putting his head through the door to do the shout. Whatever, it meant an actor found it very hard to clock off in time to get a drink. Sometimes you would be in a position to rush in just before closing, order two pints and line them up, but then you only had ten minutes' 'drinking-up time' to sink them, so that wasn't much good. It just left you with an enlarged belly and a desperate urge to pee.

Fortunately, for those difficult, dry times in an actor's life, there was Gerry's.

Gerry's was an underground cavern down a steep set of stairs between two shops on Shaftesbury Avenue. It had been opened by Gerald Campion, a short, rotund chap who, as a boy, got the part of Billy Bunter in a television series and became a bit of a child star. Like a lot of child stars, when he grew up and started seeking adult work, he found his former fame more of a hindrance than a help. Intimately understanding the profession and its needs, he opened a members-only after-dinner club for actors where you could drink and eat until two or three in the morning. So an awful lot of actors would end up at Gerry's.

I used to be excited to spot Hywel Bennett in there, when he was at the top of his game. He had acted with Hayley Mills and had been in the movie *The Virgin Soldiers* – the DiCaprio of his time, you could say. James Villiers was often in there too, another great British film actor who made me feel a bit starstruck. Ronnie Fraser was in Gerry's so much he had his own drink named after him – a tall vodka cocktail, mostly vodka. Mike Pratt from *Randall and Hopkirk (Deceased)* actually ended up serving there. I would also bump into the great John Junkin, who became a good friend and ally.

You had to be buzzed in via the intercom, once your name had been checked on the list. Then you found yourself on a narrow downward flight of stairs which quickly turned to the right through ninety degrees. A few more steps and you were in the magic kingdom. Everybody who was already in the club would turn to see who was arriving, so people liked to make a bit of an entrance as they swept down those final steps to the floor. Before you lay a dimly lit cellar, illuminated mainly by candles, and to the right, stretching back about thirty feet, were a number of what can only be described as horseboxes – booths, I suppose, would be the flattering term. In front of you was the bar, always frequented by a few diehards. To the left, two more horseboxes and the less than desirable Ladies and Gents toilets, also used as the storeroom.

It wasn't salubrious, then. But the point was, it was your club. You were among your own kind, you felt, and were very comfortable to be so. You could squeeze into a booth, if one was available, and order a meal – nothing fancy, steak and chips, mostly – and the beer and Scotch flowed freely. In those days, I stuck with beer – light and bitter, specifically. Many a night I would stagger out of Gerry's in the early hours of the morning with Malcolm Taylor, in a state of over-refreshment, having unsuccessfully attempted to woo the waitresses. Those were thrilling times altogether. I was acting in the West End, living in the West End, drinking in the West End – I couldn't have got much more West End without changing my name to 'West End'.

CHAPTER TEN

How not to make a movie. In bed with Elizabeth Taylor, but not Richard Burton. And various other adventures in the screen trade, not all of them entirely satisfying.

We come now to the portion of this narrative which must deal with my days in Hollywood – obviously an unforgettable period for me. The details are etched so vividly in my mind, it's as though it were yesterday, although, I confess, at the time I was constantly pinching myself to check that it was really me.

Really me, arriving in the entertainment capital of the world! Really me, driving on Sunset Boulevard with the sky above an incredible blue and the sun glistening in the palm trees! Really me, passing in a state of almost childish wonder through the gates of Universal Studios and onto its famous movie backlot!

Ah, what a lovely week's holiday that was. The summer of 1978, I believe. Linda Ronan, who handled this area for the Richard Stone Partnership, had got me a set of commercials for Cobb & Co., a pub-restaurant chain in New Zealand. The reason they wanted me was because of some physical antics I had got up to in a comedy series for ITV called *The Secret Life of Edgar Briggs*. The series had inspired a selection of scenarios for adverts in which I played a salesman for whom everything goes wrong and who creates chaos even as he is trying to make his pitch – a kind of anti-commercial, if you like. Anyway, among the perks of the job was a flexible air ticket, meaning that I could break my return journey anywhere I chose. I chose Los Angeles, where a great former girlfriend, who used to work in the bar at Gerry's, was now living. She had succeeded in securing a job with a publishing house and had emigrated. She agreed to put me up and show me the sights, and we had a fabulous week before I headed back to London.

Those seven days of tourism, which included trips to a number of very good burger bars, represent, even now, the full extent of my experience of Hollywood. Not for want of trying, I should say. Or perhaps I should say, not for want of dreaming. If any actor tells you their idle contemplations haven't turned longingly, at some point or other, to the prospect of a major American film deal, they're almost certainly fibbing. Yet it may be significant that, when I was actually in Hollywood that time, I didn't think about doing anything to make the dream become a reality. My agent, Richard, had a representative working in Los Angeles – his son, Tim. So, at Richard's suggestion, Tim and I met for lunch one day. Tim booked somewhere buzzing and businessy on the Sunset Strip, or thereabouts – the kind of place where you could believe everyone was talking deals and projects. He was adamant that we should get a good table – by which he seemed to mean one in the middle of the room. I was puzzled about this insistence at the time, thinking that surely all the best tables were the ones over by the wall, out of the way. But, of course, it was in order to be sitting where the maximum number of other diners would walk past you during the course of your meal, meaning you had the chance to catch someone's eye and say hello if you needed to.

I was a wide-eyed innocent throughout that trip – to an extent that seems bizarre to me now. I was an actor, in Los Angeles, with an agent – and yet it didn't occur to me to network or mingle or put myself about or turn the trip to my commercial advantage. Maybe, deep down, in my heart, for all the fantasies about a life in film, I lacked the belief. Maybe, in my heart, I thought it was far above and beyond me. It really was back to my innocent Incognito days: I suppose I wanted someone to tell me I was good. I was incapable of telling them. I was the wrong way round in LA.

This is not to say that the film world has not come a-calling for my talents on at least a couple of occasions. Reader, I have indeed graced the silver screen. However, I think it's fair to say that at no point while I was gracing it was cinematic history made. In fact, one of the films was so bad that cinematic history was almost unmade.

In 1973, I was busy in *No Sex Please* in the West End when Tim Stone got in touch and said, 'We've had some interest from a company called Border Film Productions who want to make a movie with you. They've seen you in *No Sex*.'

Well, that suggestion certainly tickled my interest, even though I had no idea who Border Film Productions were. The truth is, I'm not sure I ever properly found out who Border Film Productions were, even while I was working for them.

Tim sent me the screenplay for a film called *Albert's Follies*. That in itself was tremendously exciting – opening an envelope and pulling out a screenplay rather than just a play or script. I settled down to read it in a state of pink-cheeked glee. The screenplay was by a writer called David McGillivray. McGillivray went on to write a lot of scripts for the British sex-film industry. Perhaps you've seen his *I'm Not Feeling Myself Tonight* from 1975, or 1974's *The Hot Girls*; or maybe you've even come across the script for his sadly unmade 1976 piece, *Unzipper Dee Doo Dah*. Whatever, all that was in the future for him. What he had come up with in *Albert's Follies* seemed to be a fairly inno-cent kind of farcical comedy. The character it was proposed I should play, Albert Toddey, was a civil servant and an ordinary, rather meek bloke. But when things got tough, Albert would suddenly transform into a kind of James Bond figure, suited and sleek, and rescue the situation – or, at least, in his dreams he would. A slightly old, *Billy Liar*-style kind of set-up, you might immediately suggest; and you might immediately be right. But I was so busy being completely impressed by the simple fact that I was reading a screenplay, that I didn't really pause to have any particular reflections on its contents, critical or otherwise.

I went back to my agent and said I was definitely up for it. We weren't, I should add, talking blockbuster budgets. However, a three-week shoot was proposed, which could be tailored to fit around my nightly duties at the Strand Theatre, and the film was to be shot entirely at Twickenham Studios, which, if not exactly Pinewood or Shepperton – or, indeed, Universal – definitely sounded pukka enough.

Contracts were tremblingly signed, and soon after that, I was going through the doors at Twickenham with a spring in my step. On-set, I met my co-star – Imogen Hassall, a British actress who had on her CV an appearance in the schlocky 1970 movie *When Dinosaurs Ruled the Earth*. But, as she openly admitted herself, she wasn't as famous for that as she was famous for being famous. Because she was glamorous, the press flocked to her, and she was frequently photographed on the arm of somebody at an awards ceremony, in a stunning dress – normally backless, and quite often fairly frontless, too. For this, she had earned the nickname the 'Countess of Cleavage'.

I liked Imogen a lot and found her to be smart and sensitive in a way that, at the time, might have been at odds with the public perception of her. We had lunch together a couple of times while we were working and she mentioned being depressed about the way she was perceived. She said she felt trapped in a cartoon image of herself, and didn't quite know what to do about it. Seventeen years after all this, I was shocked to read that Imogen had taken an overdose and killed herself. She was only thirty-eight.

Also in the cast, playing men from the Ministry, were Tim Barrett, who later played Terry Scott's boss in *Terry and June*, and Hugh Lloyd, whom I knew from another Terry Scott series, *Hugh and I*. These guys were good company, and we were to have quite a laugh together on this project – at least in the early stages.

So, we started shooting *Albert's Follies* and, being totally inexperienced and knowing nothing about movie-making, I got on with doing what I was told to do. I turned up when I was told to turn up, I stood where I was told to stand, and I said the words I was told to say – which is pretty much the definition of film-acting, I suppose. I was the star of the film but I had nothing as glamorous as a trailer, I should point out. I had a utilitarian dressing room and went for lunch in the canteen with the props boys, where we all stood in line and moved along with a tray, having food slopped onto our plates by intimidating serving staff.

However, I very quickly got the sense that all was not what it was supposed to be. For one thing, we seemed to be working with extraordinary haste – with so much haste, in fact, that Ray the director didn't appear to have much time to do anything in the way of directing. Imogen and I would be put into position under the lights, and then we would hear 'Action!' and soon after that we would hear 'Cut!' and then we would move quickly on to the next scene.

A couple of times we went for a take, and afterwards, I said to Ray, 'If we do that again, I might be able to . . .'

But Ray wasn't really listening, and he would merely say, 'Right, let's get on. Next shot, please.'

Every now and again the cameraman would roll his eyes, conspiratorially, and quietly say to me things like, 'This is a big close-up that he wants. Don't do too much. You're doing a bit too much.' So, in the absence of any other instruction, I was taking direction from the cameraman. Even I, in my state of high excitement and with my eyes set on the Hollywood horizon, realised that this was not how it was meant to be.

Also, was it me, or did bits of the set keep disappearing?

No, it wasn't me: bits of the set did keep disappearing.

You would arrive in the morning and what had, the previous day, been a replica of a long corridor with numerous doors off it had dwindled to a solitary pair of doors in a small fake wall. It appeared the sets we were using weren't being built for our purposes – we were borrowing them. Essentially, we were making our film on anything we could find around the place that was free. When the sets were wanted elsewhere, they were being carted away. Which would explain, I suppose, some of the director's haste. You needed to get the scene in the sitting room done while you could because there was every chance that you would turn your back and find the sitting room had gone off to appear in someone else's film. I'm not sure Steven Spielberg would have settled for this – or even the person who directed (or should I say aimed?) the *Carry On* films.

Meanwhile, I was completely knackered. Six days a week, I was getting up at six in the morning and going off to spend the day filming – and then hurtling back to the West End in the evening to fling myself all over the place in *No Sex Please*. Most of the time I felt like I had just been run over, not by a lorry but by a fleet of lorries. After two of the scheduled three weeks of the shoot, I was nearly dead. I came offstage at the Strand on the Saturday night and headed back to the flat in Newman Street – and almost nothing happened until I was woken by my alarm clock at dawn on the Monday, ready to drive over to Twickenham again. I just crashed out and slept solidly through until about 2 p.m. on Sunday, roused myself sufficiently to fix some kind of lunch, then curled up in front of the television for the rest of the afternoon before dragging my battered body back to bed.

The crisis point was reached in the final week of filming. There came a moment in the day when Imogen and I were required to appear in a scene which involved us walking down a passage together. For some reason, within the plot, I had lost my trousers and was wearing boxer shorts printed with a Union Jack (you'll get some measure of the quality of the film's farcical humour here). Imogen and I completed our duties, and then we heard the director say, 'Cut! OK, that's good. Now we'll go again with the second cast.'

Second cast? What did he mean, 'second cast'?

Then, as Imogen and I stared open-mouthed, onto the set trooped eight girls in tiny, ragged bikinis, all of them tied by their wrists to a length of rope, one end of which was in the thick-fingered grip of a large muscle-bound man. I was completely confused. This wasn't in the script, was it? A scene involving scantily clad girls, attached to a rope, and some kind of slave master? I don't think I would have missed that. Yet here they were.

Imogen and I simply stood aside as the man, the girls and their piece of rope were filmed passing down the corridor.

Thus was it revealed to us that *Albert's Follies* was no longer, strictly speaking, *Albert's Follies*. It felt more like *Jason's Folly*. And *Jason's Folly* was now a film called *White Cargo*. A whole subplot had been grafted onto the script – a story about selling strippers into slavery. To be frank with you, I'm still fairly confused about how this all worked. But my basic understanding is that, at some point during the filming, the order had come through from the producers to switch the film from a U certificate to an X certificate, in the panicked hope, presumably, that this would give it some life in the adult cinemas – the 'gentlemen's cinema clubs', as they used to be known in the 1970s – if nowhere else. Therefore, obviously, bring on the sex-slave strippers: it was as subtle as that. So *Albert's Follies* became *White Cargo*, which was *Albert's Follies* but with some extra slave girls and a random sex scene banged, as it were, onto the end of it. Or into the middle of it. Or whenever the fancy took the director.

Brilliant. My big breakthrough into the movies – and I was essentially making a soft-porn film.

Worse than that, I was making a soft-porn film without even knowing it.

Even worse than that, I was making a soft-porn film without being in any of the soft-porn bits.

Imogen and I made our feelings known to the director and to the cameraman and to anyone else who would listen. We received only shrugs. By this time we were seven-eighths through filming, and also tied to a contract, as tightly as those girls had been tied to the slave-trader's rope. So we finished up.

Reader, it was a dreadful film: please spare yourself the trouble of looking for it on Netflix, where you probably won't find it anyway. The finished article, my shining shot at big-screen superstardom, was a patchwork of disasters. Some of the takes used in the movie were actually camera run-throughs – rehearsals, in other words. At one moment, I am seen climbing over a wall at night-time and landing on the other side of that wall in daylight. To nobody's surprise, the film duly bombed. It became one of those films where you can fairly confidently say that more people were in it than went to see it. And there weren't that many people in it. Sex sells, people will tell you. Not always it doesn't.

Why did I go through with it? Because all I could see at the time was Hollywood, of course. You have to have been in a film to be considered for a film. It's catch-22 and Equity all over again. So if you somehow do break through and get to make a film, you're off and running. That's how it works, isn't it?

How far from the truth can you get?

Mind you, in fairness, I should point out that also in *Albert's Follies/White Cargo* was a Welsh actor whom I had known since I played that part in *Softly Softly* right at the beginning of my television career. It was this particular actor who had the mixed privilege of attending a Westminster hotel, after the three weeks of principal filming at Twickenham had ended, to romp around on a bed with the actress Sue Bond for the added-on sex scene belatedly deemed necessary by the producers. His name was Dave Prowse and clearly Dave managed to put this embarrassment behind him very efficiently: he later went on to play Darth Vader in the *Star Wars* movies. What had he got that I hadn't? Well, let's put it this way: he didn't have to wear lifts.

* * *

As THIS IS an autobiography, it had better be warts and all. So my other less-than-successful attempt to storm the world's cinemas in the early 1970s had me trying to use, as my Trojan Horse, the British film adaptation of Dylan Thomas's *Under Milk Wood*, directed by Andrew Sinclair. Word had got out that Richard Burton and Elizabeth Taylor had signed up to appear. Accordingly, thousands of actors went along to the London auditions, lured, I'm sure, by the enticing prospect of being able to say they had worked with Liz and Dicky. In fact, I think almost anyone who could do a Welsh accent and who was in London that day showed up, irrespective of whether they were an actor or not.

My trump card, though, and the thing that made me stand out from the crowd, was that I had been in Malcolm Taylor's stage production of *Under Milk Wood*, both at the Vanbrugh Theatre and then, later, in its six-month transfer to the Mayfair Theatre. This helped swing me a part. (Incidentally, Dylan Thomas's daughter, Aeronwy, came to see that Mayfair Theatre production and said nice things about it, which made us proud.)

I got cast as Nogood Boyo, and off I went on the train, all expenses paid, to Wales for four days, thinking, yet again, 'Next step, Hollywood.' We were billeted in an old-fashioned, badly faded but still rather grand hotel on the west coast, which made a change from the fusty bed and breakfasts of the touring theatre scene, and many was the night that Dicky Burton and I sat at the hotel bar, drinking and yarning and putting the industry to rights until the small hours.

OK, not really. Burton played the narrator, so he wasn't around at all while I was there. As for Elizabeth Taylor, she was Rosie Probert, the tart with the heart, and none of my scenes put me opposite her. However, on one of the days that I was there, a buzz started to go around the place: 'Elizabeth Taylor's on the set!' I took care to inveigle myself into the room where they were filming and observed from a distance.

And lo and behold, eventually there she was, radiating starriness. She was in a long nightdress and filming a scene where she had to lie down on a bed. There was a lot of pampering and fussing of her and ensuring that she was comfortable where she lay. Once she was settled, the director led in an extra in a grubby costume and brought him to the bedside. This extra was clearly more nervous than he had ever been in his life.

'Miss Taylor,' the director said, hesitantly and subserviently, with the manner befitting conversation with a megastar, 'may I introduce you to Darren? He's going to play the part of the sailor.'

What Darren had to do, following this scanty introduction, was to get into bed with Elizabeth Taylor. Then he had to lie there, on top of her, not moving. This, I have to say, Darren duly did. I'm not sure she even looked at him at any point. The camera was above them, so, in the shot, all you saw was the back of Darren's head and one of his ears, filling maybe a third of the frame, and then, more predominantly, Liz Taylor's face, looking up into the camera from the pillow.

Taylor spoke her line: 'Quack twice and ask for Rosie.'

That was it. Darren then climbed off Britain's most famous film actress and walked away. But presumably that was his story forever more: 'I got into bed with Elizabeth Taylor once.' And I bet nobody ever believed him. Apart from, of course, those who were on the set that day, and the very small number of people who saw the film.

I was so impressed by my surroundings on that shoot: the huge lights, the giant 35mm camera on tracks . . . this seemed like the full monty to me, the big time. That said, I had my own embarrassing moment. As Nogood Boyo, I had to be, as the Dylan Thomas line put it, 'up to no good in the wash-house' with Lily Smalls – a brief cameo moment which required me to come up behind Lily, who was played by Meg Wynn Owen, and reach round to grab her breasts. Maybe less of a cameo moment, then, and more of a camisole moment. Either way, I was consumed with self-consciousness. It was as awkward as I have ever felt in front of a camera – a terribly clinical moment in front of about twelve gawpers.

On reflection, this was one of only two occasions in my acting life when I found myself doing anything that could remotely be described as a sex scene. The other one occurred in a production of *Micawber* when I was playing opposite Jan Francis – and that, too, was surprisingly mortifying. *Micawber* was a four-part comedy drama written by John Sullivan, the writer of *Only Fools and Horses*, who had borrowed the character of Wilkins Micawber from Charles Dickens's *David Copperfield*. Episode one aired on ITV on Boxing Day, 2001 – when it went up against the Christmas Special of *Only Fools* over on the BBC. So, that Christmas, on one channel was a production starring me and written by John Sullivan, and on another channel was a production starring me and written by John Sullivan. It's all about viewer-choice in the end, isn't it?

Anyway, Jan was portraying this rather evil woman, Lady

Charlotte, who gets Mr Micawber into the bedroom and starts to seduce him. During the course of the action, which requires her to be fairly unsubtle about things, she pulls him down on top of her very hard, essentially planting his nose in her cleavage.

We did a run-through, and Jan yanked my head down to her neckline, as per instruction. At which point, I heard a voice above us say, 'Hold on, David – stay there while we relight this.'

So, there I was, with my head stuck between the breasts of a woman whom I knew well, but whose husband I knew weller. (He was Martin Thurley, the writer of *March in Windy City*.) And there I stayed, waiting for a couple of technical hitches to be sorted out. And waiting. And waiting . . . Jan and I became quite hysterical as these long minutes ticked by, but, on my part, the hysteria was entirely to cover the embarrassment.

Obviously, when you go to the pub after a day like that, and you tell someone with a proper job that this is how you spent your working day, they tend to look at you slightly askance. But what you've got to remember about experiences like these is that they take place in excruciating circumstances: witheringly, belittlingly, in a roomful of people and with someone popping up every minute or so with a bit of powder on a puff. ('You're sweating, David.' 'Yes, I know I am.') It's not uncomplicated, is what I'm saying.

Anyway, my other key memory of the *Under Milk Wood* filming, beyond the embarrassment of the breast-grab, was having to wade out into the sea to film a scene with Mrs Dai Bread, who was played by Ruth Madoc. I had known Ruth since that Malcolm Taylor production. She was now married to the actor Philip Madoc and was three or four months pregnant with their first child at this time. And here we were, dipping in the sea, in March, in Wales, which doesn't tend to resemble the Caribbean at that time of year – nor, really, at many other times of the year. It was stunningly freezing. I was fully clothed, but

Ruth wasn't wearing all that much. This was some kind of dream sequence and Ruth had to be in the water, topless, and summon me in after her. We were in the water for about twenty minutes and did the scene about three times over. All the time, I was worrying, saying to myself, 'This can't be a good idea for a pregnant woman.' When I think of that scene, I still shiver. I shot a documentary in Norway in winter once upon a time, and even there it wasn't as freezing.

It all worked out well, though. With the birth, I mean; Ruth had a boy. The film, on the other hand, worked out less well. People around the production spoke very excitedly at the time about how *Under Milk Wood* had never been adapted into a movie, and it turned out, retrospectively, that there were very good reasons for that: like the fact that, by definition, it's 'a play for voices'. It's all about the words, and the images created by the words, and making a picture out of it was, fundamentally, beside the point, or even self-defeating. I think the film was slightly below the standing of Burton and Taylor at the time. But Burton did it because he was Welsh and he was, as he never ceased telling people, 'in love with the bard'. Well, we all were – and also, some of us, in love with the idea of making a movie.

Alas, barring a couple of other more or less regrettable excursions, that was pretty much the extent of my film career. In 1978, a half-hour comedy I'd made with Ronnie Barker a few years earlier, called *The Odd Job*, got expanded into an eighty-minute film, directed by Graham Chapman from *Monty Python*. Chapman also played the lead, a depressive who hires an odd-job man to bump him off. (Ronnie Barker had turned it down, which should have sounded more alarm bells with me than it did.) I played the unlikely hired killer, as I had for Ronnie, but I wasn't Chapman's first choice. He wanted to give the role to Keith Moon, which gives you an indication of the different direction in which he wanted to take the comedy – rather losing the essence of it in the process, I felt. Certainly this was the only time in my life when I was ever considered a substitute for the drummer of the Who.

When they tried to revive the *Carry On* format in 1992, with *Carry On Columbus*, starring Julian Clary, I was sounded out about getting involved. But I read the script and found I wasn't laughing very often. Not for me, Raymond. (I do, however, do a good Julian Clary impression. What a pity this is a book, or I would do it for you now.)

More recently, the producers of *Gnomeo & Juliet*, the children's animation, offered me a part in a film (probably not for children and certainly not an animation) about the man who invented Viagra. Don't ask me which part. Let's just say I found I couldn't get all that worked up about it.

So, that's the story of me and Hollywood . . . so far. But you know the old saying: 'This time next year . . .'

*   *   *

AT LEAST ONE good thing came out of that *Under Milk Wood* shoot in Wales, though. It was where I met an actress called Olwen Rees, who played Gwennie. She was a beautiful girl and a lovely singer, and I grew very friendly with her and her husband, Johnny Tudor, who was a cabaret artist who worked the shipping lines.

A couple of years later, in 1977, I was touring in a production of *The Norman Conquests* which, among other dates, went to Cardiff. Olwen came to see a performance and brought along her friend, a striking, red-headed girl called Myfanwy Talog. Myfanwy was a teacher turned actress and, though I didn't know at the time, quite famous in Wales on account of her appearances on Welsh television with the comedy duo Rees and Ronnie. You could say they were the Welsh version of the Two Ronnies, and Myfanwy was the leading girl in the show.

Olwen was doing a bit of matchmaking, clearly – and a very

successful piece of matchmaking, as it happened. The three of us went out for dinner together and I was instantly taken with Myfanwy, and she with me. We started to go out together – which was quite tricky at first because she was in Wales and I was either in London or off on tour. You find a way, though, if you really want to do something. We made it last for eighteen years.

CHAPTER ELEVEN

The noble art of raspberry-blowing. My apprenticeship as
a shop assistant. And the bed that rocked in Billingham.

I called Ronnie Barker the 'Guvnor'. It was a jokey nickname
at first, but it grew to express exactly what I felt about him.
The Guv'nor is what he was to me, and always will be. It wasn't
just the depth of his comic gift, the abilities he had as a writer
and a performer and a composer and an artist (even his handwriting was a work of art), it was the way he conducted himself,
the kind of man he was. I've always tried to emulate him a bit
and to feel him on my shoulder.

He was in his early forties when we first worked together,
and firmly established. His television partnership with Ronnie
Corbett in *The Two Ronnies* was already up and running and
on its way to becoming one of the biggest items in British
television history. Yet you would have been hard-pushed to find
someone less grand or starry. The trappings of show business
and the attention that it brought him were of no interest to
Ronnie. He lived quietly, kept himself out of the limelight and
wanted nothing to do with fame for its own sake. After rehearsals
or filming, he would want to go home to his family. He hardly
ever attended big social events. On television, he was almost

always in character: that was the thing he loved and the thing he absolutely excelled at – playing comic roles. The only time Ronnie really appeared on-screen as himself was in those portions of The Two Ronnies when the pair of them sat at a desk and read the spoof news headlines, quite openly chuckling at each other's gags. That's pretty much how he was, off-screen, the whole time I was around him: genial, open, always looking for what was funny in any situation, and quick-witted in a way that often, I don't mind admitting, left me trailing in his wake.

I remember one time, very early on, during a rehearsal for Open All Hours in a room at the BBC, something stupid happening and everybody ending up on the floor, which used to happen a fair bit. And when everybody had just about finished picking themselves up, Ronnie said to me, very seriously, 'It's amazing.'

I said, 'What do you mean?'

He said, 'Look at us. We're getting paid just to make ourselves laugh. It's not a bad life, is it?'

That was the attitude he took to his work, and it couldn't have made him easier to be around.

He was very quick to make me feel that he saw something in me. At first, perhaps, it was simply the fact that I could perform a reliable pratfall. In Hark at Barker, he gave me the part of Abdul the Filthy in a sketch set in a harem, with Ronnie as a sheikh, magisterially eating bananas and tossing aside the skins. Every time Abdul entered, he found a new skin to slip on. That makes the humour in the sketch sound pretty basic, but in fact it was in the context of a very sophisticated cinematic joke. The idea was to make the skit look like an old piece of film, slipping in a faulty projector – that thing that used to happen sometimes with movie reels, where the image would suddenly get out of true, so you would be seeing the top half of the frame at the bottom and the bottom half at the top. In the sketch, you saw a girl falling into the hands of an evil sheikh in the bottom half of the screen – only for Ronnie to reach down to her from the top half of the image and pull her up to safety. To make this work, they had to build two identical harem sets, one on top of the other. Ronnie simply leaned out of the top set and pulled the girl up out of the bottom set. But when you saw it, he appeared to have breached the boundaries of the actual film. It was clever stuff – cleverer than any other sketch I had seen involving banana skins.

Another time, Ronnie had this joke he wanted to do, as Lord Rustless, the baffled old aristocrat. His Lordship was going to preach the amazing advantages for a household of having a communication tube, like on board a ship – a pipe you could talk down in order to summon your staff from other parts of the house. Rustless demonstrates the use of the pipe by talking into it and waiting for a reply to come back to him – except, instead of a voice being heard, a cloud of soot puffs out of the tube and covers him. We see Josephine Tewson, playing the old spinster Bates, also attempting to communicate using the tube, and also getting a face full of soot. The tube was loaded with black powder and, out of shot, someone would puff into the other end of it and expel the soot at the appropriate moment. They tried it a few times in rehearsal, but Ronnie wasn't entirely happy with it. Eventually he said, 'I want David to blow the soot out because his timing is accurate and I need someone who can time this.' That rather put me on the spot. But I felt like I had been handed a little bit of responsibility, that I was moving up in his estimation. Fortunately, I got it right.

These were only little bits and pieces, but it was through them, I'm sure, that Ronnie grew increasingly to trust me as a comic performer and, in particular, to trust my timing. He had a scene in which Lord Rustless notices a pin on the floor, and bends down to pick it up, rather pompously intoning the old saying: 'See a pin and pick it up, all day long you'll have good –' And at that point, I come crashing through the door behind him as Dithers, and knock him flying. To get the laugh, it had to be done on the button, dead on. We rigged up a monitor on the other side of the door, so I could watch Ronnie and time the moment. When you get it dead on, that's what makes it sing, and I guess I had been up to these kinds of tricks in the theatre long enough to know what I was doing.

It was also pretty quickly clear that we knew how to make each other crack up. There was a skit where Rustless had his staff lined up like an army, including me as Dithers, all of us standing to attention and ready for his inspection. Then Ronnie walked down the line, making kind of parade-ground comments: 'Stand up straight!', 'Shoulders back!' and so forth. As Dithers, I automatically looked like I'd crawled out of a rubbish bin and was effectively wrapped in rags. When Rustless reaches me, though, he simply says, 'Buttons!' In rehearsal, I found myself thinking 'fly buttons' and responded by bending forward to look down in the area of my flies. This creased us both up. Ronnie said, 'Do that, definitely.' As we carried on rehearsing, that little moment continued to make us laugh. We were both of us thinking, 'This is absolutely going to kill them when we come to do it in front of the studio audience.'

So we get to the night of the recording, and the audience is in, and we do the inspection-of-staff scene, and Ronnie passes along the line and reaches me and says, 'Buttons!' And I lean forward and look down at my crotch. Nothing. Absolute silence from the audience. Not so much as a smile. There's just a fraction of a beat in which Ronnie looks at me with slightly widened eyes. And then he moves on. Some fall on stony ground, was the lesson here. Also, beware the in-joke.

The time I realised that Ronnie really had started to believe in what I could do was when he asked for me to appear in *The Odd Job* – part of a series of one-off comedy plays that Ronnie and Humphrey Barclay made for LWT in 1971. These pieces were brought together under the title 'Six Dates with Barker'.

Ronnie had sent me a script, by Bernard McKenna. The story featured a depressed husband, called Arthur Harriman, and the slightly loopy itinerant he hires to help him do away with himself and who, when Arthur eventually goes cold on the idea, continues to insist on the old-fashioned virtues of a job well done, and finishing what you started. I thought it was terrific, very funny but also slightly dark, and I could see myself playing the husband, which I was sure was the plan.

I said to my agent, 'I think the script's great. I'll be very happy to play Arthur.'

My agent said, 'No, Ronnie wants you to play Clive, the hit man.'

This seemed unlikely to me. Clive had all the best lines, all the zingers. Arthur was basically the feed. I rang Humphrey.

'Just to clarify, is it right that Ronnie wants me to play Clive?'

Humphrey said, 'Yes. Ronnie's going to be the husband.'

I said, 'But Clive's part has all the jokes.'

Humphrey said, 'Well, maybe. But this is the way Ronnie wants to do it.'

I was very struck by that. This was the polar opposite of my experience with Terry Scott in *Hugh and I*. It wasn't about Ronnie being the big star, the needy comedian, having to get the laughs. It was about what Ronnie, as an actor, thought worked best for the piece. That was his fundamental philosophy and one I never saw him contradict. He saw the bigger picture at all times.

So we filmed *The Odd Job* and it went well. It's hard to explain what makes two actors sit comfortably opposite one another on camera, and come across well together, and no doubt there are many contributing factors. But with Ronnie and me, I think a lot of it was about the rhythm with which lines went back and forth between us – that shared sense of timing, which can take a verbal form as well as a physical one. Sometimes you can find that rhythm with someone over the course of time. But with us, it was there pretty much straight away. It was possibly a bit competitive at first, like tennis. And, with Ronnie, the ball would come back harder than I was used to, and I would end up having to raise my game, pushing myself further to return it to him. But, at the same time, Ronnie wasn't playing to win. He was playing simply towards the end of getting the laugh. In any scene you were doing, he knew where the laugh was – the winning shot at the end of the rally, as it were. And however we got it, and whoever ended up hitting it, he didn't mind. He just wanted to make sure we got it.

The Odd Job ended up being shot in moody black and white. That wasn't an artistic decision, though. It owed itself to something far more prosaic and very 1970s: industrial action. Workers at ITV were in dispute over pay and the crews on certain productions refused to use the colour technology as a kind of strike protest. As a result, of the 'Six Dates with Barker', five were in glorious colour and the sixth – *The Odd Job* – was not. I hope that wasn't anything personal, brothers. I don't think the piece lost any of its humour for the lack of colour, however.

Incidentally, one of the other 'Six Dates' was entitled *1899: The Phantom Raspberry Blower of Old London Town*, written by Spike Milligan. It was a play in which the fog-bound Victorian city is menaced by an elusive figure who does for people by leaping out and blowing raspberries at them. I wasn't involved in that piece, but a few years later, when Ronnie revived the story for *The Two Ronnies* and presented it as a weekly serial within the show, I was given the enormous honour of providing the raspberries for the soundtrack. As Ronnie B. knew, very few people blow a raspberry as well as I do. Indeed, this may well be an area of expertise in which I could be described – without fear of contradiction – as a world leader. It has to be remembered that Ronnie was ever the perfectionist. He monitored my raspberry-blowing extremely carefully, for volume, tone and duration. At one point, he had me in the soundbooth while he stood on the other side of the glass, and he conducted me, very earnestly, in an entirely blown-raspberry version of the '1812 Overture'. (Anyone interested in seeing me restage this performance at the Royal Albert Hall any time soon, get on to my agent.) Jobs don't come much more profound than going into a BBC studio to spend a morning making farting noises into a microphone. The end credits for this portion of the show were printed on old-fashioned boards and filmed. I still have the credit board which reads 'Phantom Raspberry Blower – David Jason' and I'm enormously proud of my contribution to that little moment of comic history.

After 'Six Dates with Barker', Ronnie left ITV and went over to the BBC where, in 1973, he made another set of one-off shows, this time in a series called 'Seven of One'. (Why Ronnie left ITV for the BBC, only those in the know would know, and as I wasn't in the know, you know, I wouldn't know. You know?) The title of the series was meant to be 'Six of One', and Ronnie intended to follow it up later with another series, entitled 'And Half a Dozen of the Other', but someone at the BBC slightly ruined that gag by insisting that there should be seven shows in the first series. So, somewhat meaninglessly, 'Seven of One' it was.

Each of the shows was essentially conceived as a pilot for a possible sitcom. There was, for instance, *I'll Fly You for a Quid*, written by Dick Clement and Ian La Frenais, the tale of a Welsh family who will gamble on anything. Ronnie was especially keen on that one, and frustrated that he never got to make it into a series. There was *Another Fine Mess*, written by Hugh Leonard, which was about a pair of Laurel and Hardy impersonators. But the clear stand-outs were a play called *Prisoner and Escort*, another Clement and La Frenais piece, about a convict being carted off to prison; and a play by Roy Clarke about a penny-pinching Yorkshire corner-shop owner and the thwarted nephew who works as his assistant. That one was called *Open All Hours*.

Ronnie was really keen for me to be involved in the 'Seven of One' series somewhere and he said, 'There's a part for you in practically every one of these, but I can't have you in all of them. I think you should be in either *Prisoner and Escort* or *Open All Hours*.'

We discussed it more thoroughly, and eventually we decided that the best place for me would be in *Open All Hours*, playing Granville, the hapless nephew of Arkwright the shopkeeper.

Did I know immediately that this rather lost character in his Fair Isle jumper would end up propelling my career to another level? It would be both tidy and romantic to say that I did, but the truth is I absolutely didn't. As far as I was concerned, Granville was just another character to play. In fact, by comparison with Clive in *The Odd Job*, I secretly found him a little bit thin and disappointing. I didn't think the relationship between Arkwright and Granville was anywhere near as rich as the relationship between Clive and Arthur. Altogether, the script didn't leap out at me the way *The Odd Job* script had done. Of course, it was a very different kind of piece. But the main thing was, if Ronnie thought it was worth pursuing, I felt there must be something to it. And it meant I would be working with the Guvnor again.

* * *

IN 1974, HUMPHREY Barclay once more favoured me with encouragement and work, offering me a role in a sitcom he was producing for ITV, entitled *The Top Secret Life of Edgar Briggs*. Not just any old role, either: the lead. Humph's belief that I could carry a series was a real vote of confidence in me. I was, after all, still relatively untried on television at this point in my life. Humph was convinced that both me and the show would fly, and always spoke about it afterwards as one of the funniest things he was ever involved with. I wish he had been right about the show flying.

The Top Secret Life of Edgar Briggs was written by Bernard McKenna (who wrote *The Odd Job*) and Richard Laing. I played Edgar, essentially a humble and rather clueless pen-pusher, who is promoted, by an administrative error, to the post of personal assistant to the head of the British Secret Intelligence Service. In that position he somehow manages to be successful, despite himself, in a whole variety of espionage missions. There was a lot of deadpan stunt work, which I relished. I seem to remember getting my tie stuck in a filing cabinet in one episode – and in another, driving a car very fast over a humpback bridge, so that all four wheels left the ground. Did I vault a sofa at any point? It would be hard to imagine I didn't. I also remember hanging off a windowsill at the top of a tall house in Regent's Park while my Secret Service colleague Spencer (played by Mark Eden) tried to haul me in from inside by the sleeve of my cardigan – only for me to slip out of the cardigan and plummet to the ground. Or, at any rate, plummet to the pile of cardboard boxes carefully arranged out of shot to break my fall. I think everyone on the production was slightly surprised at my willingness to perform these stunts myself. They would quite happily have supplied me with a stuntman. But where's the fun in that? I was happier being given the chance to channel my inner Buster Keaton.

We filmed thirteen episodes in all. I can still remember the combination of deep anticipation and high anxiety just before the first show went out – feeling enormously proud and, at the same time, vulnerable and exposed. To promote the series, I was asked to do an article for *TV Times* – one of those 'boy, I've really arrived' moments in an actor's life. They knew that I could ride a motorbike, drive a car, ride a horse (more or less, thanks to those lessons in Weston-super-Mare) and fly a glider.

So I was depicted on a picture spread doing all of these things. Showing off, in other words. The photographer was called Bert Hill. I went up in the glider and he went up in the tug that tows the glider up, and did air-to-air shots. We did pictures on a trials bike, and some of me diving – not in the Cayman Islands sadly, but in a lake somewhere in Britain. When the piece came out it was entitled 'TV's Man of Action'. Of course, I made out to people that I found it a bit embarrassing, but actually I thought it was great. It made me feel pretty special – like some kind of top gun.

In the papers, critical reaction to the show was good. *Edgar Briggs* had 'style and panache', according to the *Daily Telegraph*. The *Daily Mirror* said the show revealed that 'David Jason is a modern Buster Keaton with most of that great silent actor's gift of timing, rhythm and skill'. As comparisons go . . . well, I was ready to accept that one.

One problem: ratings. They started low, and they didn't get any better. Now, it's always easy to blame external circumstances for things like this, but, in this case, bear with me: the show was scheduled to go out on ITV on a Sunday evening, at the same time as *The Brothers* was going out on BBC1. In other words, *Edgar Briggs* was pitched up against just about the most successful drama series on television at that time. It couldn't have been a worse clash. In today's terms, it would be like trying to launch a new comedy show opposite *Downton Abbey*. The only people likely to watch would be a small hard core of new-comedy fans and the bewildered. In some ways, the scheduling of *Edgar Briggs* was a compliment: it demonstrated the amount of faith that ITV had in the show. They clearly thought it was competitive. But their confidence backfired. It meant the show was badly hampered from the off. It limped on and petered out. On commercial stations, naturally, ratings rule. There was no offer of a second series. The experience was, as you will readily understand, a bit of a blow for 'TV's Man of Action'. I had the big build-up, followed by the big let-down – and then the lingering and very public disappointment, stretched out over thirteen rather gloomy weeks. I was chastened. I went back into my shell a bit.

Still, at least *Edgar Briggs* had got as far as people's television sets. In the same period, there was another attempt to launch a comedy series with me in the leading role – this time, a project of the director/producer Sydney Lotterby at the BBC. The show was by Roy Clarke, the writer of *Open All Hours*, and was entitled *It's Only Me, Whoever I Am*. The central character was meant to be a kind of Walter Mitty figure who could never quite get his act together because he was always off on flights of fancy. Again, there was loads of enthusiasm around the project and a big sense of having found something that would work.

We made a pilot, and I remember a scene outside a cinema in which my character went into dream mode and was overcome by a fantasy in which he turned into a military colonel and began ordering the cinema queue around. At the time I felt nothing other than the sense that I was making a show which would end up on telly and really connect with people. It was written by a great writer, directed by a great director. What could possibly go wrong?

The pilot was edited and finished, and Syd and I got together to watch it. Afterwards, Syd said to me, 'You know what? I'm really sorry, David, but it doesn't work.' I agreed with him: it didn't. I don't know whether there were ingredients missing, or whether we had approached it in the wrong way, or what had happened – I couldn't put my finger on it at all. All I knew was that it felt flat. Again: bitterly disappointing.

What could you do? Battle on. Somebody said to me, very early on, 'If you want to make it in comedy, you have to have an idiotic determination to succeed.' Well, I seemed to be meeting the requirements. I had the necessary determination and I had the necessary idiocy.

Incidentally, we shot some of that failed pilot for *It's Only Me* in the north of England. In the evening we used to let off steam by playing snooker back at the hotel where we all stayed. Syd's first assistant on that shoot was a bloke called Ray Butt, and Ray's accent was so East End, you could cut it with a knife. I couldn't help taking the piss out of him, walking around the table, flexing my neck and saying, 'Awright, Ray? Awright, son?' We should bear this harmless and apparently negligible piece of mimicry in mind because without it I might not have landed a certain cockney part later in my career, in a series that definitely did work.

* * *

IN 1975, *PRISONER and Escort*, from the 'Six Dates with Barker' sequence, became a series called *Porridge*, with Ronnie B. in one of his best and eventually most popular roles as Norman Stanley Fletcher, the cunning but always deeply humane lag. The series was produced by Sydney Lotterby. After my performances as Dithers, Ronnie knew I could play funny old farts and there was a character in *Porridge* called Blanco, who was meant to be a seventy-year-old prisoner whom Fletcher had a soft spot for and kept an eye on. Ronnie requested that I play him.

I was two hours in the make-up chair, doubling my age in order to become Blanco. It had been a similar time for Dithers – quite uncomfortable and not a little boring, if the truth be known, but you lump it. The way Ronnie turned into Fletcher, by contrast, was breathtakingly effortless. He'd spend a little bit of time in hair and make-up, put the chewing gum in his mouth and he was off. He put on that character like he put on a coat. When he was Fletcher, he was Fletcher. When it was time to go to the canteen, he was Ronnie Barker again. He could slip in and out of it at the click of a finger – which, I guess, is the sign of true comfort in a role. Some actors never come out of character. Apparently this is true of David Suchet when he's playing Hercule Poirot, the Agatha Christie detective. Talk to him at any point during the working day, and you'll be talking to Poirot, complete with the accent. He stays in character. Why not, if it helps you? That wasn't how it was for Ronnie, though: he was in and out.

They built HM Prison Slade, with its Victorian-looking gantries and stairways, on a special set inside an old water-storage tank at Ealing. I would come out of my cell and walk along the gantry and then go down the stairs to the ground floor and sit there in the communal area, with all the lags, playing chess. It looked and felt extraordinarily believable.

All the scenes in the prison cells, though, were filmed at Television Centre. So, too, were the scenes in the prison hospital. There was a lovely moment where Blanco is in the prison hospital bed next to Fletcher, talking about the possibility of being released on parole. 'No, Fletch. They'll never release me. They'll have to carry me out,' he says. 'I'm too old now. They'll be taking me out in a wooden overcoat.' Fletcher says, very gently, 'No, you're not old.' Then there's a pause while he thinks about it. 'You *look* old. But you're not old.' That lovely line was made up by Ronnie during rehearsal. I think all the script had for that moment was: 'Don't talk like that.' What Ronnie came up with was funny and touching, so in it went.

Porridge, of course, went on to be an extremely highly regarded sitcom, routinely mentioned right up there among the very best when the lists get written. People always say that the essence of a sitcom is people trapped by their circumstances. In that sense, *Porridge* was the essence of the essence. After all, you don't get people more trapped by their circumstances than prisoners and their wardens. The comedy that Ronnie and the cast – and, of course, Clement and La Frenais – worked up out of those ultra-restrictive confines is the stuff of genius. I feel enormously privileged to have had a small part in it.

It was on the set of *Porridge* that I met Richard Beckinsale, who played Lenny Godber, Fletcher's Brummy cell mate. Richard was a handsome, friendly guy with something rather effortlessly glamorous about him. He also had an extremely dry sense of humour. You could never quite tell whether he was winding you up or not. He could spin a story so well that you had no choice but to believe it, and he liked to spend whole minutes building those stories up. He would tell you he had been in Harrods and had seen the Queen come in and buy some make-up, and the tale would be set amid all these effortless details that made it weirdly plausible. And when you said, 'No, really?' He would say, 'You didn't believe that, did you?'

I went to see him onstage one night, in a play called *Funny Peculiar* by Mike Stott, at the Garrick Theatre in the West End. He was very good in it. I remember a moment where somebody upended a bag of marbles on the stage. I can't remember why there was a bag of marbles hanging around at that point: go and see the play or buy the script if you want to find out. But the actors ended up slipping and skating around the stage on them, as though they were on ice: it was well done and very funny.

I went backstage afterwards to say hello to Richard and congratulate him. As we left the theatre together, Richard said, 'Can I give you a lift anywhere?' I said, 'That would be very kind.' We walked round the corner and I couldn't believe it when he put his key in the door of a massive Bentley saloon car, not all that much smaller than a bungalow. He just grinned, and in we jumped.

I was most impressed. I think Richard's attitude was, if you've got it, spend it, because there's no point hanging on to it. I was the opposite, but maybe that's a wartime childhood for you. I still had, burned into my mind, the image on the huge government poster on a hoarding at the end of Lodge Lane when I was growing up – a picture of a dripping tap with the simple instruction 'Waste not, want not'. That graphic has stayed with me my whole life. Even now, I go round the house turning off lights. (In order not to waste electricity, you understand, not because I think the blackout is still on.)

Richard's life ended tragically early. One night in March 1979, we were at a party thrown by Ronnie B. He and Ronnie Corbett had both decided to take their families off to Australia for a year, to exploit some work opportunities there and also to avoid Britain's then crippling tax regime. Before leaving, Ronnie B. held a farewell bash for a few of his mates and his family. He booked a big round table at Langan's Brasserie near Green Park. There was Ronnie and his wife Joy, Richard, myself and a handful of others. We had a meal, and lots of wine and there was much jollity. Michael Caine, who part-owned Langan's, stopped by the table, I remember, and had a chat with Ronnie during the evening. At around eleven thirty, Richard got up and came round to us all individually, making his apologies. He said he had to go because he had promised he would look in at another close friend's party. So he said his goodbyes, shook hands with everyone and left.

Over the next thirty-six hours, the news gradually reached us all that Richard had died of a heart attack at home during the night. It was so shocking. We were devastated for him, and for his wife, Judy Loe. It caught all of us completely off guard but it hit Ronnie particularly hard. He couldn't work for a number of days because he was so upset.

Richard was just thirty-one years old. He had barely started.

* * *

IN 1975, THE BBC decided to make *Open All Hours* into a series, directed by Syd Lotterby. Six episodes had been commissioned, to be written by Roy Clarke. Ronnie asked me if I would be interested in resuming the part of Granville. I was more than interested. I was delighted. The chance to play opposite Ronnie in an entire series was a dream outcome.

So, in 1975, work began in what we referred to as the Acton Hilton, a purpose-built block of BBC rehearsal rooms, situated in gorgeous, leafy Acton, west of Shepherd's Bush. Dances and dramas and comedy shows and all sorts were coming together in this rather low-rent den, which made it, in fact, despite its anonymity, quite a buzzy place to be. On the top floor was the canteen, where we would adjourn for a restorative repast of egg, chips and beans, or chips, egg and beans, or beans, egg, chips and sausage, or sausage, egg, chips and beans. If you could time your lunch break to coincide with the arrival of the girls from Pan's People in their rehearsal leotards, you considered yourself doubly refreshed.

Returning to *Open All Hours* was also a chance to renew acquaintance with Lynda Baron, who played Nurse Gladys Emmanuel, the district nurse, Arkwright's thwarted lust object. Lynda was great company. She was a wonderful singer, and long before she did *Open All Hours* she had been a cabaret artist and had worked with Danny La Rue. But the most impressive thing about her – and the thing that had Ronnie and I spitting feathers – was that she had a photographic memory. She would do the first rehearsal, which was always a 'blocking' day, which is to say, going through the script and working out all the positions on the set during the scenes. Lynda would come in the next morning and she would have absorbed everything from the previous day and be able to work without a script, while Ronnie and I were still fumbling with bits of paper and looking confused. Needless to say she was also DLP (dead line perfect), unlike me, who was still prone to the occasional gentle paraphrase.

After rehearsing the six episodes, we set off up to Doncaster for a couple of weeks to film all the exterior shots. Arkwright's corner shop was, in fact, a commandeered hairdressing salon. The location scout had found the place, ideally corner-situated, and came to an arrangement with the owner, paying her to go off on a two-week holiday. The props department then moved in and turned the place into a plausible general store. Everybody in the neighbourhood seemed very tolerant of us, even when shooting went on into the night – although there was one occasion when a window flew up on the other side of the street and a bloke leaned out and, very politely, asked, 'Is this going on much longer? Only I've got to get up early in the morning.' We reassured him that we would be finished very shortly. He said, 'Well, that's all right, then,' and shut the window.

It wasn't until a subsequent series that a local man came at me on the street with a bread knife. But we'll get on to that in due course.

In Doncaster, I had to master the use of Granville's delivery bike – not as straightforward as it may look, because when you turn a corner on those delivery beasts, the fixed container at the front doesn't turn with you, which is highly disconcerting. But, of course, I was able to tap into that valuable experience I had, working for the Victor Value supermarket at the age of fourteen. You never forget, you know. Riding a bike is like . . . well, riding a bike.

With location filming completed and edited back in London, we adjourned to Television Centre to shoot the rest of the material in front of a studio audience, one episode at a time, always on a Sunday night. This was my first prolonged taste of filming television in front of an audience and the way it requires you to serve two masters: the audience in the studio and the audience at home. That was quite a difficult balance. When the audience laugh, you have to find a way to ride that laugh and absorb it and then choose the right moment to continue on with the show. You mustn't crash into the audience but you mustn't look like you're waiting for them to stop laughing, either. So there's a little beat in there which isn't catered for by the script. The director can extend time by cutting away for a reaction shot, which helps you out. But there's still a technique to interacting with the audience's laughter that you only pick up by doing it.

There was no canned laughter, by the way. We never used it. However, before the recording, when the warm-up guy went out in front of the audience to do a little routine and get everyone in the right mood, the director would always make sure he taped the audience's reaction to the warm-up man's gags. Then he knew he had some laughter in the can which he could use to cover over any dropouts at edits, should they prove necessary. That was the only sense in which the laughter was ever artificial.

During the filming of that first series of *Open All Hours*, Ronnie and I grew closer. After Sunday recordings we would set off together to a bistro in a mews near the Victoria and Albert Museum where we would order what Ronnie referred to as 'battery acid' – the house wine, which was throat-peelingly filthy. Soon I started going to see Ronnie and the family for dinner – first of all in Pinner, in north London, where he and Joy lived with their three children, and then out in Oxfordshire, at the old mill house called Dean Mill which he and Joy bought and restored. The pair of them had excellent taste and Ronnie was a great collector, with a very good eye for stuff from antique shops and junk shops. He didn't collect things because they were valuable, particularly. He collected them because they appealed to him and he liked to have them around.

Consequently his place was like a house of wonders. There was a tall cabinet, I recall, with three shelves in it, and each of the shelves was groaning with little statuettes of 1920s bathing belles: porcelain figures, in swimming costumes, all a bit risqué for their period, possibly, but with beautifully detailed china faces and bathing caps hung with jewels. When I went to Ronnie's place, I used to stand in front of that cabinet for ages. I was also struck by a statue he had of a woman in flowing robes, holding a lamp and standing on a rock. At the top of the stairs there was a cabinet full of toy soldiers, the old lead ones, beautifully finished and hand-painted. There were boxes of cigarette cards, too, some of them still in unopened packets, and there were thousands of postcards. Ronnie loved images of the seaside from the turn of the century and dedicated albums to them. I remember, too, leafing through an album entirely comprising postcards made from silk – page after page of them.

The walls of the house, meanwhile, were covered with wonderful pictures, of all shapes, sizes and styles. I said to him once, 'How do you do it?'

He said, 'It's easy. If you like something, you put it up on the wall.'

I said, 'But what about the colour, the size, the question of whether it matches the carpet?'

Ronnie said, 'Forget all that. Just sling it on the wall and enjoy it.'

But he and Joy had such natural taste that they could adopt that approach and it was bound to work. If it had been me, I would have been worried about getting it wrong. I didn't have confidence in my own taste the way they did.

Still, I got a bit of an education from Ronnie in this area. When we were on location for *Open All Hours*, we had Sundays off, and Ronnie would get his driver to take me and him off for the day and go hunting for bric-a-brac in the surrounding villages. (I didn't have my own driver in those humble days, by the way – I was just the poor errand boy in the Fair Isle jumper, don't forget.) We would seek out antique shops and junk places and spend hours nosing around. The tinier and the more offbeat the shop was, and the further it was into the middle of nowhere, the happier Ronnie was. I eventually plucked up the courage and picked up a few things which he gave me the nod on. I remember, in particular, getting hold of a large advert for Sunlight Soap, probably dating back to the 1920s and using a primitive 3-D effect. It was made using painted vanes, so that from one angle it appeared to be saying 'Sunlight Soap' and then, from a slightly different position, it read 'The Perfect Wash'. I thought that was amazing, and it was just lying around in a junk shop, where the bloke wanted next to nothing for it. Ronnie was lusting after it, but I got in there first. That advert hung in my kitchen for years.

Ronnie's house in Oxfordshire was a treasure trove, and a place where I and, in due course, my girlfriend Myfanwy were made to feel extremely welcome. But it was also somewhere where I almost met a premature death – or, at the very least, narrowly escaped life-altering injuries.

It happened one summer. Myfanwy and I were staying for the weekend, and after a very nice evening in which a certain amount of wine had been drunk, everyone went off to bed. We had been put in the spare room, at the top of the house. It was a very hot night, though, and I couldn't get to sleep, so I thought I would get up and take a bit of air. In our room, I had noticed there was an additional door, set into one of the outside walls and so clearly leading to the outside of the house. Using my by now quite intimate – but at the same time slightly inebriated – knowledge of the layout of Ronnie's place, I worked out that this door must give onto a flat roof. If I could stand out there and take the air for a while, I might find sleep came a little more easily.

So, I went and opened the door and cool air duly rushed in. Being the countryside, and not, apparently, a moonlit night, it was pitch black outside, to the extent that I couldn't see any further, really, than the threshold of the door. I certainly couldn't see anything much below me. There were no street lights – and no stars, even. I stood in the frame of the door and put a bare foot outside, over the edge. I couldn't feel anything with my toes, but I knew that one step down or so would have to be that flat roof. All I needed to do was step forward and drop down onto it. Maybe I could even sit down in the doorway, ease myself forward over the threshold and get down that way. I was all ready to do this and jump out when it suddenly occurred to me that there might be little stones on the surface of that flat roof, and that these might play havoc with my bare feet. So, instead, I contented myself with standing in the doorway and breathing in the night air for a while. Then I closed the door and went back to bed.

In the morning, I went and opened the door and had a look out again. There was no flat roof there, or indeed anywhere. What there was was just a thirty-foot sheer and immediate drop down onto the disused mill wheel below. I told Ronnie about my night-time adventures with the door over breakfast and saw the blood drain from his face. Within a few days of our departure, a builder was round there putting a nice, secure balcony across the offending door.

One small further, slightly drunk step that dark night, and I don't like to think what would have happened. Would a mill wheel break a man's fall? I'm not sure, and I'm not sure I want to find out. Maybe I wouldn't have died. But I might have struggled to play the trombone thereafter.

The first series of *Open All Hours* was broadcast at the beginning of 1976. The BBC, in its almighty wisdom, decided to put it out not on the mainstream channel, BBC1, but on BBC2, which was regarded as very much the backwater for a brand-new comedy series. The BBC's reasoning, as it filtered out to us, was that *Open All Hours* was 'a gentle comedy' and therefore better suited to the calms of the second channel than to the noisier, choppier waters of the first. Obviously, that was a slight blow – and yet BBC2 had its own kudos. What annoyed Ronnie, more than anything, was the use of the word 'gentle' in relation to the show. He told me, 'When they say it's "gentle", they normally mean they don't think it's very funny.'

What BBC2 definitely meant was smaller audiences. *Open*

All Hours did modestly well, but the first series came and went without much fanfare. There was no indication that anyone at the BBC particularly wanted to make another one, although we would have to wait and see on that.

Meanwhile, something else which came and went without really taxing the trumpet section: *Lucky Feller*. This latest Humphrey Barclay project for ITV reached the nation's screens in the autumn of 1976 and, once again, I had the leading role. You could never accuse Humph of losing faith in me. Alas, as with *The Top Secret Life of Edgar Briggs*, *Lucky Feller* didn't quite manage to flap its wings and fly.

The series was written by Terence Frisby, who wrote the wonderful sixties stage play *There's a Girl in My Soup*. His sitcom essentially revolved around two brothers living in the south-east of London. Remind you of anything? But in this case, I was the younger of the brothers – Shorty Mepstead, who was hapless and seemingly virginal – and the drama centred on a love triangle between me, my brother Randolph (played by Peter Armitage) and my fiancée Kathleen, played by Cheryl Hall. Cheryl was married at the time to Robert Lindsay, whose star was very much in the ascendant. The pair of them would go on to appear together in John Sullivan's *Citizen Smith* – Bob as Wolfie Smith, Cheryl as his long-suffering girlfriend Shirley. Cheryl and Bob invited me to dinner at the very nice little place they had in Wimbledon, and when the series ended Cheryl gave me a drawing of Laurel and Hardy as a memento, knowing how big a fan I was.

I thought Terence Frisby's writing for *Lucky Feller* was great. There was one scene in particular where Shorty takes Kathleen to a Chinese restaurant – which is clearly as exotic as dining out has ever got for either of them. They look at the menu and Kathleen says, 'Oh, look, they've got prawn balls.' To which Shorty's rather anxious reply is, 'Really? I didn't know prawns had balls.' That line would sink if it was offered with a nudge

Changing into leaky equipment for a diving lesson in Swanage. And then (right) having that diving lesson. Despite this, diving grew into one of my great passions.

As Dithers the 100-year-old gardener with Ronnie B. and company and an enormous sign so we don't forget what we're doing.

The Top Secret Life of Edgar Briggs. The beginning of my stunt career and, by the look of it, very nearly the end of it.

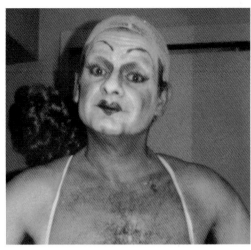

...y name in red lights in the West End – exactly as foretold.

Getting the slap on in order to play Lord Foppington in *The Relapse*. This was one of my favourite parts.

Lord Foppington fully made up and in glorious costume. Note the two poodles on my head. Getting them to sit still was hellishly difficult.

With the Guvnor. Arkwright and Granville, *Open All Hours*, circa 1981.

Richard Wilson, delighted to be posing with me during *A Sharp Intake of Breath* in the late 1970s.

At a recording of *Danger Mouse*, with Brian Trueman and Jimmy Hibbert, writers and performers. I loved that mouse.

My name, placed subtly above the title. And me pointing at it, in case you hadn't noticed.

Skiing in the Alps and wearing comedy glasses.
A good comedian is never on holiday.

The cast of *A Bit of a Do* gather round its writer, 1989. Left to right: Nicola Pagett,
Paul Chapman, Michael Jayston, David Nobbs, me and Gwen Taylor.

Derek Trotter Esquire. An unused still from the original title sequence of *Only Fools and Horses*.

My mate Nick Lyndhurst on the set of 'Miami Twice'. Barry Gibb of the Bee Gees not in shot.

Rodney, Del, Grandad. Or the Three Stooges. With Nick Lyndhurst and the late, lamented Lennard Pearce.

During 'Miami Twice', looking grubby, just after I was chased by a crocodile.

Nick and me – a pair of silly Buddhas. On location for *Only Fools and Horses*, west London, late 1980s.

and a wink, but voiced by Shorty, in complete naive innocence, it played very nicely. My brother Arthur recently repeated that line to me, so at least it made an impression on someone.

From my point of view, *Lucky Feller* was a really enjoyable piece of work. I got to drive a bright red bubble car for the opening credits – not the last time I would be associated on-screen with a three-wheeler. These were years when I felt like I was learning all the time. Nevertheless, counting this and *Edgar Briggs*, that was two opportunities I had been given to carry a television sitcom, neither of which had quite taken off with people, and I guess you have to wonder how many chances like that you'll be given in a lifetime – especially if you're now thirty-six, as I was at this point. The industry was certainly more patient in those days than it seems to be now – but even then, patience had its limits. Around this time, somebody wrote in the *Stage*, the industry newspaper: 'Somewhere there is a writer whose ideas Mr Jason can execute to great effect, but they have not yet met.' It was a point of view – and, as it turned out, a rather prescient one. But I'm not sure that was how I was really considering the situation at the time. The most important thing was not to think too hard about the longer term, but just to enjoy the work when it came up, and for as long as it continued to do so. The journey, not the arrival, as they say.

They do say that, don't they? Ah, well. If they don't, they do now.

* * *

THROUGHOUT THE 1970s, alongside the television stuff, I continued to work pretty constantly in the theatre, taking roles in the West End and going out on tour. The fact that I had spent eighteen months in *No Sex Please – We're British* without wrecking it had increased my reputation and left me in a pretty solid position to be considered for other jobs in that line. In 1974, for example, I found myself teamed up with the actress Liz Fraser, who was quite a star in the British comedy firmament, having appeared in the movie *I'm All Right Jack*, in several of the *Carry On* films, and on television in *Hancock's Half Hour* and *The Goodies*. We took over from June Whitfield and Terry Scott in the West End in a farce called *A Bedful of Foreigners*, written by Dave Freeman, who had written for Tony Hancock, Arthur Askey and Benny Hill. His play centred on two couples on holiday in France who discover, with various levels of dismay, that they have been booked into the same hotel room in a full hotel. Again, we weren't exactly talking Chekhov – but we were talking seventies-style knockabout fun, which meant that Liz had to appear at least once onstage in a basque. I'm afraid those were simply the rules for this kind of play in that era. The run lasted for six months but, in all honesty, people had been coming for Terry and June, the TV stars, and it went a bit hollow in their absence. Relations between Liz and myself were workable but slightly distant. I think Liz assumed I was gay because, in the whole of the time we were acting together, I never once made a pass at her. It was the only explanation she could come up with.

Then I went out on the road with a play called *Darling Mr London* – and rather wished, in a roundabout way, that I hadn't. This was a piece that had been co-written by Tony Marriott (one half of the team that came up with *No Sex Please*) and Bob Grant, who will be familiar to fans of the sitcom *On the Buses*, in which he played the character Jack Harper opposite Reg Varney's Stan Butler. My character in the play was an international telephone operator called Edward Hawkins – a set-up which would obviously struggle for traction nowadays, in the age of Vodafone and 3G. However, it was all perfectly comprehensible in the mid-seventies, when, as everybody knew, phone calls were only made possible by someone sitting at a switchboard with a fistful of plugs. Hawkins was meant to be a Mr Nobody kind of figure in real life, but at the same time was someone in possession of an amazingly suave and appealing telephone manner. This had enabled him to charm himself into the affections of girls in various countries around the world, with whom, in his mind, he was having a collection of hot affairs. (Mr Nobodies with rich fantasy lives: are we beginning to detect a certain theme emerging in my professional roles? Granville, Edgar Briggs, even Albert Toddey in the doomed film *White Cargo* . . . there would, indeed, seem to be a distinct thread of vulnerable wistfulness linking these characters. Though it was vulnerable wistfulness combined, commonly, let's not forget, with a properly butch ability to vault a sofa.)

Hawkins has, in the course of these international conversations, omitted to mention the existence of his wife, meaning that he's in big trouble when all these girls descend on England from their various home countries, in order to take part in a beauty pageant, and suddenly start turning up at Hawkins's house in order to meet the man behind the voice.

Could I, as an actor, do a convincingly suave and appealing phone manner? Why, yes, I have to say I could.

The aforementioned Bob Grant took the role he had created of Hawkins's lodger, who was a curate. Well, it could hardly have called itself a farce without a lodger who was a curate, could it? Meanwhile, the plot device of the beauty pageant was a convenient, if painfully thin, excuse for the girls (who were called things like Britt, Ingrid, Sylvana and Monique) to appear onstage in bathing costumes, or otherwise (in the popular phrase of the time) 'scantily clad'. Most of the girls were played by English actresses putting on accents, but Miss Sweden was played by Leena Skoog, an actress who was so popular with the tabloid photographers at the time that she virtually had her own column, and who genuinely was Swedish – to the extent, indeed, that she could hardly speak English. Also in the cast was Valerie

Leon, who had been a big presence in the *Carry On* films, and Cheryl Hall, my former co-star in the short-lived *Lucky Feller*.

You may be getting ahead of me here, but it turned out there was quite a lot wrong with the play. For starters, some of the cast couldn't act their way out of a paper hat. Also there were pieces of farce in the staging that didn't work, which became glaringly obvious when we put it in front of an audience. I kept saying to Grant, 'We should have a look at some things.' There was, for example, a moment where a male character was seen going through a door, in the room beyond which – as the audience has been led to believe – supposedly lurked one of the girls in a state of undress. From behind the door was heard a quantity of affronted screaming and various other bangs and crashes, and then the man returned to the stage, apparently the victim of an assault which had left a broken tennis racket hanging around his neck. He would then stagger about for quite some time, supposedly regathering his senses. This little piece of action went for nothing on a nightly basis. You could almost feel a cold wind blowing off the audience, and then watch a number of balls of tumbleweed bowl silently across the stalls. I gently suggested to Bob that perhaps the actor could try reining in on the staggering a bit, but no. The staggering went on in full. It was the same with another moment in which Bob, playing the curate, was obliged to come on in his pyjamas. For some reason, not explained by anything else in the play, Bob chose to have the pyjama bottoms held up by a lavatory chain, tied around his middle. Bob thought this was hysterically funny, but the audience, on the whole, tended to disagree. Again, I quietly suggested losing the toilet chain, but, again, my suggestion was ignored. It wasn't as though I could really press any of these points, because Bob was, of course, the co-writer of the play, so he essentially had the authority to do what he thought fit and to wear as many toilet chains as he thought appropriate.

An additional problem was that Bob had something that I

suppose might fall into the category of 'intellectual aspirations'. He was, I believe, a graduate of some sort of university in the East End of London, and he thought he knew about comedy, in the academic sense. In the evening, when we were on the road, I would often share a meal with Bob and his wife, who was on tour with us, and try to discuss parts of the play, only for him, invariably, to set off on a sentence which began, 'Well, what you don't understand is . . .'

My opinions clearly weren't welcome. About three weeks into the tour, I overheard Bob and Tony Marriott, in the dressing room next to mine, discussing the possibility of having me replaced. I was pretty philosophical at the prospect. I was frustrated that nobody was setting to, and rolling up their sleeves and getting rid of the stuff in the play that didn't work, and concentrating on the stuff that did. But there it was. The plot to get rid of me seemingly evaporated.

Darling Mr London wasn't, all in all, a flying success. The great shame is that there was one spectacular moment in the show that almost unfailingly brought the house down. It came where my character, Hawkins, is in bad odour with his wife, who has told him he will have to leave the marital bed and sleep on the pull-out sofa. By this point in the play, the audience have seen this sofa bed go up and down a couple of times, perfectly conventionally. This time, though, after I have readied myself and the sofa for bed, it is suddenly beholden upon me (not uncommonly in farces – but not uncommonly in certain B&Bs too, as I well knew) to find somewhere to hide in a hurry. Offstage could be heard, from all sides, the sound of the girls calling 'Where's Edward?', clearly about to come on. So, in a desperate attempt to find cover, I used to take a run the width of the stage and dive into the sheets on the bed, which was tricked so that it would close up with a snap and revert to being a sofa with me apparently vanished into the softly upholstered heart of it. From the auditorium, it looked like the sofa had eaten me whole. This, I tell you, with no word of a lie, stopped the show. People would be falling about, unable to believe their eyes. It was very difficult to achieve and relied on some cunningly removed bolts. I think it's the best piece of business I ever did on a stage.

OK, there was a night or two when Sod's Law was in operation and the bolts malfunctioned, meaning I would dive in and the sofa wouldn't spring back together around me. And then the magic rather evaporated. But that happened surprisingly infrequently, and when it worked, it was brilliant.

We opened in Billingham in the north-east of England – and not for the first time in my life as a touring player. Billingham was a famous start-up destination, where many plays, with their eyes set on the West End, seemed to begin their uncertain journey – for the fundamental reason, I believe, that it was pretty cheap to do so. Billingham was famous for a) its shipbuilding and b) its chemical factory. You could see the smoke rising gently off the latter, and if the wind was blowing in the wrong direction the entire cast ended up with terrible throats. The theatre was a municipal building – meaning that it doubled as a concert hall and a lecture theatre. It also had attached to it a gymnasium and a roller-skating rink and your best hope was that the play you were doing didn't contain too many quiet, sensitive moments. When the sound level on the stage dropped, you could hear the noise of the Wurlitzer organ pumping through the walls from next door, along with the thrum of the circling skates on the floor.

Opposite the stage door, just beyond the pedestrianised shopping precinct, was a tower block built specially to house university students. The arrival of *Darling Mr London* must have coincided with a university vacation, because we were able to get cheap accommodation for the cast in the otherwise largely empty tower. Any way you could find to save money while out on tour was always welcomed, but on the negative side, the regulations in that tower block were just as stiff, if not stiffer, than in even the most draconian B&B. There was an 11 p.m. curfew, a strict 'no guests' rule and, just to ensure the regime was enforced, there was a bloke on the door with an Alsatian. The curfew was frustrating, but we would smuggle a few beers up with us after a show, and convene in someone's room for some drinks and a chat. The facilities were spartan – a communal bathroom on the landing, and a single bed, as narrow as a plank. Yet somehow these antiseptic surroundings did not succeed in discouraging Derek Newark and Leena Skoog from letting nature take its familiar course.

One morning I went to Derek's room to knock him up for breakfast. All I could hear from the other side of the door was hysterical laughter. I tapped on the door.

Derek said, 'Who is it?'

'It's David.'

'Wait a moment.'

Derek opened the door and there was Leena, tucked up under the sheets and lying on the tiny, almost monastically narrow student bed, which was now sloping downwards at a jaunty angle. During the course of the night, both the legs at the foot of the bed had got tired of lending their support to Derek and Leena's combined exertions and had snapped clean off. They thought it was entirely hilarious. And so, I guess, did I, although I would have liked to have seen them explain it away to the bloke with the Alsatian.

CHAPTER TWELVE

Struggles with an inflatable life raft. The mouse that was
a roaring success. And if it's Tuesday, it must be Jakarta.

In 1977, I was asked to go to the London Weekend Television Studios at Elstree to meet Ronnie Taylor. Ronnie was a writer who was very influential at LWT at the time. He was – like Spike Milligan, Dick Emery and countless others – one of that generation who had been in the war and had got involved in putting on shows, to pass the time and entertain themselves. When they came back from the war, they simply carried on. He was about my height – in other words, average. (Ahem.) He had greying hair, was neatly and conservatively dressed in a shirt and tie, such that you might believe he was someone with a sensible, proper job, rather than a writer of comic material. He had a warm personality and was extremely easy to like. He was also very quietly spoken. That's often been a surprise to me, with comedy writers – it was certainly true of John Sullivan, for instance. You expect people who write funny things to be loud, and constantly saying things like, 'So, there were these two vicars, right . . .' Often it couldn't be further from the truth.

Ronnie said he was going to do a pilot for a comedy series

he'd written and he asked me to read for him. On the way home afterwards, I was thinking, 'I recognise that stuff from somewhere.' It seemed very familiar to me – the tone and pace of it. That turned out to be no surprise. Ronnie used to write radio scripts for Reg Dixon, who was a music-hall comic. Ronnie had decided he could adapt and modernise those scripts, and that was the substance of this series he'd come up with.

The show was A Sharp Intake of Breath – the breath in question being the noise people make, sucking air past their teeth, just before they tell you that they can't possibly mend your car while you wait, or fix your gutter without also having to retile your roof, or before they stress the impossibility of satisfying any number of other straightforward requests for service. I had the starring role of Peter Barnes, an ordinary bloke who is constantly thwarted by authority and bureaucracy and petty officialdom as he tries to go about his life. Again, as so often with the parts I was getting at this time, the keyword seems to be hapless. The show had this nice kind of repertory idea, which was that Richard Wilson was in every episode but played a different part in each – my boss, my doctor, my solicitor, my father-in-law, my tailor. Richard had great timing and I admired him enormously and was very pleased for him with the success he went on to have in One Foot in the Grave. Similarly, Alun Armstrong played a mechanic one week and a tourist the next and a salesman the week after that. I think Alun was a bit confused about me because he assumed I would want to go to the bar at lunchtime and sink a few drinks, and I wasn't interested. I think he found that a little uncomradely and it drove a bit of a wedge.

Still, triumph: the show made it to a second series – six further episodes, broadcast in 1979. And now, having had the chance to see how the show and the cast worked, Ronnie was able to start writing with me and Richard and Alun and Jacqueline Clarke (who played my wife Sheila) in mind, writing for our voices, and knowing our strengths, so the show got stronger.

My favourite scene from the series arose from a conversation that Ronnie and I had, and came in the episode when Peter goes to the post office to pick up a parcel that's waiting for him. Alun, as the postal worker, does the sharp intake of breath and gives Peter a thousand reasons why he can't possibly unearth his parcel for him at that moment. Eventually, though, he gives Peter permission to go and root around for it himself in the backlog of undelivered mail. So I go into this metal cage and start looking for this parcel, amid all the other packages that are stacked up inside it. Among the parcels that I keep having to move is a fairly large one, partly unwrapped and with a tag hanging out of it saying 'Pull here'. So, after some deliberation, curiosity eventually gets the better of me and I do, indeed, pull there. At which point it turns out that what the package contains is a canister holding an inflatable life raft, which now goes up inside the cage. This leaves me fighting in a confined space with a large quantity of uncontrollable and swelling orange rubber, and trying to get out but being unable to do so because the rubber is blocking the entrance. We couldn't rehearse it very thoroughly because we only had two canisters, and we needed one, obviously, for the take. So the whole thing was a bit of an improvised situation and quite hard to manage. I had to try and keep camera-side of the raft, because obviously there was no mileage in me disappearing entirely behind the inflating rubber. But this was the kind of stuff I absolutely thrived on. Again, it felt like a hark back to the pioneering days of the old silent movie. The attitude was: here's what you've got to do; see what you can get out of it; and hope you survive.

A *Sharp Intake* continued to perform OK in the ratings and, miracle of miracles, a third series was commissioned. It was, by that reckoning, the most successful programme I had been involved with – or certainly the longest-running. I couldn't have been happier about it. The comment that had been made in the *Stage* about me having yet to find a writer to release my talent – well, I really thought I had begun to find that in Ronnie Taylor.

And then tragedy struck. At the end of 1979, just after we started recording the third series, Ronnie was taken ill over a weekend. We were told that he had been rushed to hospital and taken into intensive care with encephalitis. I had no idea what that was, or even how to pronounce it. It was, as I then learned, acute inflammation of the brain, and extremely serious. Even so, for the next two weeks, I simply waited to hear that he was getting better. I couldn't imagine any other kind of news. I was sure he would soon turn the corner. It never occurred to me that he simply wouldn't.

I was knocked sideways by Ronnie's death and it must have been so awful for his family. He wrote for Val Doonican and I remember Val paying respects at the funeral, very movingly. It was a bitter blow. I'd just started to work closely with a writer whom I respected and who respected me. We were beginning to work together as a team. It was a wonderful feeling – a feeling of being part of the creative process. I had to wonder whether I would be lucky enough to find that ever again.

* * *

ANOTHER MESSAGE FROM my agent. 'There's a Manchester-based company looking for some voices for some cartoon characters. Would you be interested in going along to a studio they've hired in Soho and reading for them? They'll explain it all to you when you get there.'

As it happens, I've always loved cartoons. My love affair with them started when I was seven and my mother used to take me to the pictures with her. We used to go at least once and sometimes twice a week. Between the B picture and the A picture there would always be a section of cartoons – normally Looney Tunes or Walt Disney. We were there, ostensibly, for the John

Wayne feature but the high point for me was always those cartoons. The colour and the vibrancy and the silliness made a wonderful impression on me.

So I headed to Soho and there I met a man called Brian Cosgrove and his business partner, Mark Hall. They had been doing a lot of animation work for children's television – a cartoon series of *Noddy*, some stuff for *Rainbow*. The had also done a lovely series that I remembered seeing called *Chorlton and the Wheelies* – a very surreal piece in which characters appeared out of the ground and travelled around on a wheel. They showed me some drawings of a character they were calling Danger Mouse – a friendly-looking rodent with an eyepatch and a superhero-style 'DM' logo on his chest – and his sidekick, Penfold, a shy, slightly bald-looking, thickly bespectacled character. I said, 'I can see that DM is a mouse, but what's that supposed to be?' Brian looked a bit chagrined. 'Well, it's obvious, isn't it?' he said. 'It's a hamster.'

'We've got another actor coming in,' Brian said. 'He should be here shortly, and, if it's all right with you, we'd like you both to have a go at both parts – read a scene or two and then swap over.'

I said, 'Fine. Who's the other actor?'

Brian said, 'Do you know Bob Todd?'

My heart sank into my boots. I did indeed know Bob Todd. Bob had been a superb straight man – for Benny Hill, chiefly, but also for Sid James and Dick Emery and many others. In the process he had earned himself the memorable nickname 'Silly Todd'. But all that was by the by. What I knew Bob Todd for was for the short and not particularly distinguished time we had spent together on a cruise ship to the Canary Islands a few years previously.

Not on holiday, I should add. This was 1974, and we were filming an episode of the *Doctor at Sea* comedy series, based on the Richard Gordon books. We both had bit parts. My character went by the wholly plausible name of Manuel

Sanchez. He was a stowaway who lived in a wardrobe aboard the ship. He was eventually discovered by Robin Nedwell as the doctor – possibly it was even in Robin's wardrobe. Memory fails me. Sanchez had to be taken to the captain, but he escaped into hiding again.

On the Tuesday, the director said, 'We're going to be filming the chase sequence on Friday. I want you to go around the ship and invent the chase sequence. Give it to me by Thursday latest so I can put it in operation to shoot it Friday.' They had a wonderful swimming pool on board the boat, so I decided to run round it. I had to jump over a girl in a bikini and bump into Bob Todd, knocking him into the pool. I believe I bumped into a waiter with a teetering tray of drinks, upending it onto innocent passengers. What larks. It's highly possible that Buster Keaton would have achieved more, I concede. But slap some comic music on top of it, and I didn't do too badly.

(People who had bit parts in one or other of the *Doctor* series over the years: Arthur Lowe, John Le Mesurier, Maureen Lipman, Hattie Jacques, Roy Kinnear. I was in some very distinguished company.) The bonus attached to this otherwise quite menial job was that it required us to leave the Port of London on a cruise ship named the *Black Watch*, and voyage to Madeira and beyond. When we weren't filming, we were free to disport ourselves on the ship among the passengers. And Bob certainly did disport himself, especially in the region of the bar, but also in the region of the dance floor. In particular he disported himself in the region of the dance floor after disporting himself in the region of the bar.

One night, not long after we had set sail, we were in the bar, with the cruise-ship band plying its trade in the corner. I remember him dancing with a woman who had recognised him off the television, and, as they danced, he undid the buttons on his braces, causing his trousers to descend gracefully past his knobbly knees to his ankles, where they remained while he continued to dance. The entire dance floor – and the woman he was dancing with, in particular – was thereby treated to the experience of Bob Todd's gently sashaying Y-fronts. Bob seemed to find this most amusing – and there were quite a number of people in the room who shared his pleasure, thinking this was the act of a complete card. There were quite a few, too, who cringed with embarrassment.

The following morning, prior to filming, I was at breakfast with Robin Nedwell, who was the star of the show, and Bob joined us. He was, at least, wearing his trousers over his underpants by this time, but he had also put on dark glasses and was clearly nursing the hangover from Hades. He sat at the table with his head in his hands, for several moments.

'Are you all right, Bob?' I asked.

He replied, very quietly, 'I will be in a minute.' And with that he carefully and wincingly raised his hand to summon a waiter.

I was thinking, 'Good idea. Maybe a plate of eggs and a couple of cups of strong coffee will sort him out.'

When the waiter arrived, Bob, in a voice that was obviously causing him traumatic pain to use, said, 'Would you bring me a large brandy?'

Robin and I looked at each other and got on with our large and very tasty breakfasts. A couple of minutes later, the waiter duly brought the requested poison. Even the smell of it made the head swim. Bob downed it in one. After a beat or two, he was more or less ready to face the day.

The impression I forged of Bob over that week adrift on the waves was that he was not the most disciplined of performers. Bob was not a trained actor, so I think he needed alcohol to free himself – to get himself to the place where he could be funny. Otherwise he was inhibited. He wouldn't have been the only comic performer for whom this equation was true. There have been many over the years and it's my fortune that I've never been one of them.

And now here we were, drawn together again by the operation of fate and an agent's phone call. When Bob arrived, we greeted each other warmly enough, had a little chat, went into the studio and did a reading. Bob, it seemed to me, was off the planet. He did a lot of bawling and shouting. He seemed to think the best approach to both characters was total madness. I tried my best to fit in with him, and bounce off him, but it was like trying to bounce off a wall of flame. I was comprehensively out-shouted and out-bawled. We all shook hands afterwards, and left, and I walked away thinking, 'Well, that's blown that. And thank you very much, Bob Todd.'

A couple of days later, Brian phoned my agent and asked, would I come back to the studio to read again.

'Would that be with Bob Todd?' I asked, slightly tentatively.

Apparently not, according to my agent. They wanted me to try out with someone else.

'Great,' I said. 'So, who's the other actor?'

My agent said, 'Er . . . it's Terry Scott.'

Good grief, as Danger Mouse himself might have said. Out of Bob Todd's frying pan, into Terry Scott's fire. Memories of Terry's lordly demeanour during that BBC panto, and of the commandeering of funny lines during Hugh and I . . . Could I really share a studio with Terry Scott? Could I really pretend to be a talking mouse, while he was pretending to be a talking hamster? Wouldn't his hamster end up eating my mouse alive?

Well, no it wouldn't, as it turned out. And yes, we could share a studio. Perfectly easily, in fact. A good deal of growing up on my part, some mellowing on Terry's part – I'm sure both those things were factors. Either way, we didn't pause to revisit those days when I played the King of Gooseland to his swinging policeman. It's perfectly possible that he never realised we had been in the same room, let alone hung together from its ceiling. But our voices clicked when we read together and, under Brian's excellent direction, we ended up rubbing along perfectly well. Say what you like about Terry Scott, the man was a professional and he knew about character acting. I was Danger Mouse to his Penfold, and he was Penfold to my Danger Mouse, very happily for more than ten years and more than 160 episodes.

That first connection with Cosgrove Hall Films was the start of so much pleasure for me. If the thing you most love about acting is the chance to inhabit other characters, and disappear into them, how could you not love voicing animations? The secret, if there is one, is to treat the drawing as you would treat any other character you might be asked to play. You don't think of yourself as adding a voice to a cartoon; you think of yourself as playing a character. *Danger Mouse* led to *Count Duckula*, its vampire-spoof spin-off, and those things in turn, after auditioning, led to me becoming the voice of the Big Friendly Giant in *The BFG*, the animated film version of the brilliant Roald Dahl story. Then, perhaps most excitingly of all, there was *Wind in the Willows*, from the Kenneth Grahame classic, which Cosgrove Hall made into a feature-length film at first, and then drew out into a long and very successful television series for children.

Brian and Mark wanted me to play Ratty, which I thought would be great. But I had an idea for Toad and it started to nag away at me. Everybody I had seen playing Toad had played him as a bit of a piece of work and more than faintly unpleasant. That's the way the book seems to lead you. I thought, if that was the case, how could he have such nice friends – friends like Badger and Moly? I wanted there to be something lovable at the core of him. Sure, he's a bit of a boor and a bit of a show-off and he periodically goes off on one – but he's those things because, fundamentally, he's childlike, and I thought if you could bring out the innocence of him, you would reveal there was no harm in him.

I pleaded with Brian to let me put a tape down of my

interpretation of Toad. I wasn't aiming to get the part – I was perfectly happy at the prospect of being Ratty. But, in all honesty, I didn't think I could bear the thought of being part of it and yet hearing Toad played entirely as a wrong 'un. I thought, at least I could communicate my idea of Toad to the producers and perhaps they would impart it to whoever eventually ended up playing the part. At the very least, I would have got it off my chest and known that I had tried.

Brian spoke to me a couple of days later and said, 'You've given us such a problem. We wanted you for Ratty, but we've been listening back to that tape you made and we're now very taken with the idea of you as Toad.' It was Toad that I played, in the end, and they got Ian Carmichael to play Ratty.

What a cast Brian had managed to assemble. Ian Carmichael was a huge star. For the voice of Badger, Brian secured the services of Sir Michael Hordern. Sir Michael was, of course, one of the theatrical greats and a real hero of mine. Moly was Richard Pearson: I'd seen him many times in big television dramas. This was fairly sobering company to be lining up alongside. I felt like a bit of an interloper. Sir Michael, in particular, clearly didn't have the first idea who I was or why he should be working with me. However, between takes, I soon worked out that if you got him on the subject of fishing, he was off. We got quite friendly – to the point where I felt able to call him Michael and he felt able to call me 'My dear boy'.

Mind you, I was very proud when Brian related something to me that he had observed when we all did the first read-through together. Brian was watching from the control room, through the glass, and he told me afterwards that, when I started to read as Toad, giving it some energy, he could see the others visibly quicken, as though I had surprised them. A few chins came up and Brian said he thought there was a bit of game-lifting going on in the room from that moment as they responded to the energy. I know I could never have stood on a stage with Sir Michael Hordern doing Shakespeare and been competitive, but in the context of a recording studio, his Badger versus my Toad, I think I just about managed to hold my own.

One day, some time after these recording sessions, I went into a sound studio to do a voice-over for a commercial, and there was Sir Michael Hordern. This took me by surprise. I was a little shocked to see this giant of the theatre in these lowly environs.

I said, 'Sir Michael, what are you doing here?'

He replied, 'What am I doing here? My dear boy, I am doing what you are doing: I am being a vocal whore.'

Well, that's one way of seeing it, I guess.

Brian Cosgrove became and remains a close friend. When we were recording in Manchester, I would frequently go and stay with his family, rather than in a hotel, and sleep on a camp bed up in the attic. Which had a floor and electricity, I should add. I wasn't slung up there in the dark with the Christmas decorations. Indeed, Brian, who was deeply dedicated to his craft, had the attic kitted out for his home studio and it was, as such, the place he went to work when he came home from work.

Every morning, I had the challenge of getting to the bathroom before the rest of Brian's family, in particular his two daughters, Jenny and Laura. I'd get to the door which closed off the stairs to the attic, only to hear the patter of feet on the landing and the shutting of the bathroom door. So I would sit at the foot of the stairs until I heard the bathroom door open again. At which point, in the time it took me to stand up and begin to open the door, there would be another pattering of feet and the sound of the bathroom door shutting again. Let me tell you, when you need to go . . . Anyway, it was a tiny price to pay in order to share the good company and homeliness of Brian and his wife Angela rather than mooch around in the sterile environment of a hotel.

In the basement, meanwhile, lived Brian's collection of old fairground slot machines. These immediately fascinated me. Brian had acquired them from his neighbour, Cliff Mills. Seaside piers were going through a bit of a revolution, getting rid of their old penny machines and going over to electronics. A lot of this great, historic machinery was just dumped in bins, tragically. But this Cliff Mills was in the know, and he went round and picked up a lot of these unwanted items, virtually for the price of taking them away. Brian became one of Cliff's best customers. He bought a whole load of penny slots, some of them very intricate, including a fabulous one which enabled you to fire ball bearings at a selection of tin cats sitting on a wall. Was Angela pleased about these acquisitions? I can't comment, except to note, again, that they went in the basement.

It was in Brian's basement that I first met Marvo the Mystic. (No relation to Mystic Mavis in Birmingham, I'm pretty sure, though you never know.) Marvo is a wonderful figure, probably from the 1940s, who lives in a glass cabinet, wears a red jacket and a bow tie, and performs tricks if you cross his palm with silver. Specifically, if you put in a coin, he taps on the glass with his wand to get your attention and then, with his other hand, raises a small cone that sits on a little table beside him. Beneath that cone: nothing but air. He returns the cone to the table, and for the next few moments, his eyes go backwards and forwards and his eyebrows go up and down, in the manner of someone contemplating magic. Then he raises the cone once more – and, incredibly, there are now two coins on the table. Then he lowers the cone, taps on the window, raises the cone again – and the two coins have become one! Gobsmacking. And he's only just getting started, because if you feed him another coin, the next time the cone gets lifted, it reveals a beetle. And on it goes.

I wanted to buy Marvo off Brian, and every time I went there, I asked him to sell Marvo to me, but he always refused.

Eventually Brian said, 'If you really want Marvo, why don't we build another one?' And that's what we did: we constructed a perfect replica. We took apart the first Marvo, to see how he was made, and built another one from the ground up. Brian constructed the doll figure, and I looked after the mechanism.

While this project was under way, I would take the mechanics of the doll away with me on tour and work on them in my hotel room in the day. Something we were stuck on for a while was how to find Marvo some respectable eyes. But that was solved by a trip to an eye hospital in Manchester where very helpful staff showed us whole trays of glass eyes and allowed us to nab a couple. Marvo currently resides proudly in the hallway of our house, in full health, where he is happy to perform for a penny. (Cheaper than Mystic Mavis in Birmingham, definitely.)

* * *

EVEN THOUGH WORK was often sending us to different ends of the earth, my girlfriend Myfanwy and I were managing to grow close – although I should concede that, despite her best efforts to teach me, my grasp of the Welsh language still extended no further than 'men in y barra', which is Welsh for bread and butter. (Easy for a Londoner: you just need to say 'men in a barrow' in your best cockney accent.)

Myfanwy still had her little terraced cottage in Wales, which we went away to a lot. But in the early 1980s, I realised I had enough money to buy a place in the country nearer London that the two of us could go to at the weekends. After a little bit of hunting, I found a dilapidated cottage in Crowborough in East Sussex, a village I had always liked when visiting friends there. When I say 'dilapidated', it was, without doubt, the most ill-advised purchase I ever made in my life, with the possible exception of my first motorbike. I realised the place was, as the estate agents like to say, 'in need of renovation'. What I hadn't realised was quite how needy its 'need of renovation' was going to turn out to be. Every time I went near it, whole new layers of previously undisclosed damp and rot revealed themselves, and large areas of the building seemed to be held together with a combination of fungus and hope.

Still, I like a practical project, as you might have gathered. Myfanwy and I started going down to Crowborough when we could and digging the garden and attempting to restore this place. I also cunningly enlisted the help of friends. 'Come and stay in my country cottage . . .' was the cry, followed, in a slightly lower voice, by '. . . and help me finish building it.' When I was doing *Danger Mouse*, Brian Cosgrove, the animator, and his wife Angela came to spend time down there and pitched in. My cousin Ken had his sleeves rolled up for months on end and played a huge part in the renovation. And one day, I invited our neighbours in London, Micky and Angie McCaul, to come and inspect (and, of course, help with) the work.

Our proud tour of the building took Micky and Angie upstairs, where the floorboards were all up, meaning you could only cross the room by stepping on the exposed timber beams. Myfanwy went to put her foot on a beam, missed, hit the thin plaster instead and screamed as her leg disappeared through the ceiling into the room below. It would have been a nice bit of business, if she'd meant to do it. Micky McCaul lunged forward to grab her arms and prevent her going downstairs the quick way.

Still, I have to say I later outdid Myfanwy on the 'personal injury sustained during the renovation of the cottage' front, by causing a gruesome amount of damage to my left foot while cutting a patch of long grass in the garden. Reader: be careful with a Flymo on a slope. As I stood above the overgrown area, sweeping the machine from side to side, I basically ended up mowing my foot. 'It's nothing,' I bravely insisted, before removing my rubber shoe (a now slightly chopped rubber shoe), surveying the mess that lay beneath, and realising that it wasn't nothing at all, but actually quite something. A neighbour came out and kindly helped me wrap the foot in a towel before calling an ambulance. Off to A&E for . . . what's that, the 963rd time in this book? I ended up spending a week in bed with my foot up in the air in one of those contraptions beloved of cartoonists and *Carry On films*. The legacy is a completely inflexible big toe on the relevant foot. Ah, well. There are worse fates – and worse ways to injure yourself with a lawnmower.

* * *

SINGAPORE, HONG KONG, Dubai, Kuala Lumpur, Egypt . . . places that were just a vague rumour in a distant atlas, as far as I was concerned. Yet, as the 1970s turned into the 1980s, and as I turned from my thirties into my forties, I was to land up in all of them as a travelling actor. It turned out to be a horizon-expanding experience, in so many ways.

I owed this unforeseen and enormously privileged crash course in geography (among other subjects) to Derek Nimmo. Derek was a very successful actor in British films and television, but he was also a West End stage actor and a producer. He was dapper and very charming, and extremely well spoken. The stutter that he used to employ as the Reverend Mervyn Noote in the clerical sitcom *All Gas and Gaiters*, and also, as a matter of fact, while selling chocolate biscuits ('P-p-p-pick up a Penguin', as he used to say in the ads), was affected. But otherwise what you heard was exactly as he spoke – softly, gently, rather poshly. I don't think he was particularly posh, in fact, but he was certainly wealthy. One evening, I was invited to his house for dinner. It was a grand, four-storey, terraced place in Kensington, very tastefully fitted out. Before we ate, we had drinks in the sitting room. Derek was wearing a velvet smoking jacket and on his feet was a pair of dark velvet monogrammed slippers. I remember thinking to myself, 'I cannot believe it. Derek Nimmo actually has monogrammed slippers.' Later, I told my girlfriend, Myfanwy that I wanted a pair of monogrammed slippers, just like Derek Nimmo's, and she had them done for me. With my initials on them, obviously, not Derek's. In fact, I've still got them, although I don't wear them: they're the kind that have no backs, so you end up curling your toes to keep them on, and they've got leather soles which means you don't walk down stairs so much as ski down them.

Anyway, there we stood that evening, sipping politely at our glasses, and I found myself looking at this picture of Venice above the mantelpiece.

Derek said, 'Do you like the picture?'

I said, 'Yes, very much.'

Not wishing to appear ignorant about these things, I decided to take a flyer and dredge up a bit of my fairly minimal knowledge of art history.

I said, 'It looks a bit like a Canaletto.'

To which Derek said, in that faltering way of his, 'Yes. Well, it, er, it is a Canaletto, as a matter of fact.'

Derek's ability to buy paintings can't have been impeded, I imagine, by the highly imaginative decision he had taken to go into business exporting theatrical productions from Britain to the Far East. My understanding is that this enterprise had come about – in a very Derek-like manner – as the consequence of a 'terribly nice' conversation he'd had on an aeroplane while heading to Australia to watch the Gold Cup yacht race (a bit of a hobby of his). During the flight, he had found himself next to the chief executive of British Airways and they had got chatting about the old-fashioned concept of 'dinner theatre' – a form of entertainment which had largely fallen into obsolescence, in which clients in hotel restaurants sat down to a meal and, shortly after the serving of the coffee, watched a play.

Derek and the chief exec were wondering why that didn't really happen any more. Derek said that, if the notion were ever revived, he was very well placed to lay hands on some productions and some actors. The chief executive said that, for his part, he was very well placed to lay hands on some sponsorship from British Airways. And thus, over some spicy tomato juices and a handful of airline peanuts, were the wheels of commerce set into motion.

I think the first thing Derek did in this line was take a West End play, with himself starring in it, to the Hilton Hotel in Hong Kong. Hong Kong was still a British colony in those days and it turned out that there were a lot of people living and working there who wanted to see a play that had Derek Nimmo in it. Hilton Hotels duly expressed a willingness to stage the play at other Hiltons, elsewhere in the world. So now Derek had an airline and a luxury hotel chain on board, and suddenly, from this one play that he did in Hong Kong, he found himself dispatching productions to hotels in Cairo, Dubai, Muscat, Jakarta, Sydney and all stations east of Margate.

I went on three of these adventures in all. I was invited to take a production of *No Sex Please – We're British* to Dubai, along with the wonderful Geoffrey Davies and Sally Ann Howes (who was Truly Scrumptious in the film of *Chitty Chitty Bang Bang*). I went to the Far East with a production of *The Unvarnished Truth*, with John Fortune, Frank Windsor and Jo Kendall. And I went to Australia with Leslie Phillips and Ann Sidney in a farce called *Not Now Darling*.

Now, two of those three experiences were a pretty much unalloyed joy from start to finish. The other one starred Leslie Phillips.

Leslie was already by this stage in his career well established as a legend of British comedy thanks to his work in radio series such as *The Navy Lark* and then in British war films and *Carry On* movies. He had, under Nimmo's aegis, embarked on a long tour of *Not Now Darling*, a farce written by Ray Cooney and John Chapman, which was booked to travel round Australia and then come back through the Far and Middle East. Leslie had been playing this character in a West End run for quite a while before this. The tour was already under way when Derek asked me if I would like to take over from Andrew Sachs, who was playing the co-lead in that play. Andy had to fly back at the end of the Australian leg because I believe he had been contracted to start work playing a Spanish waiter alongside John Cleese in a television series called *Fawlty Towers*. I wonder what became of that.

Anyway, I said, 'Absolutely – fantastic'. The prospect was really appealing. I loved travelling and seeing new places, and I was also of the firm opinion that the opportunity to travel and see new places at someone else's expense and while being paid should never be batted away lightly. Wages in the bin, living like a king – what could be better?

So, the plan is for me to fly out to Australia, two weeks before the play is due to finish there, meet everybody, including Leslie Phillips, and rehearse my role. Andy will continue to play for those two weeks in the evenings, while I rehearse during the day. Then we will leave Brisbane and fly to Singapore, where I will take over from him. It all sounds perfect.

So, I take a twenty-three-hour flight from Heathrow, with a couple of stops for refuelling, which feels like a fortnight. You get a bit stir-crazy, stuck in a tube that long. But I finally land in Australia, feeling no brighter than if important parts of my body had spent an entire day and a night being squeezed through a mangle. I queue up at immigration and I show my passport and I'm asked to explain what my business in Australia is.

'I'm an actor,' I say. 'I'm joining up with a touring production.'

The man at the desk says, 'Can I see your work permit?'

Work permit? Do I need a work permit? Nobody told me I

needed a work permit. But I'm sure that, if I do need a work permit, a work permit will have been arranged for me. Derek Nimmo's company will have known about the need for a work permit, and will have sorted a work permit out. They wouldn't have flown me all this way without organising a work permit, if a work permit is necessary.

My interrogator goes away to make some further enquiries. Quite a long time passes. He returns.

'No, you don't have a work permit.'

His other piece of good news: they're going to search me. Nothing personal, just a routine, random thing, but they'll need to have a look in my luggage. So I haul my suitcase onto the table, and they go through every single thing I've got. The search is so thorough that I'm beginning to suspect that it will soon extend to me, and that I will in due course find myself naked in a side room, bending over a table and hearing the snap of rubber gloves on an Australian immigration official's wrists.

I'm right: the search does extend to me. Fortunately, though, they confine themselves merely to a vigorous pat-down. Still, all this takes quite a while, and I'm not getting any less tired, or any less irritable.

The search complete, I'm left sitting alone with my bags while, I assume, phone calls are being made and people are trying to work out what to do with me. I wait, and wait, and wait. And after that, I wait a bit more. And then, after that particular wait, I do a bit more waiting, before going back to waiting again. Eventually the waiting tips me over the edge. Through the window can be seen the plane I came in on, still on its stand. I get up, locate my immigration official and confront him with trembling lips.

'What's happening with that plane?'

He says, 'It's being refuelled and then it'll fly back to London.'

'Put me on that plane,' I say. 'Go on – put me on it. You

don't want me in the country, I haven't got a permit, I'm tired, I'm hungry, I'm fed up . . . just put me on the next plane. I just want to go home.'

The immigration official gives me an appraising look. Something in the tone of my voice, and in the twitching of one of my eyes, informs him that he is no longer dealing with an entirely reasonable human being. This could have gone either way, maybe, but it seems to cause a softening in his attitude towards me. He places a calming hand on my shoulder and leads me through to his office, where he phones the theatre company, organises for somebody to come to the airport and collect me, stamps a piece of paper and admits me to his country.

'Welcome to Australia, Mr Jason.'

I get to the hotel and crash out. The following evening I go and watch the play, which comes off very nicely and goes down well. Afterwards I'm introduced to the cast and the crew and I meet Andrew Sachs and Leslie Phillips, and everything seems very nice and very pleasant.

The next day we start rehearsals. Or sort of. The director tells me Leslie won't be turning up today. 'He thinks there's no point coming in until you've at least done some blocking,' the director says. Well, that's a bit disappointing, but given that Leslie is working in the play at night, it doesn't seem entirely unreasonable. So I spend that day doing some blocking with the director, trying to get all my positioning sorted out.

The next day I go in at 10 a.m. Still no Leslie. Still no anybody, actually, apart from the stage manager. 'Where is everyone?' I ask. 'I think they'll be in about two,' says the stage manager. 'But I can rehearse with you if you like.' The stage manager has the book with the script and all the moves in. We spend the morning rehearsing, with me playing my part, and him playing all the other parts in the play. Inevitably, this quickly becomes lunatic, on the grounds that I keep losing track of who he is. 'Who are you now?' I stop to ask – over and over again.

We break for lunch. After lunch it gets to two thirty. Still no Leslie, still no cast. 'I'll make a call,' says the stage manager. He goes out to the phone and then returns with a grave face. He says, 'I've got some bad news. The rest of the cast won't work with you.'

'Why ever not?' I say.

'Because you're not a member of Australian Equity. You're a blackleg.'

I didn't know I needed to be a member of Australian Equity, any more than I knew I needed a work permit. 'Isn't this all taken care of by Derek Nimmo's company?' I say. 'Apparently not,' says the stage manager.

We spend the rest of the afternoon and the whole of the next day sorting out my Australian Equity problem. I end up arranging to pay my subs and become a member of Australian Equity. That's twice now that Derek Nimmo's company has let me down on the basic paperwork. But hey: onwards and upwards.

On the fourth day, the cast are free to work with me without breaking union regulations, so we get some stuff done. Or, at any rate, we get some stuff done after everyone turns up, which is in the middle of the afternoon. Still no Leslie, though.

Friday is the last day set aside for rehearsals for that week, and at last, that afternoon, Leslie finally appears. I'm very grateful: something like a full run-through might now be possible. 'I'm going to be whispering,' Leslie informs me, in a whisper, at the start of the session.

'Sorry?' I say.

'I'm going to be whispering,' Leslie whispers.

'I'm sorry,' I say. 'I can't hear you. You're whispering.'

'Yes, that's what I'm trying to say,' whispers Leslie, in a now slightly irritated and slightly louder whisper. 'I'm going to be whispering. I have to save my voice because I need it for the play.'

'Oh,' I say, 'OK.'

Although, inside, I'm thinking, 'This is not great.'

Off we go, me talking, Leslie whispering. We reach a point in the play where I'm standing centre stage with Leslie and he turns his back to me and addresses one of the other characters. It all goes rather quiet for me at this point, now that I can't see Leslie's whispering lips and I realise that I've missed my cue and have no idea what's going on.

I think it's safe to say the whole thing isn't going tremendously well. In fact, I seem to be experiencing animosity and coldness from pretty much everyone in the cast. I think they all loved Andy so much, and had grown used to him: now here was this new boy barging in, whom nobody knew from Adam. The ranks closed against me. It was my first experience of that in a cast.

We try to rehearse for the second and final week – me with the stage manager and with some of the cast, on the odd occasion when they would turn up, and even less frequently with the whispering Phillips. The play finishes its Australian run on the Saturday. Needless to say, I am not invited to the last-night drinks.

We pack up and fly on to Singapore, with me feeling pretty bewildered and miserable, not to say frighteningly underrehearsed. In Singapore, we have three days while the set is being built at one end of the hotel ballroom. Derek Nimmo is due to fly in to oversee the opening of this part of the tour. Determined to talk to him as soon as I can, I sit in the hotel's splendid reception area and wait for him to come through.

'David, my dear fellow, how are you getting on?' he says.

'Derek, I need to have a word with you,' I say.

'Oh, my dear boy, we'll have some coffee, shall we?'

We sit together in the reception. He looks at me and he can tell that all is not well in the fields of Rome, or whatever that unforgettable quotation is.

I say, 'I want to go home.'

277

'I beg your pardon, dear boy?' says Derek.

'I want to go home on the next flight,' I say. 'I can't do this tour. There isn't one person in this company who will speak to me. Leslie Phillips can't even be bothered to look at me.'

Derek asks me to explain in detail the problems. He is understanding because he has to admit that he's had someone on the phone to him, expressing (albeit in possibly more choice words) that things are not exactly running smoothly. Derek has arrived expecting to have to calm the waters and now he's got me in his face as well. He knows the show will be in some serious trouble, and so will his company, if I walk out at this stage. He pleads with me to stay.

'Open tomorrow and do the show for a week,' he says. 'If you're still unhappy, I'll find a replacement.'

So I consent and on we go. The first night is, to say the least, interesting. Before curtain up, Leslie calls a cast meeting on the stage. 'Now, listen up, everybody,' he says, although I feel he's only really talking to me. 'Tonight we open. Remember: this is a farce. We've got to attack it. Keep up the pace, pace, pace.'

I thought to myself, 'Christ. Pace? I am so under-rehearsed I don't know whether I'm coming or going.' Everyone in a new play gets nerves on a first night but my nerves on this occasion are more like nightmares.

So we open. Leslie has got everybody going at breakneck speed. As the play goes on, everything is flying at me so quickly, I don't know whether it's Tuesday or a lemon. Every time I come offstage, I have pieces of paper with prompts and lines and clues written on them, stuck to the walls and the backs of the flats. Only those pieces of paper come between me and a rank, miserable, mumbling public humiliation.

Come the fourth night of the run, though, I've started to settle in a bit and the cast has calmed down. And so, I think, 'I'm here, I've got to go through with it and I might as well enjoy it. Nobody's talking to me, nobody cares, so I'll see what

I can do. I'll play the play for my enjoyment and sod the rest of them.' Because now I'm just beginning to sense that the audience is starting to like me.

The play requires Leslie to play a slightly oily fur-coat salesman who does his best to smooth his way into the affections of his female customers. I'm playing Crouch, his lowly assistant, who stitches the fur coats together, and I'm generally his stooge. As you enter stage left, there's a kind of platform area, one step up from the main floor of the stage. At one point quite early in the action, Ann Sidney comes on, playing a potential customer. Leslie and I are standing together, over to one side, on the platform. Leslie's line is something like, 'Hey, Crouch, what do you think of her, then, eh? I'll see if I can fit her with a coat.'

With that, he would give me a salacious nudge and set off across the stage towards Ann. This fourth night, he nudges me and I step down off the platform, as if propelled that way by his elbow, and give a look of confusion, as if to say, 'How did I get down here?' or perhaps, 'Blimey, I seem to have shrunk.' And there's a big laugh from the audience where there hasn't been a laugh before – much to Leslie's confusion, as he heads across the stage with his back to me. I can see him out of the corner of my eye, and I can tell by the slight pause in his stride that the audience's reaction has hit him. He thinks it's something he's done. But he carries on.

So that was fine. I got a slight reward. The next night, we do it again. Again, a big laugh. And I can see him now, thinking, 'Where's that come from? What am I doing? Or what is he doing?' This time he turns round to look at me. And I stop looking around and give him a look. Whereupon we get another laugh for that. And as soon as he looks away, I give another puzzled look, and get another laugh.

At the end of that week, Leslie has clocked what I'm doing. So now, instead of nudging me, up on the platform, he puts his arm around me, so that I can't make the move off the step. He

279

also moves across to Ann backwards, so that he can keep his eye on me. So I think, 'That's all right: I can stand to lose that moment because I'll get something else later on.'

And so, over the next week or two, I set out to explore the piece for my and the audience's entertainment. There's a portion of the play when I'm onstage and Leslie's not. That's when I decide I'll have some fun. Which I do. I'm finding laughs that haven't been there, and the occasional round to go with them – to the point where Leslie has to come up from his dressing room and stand in the wings and see what's going on.

We finish in Singapore and move on to Jakarta. On the plane, one of the cast members comes and sits next to me. They say, 'I've been asked if I would come and talk to you and ask you to go a bit easy on the rest of the cast.' I say, 'What do you mean?' They say, 'Well, you're being very ungenerous. You're getting all the laughs and you're not being very generous to anybody else.' I say, 'I suppose you realise that nobody would even talk to me at the beginning of this. Nobody helped me at all. I'm only doing what I have to.' I say that I think they ought to have a look at the billing. On the billing it says, 'Leslie Phillips and David Jason in . . .' I tell them, 'That's why I have to do it.'

From Jakarta on, to my intense relief, there's a bit of a thaw in relations between us all. Leslie becomes a touch more friendly, starts to give me the time of day a little. Our relationship duly becomes workable – settles down into the tacit respect that each of us has for what the other can do. Fair play to Leslie: he didn't have the first clue who I was and I suppose he needed me to prove myself to him. I'm glad I stuck around to do so.

It was hard to be glum for too long with audiences like the ones we got on those tours – great crowds of ex-pats, for the most part, working in the Far East on oil and engineering projects, maybe living over there with their families, working long hours and long days, and more than up for a laugh. They would book tables at the Hilton, and pitch up at seven for a drink. Then they would have dinner, and drink some more. Then at ten, we'd come on, and by that time, they were wonderfully well away.

And we did a very good job. OK, the productions could be a bit ramshackle in certain departments and less slick than they might have been in the West End. Derek's wife Pat, who was very down to earth and nice as pie, used to come with us sometimes, as part of the management team, and occasionally shortage of numbers would mean she would be commandeered to sit in the corner, just offstage, and act as the prompt. Lovely lady – terrible prompt. She never used to know where she was in the play, which is not an especially useful trait in that line of work. One night, in Hong Kong as I recall, we got a bit lost, as happens from time to time. So I came to the prompt corner and whispered, 'Next line, next line,' only to hear Pat whisper back, 'I don't know. I don't know where I am.' So I had to go back out and ad lib. But we managed to get ourselves back on track and no serious harm was done.

Nevertheless, we handsomely entertained people who desperately wanted entertainment and who longed for a bit of contact with Blighty. These were people away from home on six-month or even year-long contracts, and they missed home, and we gave them some kind of taste of it.

Meanwhile, I was earning £500 a week, which was handsome money at this time, and being required to spend almost none of it. Nearly the only time I ever had to dip into my own pocket was when it came to settling the mountainous phone bills I ran up, calling my girlfriend Myfanwy back in Britain.

I worked with some good actors, too – especially on *The Unvarnished Truth*. When the offer came up to do the trip again, I didn't hesitate. Frank Windsor was very quiet and very nice: a gentleman. John Fortune had a sense of humour so dry it almost crackled. Quite apart from being excellent comic performers, both were proper team players, which is what you need to be in a touring production, unless the whole thing is going to implode horribly. The three of us stuck together, helped each other out, and had a jolly time. The only problem I had with John, in all the days we spent together, centred on the unfortunate matter of a hair that, apparently unbeknown to him, had sprouted between his eyebrows and grown to a considerable length, and which was showing no signs of stopping any time soon. As the tour wore on, in passages of the play where John's face and mine were necessarily close, the hair grew ever more to be a source of wonderment to me – its scale and luxuriance, its ability to survive John's vision and stand alone against disaster.

One night, the pair of us were killing a bottle of whisky in my room and I felt emboldened to raise the matter of the extraordinary hair. 'John,' I said, in a voice that may well have been rather slurred, 'could you do me a favour? Can you get rid of that hair? It's becoming something I'm fixing on, and I shouldn't.' John, whose voice was also possibly quite slurred, couldn't have been more obliging. He removed the hair there and then. After which, I rather missed it, to be perfectly honest. But, on the whole, it's always best to confront these things, actor to actor, and we never had a moment's discomfort after that.

Royce Ryton, the writer of *The Unvarnished Truth*, also had a part in the play, so he travelled with us, too. Royce was quite an odd cove. On occasions he would wear a pink suit and walk around with a long feather quill in his hand, connoting to all and sundry his trade as a playwright. Well, I suppose it was easier to carry a quill around than a typewriter. Something happened which annoyed him at one of the airports – I think a three-hour delay was announced – and he lost his cool and was seen jumping up and down in his pink suit and feather – which is no outfit, really, in which to get angry.

What a lark the whole thing was, though. We were treated like lords and made to feel like stars, or thereabouts. An English-language newspaper in Dubai greeted my arrival with the headline 'SUPERMOUSE IS IN TOWN!'

OK, so, technically, that should have been Danger Mouse. But who was quibbling? Not least when beneath the headline was a large photograph of me captioned 'David Jason in A Short Intake of Breath'.

OK, so, technically, the photograph was a still from No Sex Please – We're British. But again: who was quibbling?

There was so much that was new to me. To depart from Heathrow and, a few hours later, be arriving in Malaysia and walking past a sign at the airport reading 'Dadda smugglers will be executed' ('Dadda' being the Malaysian word for drugs) – well, that was a sight to open a relatively untravelled Londoner's eyes. Ditto the sight of the river in Jakarta, a tidal reach which comes in from the sea, where people openly crouched to do their business in the water. Ditto, again, the sight of that business, equally openly floating on the surface or stranded at the side of the water.

One minute I was in Dubai shopping for a dishdash to wear – the classic long cotton shirt garment – and finding a rather fetching blue one with an embroidered neck. The next minute I was seeing the pyramids in Egypt and looking at the death mask of Tutankhamun. And the minute after that I was bartering for a carpet in Singapore and being shown the notorious Changi Prison – a leading centre for corporal punishment by caning. We were taken there by the hotel manager who thought we ought to see it – if only from the outside. I don't know whether he was issuing some kind of warning regarding the maintenance of standards in our performance, but it certainly looked like somewhere none of us wanted to end up and I'm sure that, deep down, we upped our game that night.

Derek Nimmo would frequently be having lunch with highly

important people who were highly important for reasons that were never entirely clear to me – diplomats, business executives, political players. One day he invited me along to a lunch with a highly important sheikh. After we had eaten, the sheikh asked me meaningfully, 'Would you like some tea?' At this point, Derek gave me a gentle kick under the table and a look which suggested I might want to decline. 'No, I'm fine, thank you,' I said. 'It's Scottish tea,' the sheikh added encouragingly. Again, I declined. For Scottish tea, as Derek explained later, read undercover whisky. Our pal the sheikh didn't seem to take milk.

The hotel managers were, altogether, most obliging in showing us the sights – and some of these sights were amazing. In Dubai, the sheikhs seemed to be going in for competitive airport building. We visited a massive marble mausoleum, actually a terminal building, fantastically constructed – and yet only catering at that point for the arrival of two aircraft per week. It was explained to us that it was built, essentially, out of jealousy of the scale of the neighbouring sheikh's airport. Well, it stands to reason: you wouldn't want your airport to be smaller than anyone else's, would you?

The manager of the Jakarta Hilton laid on a huge banquet for us – champagne, groaning platters of fish, shrimp, lobster and salad, servants bowing and scraping. It was like being in some kind of fairy tale. The banquet was served on a dais under a flowing awning looking out over the gardens where exotic flowers bloomed and fountains danced. The idea that acting could open up experiences like these to someone from a terraced house in Lodge Lane seemed staggering to me.

One night after a show the manager in Hong Kong arranged for cars to whisk half a dozen of us away to a restaurant in the backstreets where girls danced as we dined. Then, at the conclusion of the meal, we were all led through the restaurant's kitchens, across a courtyard and up a metal fire escape where the manager smoothed a palm with Hong Kong silver and we were ushered into what I suppose we should refer to as the 'special room', with seats for us around a small platform. We sat and drinks were brought to us. And then a woman arrived, stepped up onto the platform, danced and gradually disrobed before . . . Well, how to put this? Let's just say that – call me old-fashioned or hopelessly sheltered – I had no idea that you could use an unpeeled banana for quite those purposes. Neither, come to think of it (and, again, apologies for my naivety), did I have the merest inkling that you could press a ping-pong ball into service like that – nor that it would shoot quite so high into the air when you did so.

Table tennis has never felt entirely the same to me since.

When we'd been conversing, the hotel manager had told us that, in certain Eastern cultures, the most impolite thing you can do is point your foot at somebody's head. It's considered the worst kind of insult. Well, for the second part of our very special private show, a man and a woman entered. They also climbed onto the platform and disrobed and then commenced their act, which, suffice it to say, was as far removed from a matinee performance of *Aladdin* in Wimbledon over the Christmas period as it is possible to get. The girls who were with us were truly embarrassed – perhaps even horrified, although, it should be noted, none of them asked to leave. I'm sure I felt quite embarrassed to be sitting there too, but my attitude was, 'Well, life is notoriously short, and how many times are you likely to get to see this sort of thing?'

The couple reached a stage in their act where the female half was on her back with her legs pointing in a northerly direction, while her male partner knelt in close attendance. At this point the lady's right foot attained a position extremely close to my face. Thinking I might lighten the atmosphere, which had grown heavy and somewhat awkward, I attracted the attention of the man and, pointing to the lady's foot, feigned affront. He roared with laughter and told his partner, 'The gentleman from London has just accused you of offending him in the basest manner.'

Everybody completely collapsed at this. Well, when I say completely collapsed – the bloke on the stage didn't completely collapse. One part of him didn't collapse at all. Most impressive. But that's the difference between a professional and an amateur, I guess.

Mad times, all in all, with one sobering moment to put the madness starkly in relief. It must have been in 1982. We were heading out on a 747 which included, on its upper deck, for the use of we passengers of privilege, a cocktail bar. There we were, three or four of us, several hours into the flight, leaning on the bar, with an air hostess serving us with whisky sours, when, through the porthole, we seemed to see flashes of light on the far horizon, probably hundreds of miles away across the desert.

I said, 'What's that over there? Can you see those flashes?' A couple of the others gathered round.

The air hostess said, 'Oh, that'll probably be the war.'

I said, 'Come again?'

'Iran and Iraq,' she said. 'They're at war.'

Well, I knew that. But at the same time . . . what a peculiar and eerie moment for reflection this was. Somewhere way below us, people were firing rockets and bombs at each other. We, meanwhile, were suspended at 35,000 feet, in our unworldly little bubble, sipping cocktails, chinking glasses and saying, 'Chin-chin.'

CHAPTER THIRTEEN

Menace and hair-dye on the streets of Doncaster. Goodnight from him. And two blokes called Derek.

The decision of the Two Ronnies to decamp to Australia for a year had an upside. It meant the BBC was suddenly bereft of new material from one of its most popular comedy acts. To help fill the gap, the first series of *Open All Hours* was rebroadcast, this time on BBC1, rather than on BBC2 where it had been hidden, relatively speaking, the first time round. On this second showing it attracted some attention and got good ratings, entirely supporting Ronnie's feeling that the BBC should have gone that way with it in the first place.

So, in 1980, four years on from the initial run, and with Ronnie now back in Britain, Roy Clarke was commissioned to write a second series, bringing Arkwright, Granville and Nurse Gladys Emmanuel together again for another shot at the glory which perhaps always ought to have been theirs. It was a highly exciting prospect for me – working with Ronnie and Lynda again, larking about in Doncaster – and yet, at the same time, I did have some anxieties about it. Granville the shop assistant – my role – was meant to be around thirty years old. I was now a full decade older than that, and – reader, let us not shy away from this subject – a degree less well appointed in the hair department than I had hitherto been. In the intervening years, time had performed its evil depredations and I had endured a certain amount of typical male-pattern thinning around the crown region. Furthermore, a little snow was beginning to appear around the eaves.

Well, OK, that happens to thirty-year-olds, too. But I had other worries as well, about the nature of Granville's character. I voiced these to Ronnie when we were discussing whether to go ahead. I said, 'The relationship between Arkwright and Granville, as it's written, is great and I can see it's good fun. But I'm a bit worried about my age. Can I play down that far? Because if Granville is as old as I am, doesn't the fact that he's still on his own, failing to have any success with women still, by all implications a virgin – doesn't all that stuff stop being good fun and start feeling a bit . . . weird? It's sitting uncomfortably with me.' I guess, most of all, I was worried about making Granville, this seemingly eternal shop boy, appear not to be playing with the full deck.

Ronnie said he thought it would work – firstly because the make-up department is a wonderful thing. 'They'll believe you're still Granville,' he said reassuringly and while kindly refraining from staring too curiously at my bald spot. Secondly (and perhaps more importantly), Ronnie said there was some room for the issue to be conveniently blurred if Granville's age continued never to be mentioned in the scripts. Thirdly, Ronnie pointed out that there was a permanent justification for Granville lacking life experiences because, of course, he was snookered by his job. That was Granville's predicament and the source of all his wistfulness: the shop had become the full extent of his world and he didn't have time for anything beyond it. *Open All Hours*: Granville's problem was explained in the title. Ronnie was, as always, very wise, and if he thought it was OK, that was good enough for me.

So I was persuaded, and off we went. In the make-up department, remedial measures were duly taken. I had to pin on a hairpiece at the back and to colour up what remained of my own legitimately rooted stuff with a spot of dye. As my dear daughter Sophie once said, cutting straight to the point, as small children do: 'Can we see that programme when Daddy had black hair?'

The cast and crew were welcomed warmly back to Doncaster – except, clearly, by the man who, while we were filming on the street outside Arkwright's shop, burst past the camera, right in the middle of a take, and threatened me with a bread knife. Which doesn't often happen.

A bizarre moment, to say the least. It was night-time, but we were filming to make it look like early morning. I was outside the shop, as Granville, doing a reaction shot – dreamily looking up the road at the departing milk float containing his new, unrequited love, the milk lady. Suddenly a large, middle-aged figure in dark, shabby clothing had come striding past the camera and was now standing right in front of me, brandishing a long, serrated blade and bawling meaninglessly. Funny how a certain kind of calm can descend on you in a situation like that. I neither shrieked nor turned and ran, as I might have done if I had been in a film. And, funnily enough, I kind of *was* in a film.

I simply looked at this man rather quizzically, and said, in an attempt to be calming, 'Was there something you wanted?'

After a beat or two, a couple of guys from the crew got hold of the armed intruder and carefully led him away. Thereafter the police were summoned. The poor bloke turned out to live nearby and to be a fully paid-up member of the bewildered. Who knows what was going on in his head, but I don't think he had me or anyone else in mind as a specific target. Nor do I think this was a motivated attack on *Open All Hours* specifically, or the sitcom genre in general. The bloke was just out and about with his bread knife. As you are. We regrouped, did the shot over, and were never again menaced with a serrated blade between then and the end of the fourth and final series in 1985.

Ronnie used to refer to me teasingly as the 'Little Feed' – the small bloke who set up his funny lines for him. That was pretty much a neat summary of my role in the show. Granville had his moments, of course – not least the *Singin' in the Rain* spoof, where Granville gets caught in a downpour while sweeping up outside the shop and ends up giving it a bit of Gene Kelly. I had long conversations with Syd Lotterby, the director and producer, about this. We couldn't spoof the whole routine because it was far too long and complex, so we needed to pick out the elements that people would remember. The three main ones, we reckoned, were: splashing through the gutter; swinging round the lamp post; and spinning with the umbrella. We had the gutter and we had the lamp post, and we decided to use the broom for the umbrella. Syd got me a copy of the film so that I could refresh my memory of what Kelly did and how he did it. We rehearsed the routine for several evenings after shooting had finished. And then we filmed it in one long night shoot, into the early hours of the morning, with the song played out to me in the street.

That sequence was quite hard for me because, as we have previously discovered, my grasp of music is not the best. I also spent the evening in a state of some discomfort. The artificial rain machines used on these occasions have to pump out a really heavy quantity of water in order for it to register on the camera – actual rain would be hopeless for this purpose, funnily enough – and, as a consequence, your clothing gets soaked very fast and then stays soaked. Accordingly I was wrapped, under my costume, in cling film, to form a protective layer. Before the clothes went on, I looked like a supermarket chicken. Let me tell you, lest you are tempted to experiment with this: in monsoon conditions, cling film can just about be relied upon to keep the water off your body but it won't keep you warm. It will, however, keep you extremely fresh. It won't necessarily make you a better dancer, though.

Anyway, beyond these showpiece moments, the simple fact of the Granville/Arkwright relationship meant I was there to be Ronnie's stooge. I don't recall this being particularly chafing. On the contrary, I was having an awful lot of fun and I felt extremely lucky to be where I was.

At the same time, I can't deny that there were at least a couple of moments when I found myself wondering whether I hadn't just outgrown Granville, but whether I had also outgrown the kind of part that Granville was. One time, we finished an episode and discovered that we had overrun the thirty-minute mark by several minutes. So we sat in the editing room working out what to leave out in order to trim the show down to the requisite size. As I sat there, I could see all my funny stuff hitting the cutting-room floor. I had gone very quiet and Ronnie noticed and asked me if I was all right. I said, 'Any jokes that I have are getting cut. All I'm left with is feeding you.'

The following day, Ronnie wrote me a poem in rhyming couplets, full of mock-Shakespearean 'thees' and 'thous', the clinching lines of which were: 'The future will provide thy need / Till then be content to be a little feed.' It was his way of telling me not to get anxious, and that I shouldn't forget that what I did had value. (Ronnie often sent me poems. He was constantly playing with words and was very quick at composing verses. On my forty-second birthday, which came while we were filming up in Yorkshire, he threw a party for me in Bawtry and presented me with a handwritten poem, put together that afternoon, which included this classic couplet: 'He's here tonight, without his pinafore / The lad we're going to buy a dinner for.')

It was during the filming of *Open All Hours* that scandal threatened to engulf me, courtesy of the attentions of the British press. I was pictured in one of the papers emerging from Langan's restaurant in London, apparently a little over-refreshed and in the company of what the caption darkly referred to as 'a mystery blonde'.

That was no mystery blonde. That was Ronnie Barker's wife. Ronnie, I hasten to add, was just behind us. He, Joy and I had been out for a celebratory dinner. Langan's had a revolving door and I had been unable to resist the opportunity to take Joy for a number of full spins in it before finally emerging, slightly dizzied. I found it very funny, obviously, to be linked in the national prints with Mrs Barker. All the same, it was the first time I properly realised that my movements were now somehow of interest to photographers and their employers. I wasn't entirely sure how I felt about that.

A couple of days later, a copy of this ruinously incriminating image of Joy and me, clipped from the newspaper, arrived in the post. On it was written the message, 'Blackmail is an ugly word . . .' I thought to myself, 'What the hell is this?'

Then I noticed the signature. It was signed 'The Guvnor'.

We did three series of Open All Hours in the 1980s. When Ronnie took the decision to bring it to an end in 1985, it was regularly getting audiences of more than 15 million. Ronnie used to say that Open All Hours was the comedy series he most enjoyed doing – even more than Porridge, which was arguably the more successful of the two. He once gave an interview in which he said, 'I enjoyed Open All Hours more because of David.' I was very touched and flattered by that.

Soon after Open All Hours finished, I was talking to Ronnie and he told me that he was going to retire – not right then, but soon. Actors don't really retire: there isn't usually a formal moment. You don't give up the business, the business tends to give you up. But Ronnie wanted to make a full stop. He was fifty-six at this point. We had recently lost Eric Morecambe and Tommy Cooper and I think that was playing on his mind.

He didn't want to work himself into an early grave. In the end, he retired on New Year's Day 1988, when he was fifty-nine, bringing the curtain down on his career at the time of his choosing. For all that it disappointed me that he stopped producing work, I respected him so much for it. It gave him sixteen relaxed and contented years with Joy before his terribly sad death in 2005.

A few days after his retirement, Ronnie sent me an official declaration, handwritten on a scroll of paper in a suitably formal script, with blobs of sealing wax and gold illuminations:

> WITNESS all ye now here present that I, Ronald William George Barker, known to the world of the footlights as Ronnie Barker, have now stepped from the spotlight after forty years and WHEREAS I have no longer any claim to the title The Guvnor, being that I no longer hold sway over nor have power to command supporting actors, bit players, stooges and feeds; NOW this hereby witnesseth that it is my chosen and deliberate intention forthwith to abdicate the said title of The Guvnor in favour of my good loyal and trusty servant David Granville Dithers Jason; and that he now is entitled to bear arms in the dignity of the office and title of THE GUVNOR and to enjoy all the privileges thereunto belonging. Signed in the presence of these worthies hereunder:
>
> Arthur Arkwright, Grocer
> Norman S. Fletcher, Director
> Rustless of Chrome Hall KGB, OM
> &
> Ronnie Barker, the Ex-Guvnor
>
> GOD SAVE THE QUEEN

You can imagine how much that meant to me. I never followed the instruction to take up that title, though. Wouldn't dream of it. There was only one Guvnor.

* * *

ONE MORNING, WHEN we were rehearsing *Open All Hours* at the Acton Hilton, I was going up in the lift with Syd Lotterby when Syd said, 'I've got something I want you to take a look at.' He handed me a manila envelope. 'Don't show it to anyone,' he said. 'Take it home, have a read and tell me what you think tomorrow.'

I was intrigued. I took the envelope home and opened it up. Inside was the script for the first episode of a comedy series. I sat down and began to read, and it was one of those ones where, within about a page and a half, you realise it's got you hooked. It was about two brothers and their old grandad, living high in a council block in south-east London and making their way, apparently very unsuccessfully, as market traders. It had characters, it had some zinging lines, it had warmth – it seemed to have all the necessary ingredients. One character in particular jumped out at me: the elder of the two brothers – the irrepressible, wannabe entrepreneur. I thought to myself, 'I know this man.'

Right there in my flat as I read, I was spun back to the days of B. W. Installations, when Bob Bevil and I were going round to builders' yards and literally knocking on the door in search of electrical work. In the East End of London we had happened on a contractor called Derek Hockley – a real East End player in a camel-hair coat, with immaculately greased hair and sharp clothing. He had a cockney accent you could have rolled up and beaten someone over the head with, and a habit of bringing his top lip slightly forward and flexing his neck as if trying to get the collar of his shirt to settle down. (He also slid me and

Bob a mountain of work doing the wiring for Ind Coope pubs, so God bless him for that.) I could hear Derek Hockley's voice and see his manner as clear as day in the character on the typewritten pages in front of me.

The reason for Syd's secrecy was that we were in the middle of preparing a show and it might not have gone down too well with the rest of the cast if the director and one of the actors had come into the rehearsal room yakking about a new project. The next day, back in Acton, during a quiet moment, I returned the envelope to Syd and said, 'This is bloody brilliant. Really, really good.'

Syd said, 'If there was a part in it, what part do you think you could play?'

I said, without a beat of hesitation, 'Derek Trotter.'

Syd looked a little crestfallen. 'Not the grandfather, then?'

I said, 'No, no: definitely Del.'

Syd kind of shrugged and said, 'Well, OK, then. Thanks.' And that was the end of the exchange.

What I didn't know was that Syd was on a mission to help out his friend and colleague Ray Butt. Ray had been Syd's first assistant in the early days of *Open All Hours* and had risen through the BBC ranks to the position of director/producer. Ray had put together the highly successful sitcom *Citizen Smith*, with Robert Lindsay, and now he was trying to set up a new series by that show's writer, a man from Balham in south London named John Sullivan. The working title of the new show was *Only Fools and Horses*, although there was a feeling that they might have to change that, as it was possibly a bit obscure. Syd was helping Ray by coming up with a few casting suggestions – including potentially proposing me for the senior member of the comedy's cross-generational trio. My reaction rather changed his mind.

Syd now went back to Ray Butt and said, 'What about David Jason for Derek Trotter?'

As Ray himself later told me, he thought about this very hard for at least one and a half seconds before saying, 'No, no – he's not right.'

But Syd, bless him, persisted. He asked Ray to cast his mind back a couple of years to that location shoot the three of us had been on, for *It's Only Me, Whoever I Am*, the ultimately doomed sitcom pilot. 'Don't you remember,' Syd said, 'how he used to take the piss out of your cockney accent during those snooker games at the hotel?'

Ray said, 'Actually, I'd forgotten that.' Ray thought about it a bit longer. He had nothing to lose by seeing me. Eventually, he said, 'All right. If you think he's worth a look, let's get him in.'

I went in to read, on my own, in Ray Butt's office at BBC Television Centre. Ray was on the top floor, looking out onto the ring created by the fabled 'doughnut' building. (Alas, the BBC has, in its wisdom, seen fit to abandon Television Centre. Its rather antiseptic but nevertheless history-steeped walls are now up for redevelopment. In 2012, I was part of a tribute show to mark the Centre's closing, where I sat on a sofa with, among others, Ronnie Corbett, Miranda Hart and Dara O'Briain, sharing our memories of the place with Michael Grade. Afterwards I had a long and wistful chat with John Cleese about the enduring abundance of Noel Edmonds' hair. I miss that building and was sad to see the BBC leave it, although, of course, life teaches us that nothing is permanent. Apart, obviously, from Noel Edmonds' hair.)

John Sullivan was also in Butt's office that day – and strongly resistant to the idea of having me in his new series. John's impression was that I was a player of life's losers – of hapless characters, like Granville and Edgar Briggs and Shorty Mepstead and Peter Barnes. As that list shows, he might have had a point. In John's mind, Derek Trotter was, by contrast, an upbeat character – a winner. Not that Del Boy ever really won anything:

Myfanwy in her 'Spotlight' portrait.

Filming the 1989 *Only Fools and Horses* Christmas Special, 'The Jolly Boys' Outing'. Everyone acting their socks off except the late Ken MacDonald, right of Buster Merryfield. Trust jovial Ken.

The *Only Fools and Horses* team clinches BAFTA glory. Left to right, Nick Lyndhurst, John Sullivan, Tony Dow, me and Gareth Gwenlan. Happy days.

Publicity still shot in 1991 for *The Darling Buds of May*, my mother's favourite programme. One big happy family, with Pam Ferris, Catherine Zeta-Jones and Philip Franks. Even more happy days.

Nobody would fix the cracks in my dressing-room wall, so I did it myself. At Yorkshire Television during *Darling Buds*. I love having a practical project.

Me as Scullion in *Porterhouse Blue*, in 1987, not looking at all well. A BAFTA for Best Actor appeared shortly afterwards.

Detective Inspector Jack Frost, circa 2000. Moustache: model's own.

Peas in a pod. A happy father and his lovely daughter. Catching up on some sleep with Sophie, 2001.

A fistful of National Television Awards. Mantelpiece getting a little crowded.

Awards don't get any bigger than this. Arising as Sir David, December 2005,
the morning after my wedding. Heady, heady times.

Hanging about as Rincewind in
The Colour of Magic and waiting for
a better job to turn up.

The women in my life: my sister, June (above), my wife, Gill, and our wonderful daughter, Sophie.

by and large, he only appeared to have won things which it subsequently turned out he had lost. But he was a winner by mentality, and John couldn't see me playing that.

We hadn't met before, and my first impression of John was 'Did he really write this?' He was very quiet and, I thought at the time, a bit morose – the very opposite of the script, which was bright and full of life. John wasn't a morose person at all, in fact, as I later learned. Quiet, yes, but not morose. I think on that occasion he was simply worried. They had already tried and failed to get a couple of people for Del – I believe Enn Reitel, the Scottish impressionist and actor, was one of them.

So, I read for them – some bits and pieces from the script, remembering Derek Hockley and employing the accent I'd used to entertain Ray all those nights ago around the snooker table in Doncaster. Ray seemed to enjoy what I did, but it's very hard to judge what people are thinking on these occasions. By default, there's a lot of politeness and goodwill in the room. However, John, I felt fairly confident, was still not convinced. I thanked them both and left.

Then I went away and did my best not to think too hard about anything – to try and suppress the appetite that had started up inside me for doing this part. Because the more I thought about Del, and the more I thought about the script I had seen, the more I felt there was something potentially wonderful there for me. I had to make every effort to switch off those thoughts so that I wouldn't be too disappointed if – no, when – I didn't get the part. 'Managing your expectations', I think they call it in the training manuals. The ghost of my non-selection for *Dad's Army* was rising before me.

Stone me, though, if I didn't get a recall. Ray rang and said, 'Would you come in and read again?' So back I went to Ray's office, and this time I was not alone. I was introduced to a young actor called Nicholas Lyndhurst, who, it was explained to me, had been cast for the part of Rodney, the younger brother, and an older actor called Lennard Pearce, who was going to be playing Grandad.

Lennard was in his late sixties and hadn't really done much television. He had spent his career slogging around the repertory theatres. Nick, who was twenty, had found fame at seventeen as Adam, one of the children in *Butterflies*, with Wendy Craig and Geoffrey Palmer. I thought, as we all shook hands, that I had met neither of these people before, but it turned out I was wrong, twice in fact. By a strange twist of fate, Lennard had played Sir Lucius O'Trigger in *The Rivals* as a guest player when I was in the rep at Bromley, in the production in which I had been Bob Acres. We only worked that out much later, when we started to reminisce. As for Nick, he had been part of the cast of a semi-anarchic kind of *Tiswas*-style children's show, where the kids would interview people who were quite well known. When I was doing *Lucky Feller* for ITV, I had gone on as a guest, promoting the show, and my interviewer in the studio had been . . . a shiny-faced Nicholas Lyndhurst. Small world – with the usual qualification that decorating it would be a nightmare.

Two of the three key parts in this new show, then, were set in stone. As for the third one, it was now up to me and what I could do in the next twenty minutes or so. 'So, shall we get started?' said Ray. He proposed that we simply read through the first script, doing any of the scenes that involved the three of us. We sat round a table with our scripts and a few cups of the BBC's famously filthy coffee, and Lennard cleared his throat and began to read.

'That Sidney Potter's a good actor, ain't he, Rodney?'

With that, we were off. And, well, what can I say? When the three of us began to put our voices to the lines, the magic was in the room. Nick's deliberate, slightly dopey tone, my best Derek Hockley, Lennard's lovely growl – all the component parts just fitted. Within a few moments of that reading beginning, I was saying 'S'il vous plaît, s'il vous plaît' and calling Rodney 'a right dipstick' and 'a dozy little twonk' to his face for the first time, and the whole thing was sounding like it had been written for us. When we reached the end of our read, silence fell on the room. Ray Butt and John Sullivan exchanged looks until Ray finally said, 'Well, that'll do for me.' And with that, I was hired.

Nick, Lennard and I went to the BBC members' bar to celebrate. We couldn't order any alcohol because we weren't members. So the three of us christened the show with a cup of tea. I remember saying, as we sat there chatting, 'You know, I don't think this is a sitcom. I think this is a comedy-drama.' I felt able to say that because of the clear dimensions of the characters: they weren't Terry and June, they weren't designed-for-sitcom figures. They were real people who just happened to be funny. I felt very, very excited indeed.

Apparently, upstairs in the higher echelons of the BBC, news that I was being considered for the role as Nick Lyndhurst's older brother had caused some consternation, on the simple grounds that the two of us looked nothing alike. 'Isn't David Jason shorter and darker and rounder of face?' It had to be pointed out, as politely as possible, that this was the whole point. Two things John Sullivan always knew about Del: 1) that he needed to be shorter than Rodney, to remove any sense of physical intimidation from the interplay between the older and the younger brother; and 2) that he should look nothing like his sibling, to enable that delicious little undercurrent of suspected illegitimacy to run through the scripts, with Del and Rodney being the only two people who completely believe that they share the same father.

Before filming could start, we had to work up our characters – work out a little further who they were and work out how to become them. The way I've always thought about it is that you are trying to inhabit the character's body, not let the character inhabit your body. But what kind of a body was Del Trotter? John Sullivan had seen him with a flat cap and a fat belly, but I said, 'No, I know just the man,' and I pressed hard for taking him in the direction of the aforementioned Derek Hockley – this cockney who dressed like a fashion model but spoke like a docker. Derek Hockley became the image I took for Derek Trotter.

Incidentally, years later, I received a wonderful letter from Derek Hockley's daughter, written shortly after her father had died. She just wanted me to know that he had taken great delight in knowing he was the model for Derek Trotter. (It was something I had mentioned in a couple of interviews.) He used to dine out on the story. I was so relieved to hear that. I took inspiration from him fondly and admiringly, but I had sometimes worried over the years whether being associated with Del Boy had upset him or even ruined the poor bloke's life, and I was very pleased to discover that it hadn't.

In the days running up to the commencement of shooting, the costume designer and I went out to dress the character. This would happen at the beginning of every series of the show, when we would step out to the shops again to upgrade Del Boy's wardrobe for the adventures ahead. I hate shopping for clothes for myself and would generally rather shut my fingers repeatedly in a kitchen drawer than stand in a store on Oxford Street holding shirts up against myself and saying, 'What do you think?' Shopping for clothes for a character, on the other hand, was something different. I utterly loved it. It was a total escape. I was through the doors of those Oxford Street shops quicker than the costume designer, picking things out and hauling stuff off the racks, thinking, 'Would Del wear this?'

On that first trip, I picked out a selection of sweaters which I thought were absolutely right for him – a bit bright, a bit Jack the Lad – and I then wore them in succession throughout the series. It didn't occur to me that they were all made by the same company – Gabicci – and that the company might take a view on that. Gabicci got in touch with me and said they'd noticed I was wearing a lot of their gear. As I read their letter, I was thinking, 'This could go either way, really.' They were either going to be pleased about the publicity, or they were going to ask me to desist forthwith, perhaps even via their lawyers. Luckily, they sounded flattered.

Indeed, in appreciation of my loyalty to the brand, they invited me to come down to their warehouse, just off the North Circular Road. So I did, and I met the managing director and had a chat about the character and the programme. Then they said, 'Come round the warehouse and help yourself.' They were loading me up as I walked through – 'Have a couple of them . . . and a couple of those . . .' I came out with virtually a hamper of shirts and sweaters. I've still got some in the wardrobe. I'm not getting into whether these items are good, bad or indifferent, from a fashion point of view, because that's not really my area of expertise and never has been. I would only say that my wife Gill doesn't appreciate them anywhere near as much as I do. But I can't throw them away. It would feel wrong.

So, I had Del's clothes; now I needed Del's hair. There was a suggestion at the beginning that he should have a bubble perm, which was very popular among certain kinds of working-class bloke at the time, but which I resisted because I thought that was going over the top. Thick Elvis sideburns were also briefly on the agenda, but I argued against those, too. Ditto the suggestion that Del should have gold sovereign rings on every finger. I reckoned that he should have just two on each hand – otherwise I felt we were overcooking it and taking him towards parody, where he shouldn't ought to go. I was doing my best to think comedy-drama, not sitcom. In the event, we went for tidy, with a little bit of grease, à la Derek Hockley.

We didn't know it but the rhythms and rituals of the location shoot and the studio recording would pretty much set the pattern for the next decade of our lives. What would happen on location is that Nick and I would get to share a suite of exclusive leather soft furnishings in the Hollywood-style, luxury carpeted trailer which, in those heady days, the BBC habitually gave to the stars of its sitcoms. Oh, all right, then: we sat in the back of what was essentially a cheap second-hand motor home, but with the sink and the stove stripped out, and in their stead, a battered sofa, a knackered chair and a rack for your clothes. The smell in the place was a heady mix of damp carpet, petrol fumes and the aroma of 10,000 previously smoked Woodbine cigarettes.

Three or four of these motor homes were supplied for the cast, making any *Fools and Horses* location shoot look like an underfunded housing project, and each of the homes had its own driver. The drivers used to fascinate me. They would bring the van to the location, park it up and then sit in the driving seat, reading the paper. Come coffee time, they'd climb out, get a coffee in a plastic cup from the catering urn, and get back in the driving seat. At some point, they might swap newspapers with one of the other drivers and read that. Then they might nod off. Eventually, it would be lunchtime, over at the chuck wagon, and then they'd be straight back to the van to sit in the driving seat again, until teatime . . . and so on, through to the end of the day. The thing was, the drivers could never get out and do anything – help someone or move something – because the crew was unionised and the drivers would have got into terrible trouble if they had shown the slightest inclination to do someone else's work. So what they did was sit. I'm not sure it was a job I could ever have done. I suspect I would have been banging my head against the windscreen in frustration after about forty minutes.

Anyway, in the confines of our mobile home, Nick and I struck up an instant rapport. We had an early bonding moment on the second episode of the series when we were out on location in London with an E-Type Jaguar sports car, purportedly belonging to Boycie. I rather fancied this car and, during a break between takes, I asked if I could take it off for a quick spin. I think everyone assumed I meant a quick blast up the road and back, so no objections were raised. Nick jumped in the passenger seat, and away we went.

About twenty minutes later, I realised that I was, to all intents and purposes, lost. We'd gone left and then right, and then left, and possibly left again after that . . . or was it right and then left? To be honest, the top was down and we were enjoying ladding about in this beautiful convertible car so much that the specifics had got a bit blurry. However, somewhere behind us lay a BBC film crew on a tight schedule, and an even tighter budget . . . We began to do our best to retrace our steps. No satnav in those days, of course.

'Was it left here?'

'No, it was right, wasn't it?'

I had just about reached the point of despair when we turned into a road that neither of us recognised and saw the film crew at the far end of it. We got back with seconds to spare before our next call.

That jaunt definitely sealed something between us. Nick and I recognised in each other a kindred urge to mess about, whenever possible. I was delighted to find myself working with someone who was as ready as I was to stage a mock blazing row behind a closed door and then pretend not to be talking to each other for the rest of the day – to the cast's and the crew's deep concern. And I was equally delighted to be the colleague of someone who saw, as keenly as I did, the value of nailing Lennard Pearce's shoes to the floor. That was the night when – with the wind up us, as it frequently was – Nick and I broke into the wardrobe room, dealt with Lennard's shoes and, for good measure, turned his costume inside out. We thought we were very amusing. Next morning we came down and started getting changed and all we could hear from Lennard's side of the room was 'Who's been f***ing about with my costume? Look at it!' And then he went to put his shoes on. And, at that, I'm afraid to say, he lost his rag. 'Someone's nailed me shoes to the floor. Who would have done such a thing? I think we should get the police in here.' He said he wasn't going to work that day, and had to be talked round by means of a calming chat from Ray Butt and effusive apologies from me and Nick. I have to say it was the only time I saw Lennard lose perspective. It wasn't like him not to see the funny side.

One day, Nick arrived for rehearsals with a bag of novelty explosives. Essentially, they were thin bangers, with string at each end. You could tie these across a door, for instance, and anybody opening it would be greeted by a bang like a small bomb going off. Quality entertainment. Every morning it was the job of the production assistant, Tony Dow (who went on to become a director of the show), to set out the chairs and mark up the floor in the church hall in Hammersmith where we rehearsed. One day, Nick and I got in early and loaded up the stacked chairs with bangers. We then loaded the cubicle doors in the toilets too, for good measure. As Tony unstacked the chairs, he triggered one shocking explosion after another, until he decided he wouldn't touch another chair. Nick and I were still laughing about this when there was an explosion in the toilets followed by a female scream of gigantic proportions. We went white. The little old lady who cleaned the church hall had entered the Gents with her mop. It nearly finished her off. No more bangers.

Ronnie Barker used to say, 'You can't be funny on an empty stomach.' It's one of the great truths of comedy. Between the dress rehearsal at BBC Television Centre on a Sunday afternoon, and the recording in front of a studio audience, Nick and I would go to the BBC canteen. I would have sausage, chips and beans, and Nick would have egg, chips and beans. Always the same. It became what we did – a ritual, almost a superstition. Sometimes the others would join us, and sometimes they wouldn't. But that's where you would find me and Nick.

What Nick and I also shared were bouts of nerves before the recordings. We would be backstage and we would hear the audience come in, hear them get settled, hear the warm-up guy doing his stuff. We'd be pacing backwards and forwards, anxious as mice. We'd say to each other, 'Why do we do this to ourselves?' That feeling never changed. We were still the same, twelve years later. You couldn't not be nervous. You were presenting a new play every week to an audience. There was so much to go wrong. And you had two hours – which sounds like a lot for a half-hour show, which *Only Fools* was at first, but it really isn't, because there will be retakes and cameras have to be moved, and sets altered, so the pressure of time was always hanging over you.

Some audiences would be worried for you. It's an unusual atmosphere for the spectator, especially if it's the first time they had watched a show being filmed – very unlike watching a play in a theatre. Between them and the set were the cameras and the assistants running around the place, and the sound-boom guys. It can be pretty intimidating and sometimes the audience would catch that sense of intimidation and freeze up a bit. Sometimes we'd do the opening scene, and the laughs wouldn't come, even though you knew there were laughs there. If I could sense that the audience wasn't responding, I would do something stupid or dry on purpose, and then share it with the audience – blame Nick or the lighting crew or the director, or anyone who was to hand. And then the audience would relax. They knew they could laugh and not get into trouble, and by the same token they knew we weren't taking it too seriously. And then they'd be off. And once they were off, there was generally no holding them.

Only Fools and Horses got off to a ragged and inauspicious start, though. On the first episode, we had three directors in quick succession. Ray Butt trapped a nerve in his back and was taken to hospital in severe pain. (Nick and I went to visit him and took him some medicinal gin and tonic, pre-mixed in a disguised bottle, and some equally medicinal cigarettes, which he very much appreciated.) So Gareth Gwenlan (who was, in due course, to become the producer/director of the show and, beyond that, the BBC's head of comedy) came across from another show as a temp. Gareth hadn't seen the script before that day, which wasn't great. Then, shortly after that, Martin Shardlow was hired as a proper replacement for Ray. I rather lost my cool over this immediate chaos. It was our first night shoot, on our first series, and I so wanted us to get it right – yet here we were changing directors every three minutes. I stormed about the place, muttering, 'I think they must be trying to sabotage us.'

We survived, though, and, once things settled, it was clear very quickly that we had the makings of a tight team. There were no weak characters in *Only Fools*, and there were no weak actors. Everybody had something to bring. Roger Lloyd-Pack was RADA-trained, and his father, Charles, was a famous film and stage actor. His performance as the fabulously dim Trigger was so good that one tended to come to the conclusion that Roger must be genuinely like that as a person. He wasn't at all. He was quiet, unassuming, totally easy-going – and a consummate actor. Not all that long ago, I was watching the television and up he popped, playing a cardinal in *The Borgias* – which is about as far from Trigger as you could probably get, acting-wise, without putting on an animal costume.

The same was true of John Challis as the oh-so-superior Boycie. John was charming, well spoken, an actor of great weight, and an absolute gent to work with – another proper team player. Then, as the series grew, there was Ken MacDonald as Mike, the landlord of the Nag's Head. Every episode he was in, you could guarantee that at some point – during the camera rehearsal or in the middle of a set change – Mike would produce a beer mat from somewhere, put a nick in it and lock it on the bridge of his nose, before looking round the room and saying, 'Who threw that?' That was his number and he never tired of it. Mike loved the show and the people in it and could become quite emotional about his attachment to everyone. His character in *Only Fools* wasn't especially big, but he was utterly committed to it because he just thought it was one of the funniest shows ever and he wanted to be a part of it. I think we all felt the same.

The first series was duly broadcast in 1981 to a unanimous display of . . . well, relative indifference, really. The BBC didn't demonstrate any particular urgency to promote the show. Reviewers responded by ignoring it altogether. It was broadcast on a Tuesday evening, which isn't always the best night to drag in the big numbers. Altogether, it had a kind of under-the-radar feeling about it. We all knew there was massive potential here, but early in a sitcom's life you never really know what they're thinking upstairs, in the big rooms where the decisions are made. *Only Fools and Horses* could have been cancelled there and then, and we would have been gutted, but not entirely surprised.

* * *

I WOULD LIKE to say it was the second series in which *Only Fools and Horses* really broke through the glass ceiling, but it wouldn't be strictly true. It was, however, the series in which the show broke through the glass chandelier, so I guess that was something.

One day John, Ray and I were trading stories about working days and stupid things that had gone on in our old jobs, and

John told us one about something that had happened to his dad. John's dad and a couple of his mates would turn their hands to anything to earn a bit of money, and they were doing some odd jobs in a big country house. At some stage, the house's owner had said to them, 'We've got this pair of large Jacobean chandeliers, which need a specialist to come in and take them down from the ceiling and give them a clean. Do you know anyone who might be able to do that?' John's dad chipped in and says, 'Oh yes, guv – we can do that for you, no problem.'

Because this pair of chandeliers weighed so much, they were bolted right through into the rafters of the floor above, meaning that to detach them it was necessary to send someone to remove some floorboards from the room overhead and unbolt the mooring, while the others stood below, holding on to the chandelier and waiting to lower it to the floor. On this occasion, one of the lads went upstairs to unscrew one of the chandeliers while John's dad and another lad stood down below ready to catch . . . the other one. With predictable and expensive consequences. The story really made me laugh. I said to John, 'You've got to use that. It's too funny not to.'

John said, 'I don't know how we could do it, though.'

I said, 'But the Trotters get up to anything to earn a few quid. Surely we could cook up some way to get them out to a country house.'

John went quiet, and I thought at first he was a bit reluctant to take on the idea. In fact, it was because his brain had already gone into overdrive and he was even then working it out. Sure enough, John came back with an episode entitled 'A Touch of Glass', in which the Trotters land up in a stately home and pass themselves off as specialist chandelier cleaners. Their duties require them to remove a pair of thumping great chandeliers, one at a time, from the ceiling of the hall. Grandad disappears off upstairs with a hammer and a screwdriver to undo the bolts from above, while Del and Rodney stand beneath the chandelier with an outstretched sheet, ready to catch it as it drops. There's the noise of screws being loosened and then, with the most almighty crash, the untended chandelier drops to the floor.

There was a lot of pressure on that piece of filming. The chandelier might have been fake, but it had still cost the licence payer a lot of money and nobody wanted to have to commission another one if it smashed when the cameras weren't turning. Anticipation was high and everybody and his brother had come in to watch – all the crew and production staff and anyone who just happened to be around. When we went up the ladder, I said to Nick, 'Now, brace yourself, Rodney, brace yourself.' I wanted the audience to believe that something was about to happen to me and Nick, so they wouldn't even think about the chandelier in the background. We braced ourselves, and the chandelier beyond us dropped. There was a momentary silence and then I heard the magic word 'Cut!', followed by whoops and screams of laughter and rounds of applause. People were rolling about on the floor and Ray Butt had stuffed a handkerchief in his mouth to stifle his mirth. I don't think the crew stopped laughing for about ten minutes.

At the end of the second series, classic flying chandelier moments notwithstanding, *Only Fools* was averaging merely 9 million viewers. Contrast *Last of the Summer Wine*, the BBC's most popular sitcom at that time, which was generally getting about 16 million. We were even lagging behind *Terry and June* – and this at a time when everyone seemed to think *Terry and June* was finished. Worse than that, the previous programme in our slot, Ronnie Corbett's *Sorry!*, had been getting 10 million viewers. In other words, we had lost the BBC a million of the viewers who had previously been happy to watch the channel at that point in the week. Those are the kinds of statistics which make television executives start to get twitchy with the trigger finger. We all had to think, 'Well, it's been fun, but that's probably it.'

And then industrial action intervened – and entirely in our favour. In July 1983, a technicians' strike at the BBC temporarily caused programmes to be cancelled and drove some big holes into the scheduled output. It obliged the BBC to raid the cupboard for old material to fill the gap. The second series of *Only Fools and Horses* thereby found itself getting an early rerun. More than 7 million people were watching every week – which was quite impressive, given that this was in midsummer, when television audiences commonly dwindle. Suddenly, deep in the heart of the BBC, faith was renewed, the candle relit, the flag run back up the flagpole. John Sullivan was commissioned to write a third series, and, better still, a fourth series beyond that. 'Ordre du jour!' as Del might have put it. *Only Fools* had been granted the time to grow.

* * *

THAT MYFANWY'S AND my relationship could withstand the stresses of renovating a ruined country cottage suggested there was something fairly strong about it. One day, she said to me, 'Why don't we move in together?' All my life I had always resisted any such thing. Indeed, traditionally this was the point in any relationship at which I had always run a mile, causing no little distress along the way. But now I didn't run away. I felt ready.

The cottage in Crowborough wasn't really convenient for either of us, except as a bolt-hole, so Myfanwy and I started looking around for a house. In the process of doing up the cottage, I had realised, belatedly, how I liked the country life. As much as I loved London and was brought up in the Smoke, I found the quiet and isolation of the countryside had started appealing to me really strongly. As that noble man of letters

Dr Johnson said, 'When a man is tired of London, he has probably been living in a bachelor flat in Newman Street opposite Micky McCaul for too long.' I felt I was done with dossing down off Oxford Street, and it came to a point where I decided I would move to the countryside, make my permanent base there, and keep the flat on for whenever I needed to stay in the city for work.

I didn't really know where in the countryside to go, though. I'd been heading south, from Newman Street, across London, to get to Crowborough and that was always a bit of a chore. So I decided to look north instead. I got a map and a compass and drew circles with gradually increasing radiuses – five miles, ten, twenty, thirty . . . forty miles was where I set the limit. I eliminated the east, because it was so tricky to get out of London in that direction, and I concentrated on the north and the west, round as far as Reading.

Obviously, generally speaking, the closer to London, the more expensive the house. I decided that twenty-five miles was really as far as I wanted to be travelling – but forget it. That was totally outside the financial bracket. There was, however, a property in Wendover in Buckinghamshire that was thirty-five miles out. I thought that was probably too far, but we went to look at it anyway.

It was a lovely place: a little house with a workshop, backing on to a hill and with a big field next door to it. The garden was lovely and the hill was National Trust property, making it that much less likely, I felt, that we would wake up one morning, draw the curtains and discover that we lived next door to a brand-new chemical factory. On the day of our viewing, which was cloudless and sunny with the birds in full song, the couple selling the house gave us tea in the garden, which was a good tactic. In the car driving away, Myfanwy said, 'That's the place.'

I had to push the boat out slightly, financially speaking, to get it. When the sale process was under way, I began to waver a little. Was it too far out? What about the price? I think, even then, the prospect of commitment, solid commitment, troubled me.

But we did it. I sold the cottage to fund it and took out another mortgage. Of course, I had the traditional paranoid actor's frame of mind at this moment: 'Will I ever work again and pay for this?' But we moved in and were very happy and promptly acquired, from a rescue home, a three-legged dog called Peg, named after Jake the Peg, of course, in the Rolf Harris song.

I was working an awful lot at this time; I have always been very driven and determined to fill the hours that way, but this was a period in which I really seemed to be going for it. I was doing *Open All Hours* and *Only Fools and Horses* at the same time, for the couple of years in the early 1980s in which those shows overlapped. When the shooting schedules allowed, I was still working in the theatre as well. In 1985, I started appearing at the Strand Theatre in a farce called *Look No Hans!* with the great and lovely Lynda Bellingham. It was not the best play, perhaps, though it did have one memorable scene when a helicopter was supposed to land on a lawn, offstage, and we had a huge fan blowing and amazing lights flickering and a thunderous sound effect, so there was all this noise and an extraordinary downdraught on the set. We beat *Miss Saigon* to the onstage helicopter by a full four years.

John Junkin, who lived nearby in Buckinghamshire, was in a play in the West End at the same time, and he and I would travel up and down to London together by train. He was always good company. I had met him hanging about in Gerry's club, where I invariably had to do my impression of John Wayne for him, which amused him greatly. After our performances, we used to meet in the pub at Marylebone Station, throw a couple of drinks down our necks and then run for the train. I would get home about midnight, have something to eat with Myfanwy, who would wait up, stay up until about 2 a.m. and then sleep through until mid-morning. So life was a bit topsy-turvy but no less enjoyable for that. I was very busy and very content.

* * *

THERE'S A MOMENT in series three of *Only Fools and Horses* where Del and Rodney are squabbling about the viability of Rodney's plans to go it alone in business and invest his £200 of start-up capital in the self-catering holiday trade. Lennard, as Grandad, has had almost no lines in this scene – he's just been a silent presence in his armchair in the sitting room. But now, at the mention of Rodney's proposed £200 holiday property investment, he suddenly pipes up and says, 'What you got, Rodney – a Wendy house?'

It's hard, even now, to summon words that adequately account for the volume of the laughter this line got from the studio audience. The laugh went on so long, it threatened to run into the next episode – and all Nick and I could do was stand there and ride it, while trying not to join in. When we had completed the filming, I stepped forward to say a few words of thanks to the audience, which I always liked to do. This time, just to tease Lennard, I said, 'That's it. I'm resigning. Nick Lyndhurst and myself have worked our socks off all evening for this show. Lennard Pearce hasn't said a bloody word – and then he just says "Wendy house" and he gets the biggest laugh I've ever heard in my life.'

Thus, in 1983, was born the laughter ratings system that everyone on the show used from that day forward. Laughs would be ranked according to their perceived Wendy-ness. A decent line might be scored as a 'mini-Wendy'. A good line would get a 'sub-Wendy'. What you were hoping for, of course, was an 'all-out Wendy', or a 'full-blown Wendy'. The 'full-blown Wendy' was the holy grail. I have to say, very often, when the

Wendy came, it was Lennard's line. Nick and I used to tease him, saying he was a lazy sod and that we were basically a twenty-minute warm-up act for his one killer gag. Lennard would just say, 'I'm old – I'm allowed.'

Series three was also when Jim Broadbent came into the series as Roy Slater, Del's old enemy from school who has turned into a particularly lizard-like copper. Who would have thought that Jim would go on from here to make *The Borrowers* and then on to Hollywood? I could never work out why he didn't take me with him.

The ratings were on the rise and the show was finally getting noticed by the critics, who had done a pretty good job of turning a blind eye to it up to this point. I was, according to *The Times* of London, no less, 'a comic player of previously unexploited substance'. Well, as painful as it sounds, I was happy to have my substance exploited. We went into series four off the back of a BAFTA nomination for best comedy series, the first time the programme had been considered for such a prestigious award. We all went along to represent the show. In the end, the BAFTA went to *Yes Minister*. We were the nearlys, but not quites. We were stoic enough about it, though. And also, by that time of the night, thoroughly refreshed.

Still, in every respect, *Only Fools and Horses* seemed set fair and sailing steadily in the right direction. We could have no idea of the scale of the setback the show was about to endure.

CHAPTER FOURTEEN

The passing of Lennard. The arrival of Buster. And a
wave from the Queen mother.

In the February of 1984, we started to make series four of
Only Fools. We were a few days into external shooting, in
cold and miserable sleeting weather, and we'd taken a much-
needed break for the weekend. It was Monday morning, and
Nick and I were in make-up, trying to get warm and preparing
for the day's filming. Ray Butt tapped on the door and came in
very slowly. He was grey-faced and distraught in a way that I
had never seen him looking. He said he had some bad news
and that we should sit down. And then he told us what he had
just learned. Over the weekend, Lennard Pearce's landlady, who
lived in the flat below him, had found Lennard's body at the
foot of a flight of stairs.

The best that Ray could piece together about what had
happened was that Lennard had had a heart attack, and that
the heart attack had caused him to fall. Nick and I didn't know
what to do or say. Obviously, filming was immediately cancelled.
We all went home in a state of utter shock. Lennard was not,
essentially, a well man – and I guess we knew that. He had
smoked heavily all his life, and was still smoking when we

worked together. Yet the thought that he was gone produced only disbelief. That disbelief was stubborn. It stayed with us and wasn't dispelled even by the reality of Lennard's funeral, several days later. The funeral was a small and humble affair. Lennard seemed to have very little in the way of family. His landlady and her daughter seemed to be the closest people to him. Those of us on the show had grown to think of him as family too, though. We mourned his loss as you would mourn the loss of a family member.

In due course, we had to turn our minds to the question of what to do about *Only Fools and Horses*. Gareth Gwenlan, who had recently been appointed the head of comedy at the BBC, called a meeting with Ray Butt, John Sullivan, me, Nick and a couple of others connected with the show. The episode that we'd been working on had, of course, been cancelled. What we now had to discuss was how – if at all – to proceed in the future.

We started to talk about it. John, who was still shaken up by mourning and clearly upset about having to have these discussions so soon, made it clear very early in the meeting that he couldn't write for just Nick and me because the whole mechanics of the piece demanded the interplay between the generations. He didn't think we really had a show without that.

Somebody then tentatively floated the idea of getting in another actor who looked like Lennard and simply carrying on with the Grandad character as if nothing had happened. This was absolutely the wrong thing to suggest. John, in particular, was horrified. Both Nick and I joined in the chorus: we couldn't do that to Lennard's memory.

Somebody else then said, 'I know – let's introduce a female character. We could make an old aunt arrive, or something, and she could become the third member.'

At this point, I pitched in and said I wouldn't want to go with that. I pointed out that there had been a lot of physical antagonism between Del and Grandad and that this had been an important source of the comedy. Del could push and shove Grandad into the back of a van and tell him, 'Shut up, you old twonk,' and the audience allowed for it and found it funny. I said I didn't think this would work if the person that Del was bullying in his irritation was an elderly woman.

John had been silent for quite a long time, and he now said, 'Look, it does happen that people in a family die. It's happened to us. What I want to do is to write a funeral for Lennard – a script in which we acknowledge that Lennard has died and take that on board in the show.' I remember thinking, 'Right: how the hell is he going to make that work, in a comedy series?' But John said he would go away and write something we could look at, and with that, the meeting ended.

A while later, I got a call from Ray Butt, who wanted me to go in and see him. He said, 'I've had this letter arrive, with a picture.' I had a look at the letter. It was handwritten and it said, 'I understand that Lennard Pearce has died and without wishing to be disrespectful to his memory, if you were thinking of replacing him I would like to offer myself as his replacement.'

And there, in the accompanying photograph, was this guy with bright eyes and pink cheeks and a bushy Captain Birdseye beard. He wasn't actually wearing a sailor's cap, but when you looked at him, you felt he ought to be. The letter was signed 'Buster Merryfield'.

John Sullivan came in and we all sat in the office looking at this photograph and saying, 'What do you think?'

John said, 'He looks like a sailor. I could see him being a long-lost relative, who's been at sea, maybe. I could get him to come to the funeral.'

I said, 'Why don't we interview him then, and see how it works?' Deep down, I was pretty convinced it wouldn't work at all, but I couldn't see that we stood to lose anything by trying.

So Ray arranged for Buster Merryfield to come to the BBC. Buster had been a bank manager, formerly in charge of the

Thames Ditton branch of NatWest. He was now living with his wife in a bungalow in Byfleet. Much like me for a while, he had combined a day job with amateur dramatics and he became a bit of a leading light in his local group. He always lusted after turning professional and (again, like me) he had picked up a couple of bits and pieces by responding to ads at the back of the *Stage*. He didn't have an agent, or anything sophisticated like that. He just had his enthusiasm.

He turned up at Ray's office wearing a blazer and grey flannel trousers, a shirt and a neatly knotted tie. We asked him to read a passage from an old *Only Fools* script. Sure enough, he read extremely confidently, and very well. He was funny by instinct and he knew where the laugh was and how to get it. Plus, of course, he had that amazing look about him – an eccentric face, the face of someone whom you immediately wanted to like. He convinced us, and we convinced ourselves. So, without further ado, Buster was hired. It's an incredible story, really. Buster must be just about the only person who wrote away for a role in an established television sitcom and got it.

In the happy years to come, we went after Buster relentlessly to try and get him to tell us what his real name was, and only after ages and ages of pressure did he eventually weaken and inform us: it was Harry. He would only ever answer to 'Buster', though. He had been a fit young man and a big boxer during his time in the army, which is when the nickname was bestowed upon him. The other thing we constantly tried to do was to get him to show us a picture of himself without his beard. In that area, alas, he never weakened.

John went ahead and wrote with Buster in mind to play Del and Rodney's Uncle Albert, who was going to turn up at Grandad's funeral as a long-lost relative and then never go away. The resulting episode was 'Strained Relations'. I remember being very nervous when I read it for the first time. I desperately wanted John to get it right – and I could see how the whole future of *Only Fools and Horses* depended on him doing so. Yet I just didn't see how it was possible that he would.

I should have trusted him more. When I turned through those pages encompassing the funeral scene, I realised he had completely nailed it. I knew John wasn't frightened of hitting things head on, but what I hadn't realised before was just how extraordinarily adept he was at moving from comedy to drama and pathos. The scene was dark and sad and yet it was shot through with these bright shafts of humour, right from the beginning, with the flowers at the cemetery and the note from Del and Rodney, marked 'Always in our foughts', through to the superb kick at the end, when Del hands what he believes is Grandad's hat to Rodney and encourages him to drop it into the grave in one final, moving tribute, only for it to emerge that the hat actually belongs to the vicar. When I read that, I collapsed. It was just so . . . Trotters.

Of course, then we had to film it. What a bleak day that was. The weather matched our moods and it fed into the scene: the drama of the dark glasses at the graveside; the turning to the gravedigger, as he begins to shovel soil onto the coffin, and saying, in a fiercely protective way, 'Gently!' It was all very hard to do, with Lennard's memory so fresh. I know we were just playing around in front of cameras, but trust me: it didn't feel like that. I was very emotional. It was an episode written by John out of respect for Lennard. So I wanted to get it right for Lennard, and, at the same time, I wanted to get it right for John. He just wouldn't let television dismiss Lennard's passing, in the way that television might have done, if television had been left to its own frequently fickle devices. It was a wonderful thing – and something that nobody had done in situation comedy.

Out of adversity, of course, grew something really positive. The arrival of Buster led John Sullivan into a new rich vein – all these stories of Uncle Albert's naval derring-do, none of which you ever quite trusted, and all of which seemed to terminate in disaster and destruction. One of my favourite lines was when Buster was telling a story about being in the crow's nest, on lookout, and crashing into an aircraft carrier. 'Blimey, they would have been better off with Ray Charles in the crow's nest.' But there were hundreds like it.

The slightly tricky thing was that Buster had no experience whatsoever of television. During the first recording sessions, in an environment that was completely new to him, he wound himself up more and more with nerves. The pressure on you in front of an audience and cameras is very high and if you've never done it before it can really get to you. He kept crashing into the audience – delivering his lines without waiting for the laughter to die down, so that they were lost, which meant we kept having to stop and go back. It got to Buster badly. He was drying and losing his words, and the more he dried, the worse it got for him. The situation was becoming more and more tense. Buster was in danger of breaking down altogether and not being able to cope. So I stopped the recording. I told the audience, 'We're just going to take a little break.' I think I blamed it on the lighting crew, or the director, or one of 'them', in a conspiratorial way to keep the audience onside. Nick and I then took Buster behind the set and we had quite a long talk. He was very upset. He was saying, 'I can't do it. I don't know how.' I explained to him that it was only a lump of tape. It didn't matter. 'Look at me,' I said. 'The number of mistakes I make. But every time I do, I blame someone and make it into a joke. If you can make the audience think you don't care, the audience relax and they like you and they feel part of it.' Buster, bless him, listened very intently, and he came back out and I think that cracked it. It took a lot of the pressure off and he got better and better and relaxed more and more into the part. And we forged a new partnership and he became the lovable Uncle Albert that we know.

The audiences continued to climb. The fourth series, in 1985, averaged nearly 15 million viewers. Late in that series, there was a scene where Del did some fly-pitching in the local market – flogging super-deluxe trimming combs and urging people to save a fortune by cutting their own hair at home. Such scenes were surprisingly rare, given that fly-pitching was ostensibly Del's core business. I loved doing them – the patter, the banter, the rhythm. The time I had spent watching the illegal street traders on Oxford Street, while walking from my flat to whichever theatre I was playing in, finally paid off as research in those moments: 'Come round a bit closer, would ya? At these prices, I can't afford to deliver.' 'I haven't come here to be laughed at, charffed at or generally mucked about. I've come to sell my wares. They're guaranteed to cure hardcore, softcore and pimples on the tongue.' These were the sort of lines I'd picked up on the street and filed away, for some reason, and now I could throw them into my ad-libbed sales pitch.

That year saw the annual and now traditional *Only Fools and Horses* Christmas Special pitched deliberately against ITV's *Minder*, with George Cole and Dennis Waterman – a show which, of course, was also a comedy-drama about the black market in London, so a kind of rivalry between the two programmes was easy to confect by the press. *Minder* was a show I loved to watch, so the rivalry didn't feel particularly hostile to me, but I guess it was a good story for the papers. For what it's worth, we won the 'battle of the ratings', as it was billed, with an audience of nearly 17 million – a number I simply couldn't get my head around when I tried to think about it. What those nearly 17 million people saw was a feature-length escapade about a dodgy diamond deal involving a rogue trader in Amsterdam, although, to be perfectly frank, my most vivid memory from that show is of Nick and me following Ray Butt out of the chuck wagon one night after a location shoot. It was cold and Ray was wrapped in an anorak the size of a duvet, the hood of which made him look from behind like some kind of gnome in a horror film. This was funny itself, but what more particularly caught our attention was the noise of chinking as he walked. Nick and I caught up with him and I said, 'Ray – what *is* that noise?' He stopped and showed us his pockets, crammed full of little miniature bottles of gin and tonic. Ray had loaded himself up with supplies for the night. He did love a gin and tonic, that man. Purely recreationally, of course.

* * *

IT STANDS TO reason, of course, that you can't go on television over and over again in front of audiences of 16 million people and not get recognised on the street every now and again. Yet it hadn't really occurred to me that fame would be the inevitable consequence of all this. At any rate, I didn't realise how fame would operate to restrict my life.

The extent to which my life was changing in this area came right home to me one Sunday afternoon when I was on Dunstable Downs, doing some gliding. I was sitting there, in the glider, waiting in line to be towed up by the powered aircraft. People were walking round – it was a public right of way, so there was no reason why they shouldn't – when suddenly somebody spotted me . . . and that was it: people were coming up with their cameras and their kids and, in a couple of cases, even their dogs, and posing beside the glider. And I was sitting, as we all did, with the canopy up, strapped in and unable to move (somewhat symbolically), and silently steaming with embarrassment and frustration. Here I was, preparing to throw myself into the air in what was basically a glorified Perspex tube, and then (hopefully) to bring myself safely back down. The whole deal was pretty risky, what with the absence of that reassuring item, an engine, and when you had people going

'Look, here he is! What are *you* doing in there?' it was a little hard, shall we say, to maintain focus.

'That's me finished with gliding,' I thought. I never went back.

I spoke to Nick about being recognised. It was happening to him, too. He said that his solution was to wear a baseball cap with the brim pulled down. He could pass himself off as some bloke in a hat and go unnoticed. But, of course, when he was noticed, it would be 'Rodney! You plonker!' It wasn't so bad for me. I would generally get 'All right, Del Boy?' – and only on very rare occasions 'You wally!' For Nick, it was far harder. He got beaten around the ears with a catchphrase. But both of us were beginning to learn some lessons about fame and beginning to make adjustments.

* * *

IN OCTOBER 1986, an episode of *Only Fools and Horses* achieved an audience of 18.8 million. That episode was called 'Who Wants to Be a Millionaire', and it's the one where Del appears to be about to accept a friend's offer to emigrate to Australia and go into business over there, only to have a change of heart and return to the bosom of the family, whereupon he reflects, in a classic Sullivan line: 'If I'd taken that chance of a lifetime, it could've ruined me.' 18.8 million people, though. The show was capturing the nation's attention to an extent that none of us had conceived it would, even in our wildest and most optimistic imaginings.

On 24 November 1986, *Only Fools* was honoured with a slot at the Royal Variety Performance. We all got very excited about that. Fancy that – the Trotters on the Royal Variety. John, Nick and I sat around and had a chat. How should we play it? Should we do a piece out of a script, a bit of the current script? (We were busy on the Dorset coast shooting 'A Royal Flush', that year's Christmas Special, at the time.) Eventually

John said, 'I think we've got to have something original. Leave it with me.'

True to the Sullivan style, he came back with a really neat four-minute sketch. In it, Del and Rodney tip up in Drury Lane with Uncle Albert, looking for someone called Chunky Harris, for whom they have a consignment of knock-off whisky bottles in boxes. The idea was that they would slowly realise they were not, after all, in Chunky's renovated nightclub but, in fact, on the stage of the Theatre Royal, in the presence of the Queen Mother. Between takes on the Dorset coast, Nick, Buster and I rehearsed this piece to within an inch of its life. Here was a scene we most definitely did not wish to screw up.

The tightness of the schedule forced us to drive up from Dorset on the day of the show. There were so many acts at the Royal Variety that the dressing rooms of the Theatre Royal alone could not contain them. Our facilities were round the corner in the Fortune Theatre, which had been commandeered for the night. We had a closed-circuit television screen that showed what was happening in the show and then, as we sat in the dressing room, watching the show on the screen, we worked out that we were the only people on the bill who were doing something original. Everybody else seemed to be doing a tried-and-tested item from their honed act – not a specially written piece which they had never performed publicly before and in which they didn't really know where the laughs were. A sickly feeling entered our stomachs.

And then it was showtime, and we were called and taken up the road and in through the stage door and shown quietly into the wings. As we heard the little introductory film being played on tape to the audience, the nerves between the three of us would have powered a wind turbine. Still, the film got a laugh, and we went out there, and the laughs continued to come and the nerves magically evaporated, as they will when an audience is immediately responsive.

We reached the point in the sketch where Rodney suddenly notices the presence of royalty in the royal box and, in a frozen panic, tries to draw my attention to it. I head over to that side of the stage, peer up blindly through the lights at where the Queen Mother is sitting, and deliver the line, 'Is that you, Chunky?' At this, to my astonishment, the Queen Mother graciously waved a hand in my direction. I nearly dried. Del Boy has been waved at by the Queen Mother. I knew she was going to be up there, but I didn't expect her to wave.

Afterwards, we changed quickly out of our costumes and into dinner jackets and lined up, as is traditional, to be presented to the royal party. The Queen Mother passed along the line and when she got to me, she said, 'Thank you.' I was, of course, deeply touched. But then I noticed her saying 'Thank you' in exactly the same tone of voice to everyone else in the line, too.

We couldn't hang around, though. We had to get straight into a car and head back to Dorset to carry on filming. We had a bottle of whisky and some water to settle the adrenalin which was still coursing through us. (Buster never drank. He sat in the front. All the more for me and Nick in the back.)

Also on the bill that night: Ronnie Corbett, Nana Mouskouri, Ken Dodd and my old colleague Bob Monkhouse – not that I got to speak to him in the rush. Still, that night I'm sure we both felt like we were a long way from Weston-super-Mare.

This was a lovely interlude, but it did nothing for the scheduled shooting of 'A Royal Flush', which was already well behind. I then didn't help matters by losing my voice and needing three days off – as I recall, the only time on *Only Fools* when I ever had to call in sick. As soon as I recovered, Nick went down with the flu. The schedule was now a wreck and we were officially in panic mode. There was no time to edit the film sections so that they could be played to the audience at the studio recording; the live audience recording had to be cancelled entirely. This meant the show ended up with no laughter track.

There was also no time for music to be fitted to the soundtrack. We were shaving it so finely that, at one point, contingency plans were made to broadcast the final scene in the flat live on Christmas Day. This would have been somewhat nerve-racking. We may have been coming fresh off the back of an appearance at the Theatre Royal, but performing live to nearly 19 million people was not something of which any of us had much previous experience. It also would have played merry havoc with all our Christmases: by my reckoning, you want to be watching television on Christmas Day, not appearing live on it.

As the chaos raged and then tension rose, the answer to all questions on the set seemed to be 'F*** knows.' When are we shooting the studio scenes? 'F*** knows.' When are the script revisions going to be ready? 'F*** knows.' Frequently a hand gesture accompanied the answer – one's thumb and one's forefinger slid over one's nose. Eventually the gesture completely replaced the verbal answer. 'When's the camera rehearsal?' Hand-to-nose gesture.

Somehow, though, a broadcastable programme came together, albeit with editing continuing into the early hours of Christmas morning – Ray Butt working like one of Santa's elves on amphetamine in order to get the show finished on time. If the resulting episode was a bit patchy, one should hardly be surprised. We were just relieved there was a show at all. Afterwards, John Challis had commemorative T-shirts made for everyone, featuring a big image of a thumb and forefinger clenched around a nose.

* * *

IN 1987, IN the months between filming *Only Fools and Horses*, I was approached about the possibility of playing a part in a television adaptation of *Porterhouse Blue*, the comic novel by Tom Sharpe. Malcolm Bradbury had converted the book into a four-part series for Channel 4 and the producers wanted me to audition for the role of Scullion, the head porter of a Cambridge college. 'Do you know the book?' my agent asked. I didn't, but I went out and bought it, and I read it and thought it was really great. I was a little puzzled, though, about the connection that the director had made between me, famous for playing Derek Trotter, and Scullion, this arch-manipulator who was all about respect for your superiors and respect for king and country, while quietly co-opting power for himself. The only conclusion I could come to was that both these characters were archetypal working-class men, and *Porterhouse Blue* was, in its way, like *Only Fools*, a piece about class, albeit in a different era and a vastly different place.

I went to see the director, Robert Knights, in his office, which conveniently was not far from my flat in Newman Street. Robert was a very nice man who called everybody 'sir', in a rather old-fashioned way – as indeed did Scullion, so maybe that's where Robert got the idea from. We got on well and I was asked back for a second interview, this time with the producer and the casting director, as well as Robert. They asked me if I would mind dressing the character the way that I saw him. I said, 'No, not at all.' So I was taken downstairs to a room where there was a mound of clothes piled up on a table and I was left to get on with it. Scullion is very well described in Tom Sharpe's book, so this wasn't a tough challenge. I rummaged around and pulled out a dark suit, a bowler hat, a pipe and a stick-on moustache. Then I went back upstairs, knocked on the door again, dressed as Scullion, and did a bit of acting for them to try and convince them I could pass for a Cambridge University porter. And that was it. I took the clothes off downstairs, put them back on the table and went home.

As with all these things, I really hoped I'd get it. But it was so far removed from *Only Fools and Horses*, and so different altogether from anything I had previously done on television, that I genuinely didn't fancy my chances. I was taken aback when my agent rang and said, 'They want you.'

Porterhouse Blue was shot on film and was a beautiful production, with very little expense spared. In television the money has always gravitated towards drama, but this was something else. The exteriors were shot in Cambridge and there were some massive set-ups: the pageantry surrounding the ceremony in which a new master of the college was installed; a scene in the great hall, with hundreds of students as extras. I loved being part of those huge set-pieces. It enabled me to give some rein to my film-actor fantasies. It was certainly very different from the slightly grab-it-and-run *Only Fools and Horses* shoots.

The great Ian Richardson played the Master of Porterhouse College. Ian was a sensational actor to work with and brilliant company during downtime. There was one night shoot, when we were all sitting around, freezing cold, with our coats on, in the room that was allotted to us as a green room. The conversation turned to theatre stories and suddenly Ian was up on his feet and demonstrating how to do a properly theatrical exit in a Shakespeare play – revealing just how important you can make the simple act of walking off the stage at the end of a speech. The art (lest you wish to try this at home) is to do a kind of double exit: you go, you pause, you slightly come back, you go again. It was so funny the way he did it. Play it right, he insisted, and you could virtually guarantee a round, no matter what had happened in your exit speech.

Equally impressive to me was Charles Gray, a big man, an RSC actor – though most people probably know him as Blofeld in the James Bond movie *Diamonds Are Forever*. Charles would come into make-up and I would say, 'Good morning, Charles, how are you today?' And he would reply, in his huge, rich, thespy voice: 'Ah, dear boy. I went out for dinner last night with some friends and we drank nearly a bottle of brandy.' And you would know he wasn't fibbing because the faint aroma of

Hennessy 57 was in the air as he spoke. Or maybe it was just a strong aftershave. And yet he would be DLP – dead line perfect. He never needed the script anywhere near him. I used to feel inadequate when I rehearsed scenes with him. There would be me, with my bits of script which I had known perfectly well at home the night before but which had somehow become a little elusive in the morning, and there was Charles, effortlessly nailing it.

Some of the scenes were done on location at Apethorpe Hall in Northamptonshire – in particular a moment where there had to be a large explosion in the college quad. We were all very excited while this was being set up, believing that it was going to be some good sport, and everybody retreated upstairs to look down on the quadrangle from above. Unfortunately, the safety-conscious spoilsports rigging up the explosion gave us the severe instruction not to look out of the windows. 'Stay back from the glass, just in case,' we were told. 'You can look out until you hear the countdown commence.' There was a lot of tutting at the needless fussiness of this from the assembled thespians, but we grudgingly obeyed the letter of the law and, as we heard the countdown start, obediently stepped back towards the middle of the room.

At which point – ka-boom! In came all the windows. Glass showered onto the floor at our astonished feet. The riggers had accidentally been too generous with the explosive and it blew the glass out right across the house and cost the production a fortune in compensation to the owners. No animals were harmed in the making of *Porterhouse Blue*, and no actors either. But it was close.

This was the same quad in which we filmed the famous sequence in which Lionel Zipser, the graduate student, attempts to clear his room of an embarrassing quantity of condoms. His solution is to inflate them, using the gas pipe in his room, and then float them up the chimney under cover of night. His notion is that they will fly harmlessly away, but, of course, they descend to form a carpet of inflated prophylactics across the college's august and neat quadrangle.

It was my duty as Scullion to rescue the college's honour by spearing these condoms on the lawn with a sharp stick. In order to set up this scene, the production acquired boxes and boxes of condoms – a generous gift from the manufacturer, I believe. Two production assistants then spent the best part of a day standing at two giant gas cylinders, filling condoms, some with helium (the ones that were to fly from the chimney) and some with oxygen (the ones that had to lie on the ground). As they filled and knotted these condoms, they would lob them into an adjacent room for storage. I came past several times during the day, and was able to observe this room gradually filling with inflated condoms, until it was entirely wedged with pink rubber. It was exactly what I loved about filming: the peculiar sights you would see and walk past and find people taking absolutely for granted, as if they were the most normal thing in the world.

We filmed the condoms flying out of the chimney, which went fine. But when we came to the scene where I had to stab them as they lay on the grass, the wind was up and all our carefully laid condoms kept blowing off to one corner of the quad. Eventually, someone had to go round and pin each one down to the grass through its knot so I could jab them.

My performance as Scullion was nominated for a BAFTA award in the Best Actor category. I had been to the ceremony twice before, as a nominee for *Only Fools* in the Best Light Entertainment Performance category, and I hadn't won on either occasion. I thought about not going this time, to avoid the disappointment. Those black-tie show-business occasions don't make me very comfortable, to be honest. Plus I was up against Kenneth Branagh, for heaven's sake, who was nominated for *Fortunes of War* – a role in which, so far as I'm aware, he jabbed precisely no inflated condoms with a sharp stick. It was a bit like going willingly to your own execution, I felt. But somebody pointed out that this was Best Actor, and at the BAFTAs, and even to be shortlisted in that category was an honour so I should at least have the decency to show up and smile gamely.

So I put on my black tie and I went to the dinner in the chandelier-hung ballroom of the Grosvenor Hotel, and I sat at the table and worked on my 'stout and generous loser' expression, ready for the moment when the envelope was opened and the name was called.

Blow me down, though: 'And the winner is . . . David Jason for *Porterhouse Blue*.'

I've got to tell you, that felt incredible. When I got up from the table, my knees were shaking – but, even so, they felt like the bee's knees. For the rest of the evening, people were coming up and congratulating me – including Kenneth Branagh. I felt like I had arrived – like I was finally someone who counted. What was that thing Frank Sinatra said, as he stood at the window, high up in a luxury hotel suite, and looked across New York to the borough of his birth? 'You know, it's a lot further from Hoboken to here than it looks.' I felt a bit that way about the distance between Finchley and the Grosvenor Hotel. It was nice to be a winner. I had always been very insecure about my abilities as an actor, but that night, sitting among my peers, I allowed myself to feel very proud of what I'd done.

*　　*　　*

IN 1989, ahead of series six, I went to see John Sullivan. I was getting annoyed on John's behalf. I said, 'You're giving us these great scripts which often come in long, and in order to get them down to thirty minutes, we're cutting out more funny material than most sitcoms have in their whole episode.'

I was still particularly sore about an edit to an episode in series five, 'Tea for Three', in which Rodney buys Del a hang-gliding session, only for Del to lose control, take off and disappear off into the air for twelve hours. Del returns to the flat in a wheelchair with a neck brace. At that point I had this long, long, beautifully constructed speech, full of suppressed rage, about all the places that Del had been to and the things that he had seen on his marathon hang-gliding journey. I thought that speech was a comic masterpiece. But because the show had overrun, half of those lines got cut.

John agreed with me that the show could certainly work in longer episodes. We went to see Gareth Gwenlan, who was producing series six, and we set out our case for extending the show from half an hour to fifty minutes. Gareth said, 'Well, a situation comedy is only thirty minutes. It won't sustain more than that, really.' I said, 'Yes, that's true of average writers. But we're talking about John. And you must agree: we keep cutting gold.' Gareth gave it some thought for a while, and then gave the green light to go to fifty minutes.

This, for me, was the point where *Only Fools and Horses* really came into its own as a comedy-drama, rather than as a sitcom. It wasn't just that there was now time to get more of John's great lines in; it was that there was now more space in which things could unfold. Without the additional length of episode, the show almost certainly wouldn't have been able to develop the romances between Del and Raquel, played by Tessa Peake-Jones, and between Rodney and Cassandra, played by Gwyneth Strong. We were once again blessed in our cast members there. Tessa and Gwyneth were fine actresses: Tessa had been in Shakespeare and Jane Austen adaptations; Gwyneth had acted at the Royal Court when she was eleven and had grown up working on children's television. Those two knew what they were doing and fitted straight into the team.

Series six was also the point at which the show relocated to Bristol. Peckham had never actually been Peckham, of course;

it had been other bits of the capital. Nelson Mandela House, for example, was Harlech Tower in Acton. For series six, though, Peckham wasn't even in London. The problem was that London was becoming an increasingly tough and expensive place in which to get licences to film. It was also getting more and more difficult for us to film on London streets without very quickly attracting a crowd. Sometimes we'd get interrupted by passers-by and autograph hunters. Many were the times when I found myself standing on a pavement, waiting for the instruction to perform for a distant camera, only to find someone saying, 'What are you doing here?'

So now Nelson Mandela House was Whitemead House in Ashton Gate and all the external action was on the streets of Bristol. All the rest was implied – using the age-old trick of positioning a couple of red buses in the background.

Del changed to reflect the mood of the times. He started to fancy himself a bit of a yuppy, a wannabe Thatcherite entrepreneur, with a raincoat, a suit from Austin Reed and a Filofax. 'Yuppy Love' was the episode in which Rodney first met Cassandra, the love of his life and, after a tempestuous courtship, the mother of his daughter. But, of course, that significant piece of plot development is not what people chiefly remember the episode for; rather it is for a small piece of business I did, not unadjacent to a pub bar flap.

It came together over one of John's and my frequent chats over a glass or two. The way John originally thought of it, it was more a slip and a stumble than a complete tree-like fall. John had seen something like it actually happen at a wine bar in Balham – a bloke going to lean on the bar, just as the barman opens the flap. The bloke had to grab hold of the edge of the fixed part of the bar to hold himself up. What John had liked about the moment was the bloke's body language immediately afterwards, flexing himself and trying to recover his cool. I said I thought the way to develop it was that Del ought to go all the way over – start to go sideways, and then just continue going, and all without looking in the direction of the fall. That was the key to it, for me – the fact that Del doesn't twist his head to look where he's falling. Even with the crash mat in place, out of the shot, to break the fall, that's quite hard to do, because it runs completely contrary to your instincts, but it was a fall I'd done quite a number of times in farces in the theatre. My experience on the boards was coming in handy again.

Of course, the sweet comedy of the moment is not just about the fall, it's about Trigger's reaction – turning back from staring at the girls to find I've disappeared and then casting a startled look over to the door to see where I've gone. Altogether, though . . . well, what can I say? That little plummet through a gap turned out to be quite an item for me; indeed, some people never want to talk to me about anything else. Olivier had his Othello, Gielgud his Lear, Branagh has his Hamlet; I have my falling through a pub bar flap. And do you know what? I'm perfectly happy with that.

With episode two of the series came, unusually, controversy – or certainly controversy as it was perceived in the media. This was the one where Del acquires fifty faulty dolls – only to discover that they are not, as he assumed, harmless children's toys, but in fact the kind of blow-up dolls they sell for male recreational purposes in Soho. (Which is, incidentally, exactly where they came from, the result of a swoop on a sex shop – not by me, I hasten to add, but by the show's props buyer.) For the first time ever, the show found itself accused of overstepping the mark. One or two viewers complained to the BBC that having to explain to their young children what the joke was about these dolls had taxed their imaginations. In our defence, the dolls were clothed. But let's all move on, shall we?

By the end of that series, Rodney was married to Cassandra – an extraordinary moment. The passage through life undertaken by his character brought into focus the time that had flown by while the pair of us had been together. I'd known this guy when he was just a lad, and now here he was, getting wed. When the Simply Red song 'Holding Back the Years' was played into that episode, I'm not ashamed to say that I cried some tears for real.

That year at the BAFTAs, I won the award for Best Comedy Performance. This, to my astonishment, was getting to be a bit of a habit. I proudly set it down on my mantelpiece, alongside the one for Best Actor.

* * *

IN 1990, I turned fifty and Myfanwy threw me a surprise party at the house in Wendover. I was due back in the evening and she knew the jig would be well and truly up if I turned into the road and saw loads of cars parked up. So all the guests were under instruction, not just to arrive early, but also to park in neighbouring drives and roads. It was quite a logistical operation.

So home I come, and I walk into the completely dark house and the lights go on and – 'Surprise!' – there's Myfanwy, and my brother Arthur and his wife Joy, and my lovely sister June, and Ronnie and Joy Barker, and John and Jenny Junkin, and John and Sharon Sullivan, and David and Ellie Renwick, and Micky and Angie McCaul, and countless friends of mine from London and friends of Myfanwy's from Wales – who had all been crouching behind the sofas and hiding in the curtains.

The birthday cake was on an *Only Fools and Horses* theme, and Myfanwy was quite cross about it because the Wendover baker from whom she'd commissioned the piece had improvised a little and had chosen to commemorate in icing the scene where Del and Rodney end up with a batch of inflatable dolls. Myfanwy thought this was in poor taste on this special occasion, and she may have had a point. At the same time, the man was an artist with the marzipan and you should never hold an artist back from realising his vision.

John Junkin made a speech, and so did Ronnie B., and it was a lovely, high-spirited evening, and the nicest of surprises.

Well, when I say surprise . . . Did I twig? Of course I did. When did Myfanwy ever turn all the lights off in our house?

CHAPTER FIFTEEN

Dinner in the bath. Batman's revenge. And the saddest of endings.

If I hadn't had dinner at Langan's with David Reynolds from Yorkshire Television, I wouldn't have got a part in *A Bit of a Do* on ITV. And if I hadn't got a part in *A Bit of a Do*, I might not have ended up appearing in *The Darling Buds of May*. And if I hadn't got a part in *The Darling Buds of May*, I might not have ended up appearing in *A Touch of Frost*.

Mind you, by the same token, if I hadn't had dinner at Langan's with David Reynolds, I wouldn't have got quite so drunk. Memory has drawn a slightly headachey veil over the exact quantity of wine consumed at that fateful meeting, on that destiny-defining afternoon, but suffice it to say it was a multi-bottler.

This dinner took place as the eighties were drawing to an end, when I was as busy as I needed to be, really, with *Only Fools and Horses*. Nevertheless, I was pleased to talk to David, who sounded me out about appearing in a comedy series he was trying to get under way, written by the very talented novelist and screenwriter David Nobbs, most famous for creating the character of Reggie Perrin. Even then, as occupied as I was, there was always the drive within me – the basic actorly thing.

Be someone different. Be someone else. And take the work while it's there to be taken.

A Bit of a Do enabled me to be Ted Simcock – who wasn't an especially pleasant person to find yourself in the shoes of. He was self-centred, arrogant, chauvinistic and absolutely convinced that women were falling over themselves to get to him. But his unpleasantness was the point, as far as I was concerned. The characters I tended to be known for playing – Del Boy merely the most prominent among them – had their foibles but were meant to be essentially forgivable and lovable. They were great seekers of the audience's sympathy. Playing Ted Simcock was a chance to show another side.

It was also a chance to work with some more great actors – Gwen Taylor, who was to play my wife Rita; Nicola Pagett, who played the sexually promiscuous Liz Rodenhurst; Paul Chapman, who was Liz's hopelessly square husband. Again, this kind of company can only up your game. Nicola was one of that period's great sirens and the plot required her to seduce Ted Simcock by stripping down to a basque and stockings – a scene during which I must have been the envy of a large proportion of the male population. *A Bit of a Do* ran to two series, went down well with critics and viewers, and put me on Yorkshire Television's radar – to the extent that, in the event of a part coming up in . . . I don't know . . . let's say a family drama series set in rural Kent in the 1950s and destined to become a national, award-winning smash hit, then I would be well placed to be considered for it.

And what do you know? At the beginning of the 1990s, David Reynolds asked me what I was doing next. I told him I wasn't sure, but, like Mr Micawber, I was hoping for something to turn up. He said, 'Please don't commit to anything for another week. I can't tell you why – but please don't.' Eventually he got back to me and said Yorkshire Television had finally managed to secure the rights to *The Darling Buds of May*, an H. E. Bates novel from 1957, and they would like to offer me the part of a character called Pop Larkin.

Of course, I don't suppose any of us had even the faintest inkling at that stage of exactly how mind-bogglingly successful this project would be. I certainly didn't. I had to confess that I didn't know the book at all. But I went away and brushed up on it. I thought it was charming – a bucolic piece about a ramshackle, convention-snubbing farming family who woo the tax inspector into moving in with them in order to deflect him from inspecting their rather dodgy tax situation. But was it a television series, though? Afterwards, I had a conversation with my agent, and I said, 'I don't really know what this book is about. It's lovely, and everything, with the country setting, and all that – but nothing really happens. It doesn't go anywhere.'

I could see, though, that the characters were unusually strong – Pop Larkin, the head of the family, especially – and it was the prospect of playing Pop that made me think it might be fun to have a crack at it. I did have one condition, though: they had to shoot it on film, as *Porterhouse Blue* had been. I didn't want it to be a studio production. If they did it on film, I knew the series would at least look good and have some quality about it, even if nothing happened.

I said to my agent, 'It'll either be enormously successful or it'll fall flat on its face.' And I was right: it was enormously successful. (Though see how I cunningly hedged my bets there?)

My first question for David was: 'Who do you have in mind for Ma Larkin?' The relationship between Pop and Ma Larkin was at the centre of the drama and, whoever ended up playing Ma, we were obviously going to have to work together closely. David Reynolds said, 'An actress called Pam Ferris.' I didn't know Pam, so I rang my agent and asked about her. My agent said, 'She's great – and also a really nice, easy-going person.' That was good enough for me. Rather than meet for the first time at the read-through and rehearsals, David took us out for lunch, to break the ice between us. He was a great host as usual, though I think both Pam and I passed on the wine that time, it being lunchtime. We talked about what we'd done and a little bit about the series and our feelings about what those two characters were like: loving, cheeky, generous, trusting. She was down-to-earth, which I immediately liked about her, and we relaxed in each other's company very quickly.

Just as well, I suppose. There was a scene fairly early on in the series where the pair of us were required to be eating our supper in the bath together – and, what's more, to be doing it as if eating ham and quaffing beer amid the suds were the most natural thing in the world. I toyed with the idea of turning up on the set in a frog mask and flippers but couldn't quite bring myself to go through with it. In the event, we both wore swimming costumes and the water was coloured up to protect still further our mutual modesties.

That moment broke the ice, along with another, during a scene that brought us together in bed. We had to lie next to each other, chatting about the future of our daughter Mariette. It was Pam who had virtually all of the dialogue in this particular scene – a long and fairly complex speech. Before the shoot, I asked the stage manager, Anton Darby, whether he could get me a cucumber. I then smuggled it into bed with us and, when the director called 'Action!' and Pam began her lines, I gently laid the cucumber against her under the sheets. I expected her immediately to spring up and say, 'What the hell is that?' But I hadn't reckoned with the astonishing professionalism of Pam Ferris. She carried on, utterly undisturbed through thirty seconds of dialogue – perfectly delivered. Only at the conclusion of her lines, when 'Cut!' had been called, did she turn to me where I lay, corpsing madly on the pillow beside her, and shout, 'What in God's name are you up to?' and tore back the covers.

Altogether the cast felt like a family off the set as well as on it. We genuinely liked each other and I think an extra degree of warmth came through because of that. Philip Franks played Cedric 'Charley' Charlton, the tax inspector who pays a visit and doesn't leave. Philip was so perfectly cast. He had spent most of his career in the theatre and he was a great team player as a result of that. And then there was Catherine Zeta-Jones, who was the show's big discovery, as the Larkins' eldest, Mariette. They had interviewed simply hundreds of girls before they found Catherine. She was, it goes without saying, extremely beautiful, and you knew the camera was going to love her. She was also as lovely a person as she looked. She was twenty-two at this point and had been in musical theatre but was clearly determined to move into other kinds of acting. This series was the big step in that progression for her, but she was inexperienced in television, and she seemed very nervous at first. I remember telling her something it had taken me a while to cotton on to – about keeping your eyes still when you're doing dialogue in close-up. Normally, in the real world, your eyes range a bit around the face of the person you're talking to, but in a close-up of someone's face, that natural eye movement gets exaggerated and can look a bit odd, as if your eyes are shooting around in their sockets. If you fix your focus on one place on your interlocuter's face, it holds your eyes steady in the shot. Of course, Hollywood happened for Catherine soon after this, and obviously it was exclusively down to me. Thanks to my careful tuition at this critical moment in her budding career, she was ready for her close-up. Seriously, though, she got her part as Mariette dead on, with just the right mix of innocence and coquettishness. Hollywood stardom couldn't have happened to anyone nicer.

At the first read-through, it emerged that the production had also found some extremely talented children: the twins, Christina and Katherine Giles, and Stephanie Ralph, who played Victoria, the Larkins' youngest daughter. Kids, of course, have minds like sponges. They knew their own lines, and everybody else's as well. There was one time in the second series when I had what seemed to me to be a fairly involved speech, out in the stable. At the camera rehearsal, I got stuck and was lifting my script up to my eyes to remind myself where I was, when up piped Stephanie to give me the line. Prompted by a kid: a low blow. Frankly, I was happy a bit later in the series when the Larkins' next baby came along. A baby couldn't upstage you or tell you your lines.

The role made a few unusual demands on me. I had to drive a big old 1950s truck, an old army vehicle, painted up, which was an experience largely unrelated to what we generally think of as driving these days. It had a crash gearbox, with a lever that virtually tore your shoulder out of its socket, and steering which provided a comprehensive upper-body workout. I had to handle a few horses too, and at one point, the director said to me, 'Do you know how to milk a cow?' To which I was able to say, 'Well, yes – as a matter of fact, I do.' Years earlier, when I was going out with Melanie Parr and spending weekends at her parents' farm just outside East Grinstead, her mother Mary had taught me. If someone ever asks you if you would be interested in milking a cow, say yes. You never know when it might come in handy in your professional life.

But perhaps the biggest demand of all made by *Darling Buds* was the food. I piled on pounds doing that show. So much of it revolved around eating, and not just in the bath – great hunks of bread and ham, lumps of cheese, pickled onions, roast dinners, chocolate, all downed with a contented smile to show the Larkin family's generous spirit and carefree love of life. And then there were the fried breakfasts – cooked fresh on the set by Anton Darby, who had a little stove positioned to one side. The set constantly hummed with the smell of frying bacon and the crew would be walking around with drool hanging out of their mouths. One day, the shooting schedule meant that I actually sat down to breakfast five times. And breakfast meant a plate piled almost to the lampshade with bacon and eggs. I know breakfast is the most important meal of the day, but on that occasion it was the most important five meals of the day. By the end of filming, I felt that if I even so much as saw another bacon rasher I would begin to snort myself. I asked if I could skip the fry-ups from that point on. They said, 'Fine. We'll give you kippers instead.' Brilliant. Out of the frying pan, into the saucepan. When the kippers ran out, it was over to whole smoked haddock.

I realised what all this delightful consumption was doing to me the night I went to put on my dinner jacket for the BAFTAs and realised that I couldn't get it to button up around me. Right there, in the house, was a photograph of me taken a year earlier, wearing the jacket perfectly comfortably. Now I looked like Hardy wearing something belonging to Laurel. A few months of dieting ensued until I returned to my former, sylph-like self.

The location shooting was done in and around Bethersden in Kent – in glorious summer weather, fortunately. We used a fabulous Grade II listed house called Buss Farm which had an outhouse and an old Tudor barn attached to it. The interiors, though, were done in the studio in Yorkshire and the real genius of the show, it seemed to me, lay in making the footage from the two different sources blend. There was one scene in partic- ular in which the family were outside in the evening light – a scene in which I had to say to Charley, 'Listen to that – it's a nightingale. You don't get that in London. It makes your heart lift.' And then everyone goes inside, into the kitchen. Peter Jackson, the lighting director, whose background was in film, lit that evening scene in Yorkshire to match what we'd already got in Kent, and you simply couldn't see the join because it was done so brilliantly. The series was a high-quality piece of work altogether. We owed a lot to his brilliance, and to that of the whole team put together by David Reynolds.

I discovered something about the impact that *Darling Buds* was having, and about the sheer breadth of its appeal, when I was invited one weekend to be a guest of honour at Wycombe Air Park at a summer show for underprivileged children. This was at the point where *Only Fools and Horses* seemed to be about as popular as it was possible for a television show to get. I went along, fully expecting that when I got in front of these kids, I'd be hearing lots of shouts of 'Oi, Del Boy!' and other things Trotter-related. In fact, the minute I stepped out of the car, I was greeted by a wall of cries of 'It's Pop Larkin!' and 'Perfick!' and 'Hey, Pop Larkin – where's Mariette?'

But that's what the show did. The idyll it depicted spoke very directly to people – and to people of all ages. It was an example of a kind of television show that was already, even then, falling out of favour and which has continued to decline – a programme that families watched together. And what they saw, coming back at them from the screen, was this wonderful loving family, with kids they adored, sitting round at Sunday dinners, piling into the back of a truck and singing . . . People watched it and thought, 'Wouldn't we all love a little bit of that, if it were possible?' And that was the link, really, because the message of *Darling Buds* was the message of *Only Fools* too: that the most important thing is what happens at home and with the family.

A couple of years ago, Catherine Zeta-Jones got in touch and said she was coming to London to do some filming, and she would love to see me and Gill for a meal. She and her husband, Michael Douglas, were renting a house in Richmond and we fixed up to have lunch there one Sunday.

It was the first time I had seen her since she got married, and she greeted us at the door of this rather magnificent property and said, 'Come and meet my husband – I think he's in the pool.' It was a beautiful, sunny day and we went through the house to the garden. Michael was in the water, playing with his children. Catherine said, 'Michael, come and meet David.' Accordingly, my first sight of this great Hollywood star was as he came towards me, hand extended, just out of the pool, dripping wet, with Bermuda shorts on. All very relaxed.

After lunch, we had coffee and I sat down with Michael,

and, between doing the thing that fathers do of calling out to the kids to be careful about running near the pool and instructing them to play nicely, he said, 'I'd just like to thank you for what you did.' I said, 'What do you mean?' He said, 'Well, Catherine told me that when you did the show together, you really were very generous with her and looked after her a lot.'

Well, I was pleased he thought so, but it was very much the way of things on that show. We all looked after each other. Which stands to reason: we were one big (and overfed) family.

*　*　*

DARLING BUDS WAS my mother's favourite show – her favourite of all the things she lived to see me do before, at the grand old age of ninety, she fell asleep on her sofa. My sister June rang me. 'I can't wake Mum.' I drove from the house in Buckinghamshire and there she was, asleep and not to be woken.

She had outlived my father by fully twenty years – Dad with his arthritis, sleeping in the bed downstairs at Lodge Lane. I helped him get ready for bed one night – helped him with his pyjamas, his plastic bottle. The indignity that the elderly know. Pneumonia took him in the end. I remember visiting and holding his hand and trying to talk to him but he was already shutting down. How hard it is and how unfair it seems, letting go of someone you know so well. And now Mum too.

She had moved into a basement council flat and continued to rent it, despite the offer of other places elsewhere. She liked it there. She didn't see why she should move. Signs of my success didn't much impress her, in the main. When I bought the first house I owned in Buckinghamshire, she said, 'But I don't see why you need all this *space*.' My two-seater sports cars – the MG Midget, and then the TR7 – she referred to as 'David's mean cars', meaning they didn't have enough seats to take her and my Auntie Ede to wherever they wanted to go. Nevertheless, she came to a recording of *Only Fools*, and she quite liked that. But what she really loved was *Darling Buds*. She related to it much more closely. It was funny, though, the way she talked to me about Pop Larkin – entirely as if he were another person. I was never entirely sure she knew it was me.

* * *

MEANWHILE, I HAD finally landed the dream role of Batman – satisfying at last the burning aspiration to play a superhero which had been planted in me by the Dan Dare comic strips of my childhood. Well, kind of. Robin was Nick Lyndhurst – one of the rare occasions on which Batman has been cast shorter than his crime-busting partner. Still, that was *Only Fools and Horses* for you – never inclined to do things conventionally.

That episode, from the seventh series, in 1991, is still one that people go back to and talk about. The sight of Del Boy and Rodney running through the streets in full costume, the least likely world-savers you have ever seen, struck a loud bell with viewers which just carried on ringing. When we first read that script, we all loved it, but I had some strong feelings about the way the costumes had to go. Realistically, in the spirit of hired party costumes, Del and Rodney's Batman and Robin outfits would probably have been a bit tired, a bit tatty and quite ill-fitting. My feeling was that, in order to get the full comedy out of the moment where they save the woman from the robbers, they should look like Batman and Robin – or as close as possible – and that the costumes should be exact replicas of the originals and made to fit us. That's the way we ended up taking it and I was glad, because when we finally got that shot of them running through the smoke, it just lent itself even more to the ridiculous. If I go back to Bristol, the one they all remember is Batman and Robin. That's the one they always come up and say, 'I was there.' It really seemed to chime.

That was also the series in which Raquel gave birth to Damien, shouting words that came straight from the lips of John Sullivan's wife, Sharon, when she was in labour. 'Don't you ever come near me again, Trotter,' was, I believe, one of Sharon's, give or take the Trotter. Neither Tessa nor I had experience of childbirth at that time, and because we wanted to make the scene realistic, we took advice from midwives at the West Middlesex Hospital, where the scene was being filmed.

None of us realised that the seventh series would be the show's last. You rarely knew, at the end of a series, whether there would be another, because commissioning normally happened subsequently. So you just had to hang on and hope and see what the stars and John Sullivan came up with.

Certainly nobody had said they wanted to leave. Indeed, in the absence of a fully fledged run, each year, from 1991 through to 1993, we reconvened for a Christmas Special. The 1991 story, 'Miami Twice', saw us decamping to Florida. Which is quite a long way from Peckham. And this time, we really did go. (Spain, in an earlier episode, had actually been Dorset in the freezing cold with the lights turned up bright.) We filmed at the famous Biltmore Hotel, a giant wedding cake of a building, and were thrilled to be told that the room in which we were recording was the favoured suite of Al Capone – who was a kind of Trotter in his way, albeit a bit more violent. The hotel was being refurbished while we were there and certain parts of the building were off-limits, including a staircase up to a bell tower. The restriction was too tempting for Nick and me, who, like schoolkids, immediately shot up there to take photographs of ourselves.

The storyline included cameo roles for Richard Branson and Barry Gibb of the Bee Gees. The cast and crew were all booked to fly out on Virgin Atlantic and Richard Branson found out and, being the great publicist, asked for a part in the show. He was very charming but would it be unreasonable of me to say that I've seen better actors? His big moment came in a queue at the airport where he pushes in, prompting Del to say, 'Hey, 'scuse me, what's your game, pal, eh? Blimey. Anyone would think he owns the plane.' I assumed, after that, that a happy lifetime of free rides and regular upgrades lay ahead of me. Alas, I was wrong. Show business can be a very cruel industry.

Barry Gibb, meanwhile, had a bigger part, and even a line. Del and Rodney are shown on a tour boat, going past his house – a massive place with a big lawn that goes down to the water. As they pass, Barry is out there on the lawn with a hosepipe. Del, of course, can't resist shouting to him, 'All right, Bazza!' Cut to Barry Gibb, mumbling, 'Oh God. There's always one.' Barry was wonderfully self-effacing. He invited Nick and me into his house, introduced us to his wife, gave us tea, showed us over the place – which was, of course, a palace. He was a great fan of *Only Fools and Horses* and used to get tapes of it sent over to America.

When we reconvened for those annual Christmas Specials, it was as if we hadn't stopped. You just fell straight back into the way of things. I would put on Del Boy again and find that he fitted like a pair of wonderful old carpet slippers.

* * *

As *The Darling Buds of May* was drawing to a close, I was taken out for lunch by Richard Bates and Philip Burley from Excelsior Productions. I went along suspecting that they might have another project in mind for me and I was excited to hear what it might be. In fact, when the conversation eventually turned to business, Richard said, 'What do you want to do?'

I was a bit confused and said, 'Do about what?'

Richard said, 'I mean, what do you want to do next – on television?'

I was still a bit confused. I said, 'What do I *want* to do?'

He said, 'Yes. Is there anything that you've always had a yearning to do and never had the chance?'

I was gobsmacked. It was the first time in one of these meetings that I'd ever heard that question, or anything like it. The form had always been: 'We're going to produce x, would you like to play y?' To find myself in the position where someone was asking me what I wanted to do – effectively sitting opposite me with a blank sheet of paper in front of them and an expectant expression . . . well, this was a shock and it was a pretty stunning indication to me of the giddy heights to which I had somehow ascended.

So, straight away, I said, 'I've always had this secret hankering to put on a zebra-patterned leotard and do a Summertime Special, singing duets with Cilla Black from the top of the BT Tower.'

All right. No, I didn't. The truth, of course, is that I hadn't come along with a prepared answer. But something did come straight to mind, in fact. I said, 'The thing I like watching is detective shows. I'd love to play a detective.'

It was true. I was a sucker for sitting down in front of *Poirot*, *Inspector Morse*, *Inspector Wexford*, *Dalgliesh*, *Prime Suspect* – any of those police procedural dramas. I loved all that.

They said, 'OK. Why?' I said, 'People like to unravel a mystery, don't they? That's what *I* like to do, when I'm watching – try and beat the detective to it.' Richard and Philip said they would go away and try to find some detective stories and we would see where it all went from there.

My assumption was that they were going to ask some writers to come up with a script or a treatment, but in fact, not long after this, I received a package in the post containing five books – all works of crime fiction, all by different authors, all in slightly different areas. There was a note from Richard saying, 'See if you like any of these.' I was off on holiday to Florida, so that was my holiday reading sorted for me. I packed them and ended up reading them over the next fortnight, one by one, sitting beside the pool.

One I initially responded to was about a Victorian detective
– a Sherlock Holmes-type character in London. I thought that
was 'olde worlde' and a bit different. I could see myself doing
that. However, the idea was swept from my mind when I read
one of the other books. It was contemporary, and clever and
dark, and revolved around all manner of unpleasantness,
including the murder of a drug addict, and a robbery at a strip
club. It wasn't very Pop Larkin, in other words. The detective
at the centre of the story was this shabby, rather bitter, caustic
but very commanding character. The book was called A *Touch
of Frost* and it was written by an author called R. D. Wingfield.

That was it for me. I phoned Richard there and then, from
Florida, because I couldn't wait to tell him. I said, 'If you can
get permission for A *Touch of Frost*, I'll do it.'

Back in England, some short while later, Yorkshire Television
held a lunch for the principal members of the cast of *Darling
Buds* to celebrate the completion of the series. It was a very
jolly affair, but as everyone was leaving and I was about to sail
out the door, David Reynolds asked me if I could stay behind
for a couple of minutes. When the room cleared, I was left with
David, Vernon Lawrence and a couple of other Yorkshire TV
executives whom I didn't know. Someone closed the door, and
Vernon then said, without preamble, 'What makes you think
you can play a TV detective?' Excelsior must have been on to
them all about this *Frost* idea. I suddenly felt like I was in an
interrogation room, under suspicion. Maybe they were about to
do a 'good TV exec/bad TV exec' number on me. Anyway, I
launched into a spontaneous paragraph about how popular the
genre was and how I could see the chance to explore a slightly
darker edge in the character of Frost, while throwing in a bit
of stuff about the superiority of the English approach to TV
detective shows (audience attempts to solve crime in tandem
with the detective) to the American approach (audience is
shown the crime and the criminal at the start of the story, and

then follows the detective's trail to the guilty party). I acquitted myself fairly well, I thought. At any rate, they released me without further questioning.

Excelsior Productions did get permission to adapt *A Touch of Frost*, and Yorkshire Television did agree to get involved in it, and I did land the part. Landed it, and kept it for fifteen series and forty-two episodes, screened over a period of eighteen years between 1992 and 2010. Which is a long time to spend in the skin of a shabby detective. But, boy, I did love playing that part.

We had to clean him up a bit. In the books, Detective Inspector Jack Frost was a chain-smoker, and I had recently given up cigarettes. I'd never been heavy – just four or five a day, normally in the evening with a drink. But I didn't want to start smoking for the part and find myself drifting back into the habit again. By this time, smoking on television was starting to be a bit taboo in any case. Also, incidentally, from a purely practical point of view, smoking is a nightmare for continuity – you've got to watch the length of the ash all the time, otherwise it looks like someone has sucked down three-quarters of a cigarette in the time it takes someone else to come through the door. The less smoking you've got going on in a scene, the easier life is for everybody.

So we made Frost someone who had been a heavy smoker but who had recently quit – and actually, this ended up giving us more bits of business than if we had left him to smoke. It enabled us to give him chewing gum to occupy himself with, and it meant we could make him irritable and very grumpy about anyone else smoking anywhere near him. I remember in particular a scene in the Incident Room when one of his assistants lit up a fag to enjoy with his coffee, and Frost nipped the cigarette out of his mouth and doused it in the bloke's coffee in a fit of jealous pique. Frost's status as a reformed smoker opened up lots of little moments like that.

We didn't clean up his eating habits, though. This was another show with a tough food regime – maybe not quite as bad as the one in *Darling Buds*, but still hard on the stomach. Frost was not a healthy eater: bacon sandwiches, chips, fry-ups. People would say to me, 'You're always eating in *Frost*.' True enough. And not just that: I was always eating badly.

There was one manifest problem about me playing a detective: my height. At five foot six, Frost would most likely have fallen foul of the police height requirement and never have made it into the force in the first place. No easy way for me to get round that, really, but you'll notice I stood as tall as I could when I played Frost, and gave him a very correct, shoulders-back bearing, so that my height would be less of an issue. I also added a moustache. It was a bit ageing, but I rather liked it. I could imagine Frost growing a moustache as a younger man to give himself a few extra years and a bit more maturity. Obviously my moustache came off between series so I could play other parts. I generally needed four weeks to grow it back and had to remember to stop shaving at the right point ahead of shooting. There were a couple of occasions when I missed the mark slightly and had to help it along with a bit of colouring-in, but, one way or another, it was always ready for day one of filming.

I didn't want the show to be too formulaic. We decided that Frost wouldn't have just the one sidekick, in the traditional set-up for this kind of show, but that he would change assistants between cases: we made him a detective to whom sergeants got seconded, to learn the trade. There were a couple of regular characters – Superintendent Norman Mullet (played by Bruce Alexander), the bureaucratic superior that Frost clashes with, and Detective Sergeant George Toolan (played by John Lyons), Frost's loyal, lower-ranked colleague – but a steady supply of assistants presented us with the opportunity to keep the show fresh and to give Frost new characters to bounce off, people who would come in and challenge his slightly set view of the world. One of my favourite moments in this area was with Maureen Lawson (played by Sally Dexter) on a stake-out, the pair of us sitting in the car, eating fish and chips. Frost says, 'I expect you'll be looking forward to getting back to your boyfriend. When are you next seeing him?' Maureen very calmly replies, 'It's not a him, actually, it's a her.' Frost was old-fashioned and he needed a moment to take this on board – his chip just fractionally pausing on its way from packet to lips.

The show meant spending a lot of time away from home, at the studios up in Leeds or on location around Wetherby, Harrogate, Dewsbury and all stations local – even on Ilkley Moor without my hat. Yorkshire Television couldn't have been more determined to make it easy for me, though. I asked if it were possible to rent a cottage rather than pay for a hotel. I could cook and look after myself, after all. I wasn't after anything grand with a swimming pool and electronic gates, just somewhere simple that I could go back to at the end of the day, away from everything, and clear my head. Or as we would say now, to chill out.

They found me an old farmer's cottage in a place called Kirby Overblow off the road from Leeds to Harrogate. It didn't have central heating, so, on cold nights, I would get in and light myself a fire. Conversely, on warm evenings, I could sit out in the garden and that was always a pleasure – to come back from filming and have a large one and watch the evening go by. People used to ask, 'Don't you get lonely?' I didn't. Not at this stage of my life. I enjoyed the quiet time.

They also gave me my own driver – the magnificent Lawrence Turner. Either late on Sunday afternoon or first thing on Monday, Loz would collect me from Buckinghamshire in his spotless Lexus and take me on the three-hour drive up to Yorkshire. We'd put the world to rights for a while, then I would work on my scripts. And then we would stop halfway and have a bacon and egg roll and a cup of tea – a very Frost-like meal. Loz was on call any time I needed him.

We used to call it 'the circus'. You'd arrive at the location and all the lorries would be there and the sets and the make-up and catering. You would film for maybe three days, and then the circus would pack up and be gone, leaving just some patches of flattened grass behind it. Whenever I'm out and about and I see a film unit at work, I still feel that glow of excitement I used to get, driving onto the set to work.

And because this was a serious drama, encompassing serious matters and ugly crimes, on those sets there was an entirely different atmosphere from the kind I was used to – an atmosphere of sober, careful, almost academic concentration with none of the pranking and larking about that typically went on during the filming of sitcoms and costume dramas.

Yeah, right. I don't think any television show I've done, with the possible exception of *Only Fools*, prompted quite so much mucking about on the part of the people involved in it as *Frost* did. Certainly no show I've ever done prompted quite such *elaborate* mucking about. John Lyons was a great character who has become a good friend, but I have to tell you, the winding-up of Johnny Lyons that took place over the course of *A Touch of Frost* would make a pair of ninety-minute television specials all on its own.

It commenced when Johnny and another member of the cast went out one night and had a few jars. When they got back to their rooms at the Queen's Hotel in Leeds, Johnny went to the window and looked out and realised that he could see his drinking companion opposite, standing at his own window and also looking out. So Johnny – a sensible man in his fifties at this point, it should be pointed out – dropped his trousers and mooned him.

The following morning, Johnny's drinking companion made the mistake of laughingly telling me about this. I got hold of

David Reynolds. David jokingly said, 'We ought to do something. He's bringing the reputation of the team down.' I said, 'I know: let's create a letter from the manager of the hotel.' So gophers were employed to find some headed notepaper and the pair of us constructed a letter, ostensibly from the hotel manager to David, stating that it had come to the manager's attention that certain activities were going on in certain rooms that were bringing the hotel into disrepute and offending other guests and that, as a consequence, the manager felt he had no option but to take further action and involve the police. David then summoned Johnny to his office and, in a quiet meeting between the two of them, presented him with the letter and expressed, with much slow and solemn head-shaking, his disappointment in him. Johnny, as expected, went white with mortification.

His mortification lasted for several hours. In the hope of extending it a little longer, I went and banged on Johnny's caravan door during the afternoon, while David hid to one side. When Johnny came to the door, I said, 'What's this I hear about David getting a letter from the hotel manager?' Unfortunately, Johnny heard David suppressing his laughter, which led him to smell a rat. 'You rotten sods,' said Johnny. 'Well, that's it. You'll never get me again.'

David and I laughed and said, 'Oh, you reckon, do you? Want to put money on it?'

Johnny very misguidedly said, 'Yeah, I will. Fifty quid.'

Game on.

David and I waited for shooting to start on the next episode and, in tandem with the director Roger Bamford, devised a new and still more fiendish trap. This one involved Roger issuing Johnny, mid-morning, with a whole new page of dialogue to learn, telling him it was a last-minute script alteration, and instructing him to get it off by heart for shooting at the end of the day. This dialogue, written by David, was actually just a lengthy and deliberately convoluted recap of the episode's plot, at the end of which I, as Frost, had the one line: 'Good thinking, George.'

Johnny's face was again white – this time with terror at the task lying ahead of him. A naturally conscientious man, Johnny was always worried when he had a lot of dialogue because he liked to work at it and take his time to learn it. Accordingly, in every moment of downtime during the day's shoot, Johnny was to be found staring at the page of rogue script and cramming like mad to get the lines learned. I generously took the time to do a couple of read-throughs with him by way of rehearsal, but he really wasn't happy about it. All through lunch he was muttering to himself and telling anyone who would listen, 'I'm never going to get this learned, you know.'

That day we were on a reservoir near Leeds, doing a story about the recovery of a body from the water. At the end of the day, Roger announced, 'Right. We're going to do that extra scene.' The cameras were set; the lights were readied. Roger called 'Action' and John staggered through his massive paragraph of nonsense. Just before we reached my line, though, Roger called, 'Cut! We'll have to go again, John. You're not really in command of it.'

So Johnny went for a second take. Again he staggered, and again Roger called 'Cut!' before the end. 'No, we'll have to go again, John,' he said. Johnny went for a third take, and this time he made it through and this time we did reach my line. Whereupon I said, 'Good thinking, George. And that's fifty quid you owe me and David Reynolds.'

After much stamping about and many Anglo-Saxon words, Johnny had to admit that he'd been caught again. Yet, amazingly, came the same misguided response: 'You'll never get me again.'

Oh, but we did. And again and again, the ruses growing ever more elaborate and involving more and more members of the cast and crew, until the glorious day when Johnny found that, unbeknown to himself, he had been filming in front of a picture of his own face, blown up by the art department to fit like an advert on the back of a bus that had travelled the entire length of Leeds.

But you couldn't be winding up Johnny Lyons *all* the time, so *Frost* was also the show on which I started doing rocket launches – to great acclaim, I must say. Well, sometimes.

The problem with film shoots, I started to realise, as the years advanced, was that there were bound to be some portions of empty time – time when all you could do was sit around and wait. And if left hanging about in my caravan too long, especially in the notorious period directly after lunch, I would sometimes have to fight the urge to nod off. I needed something to keep myself going in those downtimes.

So, along with my dresser, Ned Smailes, who shared my enthusiasm for these kinds of things, I began turning my caravan into a workshop, making models from plastic kits. Sometimes I might work on a model in the evening too, for relaxation purposes. Well, as a man who passed from his fifties deep into his sixties during the course of this show (and also as a member of Her Majesty's constabulary), I wasn't likely to be knocking my pipe out until four in the morning, was I? I figured it was better to put my head in a paint pot for a couple of hours and wind down that way.

First of all, Ned and I did ships and planes. Then the planes and ships developed into rockets. And the rockets developed into launchable rockets – nice big ones, anything between two and five feet tall, with an engine and an explosive component, which could fly between 500 and 900 feet into the air – because I realised that you could get a bit of a performance with those. I would assemble a rocket using the tools that I now took around with me for the purpose, packed in an old make-up case. Loz, the driver, who was a former engineer, was invaluable in acquiring various specialist parts from obscure sources across Yorkshire. Then, once the rocket was complete, I would announce a public launch for cast and crew on a specific day after lunch.

The best venue was the big field at the back of Leeds Hospital where, for two or three years, we were allowed to film in the mortuary. Everybody would turn out and we'd have a countdown, followed by lift-off. As the launches became more sophisticated, we built a launch pad from an old lighting stand, and added our own launcher, with a key, lights and its own two-tone alarm sound effect. You've never seen anything so camp in all your life.

Ned's and my ultimate masterpiece was a *Saturn V* replica with one of the biggest engines you could get. Quite a complex build. When you launched it, it would, rather like the real thing, hover just as it lifted from the pad, and then set off into the sky – very pleasing. We used to launch that a lot. (These rockets come back, by the way. Well, they do if you're lucky. When the rocket reaches its apogee, if I may be permitted a technical term – and if you don't know it, look it up – there's a small additional explosion which blows the nose cone off and produces a parachute to bring everything back to earth again. Happy days.) Eventually, with constant use, our *Saturn V* started to char. And then, on one unfortunate day, it failed to rise off the launch pad at all, but just sat there, burning, which charred its rear end fairly terminally. So we retired it – but only very reluctantly.

And somewhere in between this mucking about, a television show got made – and a massively successful, long-running and deeply popular television show. The hunch had well and truly paid off. A lot of people seemed to be quite startled by the first episode. We made it purposefully dark, opening with the death of Frost's wife. I wanted to hit it head on, coming off the back of *Only Fools* and *Darling Buds*, because I wanted to mark the division and convince people that, despite what they might be expecting from me, I could do this too. In subsequent episodes, with the character established, it was possible to lighten him slightly. Early on, for a scene where I walked into the station, I asked if the staff sergeant could have a cup of tea beside him on the desk. Then, during some dialogue about something completely unrelated, and completely unremarked, Frost could drink the guy's tea. It was just a little bit of nonsense, but drinking other people's teas and coffees became something of a habit for Frost – a little humanising moment which chased through the series to make him more than just an efficient cop.

And how life came round full circle. David and I used to go away to a hotel periodically and have seminars to go through scripts and think about future plot developments and story ideas. It was at one of these that a suggestion came up for a character called PC Ernie Trigg, a retired beat copper who has become a police archivist. I said, 'I know someone who would be exactly right for that part.' David said, 'Who?' I said, 'My brother, Arthur.' Arthur was asked to come in and he got the role, and the role developed into a running character – twenty-seven episodes from 1994 onwards. It was great to have him around, though, oddly enough, he declined my offer of the spare room in my spartan farm cottage in favour of the comforts of the cast hotel. From mucking about in the sitting room with a mock ventriloquist act to standing together on the set of one of the country's favourite drama serials: we had come on a bit of a journey. Without Arthur's help at the beginning, my journey wouldn't even have begun. It was nice to reach this point on the road and find him alongside me.

In September 2008, a press release went out to announce Jack Frost's retirement. It was nothing to do with running out of storylines, and certainly nothing to do with falling out of love with the character. On the contrary, I would have happily played him forever. The problem was simply age: I was now sixty-eight, which meant Frost was already the oldest copper on the force. Strictly speaking, in police terms, he probably would have been obliged to retire ten years earlier, or even before that. And, yes, you can fight age hard, but unfortunately age hasn't lost a battle yet.

David and I had other irons in the fire at this point. In particular we had a programme we really wanted to do called *The Usher* – set in the world of the courtroom, where the usher is the only person able to move fluidly between everyone, on all sides, including the judge, and who might therefore imaginably assume a position of power within the politics of the court. We really wanted to do it. We had wondered whether this might be a job for Frost, post-retirement, or maybe it would have required us to develop a new character. Either way, we were keen. However, within the two or three months in which we were trying to prepare for *The Usher*, the old guard at Yorkshire Television left and the new guard came in and the wheels were set in motion for the closure of the place in a big amalgamation plan at ITV. *The Usher* didn't get commissioned.

No retirement job for Frost, then. Still, he bowed out pretty spectacularly. In the final episode, Jack married RSPCA inspector Christine Moorhead, played by Phyllis Logan, though not before poor old George Toolan had copped it in a car crash on the way to the church, the innocent victim of a jealous ram raid by the bride's alcoholic ex-fiancé. Again: what would Pop Larkin have thought?

* * *

ONE DAY I received a very strange letter. It said:

> Dear Mr Jason,
>   I noticed your performance as Toad in Wind in the Willows, *and I noticed that there was a house on the market at present which reminded me of Toad Hall, and I think you ought to consider it, you being such an expert as Toad.*

Most odd. Nobody has ever written to offer me a flat in Peckham, on the grounds of my expertise as Del Boy, nor indeed a corner shop in Doncaster, on the grounds of my expertise as Granville. But here I was, being fitted up for Toad Hall. The address the letter writer gave was about three miles away from where Myfanwy and I were living. I knew the road and the area well, and my first thought was that this place didn't actually exist. I had no knowledge of the lane that was mentioned. Nevertheless, it made me curious. One day, Myfanwy and I were driving by and we thought we would try and find this so-called Toad Hall. We failed, though. So clearly the letter was the work of a nutter.

Yet for some reason, it stayed in my mind. I couldn't shake the idea that somewhere plausibly masquerading as Toad Hall was three miles away from my house. So I tried again. This time I took the letter with me, and followed its instructions very carefully – and lo and behold, there was the lane that the letter mentioned, and there in the lane was this house. The gates were open, so I was able to see the property, down the drive. I have to confess, my first thought was, 'It doesn't look much like Toad Hall to me.' Nevertheless, I decided to look more closely and I parked and got out of the car and went in through the open gates.

Off to one side, with his back to me, there was a person on the lawn, wearing some kind of red coat, which reminded me of the menacing mad midget in the movie *Don't Look Now*. I was spooked and quickened my steps up the drive. I knocked at the front door, but there was no answer. So I walked back down the drive and plucked up the courage to address the back of the red-coated figure, who now turned round and promptly revealed himself to be not a mad midget but the gardener. He said Mr Payne, who was selling the house, wasn't in but he offered to show me round the garden. It was wonderful and seemed to go on forever, and even had a lake, fed by its own spring. I thought to myself, 'Well, it may not be Toad Hall, but I could imagine myself living here.'

I went back the next day. A friendly and very gentlemanly figure opened the door, introducing himself as Mac Payne. I told him about the strange letter, which he too found curious. He showed me the house, but, as he did so, he explained it was under offer to someone in London who had three more months to conclude the deal before their offer expired. Mac said, 'If they can't complete, it goes back on the market.' I said I wanted to put my name down as first refusal and I asked if Myfanwy could come and see the house. Mac said, 'Absolutely.' So Myfanwy came round and she too fell in love with the place.

It was on that second visit that Mac said to me, 'Do you mind if I ask what you do for a living?'

I said, 'I'm an actor.'

Mac roared with laughter. 'You're an actor and you want to buy this house? Actors don't have a pot to piss in!'

I said, 'Well, some of us do.'

So, we now faced a three-month period of hope and anxiety, waiting for the other offer to expire. Except that anxiety about the house came to be completely outweighed by other anxieties. Because in that period came the most terrible blow. Myfanwy was diagnosed with breast cancer.

She felt a lump. I said, 'We'd best go to the doctor's about that.' The doctor sent her to the local clinic for a scan and the diagnosis came back that it was cancer. You can imagine: tears. It was terrible. Then she met a specialist who said she should have an operation to remove her breast because radiotherapy wasn't going to shrink the cancer on its own. That was so hard for her to take. Neither of us had known anything like this in our lives before. It was a whole new reality to get used to. It was a very stressful time, a terrible, difficult emotional time.

It was while Myfanwy was recovering from the operation that Mac sent me a note. 'Dear David, the chap in London has fallen out of the running. If you're still interested and can raise the finances, the house is back on the market.' I went straight there. Just driving up to the house again made me realise how much I wanted it. But now there was the dimension of Myfanwy being ill. I didn't mention that to Mac. I simply told him that I thought I still wanted to buy the house, but I asked him if I could have a week to think it through.

That weekend, Myfanwy and I went down to the cottage in Wales, with Peg the dog. On the journey, and all across the weekend, we discussed the house. Should we? Everything seemed to be up in the air again. I was thinking to myself, 'What would make her happy? Would getting this big house actually be stressful for her?'

On Sunday morning, I took her breakfast in bed, and told her I was going to take the dog for a walk. Behind the cottage flowed the River Taff, and behind the river was a grassy mountain. I walked down the lane to the end of the village and down another lane, across the River Taff, and followed the path up the mountain, really striding out until I got right to the top of the mountain, with its wonderful view. I sat up there, thinking, 'What should I do? What should I do for the best?' I went backwards and forwards and sideways with everything until eventually I had it settled in my mind. If I bought the house, she would get better and all would be well.

Peg and I came down the mountain and walked into the house. Myfanwy was still in bed, because she was very debilitated, even at this stage. I made coffee and sat on the bed and said, 'I think we should go for it.' She looked so happy.

I went back to Mac. His place was pretty much twice the value of the house I already owned in Wendover. So – because they don't call me Derek Trotter for nothing – I made him an offer, slightly lower than the asking price. Mac suggested we toss for the difference. I said, 'All right then. You're on.' He called heads. And heads it was. He laughed like a drain. I said,

'All right, I'll pay you the full price.' So much for my standing as a wheeler-dealer.

Soon after this, Mac rang me and asked if I would mind dropping in again. He showed me a letter he had received. It was from the previous bidder for the house, the person whose offer had fallen through. It said that he understood Mac was selling the house to me and then went on to warn him that he doubted I would be able to buy the house as my partner had cancer. He then went on to make an increased offer.

It was like being hit with a cricket bat. First of all, how did this person know about Myfanwy being ill? Secondly, how, knowing that, could anyone use the information in that way?

I said, 'It's true, Mac. She has cancer.'

He said, 'Can you tell me whether you can pay for the house?'

I told him that I could.

'Then it's done and dusted,' he said, and tore up the letter.

Mac moved into the cottage at the foot of the garden which he refurbished and, over the ensuing years until his death, he and I became firm friends, often spending an evening sitting outside on his terrace with a drink.

Meanwhile, Myfanwy and I moved in – and everybody who's moved house knows how stressful that is. I tried to keep the burden of it from Myfanwy as much as possible. She was going backwards and forwards to the hospital for chemotherapy all through this period, but there was no sign of remission. It was slowly getting worse and worse.

During this time, leading up to 1995, I was filming episodes of *Frost* and away on location a lot, but Myfanwy was able to come with me sometimes. When she did, I would ask if a nice hotel could be found for us, so that she could be somewhere comfortable. And that way we were able to be together.

We were helped a lot at this time by John Junkin and his wife Jenny. But breast cancer is such a blight. Myfanwy just started to fade away. She grew steadily more ill. Macmillan nurses came to our aid and they were amazing, caring for Myfanwy, even staying with her overnight. Eventually, though, it became too difficult for her to be at home. They suggested she go to the Florence Nightingale Hospice near Stoke Mandeville, where she could be looked after properly.

The day we moved her into the hospice, it really came home to me how much the illness had diminished Myfanwy physically. She was now taking very strong painkillers, and she had lost so much weight and was terribly frail, and she was out of it a lot of the time, with the drugs. I went to visit her at the hospice every day for the next couple of weeks and sometimes we were able to talk a little but much of the time she was barely aware I was there.

One morning, in March 1995, the hospice rang and said they thought I should prepare myself and come and see her because it wasn't going to be long. I phoned her family. Her brother Gwyl, whom she dearly loved and who dearly loved her, came up and we went to the hospice together. The day before, I had been to see her and she had been sound asleep the whole time I was there – a shadow of herself, really. I warned Gwyl, on the way, that she may not wake up and talk to us. I wanted him to be ready for that. But now, when I went with Gwyl, she was awake and quite bright.

'Gwyl! What are you doing here?'

'I just came to see you.'

'Lovely!'

The three of us talked a while. Then the nurse came in and said, 'It might be time to let her rest now, because she's getting tired.' So Gwyl and I kissed her and we left.

They phoned very early the next morning and said that she had passed away. They asked, 'Would you like to come and see her?' So Gwyl and I went down to the hospice and we were shown into the room and it's not a thing I would want anyone to go through, nor a thing I find easy to go back over.

We said our goodbyes.

But here is the most amazing thing, which they told me is not uncommon. In the middle of that night, Myfanwy had pressed the call button and the nurse had gone to her, and, almost as if there were nothing wrong with her, Myfanwy had asked the nurse if she could have a pen and some paper. Which, of course, she brought to her. And Myfanwy wrote down a number of things that she would like to happen – gifts she would like to give, a certain amount of money for Gwyl, some ornaments and possessions for her nephew and niece. She wrote down these instructions, and then she passed away. They gave me the piece of paper and the handwriting was pretty good – firmly written, lucid. She had woken up to do that. It was as if she knew it was on its way. I drew some comfort from that – perhaps not then, not immediately. But since.

We went back to the house, Gwyl and I. I opened a bottle of whisky. Over the course of the next few hours, we finished it.

CHAPTER SIXTEEN

Marriage, birth and matters arising.

In the months after Myfanwy died, I threw myself deep into work, hoping it would get me through. Once, there had been a time when I could work to the exclusion of everything else. Once, I could immerse myself in work the way I could immerse myself while diving. I could let it fill my ears and sink right down into it until I was entirely absorbed by it, and until it was the only thing that was going on and the only thing that mattered. Not this time. Work wouldn't get me over this one. I needed other people. I fell back on the love and support of my family – my brother Arthur and his wife Joy, my sister June – people who must so often have tried unsuccessfully to attract my attention while I was sunk fathoms-deep in work but who, to my unending gratitude, were loyal and still there now that I was thrashing around on the surface. I felt as needy as a baby in those times – utterly lost – and they took care of me.

And so, in due course, did Gill. Gill was a floor assistant at Yorkshire Television in Leeds. The first time I set eyes on her, I was climbing out of a car and Gill was coming out of the double doors from Yorkshire TV's reception, having been sent down to meet me and show me to the studio. She later told me that, right there, she had felt an almost physical jolt and a voice in her head told her, 'This man is going to affect your life.' Her other immediate thought was that I looked lonely, which was how I felt. At that point the notion that we would start a relationship would have struck both of us as unlikely. She was twenty years younger than me and we were living different lives in different parts of the country, and I was still numb with grief. Yet work kept bringing us together, and when it did, we would snatch conversations, and when we talked there was, unquestionably, a connection that neither of us had ever felt before. On my days off, Gill would take me to some of her favourite places: the Yorkshire Dales, the tea rooms at Bolton Abbey or across the North York Moors to Whitby and the coast. Sometimes she made me meals at her house in Mirfield and our fondness for each other grew and grew.

I didn't expect to find someone new and settle down. I thought I'd had my chance of that and it had gone. How fortunate for me that I was wrong. One weekend, I invited Gill to come and stay with me in Buckinghamshire. And very quickly I realised, as surely and as firmly as I had ever known anything, that I was in love with Gill and that I wanted us to live together. It was a huge leap for her. She hadn't moved in with anyone before. Also, she had now been promoted to floor manager at Yorkshire Television and was only a couple of months into the new job. Her career was on the up. Yet, to my relief, she didn't hesitate. She put her little house up for sale and she came down to Bucks and we started building a life together and being happy.

Of course, even though work was no longer the great healer, I still had work to do – doing *Frost*, mostly, at this time, but also, at the end of 1996, reconvening with the cast of *Only Fools and Horses* to do the set of Christmas Specials, marking, for many people, the story's true conclusion. Which meant that Gill was there, in the studio, to share the moment when the curtain came down. Three years had gone by since we had made the show's previous Christmas Special and most of us assumed it was all over. But John Sullivan was still keen to tie up the ends of the story. He wanted the Trotters finally to become millionaires. In 1996 he wrote three one-hour episodes which were screened consecutively across that Christmas and in which Del and Rodney at last saw it all come good and made some money. Everything about the narrative pointed to these being the last ever episodes of *Only Fools*. The first two shows got audiences of 21.3 million. The third episode got 24.3 million. That's still a record for a British sitcom. It was a staggering number. It made me dizzy to think about it. You simply couldn't get it into your head how popular this show had grown to be.

At the end of the studio recording for that third episode, with the Trotters now officially on their way to wealth, we got a standing ovation from the studio audience that went on for longer than any I have ever heard – just on and on and on. Nick and Buster and I and all the fantastic cast were joined by John Sullivan and we had a group hug on the set, all of us in tears. It was very emotional and difficult to compute. We all knew this wasn't the kind of experience that comes twice in your life. What a series. So many brilliant moments and lines; such clever writing. Sullivan was a traditionalist, in a way: he made the characters do the work and they didn't need to resort to extremities of language or action. Yet there was such tremendous light and shade. *Only Fools* had a death, it had a miscarriage, it had a birth . . . The more John saw how we worked together, the more he felt he could push into areas where comedy didn't ever go. It was great, honest stuff and it touched people's lives. We had most of the nation behind us, really, when we properly got going.

The impact of *Only Fools and Horses* and the way that people responded to it was constantly surprising me and continues to do so. In the early 1990s, during the Gulf War and its aftermath, I met a bloke in a pub who worked at the RAF Command headquarters at High Wycombe. He said, 'Do you know what they do in their downtime? They race three-wheel vans against each other, and they paint them yellow and put "Trotters Independent Trading" down the sides of them. Why don't you come up and see the lads? They'd love to meet you.' So I did. I didn't get to see a three-wheeler race when I was there, but I did see the lads and was in awe at what they do and their bravery and their spirit. With the bloke from the pub, I then hatched a plan, along with Nick and Buster, to send a Trotters van out to Kuwait. We could slip it into a Hercules plane among all the other stuff on a supply run and then, when the lads and the lasses unloaded the plane at the other end, they would find this Trotters van in the middle of everything. And we could fill it up with stuff – sweets and treats and bits and pieces to amuse them.

I said I didn't want there to be any publicity around it because I didn't want anyone to think it was just for that. I wanted it to be a kind of private joke – something between the Trotters and the RAF. And it happened. We got the van and we stuffed it full of chewing gum and toothpaste and cake and all sorts. Brian Cosgrove gave us a load of *Danger Mouse* and *Count Duckula* tapes on which we stuck labels saying things like 'Debbie Does Dallas' and 'Unzipper-de-doodah' (possibly). They put this van into the middle of the giant hold of a Hercules and covered it up with important things like medical supplies and ammunition and flew it to Kuwait, where its discovery brought a bit of light relief.

It was just a TV sitcom, and yet how the tentacles of that programme reached out. In 2011 I was filming a series called *The Royal Bodyguard* and a chap called Liam Byrne came up to me. Liam was the armourer on the show, looking after the weaponry that was needed. He said he wanted to speak to me and had promised some friends of his that, given the opportunity, he would tell me his story. So I sat down with Liam. He explained that he had been a sergeant in charge of a platoon on a tour of Afghanistan. Before he had flown out, his wife told him she had packed a few things at the foot of his bag which might cheer him up in the event of bad times. Liam was touched, but he didn't think too much about it. Then one day he found himself leading his platoon on reconnaissance. On that particular mission, one of his lads was hit and killed. It was a tight unit of men, and when they got back to the camp, everyone was distraught – so unbelievably down at what had happened. Liam didn't know what to do to pull everyone back together. Then he remembered what his wife had said, about packing him things for bad times. These, surely, were those bad times. Liam went to his bag. At the bottom of it were some Pot Noodles and a copy of 'The Jolly Boys' Outing', the *Only Fools and Horses* Christmas Special from 1989. Liam's heart sank a bit. He wasn't sure, in the circumstances, that these particular items could be relied upon to do much at all. Still, he gave it a go. They boiled up the Pot Noodles; they put on 'The Jolly Boys' Outing'. It helped. Watching these wally-brains on the screen, mucking about on a trip to Margate, being ridiculously British, took those battered lads out of themselves. Somehow it lifted their morale out of the dust and it began to stand them the right way up again. It was the start of the healing process, after which they could go on. I was staggered by Liam's story and deeply moved by it. It made me realise that I had no idea how far what we did carried, and only the vaguest sense of its true repercussions. Yes, *Only Fools* was just a sitcom – and what could be more frivolous or irrelevant? You're just arsing about in front of a camera and getting paid to make yourself laugh. Yet what you do goes out there and has effects beyond any you could ever have imagined at the time.

There was a further *Only Fools* trilogy, filmed in 2001. A few critics felt we shouldn't have gone back to it – that the bow neatly tied in 1996 was now undone again. But people seemed to want it, the BBC definitely wanted it, and that weight of anticipation is very hard to resist. And John was writing it, so all of us had no hesitation in saying yes. Even beyond that, in 2011, I had a meeting with John and Gareth Gwenlan, the producer, at John's favourite restaurant, the Chinese in the Dorchester, and discussed coming back yet again – with Del at sixty-five and finding out what had become of everyone. I was up for it. I thought anything was possible in John's hands. But fate had decided this wasn't to be. A couple of weeks after this meeting, Gareth phoned me to say that John was in intensive care with viral pneumonia. He seemed to be getting better, though, and actually came out of hospital and went home at one point. We all thought he was on the mend. But then he relapsed and they took him back into hospital. He died soon after – too soon. His loss devastated us all. Again, I could only meet his death with disbelief. You can't believe you're never going to see that person again, that they're just gone. It's the most difficult thing in the world.

Now the show really was over. While it's up and running, a programme such as that is like this complete world that you exist in. But when it's done, the sets get packed up and removed, and the costumes go away, and the whole thing lives on only on a piece of tape. You can't actually go back there. So you have to consign it to the list of those things that were great and wonderful and fun . . . and utterly gone. I do miss it badly.

* * *

GILL AND I started to talk about having a family. By this time, I was sixty, she was forty. We were older than people conventionally are when they think about these things. The idea scared us a lot. We batted it back and forth.

'What do you think?'

'I don't know. What do you think?'

As you can tell, we were a pretty decisive pair. In the end we decided to leave it to fate and fate answered us very quickly. So now, in 2000, Gill was pregnant and, as long as it all worked out, I was going to be a father – something else I thought I had missed, something else for which I thought the time had swept by while I was below the surface, at work. How lucky is that?

We had names ready. I thought David would be a good name for a boy – kind of resolute, and noble. Gill pointed out that in the TV comedy show *The Royle Family*, they had a 'baby David' and we'd get mocked. It didn't bother me. Then one evening Gill tested me.

'David?' she said.

I said, 'What?'

She said, 'I wasn't talking to you. I was talking to baby David.'

So I realised that David might get complicated. I still quite liked it, though. I quite liked the idea of continuing the line.

As for a girl, I was watching breakfast television and Sophie Raworth came on. I had seen her read the news many times before and she always had my attention. Sophie was also the name of the girl in Roald Dahl's *The BFG*, for which I had done the voice when Cosgrove Hall made their animated version, so the name had extra resonance for me. I went through to Gill and told her I rather liked the name Sophie. We thought we might add Mae for a middle name, for no reason other than because it sounded nice when you put the two together.

Three weeks before Gill was due to give birth, we discovered the baby was over nine pounds in weight and breech. It was too risky for Gill to go into labour so she had to be booked in for a Caesarean. So much for her plans for a water birth. Still, the baby was now a date in the diary, which I at least found reassuring amid the mounting anticipation. Come the day, in March 2001, Gill's mum, Shirley – known to me exclusively as Burley, for no other reason, I hasten to add, than I like the rhyme – and I went with Gill to the hospital and I put on the gown and mask and was admitted to the inner sanctum to watch as the doctors delivered a 9 lb 6 oz girl: my Sophie Mae. After Gill held her, she was handed to me and the room seemed suddenly very still and I had my first moments with my daughter.

The day after she was born, the press were in the hospital car park, and they were still there a week later when Gill had recovered from the operation and we left, gingerly carrying Sophie in the brand-new car seat. We didn't have public relations people to help us. We just bundled our way out and went home in the mid-afternoon through a flurry of snow. And everyone who has done it knows what it's like to bring a newborn baby home for the first time – knows the nervousness and the anxiety and the warmth and the wonderment. I had hung a little banner in her room, ready for her: 'Welcome Home, Sophie'.

And before you ask: no, on the night of Sophie's birth, back in that hospital, I didn't carry her to the window and talk to her in the moonlight about the life that lay ahead of her, the way that Del did with Damien at the end of series seven of *Only Fools and Horses*. But I could have done. I could have spoken those lines of Del's in that episode:

'You're gonna have such fun. You are. And when you get the hump, cos you're bound to get the hump sometimes, I'll muck about and make you laugh. Cos I've mucked about all my life, and I never knew the reason why until now.'

* * *

WE LIVE VERY privately, which is how we prefer it. The garden, the workshop – those are the places I'm happiest. I like to have a project on the go – something to restore, something to fix. The pond needs cleaning? That's my idea of a good time. I love anything in the garden, actually. I've built two steam engines which you can sit astride, and a raised five-inch gauge track in the garden, which travels between two stations, with a bridge over the pond and a tunnel. I used to plonk Sophie on the back when she was smaller, sit there with my knees up around my ears, stoke the coal in the tender, sound the whistle and steam out around the perimeter of the garden.

We go on holiday to a quiet place in south-west Florida where we can take boats out and I can dive. We are blessed in what we have, of course, but I think you would struggle to describe ours as a 'celebrity lifestyle'. That's not how we see ourselves and it's not what we want. Very occasionally, we might find ourselves on the red carpet at a film premiere or at an awards ceremony. But it amuses Gill and me how bad we are at that stuff. We know the score: you should linger in front of the photographers, smile graciously and lap up the attention, for it may not be yours forever, not even next week. But I'm normally clammy-palmed with a combination of fear and embarrassment, and we end up making a poorly disguised dash for it, rushing along the carpet, blinking blindly into the flashlights, hanging on to each other like a pair of silly old fogeys. Any photograph taken of us at any point on this dash will be nearly guaranteed to make us look uneasy. We don't care. That's not who we are.

I get recognised when we're out, and it can get a little out of hand. Gill and I were once invited to watch the tennis at Wimbledon by Bruce Gyngell, who was then the managing director of Yorkshire Television: champagne lunch, seats on Centre Court, the works. In the row in front of us, and just along a bit, was Jack Nicholson. Gill and I thought, 'Great: no question of us getting bothered here. People will be too busy bothering Jack.'

Wrong. While Jack sat there, utterly untroubled, watching the tennis, a steady stream of well-wishers made their way along our row to say hello – to the point where, eventually, people around us felt obliged to intervene: 'Leave the poor bloke alone.' Now, who's the bigger star, do you suppose: me or Jack

Nicholson? Well, naturally, it's Jack Nicholson. But he's *such* a big star that there's something slightly intimidating about him. People kept their distance. Whereas I'm Del, I'm Pop Larkin: I'm approachable. Which is lovely of course, and better than having people cross the road to avoid you, I'm sure. And better still than having people cross the road to your side in order to poke you in the eye with a burnt stick. And yet . . . well, sometimes you end up deciding it'll be more comfortable for everyone if you stay at home.

Inevitably, it affects my life with Sophie a little. There are things I can't do with her. I just have to accept that. Legoland, Thorpe Park . . . we've tried those places, but people gather. Still, what we do instead is go to matinees in the West End: *Mary Poppins*, *The Sound of Music*, *Wicked*, you name it. Anything with songs and ice cream in it is fine by us. That's our time together and it's a precious thing. I show her the theatre. I show her where I come from.

And then, if it's a nice day, I might fly my helicopter. Which sounds a bit flash, I suppose: a bit 'TV's Man of Action', as the *TV Times* once had it – you might even say a bit 'celebrity lifestyle'. But there it is. It's all Gill's fault anyway. For my birthday about twelve years ago, she bought me a chance to go up in a helicopter, flying out of High Wycombe. I really loved it and I decided to learn to fly one myself. It's the most difficult thing I've ever mastered: your hands and your feet have to work in contrary motion to one another. It's a bit like playing the drums, I guess, although with greater risk of death. Yet I did it, and I did it when I was in my sixties, and I'm very proud of that.

With helicopters, you work your way up gradually: a little solo trip around a field at first, and then, as part of your exam, a solo cross-country flight to designated points. The first time I attempted that, I managed to get lost and I had to land in a field to ask a farmer for directions. Poor bloke. He was surprised enough to see a helicopter come down on his land and even more surprised to see Del Boy get out of it. I failed the exam, needless to say, and by next week the story of the bozo who got lost on his cross-country test was all around the airfield. Still, I passed eventually, and with the need I now had to get to meetings and locations up and down the country, I managed to rationalise buying my own little machine – a four-seater Robinson R44, my mechanical pride and joy.

So, a wife, a daughter, a helicopter . . . the good fortune showered upon me in these recent years is, I am truly aware, more than any man would have a right to dream of.

Oh, and the knighthood. I nearly forgot the knighthood.

One morning early in 2005, Gill brought the post to the breakfast table. Among the usual bills, there was a letter from Downing Street. The Prime Minister, Tony Blair, and his government wished to know whether I would be prepared to accept the honour of becoming – to use the official title – a Knight Bachelor. There had been no word of warning of this. It was totally out of the blue. Naturally, I assumed a wind-up and checked the envelope for evidence of the hand of the usual suspects: David Reynolds, say, or Brian Cosgrove, or Micky McCaul. Micky had once sent Gill a very convincing summons to jury service at the Old Bailey. This kind of deception wouldn't have been beyond him.

But no. It wasn't a wind-up. It was true. I was made a Sir in the Queen's birthday honours of 2005. I felt very humbled – and maybe even a little awkward about it. For me, those kinds of titles go to heroes in battle or to heroes in charity. To get one for acting, which doesn't seem to me to have any parity with those things . . . well, I found that a bit hard to get my head around. Still, it was on offer. I was hardly going to turn it down, was I?

The date was set for my investiture on 1 December. On its own, it was a thrilling and momentous prospect for Gill and me, but just to make it even more interesting, we decided to combine it with our wedding.

Gill and I often spoke about getting married, and especially after Sophie came along, but we could never come up with quite the right plan for doing it – a way that wouldn't create stress and fuss. If someone could have come into the kitchen and quickly spliced us over breakfast, we would both have been happy, though friends and family might have felt a bit let down. I suspect Burley would never have spoken to us again. Now, there's a thought . . .

Anyway, the investiture solved our problem – and kind of obliged us to act, because Gill really wasn't keen to go to the Palace as an unmarried mother. While she was organising a special lunch for the investiture at the Dorchester Hotel in London, Gill noticed that they do private wedding ceremonies there. We hatched a plan to get married, quietly and in semi-secret, on the eve of the investiture.

We invited a handful of people to come to the Dorchester on 30 November 2005 – close family members and Gill's best friend Sue Hallas. The only people who knew why they were really there were Sue, my soon-to-be mother-in-law Burley and my sister June – and, of course, Sophie. The others (Arthur and Joy, June's husband Miggy and Gill's two brothers, Michael with Paulette and Mark with Susan, and her nephews, Peter and Declan) thought they were coming to a party for the investiture. Only when they walked in did they find out they were guests at a wedding.

The marriage took place at 5 p.m. in a beautiful room at the hotel. Gill wore a gold lace dress with a little jacket and I wore a lounge suit with a buttonhole. Sophie, who was four, was our bridesmaid. It was intimate and romantic and just the happiest time. Afterwards everyone came back to our suite for cocktails and canapés and to cut the cake. Even though it was a set of rooms with a separate sitting room, the hotel staff had put up a little bed for Sophie at the end of our four-poster. Sue quietly wondered whether we were OK with that on our wedding night and we laughed because it hadn't even occurred to us that it was odd.

The following morning, I arose a married man and went straight off to become a bachelor. Or, at any rate, a Knight Bachelor. I was allowed to take my new wife with me to the Palace and two further guests. I chose June and Arthur to be with me, we three siblings thus, in a manner of speaking, completing the totally implausible journey from Lodge Lane to Buckingham Palace. Well, if the royal family never showed up to use the front room the Whites kept ready, we'd just have to go to them instead. Sophie, of course, was too young to attend the investiture, but Burley brought her to the Palace for the photos outside afterwards.

At the Palace, as Gill and June and Arthur watched, I went down on one knee on the foot stool and the Queen stepped forward and touched me on both shoulders with the sword. I'll let you into a little secret here: she doesn't actually say 'Arise, Sir David'. The whole 'arise' thing turns out to be an urban myth and is not a part of the ceremony. Shame, really. It's a good line. She should use it. However, afterwards, I stood and the Queen said, 'You've been in the business a long time.' I don't know why, but I found myself telling her I hoped I hadn't done anything to offend her at any point. She laughed and said that so far as she was aware, I hadn't.

And then it was back to the Dorchester, and a slap-up lunch for fifty. Nick Lyndhurst, sadly, couldn't make it, but so many other pals and companions were there: Humphrey Barclay, Micky and Angie McCaul, Johnny Dingle, Malcolm Taylor and his wife Annie, Brian and Angela Cosgrove, John Sullivan and his wife Sharon, Meg Poole, Johnny Lyons and his wife Anne . . . At the beginning of my speech, I stood up and said, 'First of all, Gill and I were married yesterday . . .' and the place erupted with cheering and thumping on the tables.

Amazing. A married man, a Sir, and all inside twenty-four blissful hours. I would have loved Ronnie Barker to have been there that day and shared this with us all. He was a man whom I thought more deserving of a knighthood than me. Alas, Ronnie had died two months previously. But earlier in the year, when my knighthood was announced, he had, typically, sent me a poem to commemorate the event, and at the lunch I declaimed it, so at least he was there in word:

> Congratulations, Little Feed,
> Her Gracious Majesty decreed
> That Granville, little errand lad,
> And Del Boy, Frost, and others had
> All served their nation passing well,
> So here's to Granville, Frost and Del!
> The old ex-Guvnor's proud to see
> His comrade reach such high degree,
> Knight of the Realm, and TV star
> Who never thought he'd get this far.
> 'Arise, Sir David,' she will say,
> The sword upon your shoulder lay.
> I raise a glass filled to the brim
> And truly say, 'Good Knight from him.'

INDEX

David Jason is referred to as DJ throughout.